PERSPECTIVES ON SEX, CRIME AND SOCIETY

Second Edition

Cavendish
Publishing
Limited

PERSPECTIVES ON SEX, CRIME AND SOCIETY

Second Edition

David W Selfe, BA (Hons), MPhil
Deputy Director, School of Law
Liverpool John Moores University

Vincent Burke, LLB (Hons), MPhil
Lecturer in Law
Liverpool John Moores University

Cavendish
Publishing
Limited

London • Sydney

Second edition first published in Great Britain 2001 by Cavendish Publishing Limited, The Glass House, Wharton Street, London WC1X 9PX, United Kingdom

Telephone: + 44 (0)20 7278 8000   Facsimile: + 44 (0)20 7278 8080

Email: info@cavendishpublishing.com

Website: www.cavendishpublishing.com

© Selfe, D and Burke, V   2001
First edition   1998
Second edition   2001

British Library Cataloguing in Publication Data

Burke, Vincent
Perspectives on sex, crime and society – 2nd ed
1 Sex crimes – England 2 Sex crimes – Wales
3 Sex and law – England 4 Sex and law – Wales
I Title II Selfe, David
345.4'2'0253

ISBN 1 85941 600 4

Printed and bound in Great Britain

PREFACE

It is three years since the first edition of this book was written. In that time, there have been numerous statutory and case law developments. These have covered issues of substantive law, as well as issues relating to sentencing and post-sentence disposal of offenders. In particular, the second edition has incorporated new material on the operation of the Sex Offenders Register and Sex Offender Orders.

Perhaps of even more significance, the last three years has seen a wealth of new cases involving the interpretation of recent statutory provisions and common law principles. The major House of Lords decision in *B v DPP* on strict liability and mistake of age is included. The Court of Appeal has been particularly active. New cases include *Tabassum* on consent and fraud, *Thornton* on sentencing, *Bowden*, *Atkins* and *Goodland* on indecent photographs of children, and *AB and CD* on confidentiality and disclosure of information relating to paedophiles.

The second edition has been amended also to take account of social and political changes and inputs. There have been significant parliamentary debates relating to the age of consent, as well as proposals for reform contained, for example, in the Sexual Offences (Amendment) Bill 2000, and these are incorporated in relevant chapters. Most noticeably, the text incorporates the Government's comprehensive review of sexual offences law. In this respect, the major recent proposals contained in the Home Office Review, *Setting the Boundaries*, 2000, are fully discussed.

A number of sections dealing with comparative law and the increasing influence of decisions of the European Court have been enhanced. These include the decision of the Supreme Court of Canada in *Cuerrier* and the European Court ruling in *ADT v UK*.

We have stated the law as it stands at 15 November 2000. At the time of writing, the Sexual Offences (Amendment) Bill 2000 has not yet been enacted. However, following its third defeat (on 13 November) in the House of Lords, the indications are that the Government will use the Parliament Act to ensure the enactment of the Bill. Consequently, references in the text (especially in Chapters 2 and 5) to the 2000 Bill should be read as the Sexual Offences (Amendment) Act. Similarly, those parts of the text which relate to indecency with children and indecent photographs of children must be read in the light of ss 39 and 41 of the Criminal Justice and Court Services Act 2000, which increase the maximum sentences available for the relevant offences.

We would like to take this opportunity to record our most heartfelt thanks to our wives, Elaine and Betty, for their encouragement, support and considerable patience extended to us during the preparation of this edition. We wish to say thank you also for the invaluable help provided by Nick Spalton, from the Aldham Robarts Learning Resource Centre.

Finally, our thanks go to Cavendish for all of their support, help and encouragement.

David Selfe
Vincent Burke
Liverpool
November 2000

CONTENTS

Contents

Contents

TABLE OF CASES

TABLE OF STATUTES

CHAPTER 1

HOMOSEXUALITY: THE SOCIO-LEGAL CONTEXT

1   INTRODUCTION

It is axiomatic that heterosexuality and heterosexual behaviour are as old as mankind, and therefore it seems beyond dispute that homosexuality has a history equally as long. It is true also that whilst the law has long been used both to define and regulate heterosexual activities, the law (and especially the criminal law) has been most rigorously utilised in establishing parameters around the concept of homosexuality and the activities of homosexuals. However non-controversial it may be to say that the (criminal) law does circumscribe homosexuality, it remains crucial to investigate *how* and *why* it does so.

Thus, we need to consider the various ways in which 'homosexuality' interacts with 'the law'. Why have Western societies in particular traditionally sought to regulate and control homosexuality? How have they done so? Is it right that they continue to do so? Is there, perhaps, any significance in distinguishing between homosexuality *per se* and specific physical manifestations of homosexuality?

In order to begin even to consider answering such questions, the phenomenon of homosexuality needs to be placed into context, that is, historical, cultural, religious, moral and social.

2   HISTORICAL AND CULTURAL PERSPECTIVES

It is essential not to ignore discussion of the 'minority forms' of sexual experience, which are so important if we are to understand fully our social and legal development. By ignoring the historical and social perspectives, we may run the risk also of overlooking the fact that social control of 'different' sexual behaviour is nothing new:

> The regulation of extra-marital sex has been a major concern for the forces of moral order throughout the history of the West ...[1]

This desire for sexual regulation has been, and continues to be, widespread. It can be seen as deriving from the Judaeo-Christian Church's traditional condemnation of all sexual physical activity outside marriage. This would

---

1   Weeks, J, *Sex, Politics and Society*, 1989, Longman, p 96.

extend, for example, to disapproval of adultery and sodomy in the Middle Ages, through to the State's present-day control of, *inter alia*, prostitution-related activities, homosexuality and sado-masochism.

2.1   Attitudes towards homosexuality

Although homosexuality is just one of the 'variations' on traditional, 'normal' sexual behaviour (that is, heterosexual, marital, reproductive), it appears to be the one which has been subjected to the strongest and most concerted socio-legal pressures. After all, both adultery and the use of contraception challenge the traditionally held view of 'acceptable' sexual behaviour, but they have not been subjected to the same sustained regulation as homosexuality.

It is generally agreed that homosexuality is not new: it has existed at all times and in a wide variety of cultures. But what do seem to vary are responses to homosexuality. Attitudes are culturally specific: there is no one single theory to explain socio-legal attitudes and responses to homosexuality; instead, they must be understood in their social, historical and individual contexts:

> [T]he various possibilities of same-sex behaviour are variously constructed in different cultures as an aspect of wider gender and sexual regulation. The physical acts might be similar, but their social implications are often profoundly different. In our culture homosexuality has become an excoriated experience, severely socially condemned at various periods, and even today seen as a largely unfortunate, minority form by a large percentage of the population.[2]

This view of homosexuality activity as a 'minority form' is interesting. If it is such a 'variation', it is arguable that the 'normal' majority should have nothing to fear. But, paradoxically, it is the very fact of *being different* which seems to militate against homosexuals, as West, for example, notes:

> Hostility towards groups or minorities whose habits and ideas differ from one's own is an almost universal human characteristic ... Prejudice against gays is but one example ... Their very existence challenges fundamental assumptions about life's purpose and the natural order of things.[3]

What West refers to as the 'origins of the taboo' of homosexuality are clearly to be found in traditional religious condemnation of such acts. In particular, the Judaeo-Christian condemnation was based firmly on the belief that procreation was a duty essential to preserving and continuing mankind. This view continued to be developed throughout the Middle Ages, especially in the teachings of St Thomas Aquinas. The Thomist position held that the law

---

2   *Op cit*, Weeks, fn 1, p 97.

3   West, DJ, 'Homophobia: covert and overt', in Mezey, G and King, M, *Male Victims of Sexual Assault*, 1992, OUP, pp 13–25 (at p 14).

should prohibit those acts which were 'unnatural'; as continuation of the species is a natural (that is, good) objective, it ought to be encouraged. Anything contrary to this aim is unnatural (that is, bad) and thus is to be prohibited. In the late 20th century, this remains a central argument in the Catholic Church's general condemnation of homosexual acts.

Historically, in England, the laws used to prohibit buggery – whether ecclesiastical (pre-1533) or statutory (post-1533) – were directed at the physical act of buggery, rather than against homosexuals as a group or homosexuality as a concept.

It has been argued, for example, by Weeks, that:

> [A]ll acts of buggery were equally condemned as being 'against nature', whether between man and woman, man and beast, or man and man. The penalty for the 'abominable vice of buggery' was death, and the death penalty continued on the statute books ... until 1861.[4]

Clearly, the early law prohibiting buggery was aimed at the physical act *per se*, rather than any particular type of person. The law did not distinguish between acts of buggery involving two men and acts of buggery involving a man and a woman. However, in practice, it was most commonly used in prosecutions against homosexual men engaging in acts of sodomy. Even at this relatively early stage in the criminalisation process, we can see a firm link developing between the offence of buggery and the control of male homosexuals.

2.2 'Homophobia' and perceptions of homosexuality

Although we have identified an historical culture of animosity against homosexuality, there remains the question of why that culture has continued to be nurtured and, indeed, why, arguably, social and legal attitudes have hardened in favour of extended regulation in some respects. A number of wide ranging factors exist, all of which may be significant in influencing socio-legal attitudes.

2.2.1 The concept of 'homophobia'

West has argued that the concept of 'homophobia' has two potential meanings: a 'proper' meaning and a 'popular' meaning. In its strict or proper sense, homophobia 'refers to an intense, irrational fear of homosexuality, a pathological over-reaction presumably caused by intra-psychic conflict'.[5] Such a conflict may occur when a heterosexual man, with his own perceptions of heterosexuality, is unable to repress unacceptable (to him) homosexual

---

4   *Op cit*, Weeks, fn 1, p 99.
5   *Op cit*, West, fn 3, p 13.

impulses. He will feel threatened by these subjectively unacceptable impulses which, in their most extreme manifestation, may result in violence against the homosexual.

Alternatively, in its popular or commonly used sense, the idea of homophobia refers to the demonstration of an intolerance towards or dislike of homosexuality or homosexuals. It is arguable that this latter manifestation of homophobia has declined; that there is genuinely less 'dislike' of homosexuals, due to an honest liberalisation within society and greater tolerance towards all forms of 'different' sexuality. Despite the plausibility of such a view, West concludes:

> [D]isapproval, both overt and covert, remains pervasive and reveals itself in many forms, not least in the way laws and social standards are applied differently to homosexual and heterosexual behaviour.[6]

Even taken in its less extreme, 'popular' sense, the phenomenon of homophobia is worrying. The dislike of homosexuals/homosexuality, at whatever level, indicates a clear relationship between social norms and legal attitudes and responses. If society were not so homophobic, then, in all likelihood, judicial values and attitudes, as well as legislative intervention, would be less extreme. A major difficulty which now presents itself is how to break the cycle of unfavourable legislation, judicial interpretation and social attitude, as seen for example in the failure to equalise the age of consent to heterosexual and homosexual intercourse in the Criminal Justice and Public Order Act 1994 (discussed below).

It is important not to underestimate the potential impact of wider societal views upon the development of legal attitudes in these areas. For instance, research undertaken in 1994 by the Wellcome Trust into British sexual attitudes and lifestyles, found that:

> [V]iews on active homosexuality are more polarised than on any other subject ... 70% of men and 58% of women believe that sex between two men is always or mostly wrong ... [O]n homosexuality, we are almost as censorious as the Americans, of whom three-quarters judge such practices to be always or almost always wrong.[7]

Merely to identify the existence of a concept of homophobia in the sense of a certain degree of 'hostility', does not explain fully *why* such attitudes exist. The historical and religious influences are unquestionable, but there still remains a need to explain the continuing stigmatisation (both social and legal) of homosexuality, and why the responses are, in general terms, essentially hostile.

---

6   *Op cit*, West, fn 3, p 14.
7   (1994) *The Independent on Sunday*, 23 January, p 10.

2.2.2   Role creation

Throughout its history, the concept of homosexuality has been subjected to varying degrees of ignorance, hostility and ridicule. For the most part, when the term has been used, it has been used pejoratively. It is difficult to disagree with West's conclusion:

> Male homosexuals are regarded as child molesters, traitors, transvestites, and effeminates ... Doubtless some are, but that is not to say they are in any way typical or representative.[8]

McIntosh has argued that there exists a (hostile) regulation of homosexuality because there is a perception of homosexuality as a 'psychological or emotional condition peculiar to some people and not others'.[9]

Such perceptions have resulted in the creation of a 'homosexual role', that is, from the late 17th or early 18th centuries, there emerged a very particular, censured and punished male homosexual role. McIntosh sees this role as acting in much the same way as certain criminal laws: just as some criminals are treated or punished in order to keep the rest of society law-abiding, the same is true with the response to homosexuality – to keep the bulk of society 'pure'. The effect of this role-creation may be seen as twofold: it assists in the provision of a clear demarcation between permissible and impermissible behaviour; and it helps to separate those labelled as 'deviant' from others ('normal') and thus controls and restricts patterns of behaviour.

Whilst the 'role-model' approach does not deal with all of the theoretical issues surrounding homosexuality, it is important for showing how some societies have tried to categorise homosexuals (by creating a 'them and us' situation), as well as for highlighting the purpose for so doing, that is, the perceived need for social control and protection. It is to this aspect of societal protection that we turn now.

2.2.3   The 'dangers' of homosexuality

One of the most pervasive arguments in favour of the control and prohibition of 'homosexuality' is that it is somehow dangerous. Whilst such arguments may prove to be fallacious upon closer inspection, they nevertheless remain popular in some areas of the public domain. Therefore, it is important to identify the reasons for such commonly held beliefs.

2.2.3.1   Threats to 'the young'

This particular 'threat' can in fact take one of two quite distinct forms. First, there is an argument that homosexuality 'corrupts':

---

8   *Op cit*, West, fn 3, p 15.
9   McIntosh, M, 'The homosexual role' (1968) 16(2) Social Problems 184.

> Homosexuals, in general, are exhibitionists and proselytisers and a danger to others, especially to the young. I shall give no countenance to the view that they should not be prevented from being such a danger.[10]

Legal responses to such fears are not uncommon, and two examples may serve to show the legislature's attitude to the corruption argument. The exclusion of men under the age of 21 (and subsequently of men and women under the age of 18) from the decriminalising provisions of the Sexual Offences Act 1967 (as amended) can, to a large extent, be explained by the acceptance of the majority of Parliament that the young in society are still in need of a degree of protection from corrupting influences.

Equally, the much maligned s 28 of the Local Government Act 1988 states that local authorities shall be banned, *inter alia*, from 'promoting homosexuality by teaching or by publishing material' and from 'the teaching in any maintained school of the acceptability of homosexuality as a pretended family relationship'.

It is interesting to note that such arguments are often not supported by research. West, for example, suggests that 'primary homosexuals' – those who have never experienced a heterosexual drive – develop their homosexual urges very early in life, that is, before any social, educative or peer experiences.[11] On the basis of such evidence, legislation which seeks to 'protect' the young would be, at best, ineffective and, at worst, politically motivated and biased.

The second aspect to the threat of homosexuality is that of 'child molestation'. Once again, there appears to be a popularly held view that there exists a causal relationship between (male) homosexuality and child molestation. Is there any foundation in fact to such a belief or is it yet another of the myths of homosexuality? Whilst there clearly is some truth in the common perception that some homosexuals do prey upon the young, there is equally a lack of any such causal link being firmly established by evidence. Moreover, indeed, the evidence would tend to suggest the contrary. Many adult males with paedophile tendencies are interested, sexually, in girls, not boys, thus rejecting clearly the 'homosexual link'. Furthermore, most older men who regress to paedophilia do so from heterosexual adult relationships and are very rarely homosexual.

There is a strong suggestion here that society, often through the medium of the law, is being at least disingenuous, if not positively hypocritical, in relation to its views on homosexuality and heterosexuality. Thus, society portrays the mature, heterosexual male, who displays sexual interest in youthful, teenage girls (over 16), as being 'healthy' and 'normal'; someone to

---

10 Home Secretary, Sir David Maxwell-Fyffe, *Hansard*, HC Debs, 1953, Vol 521, Col 1298.
11 *Op cit*, West, fn 3, p 16.

be admired, even 'envied'. But a similarly aged homosexual relationship (irrespective of the fact that it may also be criminal) is regarded as immoral, 'wrong' or tending towards corruption.

2.2.3.2 Threats to 'family life'

Until quite well into the 20th century, there was widespread misunderstanding about, and ignorance of, the concept of homosexuality. This was true not only within 'popular society', but also, more importantly, within governmental, legal and medical circles. The various misconceptions of homosexuals as effeminate, transvestites, often bisexual, yet also often married, and attracted to young boys, had held sway from the 17th century onwards. This traditional stereotypical mythology was important, as it denied recognising the possibility of a stable, adult, two-party homosexual relationship. If these latter relationships had been recognised, then the traditional view of homosexuality and homosexuals as a threat to the normal pattern of social mores and family life could be open to challenge, and those persons charged with the regulation of such activities would lose one of their main bases for the exercise of control. Consequently, it seems clear that political or State ideology fed the myth of the married homosexual, with a number of unacceptable traits (such as effeminacy, transvestism, etc), who was an undoubted threat to the very fabric of 'normal' society.

2.2.3.3 Threat to 'the State'

In one general sense, all the 'threats' considered above could be regarded as involving some form of danger to the State, that is, the dangers of child molestation or the danger to family life (if they exist at all), may be construed, in a Devlinesque sense, as a danger to the very fabric of society itself as we know it.[12] However, we are intending to refer here to the narrower and more specific 'threat' to the State, namely dangers to State security. There has long been a common perception that some homosexuals are not best suited to positions of seniority and responsibility, because they are made vulnerable by the threat of 'disclosure'.

There appears to exist a popularly held view in Western societies, and in Britain and the US especially, that homosexuals cannot be 'trusted' to hold certain positions of authority and control; that such men are somehow very susceptible to blackmail or other undue influences because of the situations in which they may find themselves. Of course, the simple response to such an argument is that heterosexuals can be, and frequently are found in equally compromising sexual situations, and there are numerous examples (such as the Profumo scandal) where resignations have resulted from these heterosexual liaisons. Yet the fact remains that society collectively seems more

---

12 See, generally, Devlin, P, *The Enforcement of Morals: Maccabean Lecture in Jurisprudence*, 1959, OUP.

censorious of homosexual indiscretions than it does of heterosexual ones. The political history of the late 20th century abounds with examples of such mistrust.

For instance, as Weeks notes, the fear of and mistrust surrounding homosexuality in America in the early Cold War period had significant political repercussions:

> In the early 1950s, homosexuals emerged as scapegoats in the new international climate. The US State Department under the influence of McCarthyism had already conducted a purge on homosexuals in its echelons, seeing them as 'security risks' by reason of their 'lack of emotional stability', the 'weakness of their moral fibre' and their susceptibility to blandishments and blackmail.[13]

In 1998, attempts to remove from office, by impeachment proceedings, ex-President Clinton, following his relationship with Monica Lewinsky, failed. We have no doubts that, if this had been a homosexual relationship, the scandal would have been such that the resulting public and political opinion would not have allowed Clinton to survive in office.

Similarly, nearer home, British political and public disquiet was generated by the defection to Russia in 1950 of two spies (the homosexuals Guy Burgess and Donald Maclean) who had reached positions of considerable influence within the establishment. Subsequently, revelations that Sir Anthony Blunt (who made no secret about his homosexuality) was a Soviet agent reinforced the popular conception of a link between homosexuality and State (in)security.

2.2.4   The medical issues

A number of diverse strands of thought may be found to exist within the ambit of a general discussion of homosexuality and medicine. Some of these strands relate to the more obvious 'medical threats', whilst others are better regarded as specific psychological concerns. Whatever the particular slant, each of these 'medical issues' has considerable potential impact upon perceptions of homosexuality.

For approximately the last 200 years, there has been a strong medical argument which sought to equate homosexuality with psychiatric illness. Indeed, the American Psychiatric Association only removed homosexuality from its list of psychiatric illnesses as recently as 1980. The 'medicalisation of homosexuality' was especially prevalent in the late 19th and early 20th centuries. Of course, the traditional 'explanations' of homosexuality as deriving from 'immorality' or 'sin' still existed strongly in the popular mind, but, increasingly, they began to move alongside conceptions of sickness, mental illness and heredity. Thus, Weeks poses the questions:

---

13   *Op cit*, Weeks, fn 1, pp 240–41.

[W]as homosexuality congenital or acquired, ineradicable or susceptible to cure, to be quietly if unenthusiastically accepted as unavoidable ... or to be resisted with all the force of one's Christian will?[14]

Whilst the 'nature v nurture' debate within criminological theory generally has existed for well over 100 years, in recent years, there has been a specific and expanding body of research (contrary to, for example, traditional interactionist theories of deviancy) which argues that homosexuality is a natural trait linked to individual genes. The 'gay-gene debate' is central to the 'nature v nurture' dichotomy, but, interestingly, it may in fact operate as a double-edged sword. If it could be proven scientifically that homosexuality is an inevitable genetic phenomenon, then much of the present stigma may well be removed. It would also counter certain arguments, such as: as homosexuality has been learnt, it can/should equally be unlearnt; and heterosexuals, especially the young, need to be 'protected' from the threat of conversion or corruption.

But, conversely, if a gay gene were to be identified, then there are undoubted fears that this may lead to a search for a medical/scientific 'solution' to the 'problem', and that we may witness a modern equivalent to the aversion therapy undertaken by many homosexuals in the 1950s and 1960s.

Irrespective of whether homosexual behaviour is learnt or inevitably hereditary, it is beyond dispute that this behaviour has been linked historically with an incidence of sexually transmitted diseases, such as syphilis and gonorrhoea. Whilst, today, these diseases are both less common and more easily controlled and treated, homosexuals face the much greater threat of being labelled as the carriers of AIDS. Throughout the 1980s in particular, AIDS was represented by much of the popular press as 'the gay plague'. In fact, this perception appears to be yet another example of, at best, popular mythology and, at worst, homophobic propaganda, as the incidence of AIDS-related illness is proportionately lower in the homosexual community (where 'safe sex' has long been the norm) than it is in heterosexual communities in many parts of the world. Nevertheless, another link between male homosexuality and danger (this time medical) has been forged.

3   HISTORICAL ATTITUDES TOWARDS HOMOSEXUALITY: PRE-20TH CENTURY

In order to understand fully the key legal and theoretical developments surrounding homosexuality in the 20th century, it is necessary to have an awareness of the origins of the phenomenon and responses thereto.

---

14   *Op cit*, Weeks, fn 1, p 104.

3.1 The origins of legal control

In England prior to the 16th century, sodomy was classified as an ecclesiastical offence, governed in all aspects by the ecclesiastical courts. The first Act of Parliament to deal directly with homosexual behaviour referred to buggery and was contained in the 1533 Act of Henry VIII. Although this Act proscribed and punished all acts of buggery, whoever the parties may have been (for example, buggery between a male and a female), it rapidly became most quickly used in practice against men, frequently homosexuals. The penalty for this most heinous of offences was death, which penalty lasted, at least formally, until well into the 19th century.

It is perhaps indicative of the law's rather naive and unrefined attitude towards homosexuality at this time that sodomy was the only offence recognised within the law. Any homosexual activities less than the act of buggery had to be dealt with by alternative existing laws, such as assault or attempted buggery.

3.1.1   Enforcement

The implementation and enforcement of the laws relating to buggery are difficult to trace during most of the 16th and 17th centuries, due to the relative lack of reliable statistical information. However, the picture becomes considerably clearer during the 18th and 19th centuries.

Emsley, for example, has argued that whilst the percentage of executions, of those capitally convicted actually being carried out, was beginning to fall for many offences from the mid-18th to the early 19th century, this was not so for several of the most serious offences, including sodomy and buggery.[15]

Similarly, Weeks argues that whilst there was no single discernible pattern of enforcement, there did nevertheless appear to be a series of 'troughs' and 'peaks' of enforcement, varying both with times and in relation to social classes.[16] Thus, one such 'peak' saw a spate of convictions for sodomy in 1720, coinciding with a series of 'morality crusades' at the time and related to the high profile (presumably negative) of sodomites in certain cities.

Despite the relatively high rate of convictions continuing throughout the 19th century, there remained an apparent lack of homosexual conceptualisation and a continuing non-awareness of homosexual nature and identity. In fact, more than just non-awareness, there was arguably a positive misconception about the very nature of sodomy, so that both within and outside circles of authority, sodomites (and, in later centuries, homosexuals) began to have developed around them a number of stereotypical mythologies which have remained to the present day.

---

15 Emsley, C, *Crime and Society in England 1750–1900*, 1996, Longman, pp 255 and 262.
16 *Op cit*, Weeks, fn 1, p 100.

3.2 Legislative changes

There were two major legislative changes introduced during the 19th century in relation to the criminalisation of homosexual behaviour.

As a result of the Offences Against the Person Act 1861, the death penalty for the offence of buggery was removed and it was replaced with, at that time, a sentence of a term of imprisonment of between 10 years and life. This reduction must be viewed in the light of the overall climate of penal reform being undertaken in the second half of the century. It did not indicate in any way a relaxation of the still strict social, legal and political views surrounding homosexuality, but rather was merely a small step in the general move towards a more liberal and humane penology.

By the famous 'Labouchère Amendment' to the Criminal Law Amendment Act 1885, acts of gross indecency between men, in public or private, were made misdemeanours, punishable with up to two years' imprisonment with hard labour. This offence widened the criminal law's overt control of homosexuality by covering all aspects of male homosexual behaviour, not just the act of buggery. Its recognition of 'lesser' homosexual acts, together with considerably less repressive penalties when compared with the old sodomy laws, might be taken as indicating a gradually enlightened attitude. But, on the other hand, specific private consensual acts were now criminalised, whereas, previously, they had not been explicitly within the scope of the criminal law. Of course, the 1885 amendment broadened the range of criminal responsibility only in respect of male homosexual acts. Female homosexuality, often referred to as lesbianism, was not, and is still not, specifically covered by the legislation on gross indecency between adults, although there may today be alternative charges, such as indecent assault or gross indecency with children.

Furthermore, and somewhat ironically, there appeared to be a considerable inequality of application of the new offence, and a number of anomalies developed. For instance, the authorities exerted some pressure not to over-utilise the offence and thus give too much publicity to the existence of acts of gross indecency. There was also occasional reluctance on the part of the police to be too active in enforcing the offence, and discretion was exercised in ignoring overtly private activities. Even when prosecutions did ensue, several juries displayed a marked reluctance to convict, in the face of the evidence, indicating strongly that some private actions should not be heavily policed.

However, in spite of such reticence on occasions, prosecutions for acts of gross indecency occurred frequently; and when the law was used, it tended to be used in its full force. Thus, in 1895, there occurred the celebrated trial and conviction of Oscar Wilde, following Wilde's action against the Marquis of Queensberry for libel after Queensberry had written on a card to the poet referring to him as 'Oscar Wilde, the somdomite' (*sic*). During the course of the libel trial, evidence was adduced to show that Wilde had had a number of homosexual relationships, especially with young men. The law proceeded with haste to prosecute Wilde and, despite a vigorous defence by Edward Clarke KC, a leading counsel of the day, Wilde was convicted and the maximum penalty of the law (two years with hard labour) was imposed. It is difficult to avoid at least the feeling that the popular view of Oscar Wilde, exacerbated by media attention, of the archetypal homosexual (an effeminate corrupter of youth), somehow played its part in the sentence.

It was a final irony that, when the full rigour of the law was applied, often following comprehensive and sensational media coverage of the trial, two opposite effects emerged. First, there began to develop, almost for the first time, a public awareness and perception of homosexuality. And, whilst this may not always have been the most positive perception, it did at least introduce homosexuality to the common consciousness. Secondly, high-profile media coverage began to create a homosexual identity; to create a much more positive awareness, knowledge and openness about the phenomenon itself. As Ellis states, such publicity 'generally contributed to give definiteness and self-consciousness to the manifestations of homosexuality, and to have aroused inverts to take up a definite stand'.[17]

4   HOMOSEXUALITY IN THE 20TH CENTURY: THEORIES, ATTITUDES AND IDEOLOGIES

Notwithstanding the importance of historical factors in shaping the development of homosexuality and socio-legal attitudes thereto, it is clear that some of the major debates surrounding the phenomenon have evolved during the course of the 20th century. Whilst these issues have been diverse, we wish to concentrate in this section upon three key areas which appear to have been instrumental in the continuing development of theories about homosexuality, especially in the second half of the century, namely the concept of 'permissiveness', the Wolfenden Committee Report and the perceived relationship between secularisation and social change.

4.1   Permissiveness

The idea of 'permissiveness', whatever subsequently it may prove to mean, is generally accepted today as emanating from and being applicable to the 1960s. Thus, according to Newburn:

---

17   Ellis, H, *Studies in the Psychology of Sex, Vol 2, Sexual Inversion*, 1936, Random House, p 352.

Contemporary politicians have singled out the 1960s as the source of almost all our current social ills. According to these ideologues, what we have failed to recover from is a period of moral decline, or permissiveness, that they suggest characterised 1960s society.[18]

4.1.1   What is 'permissiveness'?

At one level, permissiveness signifies a process of major social transformation, of change and decline. It represents the changing balance of power between social groups and the declining influence of the established church. To many commentators upon this period, there exists a causal relationship between social change/changes in power relationships, and the creation of a 'morally pluralistic society'. For Newburn, therefore, it is as a result of these changes and processes that 'post-war British society must be described as morally pluralistic, and ... consequently, it has become increasingly difficult to sustain the argument ... that we live in an age of moral consensus'.[19]

4.1.2   Defining 'permissiveness'

Although a number of different approaches may be identified in relation to the interpretation of the term, they are linked together by being almost exclusively critical. Contemporary analyses of permissiveness are couched, virtually without exception, in pejorative terms. It is necessary to outline only a selection of these perspectives in order to see the generally critical stance which has been adopted by a wide range of commentators.

4.1.2.1   Conservative-Historicism

Essentially, the Conservative-Historical approach evinces a desire to return to some perceived 'lost Golden Age' of morality, a desire fuelled by the apparent loss of moral consensus during the early part of this century. This school of writers displays a yearning to return to the consensus and agreement of 'Victorian morality', and to retreat from the new (that is, 'bad') sexual and moral freedom epitomised by the 1960s. There is a shared belief that moral consensus has collapsed, to be replaced by division, confusion and uncertainty in relation to moral codes and standards. The essence of this view is encapsulated, for example, by Gummer:

> In the 19th century, men ... accepted that the State had a duty to uphold morality and that private morality ought to be subject to the law as it affected society. They ... experienced little difficulty in deciding of what private morality consisted. There was a consensus – at least among the articulate.[20]

Whilst this was, and remains, a popularly held view in several quarters, it is open to a number of obvious criticisms. Foremost amongst these is the

---

18   Newburn, T, *Permission and Regulation: Law and Morals in Post-War Britain*, 1992, Routledge, p ix.

19   *Ibid*, p xi.

20   Gummer, JS, *The Permissive Society*, 1971, Cassell, p 7.

question as to why any such consensus should be limited to 'the articulate'. At the same time as being a somewhat meaningless term, it is also highly condescending to suggest that such a sub-group of society has a monopoly on morality. Furthermore, it is, at best, naive and, at worst, disingenuous to suggest that Victorian society possessed such a consensus (even amongst the articulate!). This notion implicit in this suggestion is contradicted by the often promiscuous and hypocritical nature of much of Victorian society vis-à-vis sexual mores.

4.1.2.2   Liberal-Historicism

The Liberal-Historical school agrees that the old moral order has collapsed, but disagrees that this fact *per se* should be interpreted as a negative development. Instead, they view some changes as potentially beneficial, for example, by increasing choice, removing restraint and reducing individual frustration and fears.

However, writers who favour this perspective do also see a 'negative' side to permissiveness, namely the increasing crime rate (especially in relation to serious crime) from the mid-1950s onwards. Thus, a series of infamous incidents (such as the Moors murders, the Great Train Robbery, gangland convictions of the Nashes, Richardsons and Krays, etc) were all indicative, even to the Liberal-Historicists, of increased criminality, which derived in turn from 'permissiveness' in the sense of an emerging aggressiveness towards and disrespect for authority.

4.1.2.3   The Marxist approach

It has been noted by Newburn that 'as the ability of the State to mould popular consensus diminishes ... the method by which hegemony is achieved moves from consent to coercion'.[21]

In essence, the Marxist school recognises that the late 1950s and the 1960s was a time of 'discrete moral panics' over a number of issues, a prime concern being that of homosexuality. These 'panics' arguably led to a wider and more general fear about the State's ability to exercise control, and thus to a direct challenge to the authority of the State. Consequent to these panics, there developed a feeling of 'moral indignation', so that, whereas, prior to the 1960s, the State had ruled predominantly by consensus on moral issues, it was now forced to rule by coercion.

4.1.3   *Critiques of permissiveness*

Clearly 'permissiveness' possesses no one single, simple definition. It is a nebulous and confusing (perhaps deliberately so) allegorical term, which is often used to epitomise some fundamental slip in moral and social standards. It has been argued by Weeks, for example, that:

---

21   *Op cit*, Newburn, fn 18, p 7.

... for the defenders of 'traditional' (and largely authoritarian) values, 'permissiveness' became an almost scatological word of abuse ... And by erecting that symbol of sexual relaxation, of loose moral standards, of disrespect for all that was traditional and 'good', it became easier in the 1970s to recreate a sense of crisis around social changes ...[22]

Notwithstanding the general pejorativeness inherent in the use of the word itself, it remains possible to evaluate 'permissiveness' in more specific ways than merely to condemn it as being a reactionary term of abuse. It may be useful to make this evaluation from two perspectives.

4.1.3.1   The 'politico-legal' perspective

At one relatively straightforward level, permissiveness can be viewed as little more than a particularly legislative phenomenon (covering roughly the decade 1958–68), during which a number of key 'moral' issues were addressed by Parliament, resulting in a general 'liberalisation' of the law. This view would serve to explain legal changes pertaining to a range of diverse conduct from gambling and suicide to capital punishment, abortion and sexual activities, including of course homosexuality.

4.1.3.2   The 'sociological' perspective

A potentially more profound level sees permissiveness as indicative of a wider series of social changes, including, for example, economic changes, alterations in relationships between genders and age groups, and the creation of new sub-classes and cultures. Each of these changes or developments may be linked to the perceived 'permissive' legal reforms of the time.

Thus, the relaxation of many gambling controls (regarded by some commentators at the time as a permissive loosening of morals) may be seen as a direct response to major economic changes, that is, increased social affluence and financial opportunities, deriving largely from the post-war boom.

Similarly, the decriminalisation of suicide, effected by the Suicide Act 1961, may be regarded merely as a 'humanising' modernisation of an outmoded law, or it may be indicative of a more fundamental move towards the essence of individual autonomy away from the dictates of public morality. In other words, the decade of the 1960s represents the apogee of the move from the public to the private sphere in terms of control over 'moral' concerns. It is too simplistic to regard the major legislative changes of the 1960s as simply the piecemeal reform of a series of antiquated and outmoded laws, but rather that they represented a move towards individualism and away from the rigours of collective disapproval via State controls.

In terms of the debate surrounding homosexuality, and legal reforms thereof, the key theoretical issues thus centre around two dichotomies: the 'liberalisation v control' debate and the 'private morality v public morality'

---

22   *Op cit*, Weeks, fn 1, p 249.

debate. These issues were epitomised by and evaluated in subsequent analysis of the Wolfenden Committee report.

4.2   The Wolfenden Committee Report on Homosexuality and Prostitution 1957

The Wolfenden report was, and remains, one of the most controversial and most analysed government reports of the century. For present purposes, we wish to place our discussion of Wolfenden specifically within the ambit of homosexuality, in order to consider the objectives of the report, its short and long term impact, and any theoretical basis to its content.

4.2.1   Background to Wolfenden

In the immediate post-war years, there emerged a distinctive 'moral panic' about the phenomenon of homosexuality. There was no one single cause for such panic, but rather a series of interrelated factors. It will be useful to summarise the more important of those factors as follows:

- the Kinsey Report of 1948 suggested that the prevalence of (male) homosexuality was, in fact, considerably more widespread than had previously commonly been thought;

- statistical data appeared to indicate a significant increase in prosecutions for 'homosexual offences'. For example, in 1938, there were 134 prosecutions for sodomy (although this figure included also prosecutions for bestiality), which rose to 1,043 in 1954. Similarly, the number of prosecutions for the offence of gross indecency escalated from 316 in 1938 to 2,322 in 1955. Of course, any such statistics have the capability of being misleading. Do they necessarily show a marked increase in the incidence of homosexual activity/offences? Or do they merely indicate a higher reporting rate and/or more assiduous policing?;

- political/official concerns. There was an undoubted increase in political pressure and general official concern for the need to 'stamp down' on the perceived threat of, and increase in, homosexuality. The general official impetus for 'something to be done' was given momentum in the post-war period by a number of key appointments, including, for example, a new Director of Public Prosecutions in 1944 (the committed Roman Catholic Sir Theobold Mathew) and a new Metropolitan Police Commissioner (Sir John Nott-Bowes) in 1953, who was directly responsible to the then Home Secretary, Sir David Maxwell-Fyffe, generally regarded as a moralistic anti-homosexual;

- such official concerns were mirrored by society itself. There were widespread public and social worries, bordering almost on a McCarthy-like homophobic witch-hunt in the late 1940s and the 1950s. The public seemed to express a collective concern that London was becoming the 'vice capital' of Europe during a time of high-profile events, such as the Festival of Britain in 1951, and the Queen's coronation in 1953. Also, in a development remarkably similar to that of the trial of Oscar Wilde 60 years earlier, public anxiety was increased as a result of high-profile media representations of homosexuality, including especially coverage of the Lord Montagu/Peter Wildeblood trial for homosexual offences in 1954.

The combination of such factors culminated in an almost inevitable call for action, and faced with a diversity of mounting pressures and concerns, the Government was 'persuaded' to set up the Wolfenden inquiry.

4.2.2   Aims of Wolfenden

It is often argued, even assumed, that the Wolfenden Report is a great and influential 'liberal' document. But care needs to be taken in adopting an overly one-sided view of the Committee's purpose and recommendations.

Arguments have been made, for instance, that the original pressure for some form of inquiry came not from those sections of society seeking reform or change to the laws of homosexuality (as is frequently believed), but actually from those groups identified above who had serious concerns about the extent of homosexuality. Ironically, therefore, the impetus for investigation came from a majority of the public, encouraged by media representation, which was still very much anti-homosexual in the early/mid-1950s.

Given this impetus, it must be emphasised that Wolfenden was not established merely to consider how to 'liberalise' the existing law. Indeed, the remit was much wider, and included consideration of whether 'the law' was in fact the best method of control at all in, say, the area of homosexual conduct.

It is equally ironic that many members of the Committee, including the Chairman (Sir John Wolfenden) himself, made little secret of the fact that they found the very subject matter of homosexuals and homosexuality both offensive and unpleasant. They possessed little real grasp of the statistical data relating to homosexuality, but still insisted that the research that was available, such as the Kinsey Report on findings in America, were not relevant to Britain. Furthermore, members of the Committee seemed to hold stereotypical Victorian views about homosexuality, including drawing distinctions between 'inverts' (effeminate inadequate types, often regarded as 'victims'), and 'perverts' (the 'classic' wicked proselytiser). In a typical homophobic paradox, it was believed that homosexuals formed a sick, albeit minute minority, which, at one and the same time, was capable of threatening the very fabric of heterosexual society.[23]

---

23 For a general account of these issues, see, eg, Higgins, P, *Homosexual Dictatorship: Male Homosexuality in Post-War Britain*, 1996, Fourth Estate.

To what extent, therefore, should the Wolfenden Report be viewed as consisting of a combination of 'liberal' and 'non-liberal' aspects?

The Wolfenden Committee[24] drew heavily upon two traditional 'liberal' concepts. It adopted the Benthamite principle that there are 'changing concepts of taste and morality', that is, a positivist belief that morality changes with time and within different cultures. Furthermore, the Committee relied upon the Millsian doctrine that legal intervention in private life is only ever justified in order to prevent harm to others.

Starting from these principles, Wolfenden went on to argue that the purposes of the criminal law were to protect from 'offensive and injurious' matters, to protect from 'exploitation and corruption', and to preserve 'public order and decency'. But it was not part of the criminal law's purpose 'to impose a particular pattern of moral behaviour on individuals', as there are certain activities within the private sphere which, put simply, 'are not the law's business'.

In addition, it was accepted by Wolfenden that whilst male homosexuality *might* threaten (traditional) family life, so too do adultery and divorce, but neither such activity is illegal. Therefore, on grounds both of pragmatism and equity, there exists a further reason for reconsidering the proper scope of the law's involvement in the regulation of homosexuality.

As a result of these considerations, the so called 'liberal' part of Wolfenden recommended the partial decriminalisation of some aspects of homosexual activities.

Wolfenden itself described its own recommendations as 'limited' and stressed that the proposals 'should not be interpreted as an indication that the law can be indifferent to other forms of homosexual behaviour, or as a general licence to adult homosexuals to behave as they please'.[25] Given the views about homosexuality generally held by many members of the Committee, referred to above, this conclusion was hardly a surprise.

Thus, whilst *prima facie* 'liberalising', this was really only so vis-à-vis private acts. For public acts, the official censure and legal controls remained. Indeed, it is arguable further that one reason why the 'reforms' initiated by Wolfenden were 'limited' was to emphasise the continuing protection afforded by the law to 'the young', that is, under-21 year olds at the time. Although it may be accepted that young males probably will not be 'converted' to homosexuality *per se*, they may be tempted to homosexual acts by inducements. By permitting limited homosexual acts in private, this 'threat' may be alleviated.

---

24 See, generally, *Report of the Committee on Homosexual Offences and Prostitution*, Cmnd 247, 1957, HMSO (the Wolfenden Committee Report).

25 *Ibid*, para 124.

Both Wolfenden and the subsequent public and parliamentary debates thereon were keen to stress the balance between the liberal aspects and the inbuilt checks within the recommendations (for instance, to protect the young). In particular, Wolfenden emphasised that it was recommending a partial decriminalisation; it was not defending homosexuality *per se*, but just some manifestations of it:

> In fact what the members of the Committee wished to do was alter the law, not expressly to encourage or legalise such practices, but to remove them, like adultery and other sins, from the realm of the law.[26]

In effect, the Wolfenden 'package' taken as a whole was not seeking to lessen controls, but rather to change to different methods of control, that is, away from 'external' legal control and towards private regulation, in the sense that whilst certain homosexual acts in certain circumstances were decriminalised, it did not follow in the opinion of several members of the Wolfenden Committee that those acts were being approved of in moral terms. The 'Wolfenden strategy' – the balancing of public v private, liberal v non-liberal, and control v autonomy – thus became the central theme in the debate.

Underlying all of this analysis lay the key argument, recognised and accepted even by proponents of the Sexual Offences Bill, that the 'safeguards' of protection outweighed the permissiveness of the recommendations:

> The Bill lays down very clearly that under certain circumstances the House is increasing the penalties, that it is trying to stamp out corruption of youth and minors, which is possibly the most important element in the Bill.[27]

4.2.3 Critiques of the 'Wolfenden strategy'

> [T]he entire Wolfenden strategy may be read as a complex discourse on the subject of sexual vulnerability, anxiously protecting those held to be at special risk from potential 'corruption'. Thus a normative yet somehow ever-threatened heterosexuality is inscribed at the heart of the institution of law.[28]

It is easy to view the complete set of proposals that constitute Wolfenden as a package designed to protect certain vulnerable groups. Here, that would explain the need to protect young males from the permissiveness of homosexuality, on the basis that heterosexuality is 'right'. Indeed, the immediate post-Wolfenden legislative changes complied with that strategy: the partial decriminalisation of some homosexual acts, for example, both accorded with the public/private dichotomy, as well as confirming protection for one of the vulnerable groups (the young).

However, this line of reasoning gives rise to two key questions. Why were the 1960s regarded as 'permissive'? And why did the young need 'protection'?

---

26 Home Secretary RA Butler, *Hansard*, 1958, HC Debs, Vol 596, Col 369.

27 Owen, David (Dr), *Hansard*, 1966, HC Debs, Vol 738, Cols 1108–09.

28 Watney, S, *Policing Desire: Pornography, AIDS and the Media*, 1987, Methuen, p 64.

Newburn has argued[29] that in post-war Britain, traditionally unequal groups (for example, the young/the old; men/women) were becoming less unequal in terms of 'power relationships'. Formerly, less powerful groups, especially the young, were more able to exert control and influence, and to articulate their own aspirations and desires.

Whilst these developments were, to a large extent, one consequence of vastly altered economic relations, the 'changes' themselves were often manifested by the expression of new and different moral codes and values. For arguably the first time, the young (as a generic group) were able, effectively, to express views at variance with traditional adult normative values. Interestingly, this partial shift in the 'power relationship' had two contrasting consequences.

First, the challenge to the traditional view of a belief in a single, uniform moral code, led directly to a increased belief in pluralism vis-à-vis moral issues. Thus, as sub-groups within society became more equal (or at least less unequal), the traditional moral consensus declined in favour of pluralism. Both society and its laws were placed under increasing pressure to reflect different or alternative values and moralities.

But as an interesting corollary to this 'new pluralism', there developed also a number of counter-movements – 'moral entrepreneurial groups' – who sought to 'defend' their (traditional) social position by reversing the threatened moral changes and thus restoring the status quo of consensus-based moral norms.

The other major strand in the supposed permissiveness/moral decline of post-war Britain was the phenomenon identified as 'secularisation'.

Although the process of secularisation is far from simple, one relatively straightforward account of the phenomenon is that Britain, from the mid-1940s, was seeing a general decline in the influence and importance of 'religion' as the framework for moral guidance. The traditional view was that Christianity had formed the basis of existing moral consensus and, therefore, as the impact and cohesion of religion declined, so too did the belief in a single cohesive body of moral rules.

To many 'traditionalists' and 'moral entrepreneurial groups' such as Mary Whitehouse's National Viewers' and Listeners' Association, it was this decline in the influence and status of the Church which explained the decline in moral standards and the 'invasion' of the new moralities. This crisis in the Church meant it was unable to speak with a clear, authoritative, single voice on moral issues, as it had once done. The Church's traditional hold on representing the nation's morals was being loosened, and it could no longer present a 'united front'.

---

29 *Op cit,* Newburn, fn 18, p 159.

Within the Church in the 1960s, there were two opposing solutions to the problem of religious decline, namely 'theological traditionalism' and 'theological radicalism'.

The traditionalists wished to re-assert the traditional, fundamental Christian position on ethical and moral issues – to 'stress the value of the old currency' – which would have entailed, for example, reiterating the Church's stance against homosexuality.

By contrast, the radicalists wished to construct a new and more realistic/relevant religious doctrine for the late 20th century – to 'refloat the currency'. As a result of a number of publications, the radical view appeared to hold sway. For example, John Robinson (then Bishop of Woolwich) argued that traditional religious images, when used in the late 20th century, were out of date and irrelevant to modern society. Only lack of love was inherently evil *per se*, whereas his concept of 'situational ethics' demanded that morality should be determined by the relationship between people at particular times and in particular situations.[30] In essence, Robinson's desire to contextualise ethics asks us to criminalise 'immorality' only if there is some perceived 'harm'. This contrasts totally with the traditionalists' view that criminal law is based upon Christian principles, and is therefore justified in condemning certain types of behaviour (for instance, buggery), regardless of whether or not there is harm to anyone else.

Despite a strong counter-response from the traditionalists, the radical movement prevailed, and proved quite influential in its impact upon attitudes about homosexuality:

> Surely it is the nature and quality of a relationship that matters; one must not judge it by its outward appearance but by its inner worth. Homosexual affection can be as selfless as heterosexual affection and therefore we cannot see that it is in some way morally worse.[31]

The two factors of 'changing power relations' and 'secularisation' gave rise, throughout the 1960s, to the emergence of 'new moralities', that is, a system of moral pluralism, rather than moral consensus. Many of the important legal changes of this period, such as the partial relaxation in the law of buggery, may be taken as reflecting this increase in 'moral pluralism'. Social sub-groups were beginning to have their own moral views recognised and protected, even if only to a limited extent, as Newburn notes:

> It became increasingly clear that British society ought more accurately to be described as 'morally pluralistic'. This pluralism was interpreted by some as

---

30 See discussion in *op cit*, Newburn, fn 18, pp 39–40, 174–77.

31 Heron, A (ed), *Towards a Quaker View of Sex: An Essay by a Group of Friends*, 1963, quoted in *op cit*, Newburn, fn 18, p 176.

indicating a lack of moral rules and regulations, when in reality, there were a variety of moral codes which were in competition ... yet for a time at least, one moral code could not be identified as dominant.[32]

4.3   The current debates: 1994–2000

4.3.1   *The Criminal Justice and Public Order Act 1994*

It is now over three decades since Parliament first introduced a limited exception to the criminalisation of certain homosexual acts. In that time, there has been a wealth of judicial activity, academic comment and public debate on the subject of homosexuality. By contrast, Parliament, until recently, had been relatively inactive. That inactivity ceased initially in 1994 with the enactment of the Criminal Justice and Public Order Act. The purely legal implications of the Act in relation to homosexual offences will be considered in Chapter 2. For present purposes, it is the parliamentary debates surrounding the passage of the Bill which are illustrative of many contemporary attitudes towards homosexuality.

The central debate relating to the age of consent for homosexual activities took place in the House of Commons on 21 February 1994. During that debate, many of the traditional arguments, both for and against a further change to the law, were heard. On behalf of those opposed to any further change, these ranged from moral and religious arguments, that is, that homosexual acts were 'abnormal' and contrary to the 'happy' and 'divine way' of biblical teaching, through fears of conversion and corruption of the young, to claims about the relative lack of maturity (psychological and biological) in respect of males as opposed to females. Outside Parliament, fears were even expressed that the small homosexual minority which existed in this country had 'too much cultural clout' and that that fact alone was reason enough to resist any reduction in the age of consent.

Those within Parliament who supported an equalisation of the ages of homosexual and heterosexual consent at 16 likewise did so for a variety of reasons. Prime amongst these was the belief that there was no psychological or biological reason for discriminating against young males, a view supported by the Royal College of Psychiatrists:

> [T]here are no psychiatric or developmental reasons why the minimum age for homosexual practices should be other than 16 years.[33]

Equally forceful arguments centred around a rejection of the belief that homosexuality is something into which one can be 'corrupted', and the general issue that the entire debate can be reduced to a question of equality,

---

32   *Op cit*, Newburn, fn 18, pp 177–78.

33   This view of the Royal College of Psychiatrists was quoted by Watson, M, MP, in *Hansard*, 1994, HC Debs, Vol 238, Col 107.

that is, as valid, autonomous individuals, homosexuals have the fundamental right to be treated equally to heterosexuals. As Edwina Currie MP said during the debate:

> There is no such thing as partial equality. People are either equal or they are not.[34]

The issues of equality and non-discrimination had, to many advocates of change, become central by this stage. In the same debate, Tony Blair, then Shadow Home Secretary, stated clearly:

> [The issue] is not at what age we wish young people to have sex. It is whether the criminal law should discriminate between heterosexual and homosexual sex. It is therefore not an issue of age, but of equality ... It is simply a question of whether there are grounds for discrimination. At present, the law discriminates ...
>
> [P]eople are entitled to think that homosexuality is wrong, but they are not entitled to use the criminal law to force that view upon others ...
>
> [I]t is wrong to treat a man as inferior because his sexuality is different. A society that has learned, over time, racial and sexual equality can surely come to terms with equality of sexuality.[35]

At the end of an often heated debate, the vote resulted, it has been argued, in a disappointing compromise which satisfied neither side. Edwina Currie's amendment, proposing a reduction in the age of consent to 16, was defeated by 307 votes to 280. This was followed immediately by a vote on Sir Anthony Durrant's amendment, proposing lowering the age of consent to 18. That amendment was passed by 427 votes to 162. The age of consent was reduced to 18, not 16, and to those who had fought for an equal age, this represented very little effective change to the perceived discrimination of the existing position. Thus, Roger Goode, of the gay pressure group Stonewall, stated:

> It retains the discrimination and it is discrimination which is at the core of the problem ... Instead of the police having an obsolete law on their books which they are under no pressure to enforce, they will have a fresh law that they may be obliged to uphold.[36]

Since the reduction of the age of consent to 18 in 1994, there has been an increasing concern that failure to equalise the age of consent for homosexual and (most) heterosexual acts is insupportable on the basis of discrimination, inequality and the infringement of human rights. The impetus towards change has increased further as a result of the significant alteration in the composition of the House of Commons following the General Election of May 1997.

It has been argued that the present unequal age of consent violates an individual's rights under both Art 8 of the European Convention on Human

---

34 Watson, M, MP, in *Hansard*, 1994, HC Debs, Vol 238, Col 81.

35 *Ibid*, Cols 97–100.

36 *(1994) The Independent*, 22 February.

Rights on the right to privacy, as well as Art 15 in respect of being discriminatory.

This contention was tested by Euan Sutherland and Chris Morris before the European Commission of Human Rights, where it was ruled, on 7 October 1997, that English law should be changed, because it contravenes the European Convention on Human Rights.[37] In particular, the European Commission ruled that different ages of consent between heterosexuals and homosexuals was a violation of Art 8, which provides that 'everyone has the right to respect for his private and family life, his home and his correspondence', in conjunction with Art 14, which prohibits discrimination. The Government's reaction was immediate and it was announced that it would no longer seek to defend the case. It was agreed further that MPs would be allowed a free vote, at the earliest opportunity, on whether the age of consent for homosexual acts should be reduced to 16.

4.3.2   The Crime and Disorder Bill 1997–98

Following the ruling of the European Commission in the Sutherland and Morris case, above, the Government had committed itself to a vote in Parliament at the earliest opportunity and, if there were a majority in favour of equalising the age of consent, introducing legislation before the end of the next parliamentary session.

The first opportunity for such a debate arose during the passage of the Crime and Disorder Bill, when Ann Keen MP proposed an amendment whereby the age of consent would have been lowered to, and equalised at, 16. The proposed amendment to cl 1 would have lowered the age of consent for both heterosexual and homosexual buggery, as well as the age of consent for acts of gross indecency between men.

The debate, on 22 June 1998, produced arguments which were divided along expected and traditional lines.[38] Those in favour of lowering the age of consent argued that it would produce equality and fairness in the law, would assist in the battle against AIDS and other sexually transmitted diseases (by creating openness and non-prejudice), and would lead to the protection of young people. Those opposed to the change argued from largely moral perspectives. These included views that homosexual relationships were morally wrong, that homosexual practices were not as equal or equivalent to heterosexual ones and that a reduction in the age of consent to 16 was merely one step towards further measures, such as an even lower age of consent and an undermining of (heterosexual) family life by allowing gay marriages and the adoption of children by homosexual couples. Ann Keen's amendment was passed by 336 votes to 129.

---

37 *Sutherland and Morris v UK* [1998] EHRLR 117.
38 See *Hansard*, 1998, HC Debs, Vol 314, Cols 754–811.

A much stronger opposition was met, as expected, when the debate took place in the House of Lords on 22 July 1998.[39] Even before the substantive merits of the Bill were debated, strong concerns were expressed about the timing of Ann Keen's original amendment and its place within the much wider context of the overall Bill itself. There were concerns that insufficient time had been allowed for a full debate on the amendment. It was argued that the age of consent would have been more appropriately discussed in the wider context of reform in sexual offences (including the proposal to introduce measures dealing with abuse of positions of trust), but that these opportunities had been lost by accepting the amendment to the Crime and Disorder Bill. Baroness Young then tabled a motion seeking to overturn the amendment from the House of Commons. A host of different arguments were put in favour of Baroness Young's proposal during a wide ranging debate. Baroness Young herself spoke about public opinion being against such a reduction, and health risks, as well as reiterating the 'thin end of the wedge' argument.[40] Several religious and moral views were expressed. These included the Lord Bishop of Winchester, who stated that Parliament 'should be very wary indeed about deserting the wisdom in these matters not only of the Christian faith but of the other major faiths too',[41] and Lord Jakobovits, a former Chief Rabbi, who averred that the Sexual Offences Act 1956 was a violation of the laws of God and nature.[42] By contrast, the usefulness of utilising public opinion was questioned by many, including Lord Dholakia, who argued that, in this instance, Parliament should lead public opinion not follow it, and Lord Lester of Herne Hill, who argued that such basic rights and freedoms should not be determined by 'majoritarianism' or opinion polls. Baroness Mallalieu found it extraordinary that a person was deemed sufficiently mature to take one sexual partner, but not another, and stated further that the present law neither protects the young nor prevents consensual private acts. On similar lines, Lord Annan reminded the House that there was a difference between paedophilia and the age of consent.

After a lengthy debate, Baroness Young's motion was carried by 290 votes to 122 and, consequently, the issue returned to the House of Commons. The dilemma facing the Government was acute. If the House of Commons did not accept the Lords' position and returned the Crime and Disorder Bill to the Lords for further consideration, there was a real risk, due to pressure of time, of losing the Bill in its entirety. The Bill itself was important to the Government: it contained a number of significant manifesto pledges and, apart from the issue of the age of consent, generally had wide support in both Houses and the country. Therefore, the Home Secretary reluctantly proposed,

39   See *Hansard*, 1998, HL Debs, Vol 592, Cols 936–76.
40   *Ibid*, Cols 939–40.
41   *Ibid*, Col 943.
42   *Ibid*, Col 950.

and the House of Commons agreed, not to challenge further the Lords' amendment, by insisting on the inclusion of Ann Keen's original amendment. It was dropped from the Bill in the House of Commons, and the Bill received the Royal Assent on 31 July 1998.

4.3.3   The Sexual Offences (Amendment) Bill 1999–2000

The Sexual Offences (Amendment) Bill was presented to the House of Commons on 16 December 1998. The detailed legal implications for the criminal law, especially buggery and other homosexual offences, will be considered in Chapter 2.

Clause 1 of the Bill deals with the age of consent. Its intended effect is to reduce and standardise the minimum age at which a person may consent lawfully to buggery and certain other homosexual acts. In effect (and subject to some qualifications, especially in relation to abuse of position of trust, below), the age of consent for homosexual and heterosexual acts will be reduced to 16.

Clause 2 is concerned with defences available to persons who are under the (new) age of consent. This is also discussed fully in Chapter 2.

Clauses 3 and 4 are intended to create a new offence of 'abuse of position of trust'. It shall be an offence for a person aged 18 or over to have sexual intercourse with, or engage in any other sexual activity with, a person under the age of 18, where the person aged 18 or over is in a 'position of trust' in relation to the younger person. The 'position of trust' criterion must satisfy the detailed circumstances specified in the Bill.

The parliamentary passage of the Bill has been turbulent. The Bill was re-introduced to the House of Commons on 28 January 1999, following an earlier defeat in the House of Lords. Subsequently, it was defeated in the House of Lords on its second reading on 13 April 1999.[43] It received its third reading in the House of Commons on 10 February 2000 and the Government made clear that it would use the Parliament Acts, if necessary, to ensure enactment.

As with all the previous parliamentary debates on the issue of homosexuality and the age of consent, those relating to the 1999–2000 Bill have continued to show a vast range of often polarised views. The following arguments are typical of those presented in favour of reducing the age of consent to 16. First, having different ages of consent shows inequality and discrimination, whereas an equal age of consent is a laudable objective *per se*. It is non-discriminatory. Secondly, there is no moral justification for different ages: a girl aged 16 can consent to vaginal intercourse, but not anal intercourse; two males aged 18 can consent, but not one male aged 18 if his partner is aged 17. There are no valid moral distinctions to be drawn here. Thirdly, the introduction of the new offence of abuse of position of trust

---

43   For the full and extensive debate, see *Hansard*, 1999, HL Debs, Vol 599, Cols 647-761.

would assuage fears relating to corruption of the young. Fourthly, there would be health advantages, in the sense that many young males who were criminalised at the ages of 16 and 17 would be much more willing and likely to seek medical advice as a result of their behaviour being decriminalised. Fifthly, an equal age of consent will create more positive attitudes and 'openness'. Whilst this may take time, youths (especially male homosexuals) will no longer face the stigma of criminality, bullying, adverse public opinion, etc. Finally, a most compelling argument is that it is both illogical and unrealistic to believe that the current criminalisation of males under 18 operates in any way as a deterrent. It is naïve to assume that criminalising, say, two male youths aged 17 will act as a deterrent to them from engaging in homosexual activity. The idea that, in the area of sexual activity, criminalisation can operate as deterrence is misplaced. An analogy with heterosexual intercourse is interesting. The fact that Britain has the highest rate of 'underage' pregnancies in Europe shows that the serious offences of unlawful sexual intercourse with girls under 16 or 13 (ss 6 and 5 respectively of the Sexual Offences Act 1956) have failed to act as deterrence.

The following arguments in the 1999/2000 debate may be taken as typical of those opposed to a reduction in the age of consent. First, there is a biological difference between males and females. Girls aged 16 are physically and emotionally more mature than boys of the same age, so that a different age of consent is not, in fact, discriminatory.[44] Secondly, and following from the first point, a higher age of consent for homosexuals is required for the purpose of protecting the young. Male youths under the age of 18 need to be protected from proselytism, corruption and undue influence. Thirdly, a reduction in the age of consent will be the 'thin end of the wedge'. It will lead to calls for further reductions, as well as contribute to a general erosion of respect for traditional (namely heterosexual) family life. Fourthly, public opinion is strongly against such a reduction. Fifthly, there are a number of potential health risks concerning sexually transmitted diseases generally and AIDS in particular, which would be exacerbated by a lowering of the age of consent. Finally, the change should be opposed on the grounds that it is non-Christian and contrary to the religious teachings of most major faiths.

It is important to remember that the 'age of consent' debate is only one aspect (albeit admittedly a central one) of a much larger legal picture. The proponents of a reduction in the age of consent were very keen to stress the 'safeguard' to be provided by the introduction of the new abuse of position of trust offence (see below). In addition, it is now widely recognised that the

---

44 This argument fails to give full consideration to the fact that the law prohibits heterosexual, as well as homosexual, buggery at the age of 16. The unequal ages of consent are unequal not only in terms of genders, but sometimes also in terms of acts. A girl aged 17, for example, can consent to vaginal intercourse, but not anal intercourse (with, say, her male partner aged 19). If girls mature more quickly, logic demands that she should be able to consent to both.

laws which constitute our sexual offences are amongst the most outdated, contradictory, unfair and illogical in the entire legal system. It was in this context that the Government first announced a major review of sexual offences legislation as long ago as 1998.[45] Subsequently, this was confirmed by Paul Boateng MP, Minister of State in the Home Office, who emphasised both the general problem of sexual offences and the specific issue of protection of children:

> We are committed to undertaking a wide ranging review of the sexual offences and penalties, with a view to reforming them and bringing them up to date. However, the Government will not consider reducing the age of consent below 16 – indeed, one of the principal aims of the review will be to ensure that the legal framework, as far as possible, protects children and deals effectively with those who use and abuse them.[46]

---

45 See the statement by Alun Michael, then Minister of State in the Home Department, *Hansard*, 1998, HC Debs, Vol 314, Col 10; and Home Office Press Notice 222/98, 'Sex offence laws to be reformed', 15 June 1998.

46 *Hansard*, 1998, HC Debs, Vol 319, Col 50.

CHAPTER 2

HOMOSEXUALITY: CRIMINALISATION AND CONTROL

1 INTRODUCTION

Homosexuality *per se* has never been subject to criminalisation in English law. Instead, the criminal law has concentrated its efforts upon the regulation and punishment of certain physical activities relating to the phenomenon of (male) homosexuality. Thus, whilst the fact of *being* homosexual was not proscribed, many (if not all) manifestations of such sexuality were (and still are) controlled vigorously by the law. It is interesting to note, however, that in respect of the two major offences (buggery and gross indecency), regarded traditionally as being used 'against homosexuals', the male perpetrator is not necessarily homosexual and would not identify himself as such. Similarly, where, today, an offence of non-consensual anal intercourse (that is, anal rape) is committed, it does not follow that the defendant is 'homosexual'. Nevertheless, in terms of consensual sexual acts between two men, the overwhelming majority of offences are committed by men who would identify themselves as homosexual.

The main offences which have been used by the criminal law as the central tools by which homosexual activities have been regulated are buggery, gross indecency between men and soliciting by men for immoral purposes. We will argue that the definitions of these offences and, indeed, often, the interpretations of those definitions by the judiciary are indicative of the general social attitudes displayed towards homosexuals. Furthermore, the perceived justifications for such offences (resting as they do upon outmoded notions of 'wrongdoing', social harm and the need for protection from a variety of potential threats) may be viewed as no longer sustainable from either social or strictly legal perspectives.

2 BUGGERY

The offence of buggery was subjected to significant amendment as a result of the Criminal Justice and Public Order Act 1994 (the 1994 Act). One major effect of the amendments was to create a partial synthesis of the then existing offences of buggery and rape. The potential impact upon the 'new' definition of rape will be discussed in detail below, but, for now, consideration is needed of how the 1994 Act altered the offence of buggery *per se*, and how, if at all, those alterations may be significant for the future.

2.1   Buggery pre-1994

Section 12(1) of the Sexual Offences Act 1956 provided:

> It is an offence for a person to commit buggery with another person or with an animal.

'Buggery' itself was not, and, indeed, even since the 1994 Act, is not defined by statute. Rather, its definition was that developed by the common law, namely buggery was intercourse *per anum* by a man with a man, or by a man with a woman irrespective of consent or of the age of the parties, and intercourse *per anum* or *per vaginam* by a man or a woman with an animal (in which case, it was specifically identified by the law as the offence of bestiality).[1]

The offence was subject to the 'exception' derived largely from the Wolfenden Committee Report (which clearly was limited to acts of a homosexual nature) whereby no crime was committed by two men if their actions fell within the ambit of s 1(1) of the Sexual Offences Act 1967:

> Subject to the provisions of the next following section, a homosexual act in private shall not be an offence provided that the parties consent thereto and have attained the age of 21 years.

It was confirmed in *Spight* ([1986] Crim LR 817) that the defendant had the evidential burden of raising and satisfying the trial judge of the issues of privacy, consent and exempted age, although then it was clear that s 1(6) imposed the legal burden upon the prosecution to negative the defence.

2.1.1   'Categories' of buggery

Prior to the 1994 Act, the maximum punishment for any particular act of buggery was dependent upon the specific factual ingredients of the case in question. As a result of Sched 2, para 3(a) to the Sexual Offences Act 1956 and s 3(1) of the Sexual Offences Act 1967, Parliament had created four different categories of buggery, depending upon factual circumstances, such as gender, the specific ages of the parties and consent. These categories may be summarised as follows:

- a maximum of life imprisonment where the defendant committed buggery and the other party was a boy under the age of 16, or a woman, or if the offence was committed with an animal;

- a maximum of 10 years' imprisonment if the other person was aged 16 or over and that other person did not consent;

- a maximum of five years' imprisonment if the other person was aged 16 or over but under 21, where that other person did consent and the defendant was aged 21 or over;

---

1   See, generally, eg, *Wiseman* (1718) Fortes Rep 91; *Bourne* (1952) 36 Cr App R 125; and *Jellyman* (1838) 8 C & P 604.

- a maximum of two years' imprisonment in all other circumstances, for example, if the other person was a man aged 16 or over who did consent, and the defendant was aged under 21 – or where both parties were aged 21 or over, and both were consenting, but the act of buggery did not occur in private, thus removing the act from what otherwise would have been within the ambit of the exception.

In *Courtie* ([1984] 1 All ER 740), the leading House of Lords decision on the effect of these maximum punishments, the categories were described as 'the life offence', 'the 10-year offence', 'the five-year offence' and 'the two-year offence' respectively. In *Courtie*, the appellant had been convicted of committing an act of buggery with a male person under the age of 21 (the other person in fact being aged 19 at the time of the offence). The indictment contained no allegation of lack of consent, but, before imposing sentence, the trial judge heard evidence on the question whether the other person had consented, and found that he had not. Thus, the trial judge clearly was of the opinion that he was dealing with a '10-year offence' and that he could impose such a maximum sentence. The appellant was sentenced to three years' imprisonment and he appealed. The House of Lords upheld the appeal against sentence on the basis that the appellant had been charged only with the 'five-year offence'. As the indictment had contained no reference to the extra factual ingredient demanded by the law, that is, lack of consent, it was wrong for the trial judge to sentence the appellant as if he had committed the more serious '10-year offence'.

Courtie established that, in respect of male buggery, absence of consent was the key distinguishing feature which needed to be proven in respect of 'category two' buggery. Post-*Courtie*, but before the 1994 Act, if there was an allegation of buggery with a male who did not consent, then absence of consent on that male's part needed to be asserted and proved as a distinct and distinctive feature of the *actus reus* for that offence.

2.1.2 Buggery with females

Although this chapter is concerned predominantly with the use of buggery to exercise control over homosexuals, it is worth noting that a particular problem had existed prior to 1994 in respect of defendants who were charged with acts of buggery with a female. In these cases, as the *Courtie* categories made clear, the issue of consent was irrelevant as far as the question of guilt was concerned: buggery with a female always came within category one, the 'life offence'. However, this fact then gave rise to a different problem, namely how to deal with the defendant who claimed that the female whom he had buggered had consented *de facto*, even though that consent was not recognised by the law. Undoubtedly, if there was *de facto* consent by the woman, this should be taken into consideration by the trial judge in terms of sentence, but how and by whom was this issue to be determined?

In *McGlade* ([1990] Crim LR 527), the defendant was charged with rape and buggery of a woman aged 18. The defendant claimed that she had consented to vaginal intercourse and, further, he denied that buggery had occurred, although there was medical evidence to support the prosecution's allegation that anal intercourse had taken place. The trial judge asked the jury to indicate in a special finding of fact, if they returned a verdict of guilty on the buggery charge, whether they believed the victim had consented. The jury could not agree a verdict on the rape charge, but found the defendant guilty of buggery, although without making any reference to the issue of consent. In passing a sentence of five years' imprisonment, the trial judge indicated clearly that, in his opinion, the victim had not consented. In upholding the defendant's conviction, the Court of Appeal held that the trial judge had merely invited the jury to indicate if they thought the victim had consented. This was not a case where the jury's verdict must lead inexorably to one version only of the facts being found to exist. Consequently, where a jury's verdict leaves open an important issue (consent or lack of consent) which, obviously, may affect sentence, the trial judge (who, after all, has heard all the evidence) is obliged to decide the matter himself. Here, he was quite entitled to conclude that this was a case of buggery without consent.

A different method of tackling the problem of consent in relation to the buggery of a female was adopted in *Young* ([1990] Crim LR 752), albeit with considerably less success. Again, the defendant was charged with rape and buggery. He claimed that the vaginal intercourse had been consensual. He admitted that buggery had occurred, but claimed that that too was consensual. At this point, the trial judge allowed the prosecution to amend the indictment so as to include a specific charge, namely 'buggery without consent'. The defendant was acquitted of rape, but convicted of 'buggery without consent' and sentenced to four years' imprisonment. In quashing the conviction, the Court of Appeal noted that there were no different categories of female buggery (as there were with males) and that consent was never an issue in respect of guilt. Consequently, whilst the trial judge's reasons for acting were understandable (in the sense of seeking to determine whether or not consent existed), those actions were not permissible in law. His decision had left to the jury an issue which they were not entitled to consider in determining guilt.

The legal anomalies in such cases were difficult to explain, and the procedural problems, whilst not insurmountable, as *McGlade* showed, provided merely a further obstacle to the smooth running of trials involving the buggery of females. Fortunately, however, one consequence of the changes to buggery and rape effected by the 1994 Act is the removal of these difficulties. As we will see in Chapter 3, where the prosecution today wish to allege anal intercourse without consent, the charge must be one of rape. This automatically imposes upon the prosecution the obligation to prove all elements of the offence, one such element being that the victim (male or female) did not consent.

2.2 Buggery post-1994: the Criminal Justice and Public Order Act 1994 and the Sexual Offences (Amendment) Bill 1999–2000

The current law relating to buggery remains governed by s 12 of the Sexual Offences Act 1956, as amended by the 1994 Act. The following sections will evaluate also the likely consequences once the provisions of the Sexual Offences (Amendment) Bill are enacted and brought into force.

As a result of the 1994 Act, buggery in English criminal law is now retained as an offence for consensual acts. Non-consensual anal intercourse is charged now as rape (see below).

Section 12 of the Sexual Offences Act 1956, as amended by s 143 of the 1994 Act, provides:

(1) It is an offence for a person to commit buggery with another person otherwise than in the circumstances described in sub-s 1A below or with an animal.

(1A) The circumstances referred to in sub-s (1) are that the act of buggery takes place in private and both parties have attained the age of eighteen.

(1B) An act of buggery by one man with another shall not be treated as taking place in private if it takes place:

(a) when more than two persons take part or are present; or

(b) in a lavatory to which the public have or are permitted to have access, whether on payment or otherwise.

(1C) In any proceedings against a person for buggery with another person it shall be for the prosecutor to prove that the act of buggery took place otherwise than in private or that one of the parties to it had not attained the age of eighteen.

The 1999–2000 Bill would substitute 'eighteen' with 'sixteen' on both occasions that it appears. In addition, the Bill will introduce a new s 12(1AA), providing a second circumstance whereby buggery will not be an offence, as follows:

(1AA) The other circumstance so referred to are that the person is under the age of sixteen and the other party has attained that age.

2.2.1 Actus reus

Insofar as the requisite physical act necessary to establish buggery is concerned, the 1994 Act made no changes: there must still be a deliberate act of anal intercourse or, in respect of animals, anal or vaginal intercourse. In order to establish intercourse, the prosecution must prove penetration, although the slightest degree of penetration by the penis suffices, and there is no need to prove ejaculation.[2] These criteria will remain unaltered after the

---

2   See *Reekspear* (1832) 1 Mood CC 342 CCR; and *Cozins* (1834) 6 C & P 351.

enactment of the 1999–2000 Bill, which makes no amendments to those aspects of the *actus reus*.

2.2.2 Parties

In relation to the parties to the offence of buggery, it is important to remember that the law, strictly speaking, is not limited to the control of homosexuals: subject to an amendment to be effected by the 1999–2000 Bill in respect of some persons under the age of 16, all consenting parties to the act of buggery (whether those persons are both male, or male and female) will be guilty as principal offenders. In reality, however, buggery continues to be an offence which is used predominantly to censure and regulate male homosexual activity.

By s 144(2)(a) of the 1994 Act, the penalties for buggery (as contained in Sched 2 to the Sexual Offences Act 1956, and interpreted in *Courtie*) have been amended so that the following categories now exist. First, where the act of buggery is with a person under the age of 16 or with an animal, the maximum sentence is life imprisonment. Secondly, where the defendant is aged 21 or over and the other person is aged under 18, the maximum sentence is five years' imprisonment. Thirdly, in all other instances of consensual buggery, the maximum sentence is two years' imprisonment. In the period after 1994, the last category was relevant, where, for instance, both parties were over the exempted age, but the act did not take place in private. This would also have been applicable where the parties were aged, say, 17 and 16. Interestingly, these sentencing categories do not appear to be altered by the 1999–2000 Bill. This is most surprising in respect of the 'five-year' category. Clause 1(1)(b) will make amendments to sentencing provisions in respect of gross indecency offences, but there will be no amendments to the sentencing of those convicted of buggery or attempted buggery. Consequently, despite the fact that the age of consent will be reduced to 16, the five-year category will be retained for those situations where the exemption does not apply. Thus, a man aged 21 who commits consensual buggery with a male aged 17, but not in private, will continue to be liable to a maximum of five years' imprisonment. An identical situation, but with parties aged 19 and 17, will continue to attract the maximum of two years' imprisonment.

In addition to these categories, s 144(2)(b) provides that identical maximum sentences apply to the offence of attempted buggery, operating in parallel to the substantive offences. Thus, where the defendant (aged 30) is found guilty of attempting to commit an act of buggery with another person (that person being a boy under the age of 16), the defendant is liable to a maximum sentence of life imprisonment.

The categorisation of buggery after 1994 (and prior to the changes that would be effected by the 2000 Bill) was relatively straightforward vis-à-vis the defendant, where that defendant was an adult male. The maximum sentence depended upon the age of the other party and/or the precise age of the defendant himself (that is, whether he was under or over the age of 21).

However, the position was, and, until any amendment, is far less clear in relation to the potential criminal liability of the other party, where that other person is a child. It is clear that all consenting parties technically are potential principal offenders, but whether that would necessarily extend liability to children is a debatable point.

In order to consider the possible criminal responsibility of persons under the age of 16, it is important to distinguish between two different physical ways of committing the act of buggery, namely the person who is the 'agent' and the person who is the 'patient'. The person who effects the act of penetration is regarded in law as the 'agent', and the person who is penetrated is the 'patient'. It follows logically from this that for a female to commit buggery as a principal offender, she must always be the 'patient'.

But why has this essentially physical distinction proved to be a legal difficulty in respect of children? Traditionally (that is, prior to an amendment made in 1993 (see below)), boys under the age of 14 were presumed irrebuttably to be legally incapable of performing the act of sexual intercourse. This fiction accounted for the legal impossibility of substantiating any charge requiring sexual intercourse (for example, rape) against a boy of that age, and automatically excluded a boy below 14 from being liable as the agent in buggery. Similarly, girls (of any age) were incapable of being the agent, as they were physically incapable of performing the requisite *actus reus*, that is, penile penetration. Thus, the position in respect of the child-agent was clear: boys were legally incapable and girls were physically incapable of penetration. But what is the child's position in respect of being the patient in buggery? There appear to be two contrasting views. On the one hand, it is arguable that, providing a 'mischievous discretion' can be proven in respect of a boy or girl aged 10 to 13,[3] then such a child is legally capable of being the patient in buggery and thus guilty as a principal offender. The alternative view suggests that a boy or girl under the age of 14 is incapable of being the principal offender in buggery as either the agent or patient, but, if this is so, it clearly cannot be based upon the sexual incapacity of the child, that being irrelevant to liability as a patient. Instead, the 'rule' that a child cannot be the

---

3   For the position of the law generally on *doli incapax* and 'mischievous discretion', see, especially, *C v DPP* [1996] 1 AC 1. The Home Secretary, the Right Hon Jack Straw MP, addressing the Police Federation's Annual Conference, informed delegates that the Government proposed to facilitate the abolition of the doctrine of *doli incapax* at an early date: see (1997) *The Daily Telegraph*, 22 May, p 1. Subsequently, the rebuttable presumption was abolished by s 34 of the Crime and Disorder Act 1998, although the precise impact of that section upon such a defence remains open to debate. It may have been assumed that the abolition of the presumption (effected by s 34) would also amount to the abolition of the defence of incapacity due to age. But a presumption of incapacity and a child's right to raise incapacity are not the same. See, eg, Simester, AP and Sullivan, GR, *Criminal Law: Theory and Doctrine*, 2000, Hart, pp 584–85, and the fuller discussion in Chapter 3, below.

patient seems to rest upon an interpretation of the old decision in *Tatam* ((1921) 15 Cr App R 132). Here, the defendant had committed buggery with three boys, all aged under 14. The main question before the Court of Appeal was whether the boys were accomplices to the offences. It was held that they were not accomplices, as they were 'unable at law to commit that offence'.[4] But if this statement can be taken to suggest that boys under 14 cannot be guilty as patients, it still cannot be based upon any notion of their incapacity. Instead, the Court of Appeal seemed to rely upon a number of older judicial statements, notably by Sir Matthew Hale and Sir Edward Coke, to the effect that such a child was not guilty as he 'lacked discretion'. Confusion appears to have resulted from the use of the word 'discretion'. Hale and Coke presumably meant no more than a reference to 'mischievous discretion', but the court in *Tatam* appears to have confused this with physical incapacity. It is possible to interpret this decision as being based simply upon a desire to protect the child-patient by regarding children under 14 as the victims of the offence, and thus not meriting criminal sanctions. This interpretation gains some support from the earlier decision in *Tyrell* ([1894] 1 QB 710).[5] However, there are two difficulties with this interpretation. First, the notion that a child under the age of 14 is inevitably the 'victim' of the offence is not substantiated by the facts of many such cases. It is, at best, a fiction and if the law wishes to recognise that fiction, then it should do so overtly. Secondly, and more significantly, Parliament enacted in 1993 that a boy aged under 14 is no longer to be presumed incapable of sexual intercourse. Thus, s 1 of the Sexual Offences Act 1993 provides:

> The presumption of criminal law that a boy under the age of 14 is incapable of sexual intercourse (whether natural or unnatural) is hereby abolished.

Clearly, the effect of this section is to make a boy under 14 (but aged at least 10) capable of sexual intercourse, and thus potentially liable for, *inter alia*, the offence of buggery as agent (assuming mischievous discretion is established). But does the section necessarily impact upon the position of child patients? If *Tatam* was exempting children on the basis of their physical incapacity to perform the act of sexual intercourse (however untenable this argument may be), then, at least in terms of boys, if not girls, it appears to have been overruled by s 1. If the rule was based upon a desire to protect the victim, then it is possible that the section has made no difference and the law will continue to regard child patients as the victims, not deserving of punishment. It seems most unlikely that, as Parliament has expressly legislated to criminalise the boy-as-agent, future courts would fail to consider the inconsistency if they were to continue not to criminalise the boy-as-patient. Irrespective of whether, on policy grounds, a prosecution should be brought in such circumstances,

---

4   (1921) 15 Cr App R 132.

5   See Wasik, M and Taylor, R, *Blackstone's Guide to the Criminal Justice and Public Order Act 1994*, 1995, Blackstone, p 106.

such uncertainty is undesirable. However, these uncertainties and anomalies will be removed if cl 2 of the 2000 Bill is enacted. Clause 2 recognises the *Tyrell* principle, whereby children under a certain age should receive the protection of the criminal law, not its censure. Clause 2 will remove criminal liability from any child aged under 16 where sexual activity takes place with a person over the age of 16 (see, further, below). As far as buggery is concerned, the law will be simplified, in that there will no longer be a potential distinction between the child-patient and the child-agent: both will be exempted from criminal responsibility.

2.2.1.2   Privacy

The amended s 12 of the Sexual Offences Act 1956 provides that buggery will not be an offence where the act of buggery 'takes place in private and both parties have attained the age of 18'. The 1956 Act does not contain a complete definition of the phrase 'in private'. Rather, the new s 12(1B) of the 1956 Act states that an act of buggery shall not be treated as being done in private: (a) when more than two persons take part or are present; or (b) when it takes place in a lavatory to which the public have access. According to s 12(1B), this limitation upon the meaning of 'in private' applies to 'an act of buggery by one man with another'. This was an unambiguous phrase, whilst the exception was applicable only to acts of male buggery. Since 1994, many acts of male/female buggery are also decriminalised. There is a strong consensus of opinion that the s 12(1B) definition of 'in private' does not apply equally to an act of buggery with a female. Rather, the reference to 'another' should continue to be limited to 'another man' and should not be extended to include 'another person'. It has been argued by Wasik and Taylor, for example, that the section does not apply to an act of buggery by a man with a woman.[6] However, whilst this appears to be the case, it will cause obvious anomalies to arise. If A and B (two males over the age of 18) committed an act of buggery in a public lavatory, they are denied automatically the protection of the exception, their act being regarded as not in private. If the same act were committed by C (a male) and D (a female) in the same circumstances, it seems illogical and inequitable to say that their act is not automatically to be treated as not taking place in private. By interpreting 'another' as meaning 'another person', there would at least be consistency between acts of buggery involving different genders.

The second limitation contained in s 12(1B) on the meaning of privacy relates to 'when more than two persons take part or are present'. An act of buggery (or gross indecency between men) is automatically not in private if it involves the participation of, or takes place in the presence of, more than two persons. This qualification has been the target of much criticism, and has recently been the subject of a decision before the European Court of Human

---

6   *Op cit*, Wasik and Taylor, fn 5.

Rights. In *ADT v UK* ((Application No 35765/97), ECHR), the European Court of Human Rights held (albeit in a case of gross indecency, rather than buggery) that legislation prohibiting consensual non-violent sexual acts between more than two men in private went beyond what was necessary in a democratic society for the protection of morals or health, or the rights and freedoms of others. The applicant, referred to as ADT, had been convicted of gross indecency after engaging in sexual acts, involving oral sex and mutual masturbation. The acts had involved up to four other men and had taken place in the applicant's home. Although the acts had been video recorded, the charges related to the acts themselves, not the recordings, and it was accepted that the videos were unlikely to have been viewed by any other persons. The Court accepted that the conviction of the applicant for gross indecency constituted a violation of his right to respect for his private life contrary to Art 8 of the European Convention of Human Rights. The Court held that although there may be a point at which sexual activities could be carried out in such a manner that state interference *might* be justified, this was not such an instance. There was a restricted number of friends involved and it was most unlikely that persons other than the participants would become aware of the activities. On the precise facts, therefore, the activities were genuinely 'private', and the Court would adopt a narrow margin of appreciation in respect of the State's right to interfere. Whilst the decision itself is important for the parties concerned, it should not be forgotten that the Government has expressed already its commitment to widespread reform of sexual offences, including buggery and gross indecency, (see below). The long awaited rationalisation of the meaning of privacy will form one small part of that reform. Until those reforms take place, the decision in *ADT* will be of considerable importance. It shows that the courts, including presumably English courts now that the Human Rights Act 1998 is fully in force, will consider individual circumstances in deciding whether consensual sexual activity involving more than two persons infringes the parties' right to privacy. The decision in *ADT* does not say that all acts of group sexual activity will now be regarded as in private and thus lawful. But it is likely that the courts will need to find compelling reasons for upholding the State's right of interference. This might include, for example, a finding that the acts were not 'truly private' if video recordings had been produced for future distribution and profit.[7]

Notwithstanding the above developments, it is clear that the statutory definition of what is not in private is partial and not exhaustive. Apart from

---

7   The applicant had argued also that the State's interference, and his conviction, amounted to a form of sex discrimination in breach of Art 14, because domestic law neither regulates private homosexual acts between consenting adult women nor prohibits acts of gross indecency between heterosexuals. The European Court, having decided in the applicant's favour in respect of Art 8, held that there was no need to consider the case under Art 14 as well.

the two specific instances referred to in the statute, whether a particular place where the act occurred is private or not is a matter of fact to be determined by the court with reference to all the circumstances.

In *Reakes* ([1974] Crim LR 615), the defendant engaged in an act of buggery in an enclosed, unlit private yard at 1 am. In the yard was a toilet used by patrons of nearby restaurants and employees of a local taxi firm. Access to the yard was via a gate adjoining a public road. On the question of privacy, the trial judge directed the jury as follows: 'You look at all the surrounding circumstances, the time of night, the nature of the place including such matters as lighting and you consider further the likelihood of a third person coming upon the scene.'[8] The Court of Appeal upheld the conviction and approved the trial judge's direction. In so doing, the law appears to be adopting an objective and highly restrictive test of privacy. Providing there is at least a possibility, however remote, of a third person coming upon the scene, then the defendant's claim as to privacy will be defeated.

However, a more generous interpretation was adopted in *Ghik* ([1984] Crim LR 110), where the defendant was charged with committing not buggery, but an act of gross indecency with another man in a public place, namely the underground car park at Euston Station. The act allegedly occurred on stairs in the car park at 12.35 am; the station itself closed at 1 am. Counsel for the defendant argued that the prosecution had to show some evidence of the likelihood of a third party coming upon the scene and, further, that as Parliament, in the 1967 Act, had expressly excluded private acts done in a public lavatory from being in private, then 'privacy' could be found to exist in other public places. The trial judge (Martin J) accepted this submission and directed an acquittal. As there was no evidence of the likelihood of anyone coming upon the scene, nor even evidence that the car park was open, it could not be established that the act had occurred 'in public'. In his commentary upon the case, Professor Smith agreed with the need to look at all of the surrounding circumstances:

> The mischief aimed at is the doing of an act in the presence of third parties. If it is done in such circumstances that there is a risk of its being observed by third parties, then it may well be held not to have been done in private; but if there is no chance of it being observed by anyone, then it should be regarded as within the defence.[9]

On considering the mischief with which Parliament was concerned, we agree with Professor Smith's argument that an act of buggery (or gross indecency) which took place in the back of a locked and enclosed van in a public car park should nevertheless be regarded as in a private place. However, we are less optimistic that the courts would adopt such a broad view of privacy.

---

8   [1974] Crim LR 615.
9   [1984] Crim LR 110.

2.2.3 Mens rea

It must be established that the defendant's act of penetration was deliberate, that is, intentional. Whilst the notion of 'accidental' buggery may seem implausible, the issue was considered in *Watson* ([1992] Crim LR 434). Here, the Court of Appeal quashed the defendant's conviction for buggery, one reason for which being that the trial judge had failed to stress properly to the jury that anal penetration had to be deliberate, and that accidental penetration would not suffice. Although, on the facts, there had been no defence of accident raised, it was nevertheless incumbent upon the trial judge in the circumstances to emphasise the requisite deliberate nature of the act. Of course, *Watson* was decided before the changes to buggery effected by the 1994 Act, but it is submitted that the principle is accurate and should remain. Thus, if D (aged, say, 19) was engaging in sexual acts with his girlfriend (aged 16) and, whilst attempting to penetrate her vagina, he accidentally penetrated her anus, it seems beyond dispute that no offence of buggery would be committed: the intentional physical act necessary to establish the *actus reus* is missing. However, it is possible that D (and indeed his girlfriend) in this situation may commit buggery if he fails to withdraw upon realising the nature of his act, assuming that intercourse in buggery will be construed as a continuing act as it is in rape (see below).

The second, and more significant, aspect to *mens rea* in buggery relates to the ages of the parties and the defendant's knowledge thereof.

In particular, difficulties can occur where the defendant makes a genuine mistake about the age of the other person involved in the act of buggery. Two examples, based upon the law as it stands prior to the 2000 Bill, should suffice to illustrate the problem. Suppose that D1 (aged, say, 22) commits buggery with X in private, with consent. X is aged 17, although D1 genuinely believed him to be 18. If the facts were as D1 believed, he would be committing no offence. Therefore, should he be acquitted due to his mistake? Or has he committed the 'five-year' offence?

Similarly, suppose that D2 (also aged 22) commits an act of buggery with Y (a boy of 15), whom D2 genuinely believed to be aged 16. Has D2 committed the 'life offence' (on the basis of the facts as they actually are) or the 'five-year' offence (on the basis of the facts as he believed them to be)?

At present, there is no definitive answer to these questions, but, for many years, the consensus of academic opinion has suggested that, in relation to mistakes about age, the courts are likely to adopt the approach taken in *Prince* ((1875) LR 2 CCR 154) and construe buggery as an offence of strict liability vis-à-vis age.[10] However, this approach must now be considered in the light of the recent decision of the House of Lords in *B v DPP* (considered fully, below,

---

10   Smith, J and Hogan, B, *Criminal Law*, 1999, Butterworths, p 480; Rook, P and Ward, R, *Sexual Offences*, 1997, Sweet & Maxwell, p 139.

in Chapter 5), which re-emphasised the importance of the presumption of *mens rea* and the need for compelling reasons to impose strict liability. The consequences of imposing strict liability, in the above examples, would be to make D1 guilty of the 'five-year' offence, and D2 guilty of the more serious 'life offence'. This, it is submitted, would not produce an acceptable situation. Notwithstanding the likely 'rationale' for such an interpretation, namely that young victims (even though consenting *de facto*) are deserving of the law's protection and thus more severe penalties need to be attributed to the defendants, it is clear that unsupportable anomalies could arise. In particular, there are conflicts between the law's attitude to heterosexual acts as opposed to homosexual acts, and even conflicts pertaining to the nature of different sexual acts within a heterosexual relationship. For instance, it is clear that young girls of, say 14 or even 12, can and do consent *de facto* to acts of (vaginal) intercourse, thus removing an essential element of rape. But, in such circumstances, a defendant could face a charge of unlawful sexual intercourse with a girl under the age of 16 and 13 respectively.[11] Similarly, if a youth (male or female) under the age of 18 consents to anal intercourse, or if the circumstances are such that proving lack of consent for the purpose of rape would be very difficult, then the defendant could face the alternative charge of buggery. It is here that the anomalies begin. The defendant (aged 18) who has vaginal intercourse with a girl of 15, wrongly but reasonably believing her to be 16, may be able to rely on the 'young man's defence contained in s 6(3) of the Sexual Offences Act 1956. But the defendant who has consensual anal intercourse with his male partner aged 17, wrongly believing him to be aged 18, has no corresponding defence and, assuming strict liability to be applied, will be guilty of buggery. This is no less than discrimination on the basis of the gender of the other party. But an even less satisfactory situation results where the relationship remains heterosexual and only the physical acts differ. Thus, the young man's defence may be available where the defendant makes the mistake outlined above, but if the same defendant were to engage in an act of buggery with his female partner (aged 17), and he mistakenly believed her to be 18, then, again, he would have no defence. The non-availability of an analogous defence in this scenario can have nothing to do with homophobic attitudes, but, instead, must be based upon some implicit discrimination surrounding the physical act of heterosexual anal intercourse. The only consistent and fair solution would be to make available on a charge of buggery a defence whereby a defendant could argue that his (or her) genuine, and, if necessary, reasonable, mistake as to age removed the requisite *mens rea*.

---

11   Offences under ss 6 and 5 respectively of the Sexual Offences Act 1956: see Chapter 5, below.

2.3 Reform

As noted above, the Government had announced in 1998 its intention to undertake a comprehensive review of sexual offences laws. But even before that, there had been a number of important reform proposals. In 1984, the Criminal Law Revision Committee proposed the creation of four offences of buggery.[12] Subsequently, these proposals were incorporated into the draft Criminal Code Bill as cll 95–99, whilst, in addition, buggery itself was defined within cl 87 as follows:

> ... 'buggery' means anal intercourse between a man and another person and is complete on penetration, whether or not there is an emission of seed, and continues until the man's penis is withdrawn; and 'commit buggery' means take part in an act of buggery either as agent or as patient.

Of course, it is important to remember that some of these proposals were overtaken subsequently by legislative events. Thus, cl 95 (non-consensual buggery) is now redundant in the light of the changes to rape brought about by the Criminal Justice and Public Order Act 1994.

With regard to the proposals relating to consensual buggery, it is worth noting that the Law Commission, in its commentary upon the Bill, was not in universal agreement with the Criminal Law Revision Committee's recommendations. In particular, there remained a discrepancy between the minimum ages at which males and females could give a valid legal consent to an act of anal intercourse; namely, 16 for females and 18 for males. Furthermore, there was some disagreement over the extent to which (if at all) a defendant could be entitled to rely upon a mistake about the other party's age as a defence to a charge of buggery. Here, the proposals cll 96–99) were made unnecessarily complicated by the fact that they continued to differentiate between the ages of the parties depending upon gender. There was also a feeling expressed within the Commission that, in relation to the offence of buggery with a child under the age of 13 (cl 96), any defence of mistake as to age may be easy to make and difficult to rebut, thus diminishing protection for child victims.[13]

However, these initial proposals must be read in the light of two major reform initiatives, namely the Sexual Offences (Amendment) Bill 2000, and the Home Office Consultation Paper, *Setting the Boundaries: Reforming the Law on Sex Offences* (July 2000).

---

12 Criminal Law Revision Committee, *Fifteenth Report on Sexual Offences*, Cmnd 9213, 1984.

13 For a full discussion of the initial reform proposals, see the first edition of the current text at pp 35–37.

2.3.1   Sexual Offences (Amendment) Bill 2000

The passage of the Bill through Parliament, as outlined above, has been somewhat turbulent. It met stiff opposition in the House of Lords, eventually forcing the Government to make clear its intention to utilise the Parliament Acts to force through the legislation if necessary.

However, the 2000 Bill, when enacted, would make the following changes to the law of buggery.

Clause 1 of the Bill deals with the age of consent and would substitute the word 'eighteen' with the word 'sixteen' where it appears in s 12 and para 16 of Sched 2 to the 1956 Act (as amended) and s 1 of the 1967 Act. The effect of these changes would be that consensual buggery with another person will cease to be an offence if the act takes place in private, and both parties have attained the age of 16 (rather than 18, as at present).

Clause 2 deals with defences that are available to persons under the age of consent. It provides that a person under the age of 16 commits no offence of buggery under s 12 of the 1956 Act where he or she 'is under the age of sixteen and the other person has attained that age'. This simple-looking clause, which in essence is much welcomed, has a number of interesting features. Its purpose is to exempt automatically from criminal liability (for gross indecency as well as buggery) persons who are under the age of 16, where the other person is aged 16 or over. The clause says nothing about a young person's 'incapacity', but rather seems to be justified on the reasoning adopted in *Tyrell*, above, that a young person deserves the law's protection, not its censure. The clause makes no distinction between the agent and patient in buggery, and, thus, it will provide equal exemption to young persons, however they participate in the act. The older person (although that person may be only 16) will not, of course, be exempt from liability. However, under changes effected by cl 1(2)(b), proceedings can only be instituted against the older males, where the other party is under 16, with the consent of the Director of Public Prosecutions. Finally, it is clear that cl 2 will not apply where the two parties are both under the age of 16: they both remain criminally liable. In reality, it must be doubted whether many (or any) prosecutions would ensue where, for example, two youths aged 15 engaged in consensual buggery, in circumstances where, if the youths were aged 15 and 16, the younger would be automatically exempt from criminal liability. It is possible that a prosecution may be appropriate where, for example, an element of pressure from one of the youths existed, albeit not sufficient to vitiate consent.

During debates on the 2000 Bill, a number of concerns were expressed about the effects of lowering the age of consent in respect of vulnerable teenagers, especially those aged 16 and 17. Partly as a result of those concerns, cll 3 and 4 were introduced to provide a 'safeguard', by creating a new offence of 'abuse of position of trust'. As this deals with 'sexual activity' generally, rather than buggery specifically, it will be considered in more detail below in Chapter 5. In essence, however, it will be an offence for a person aged 18 or over to have sexual intercourse or engage in any other sexual activity with a person under the age of 18, where the older person is in a designated 'position of trust' in relation to the younger. The Bill sets out four specific conditions, any one of which will constitute a position of trust. In addition, the Secretary of State, by statutory instrument, may add to those conditions, effectively broadening the scope of the offence by creating further positions of trust.

2.3.2   *Home Office Consultation Paper:* Setting the Boundaries, *July 2000*

The recommendations in the Consultation Paper relating to the offence of buggery should be considered in the light of the Government's previously stated objective of equalising the age of consent, and of creating laws which do not discriminate on grounds of either gender or sexual orientation. Equally, the proposals relating to buggery (as with many of the other proposals) do not exist in isolation; there are 62 recommendations in total in the Paper and several of them need to be viewed in conjunction with others.

Recommendation 17 proposes that 'as a matter of public policy, the age of legal consent should remain at sixteen'. The Report states at para 3.5.7:

> In line with our general principles of fairness, protection and justice, we see no strong argument or evidence for differentiating between boys and girls or types of sexual activity in setting an age of consent.

The law's current approach to sexual orientation and the specific offence of buggery are dealt with in a number of different recommendations. Recommendation 44 proposes that 'the criminal law should not treat people differently on the basis of their sexual orientation. It should offer protection from all non-consensual sexual activity. Consensual sexual activity between adults in private that causes no harm should not be criminal'. Further, Recommendation 45 proposes that 'the present offences of buggery and gross indecency should be repealed, with separate provision made for the protection of children and animals and for regulating sexual behaviour in public'.

The effect of these recommendations would be to decriminalise buggery, as currently defined between persons, as a discrete offence. It would be replaced by other offences to deal with sexual intercourse (including anal intercourse) between adults in public, and offences aimed specifically at protecting children. These would include proposed offences of adult sexual abuse of a child[14] and sexual activity between minors.

2.4   Sentencing buggery

As has already been noted (and will be discussed in detail in Chapter 3), one main effect of the 1994 Act was to re-classify non-consensual buggery as rape, with the consequence that, today, all acts of non-consensual anal intercourse carry a potential maximum penalty of life imprisonment. A further consequence of the amendments is that the old '10-year' category (identified under *Courtie* as the only category where absence of consent was a relevant factor) no longer exists. Instead, there now exist three categories of consensual buggery: the 'life offence'; the 'five-year offence'; and the 'two-year offence' (see, above, at 2.2.1.1).

Prior to 1994, the leading authority on sentencing buggery was *Willis* ([1975] 1 All ER 620, where the Court of Appeal set out detailed guidelines specifically in relation to the 'life offence', that is, the buggery of boys under the age of 16. Insofar as that aspect of the life category has remained unaltered by the 1994 Act, we submit that *Willis* remains good authority on the question of how a trial judge should approach the sentencing of a defendant convicted of buggery with a boy under that age. In *Willis*, the defendant, aged 24 at the time of the incidents, was convicted both of indecent assault (by touching the penis of a boy aged nine) and of buggery of a boy aged 8, after he had become involved with a group of young boys who had been playing games involving undressing. The defendant was described in reports to the court as being of 'dull intelligence', very immature, irresponsible, and as possessing a 'personality disorder', although specifically not a mental disorder. In upholding the sentence of five years' imprisonment, the Court of Appeal stated the following general proposition:

> In our judgment the sentencing bracket for offences which have neither aggravating nor mitigating factors is from three to five years; and the place in the bracket will depend on age, intelligence and education.[15]

However, as the court emphasised, very few such offences have neither aggravating nor mitigating factors. Indeed, most will possess both, and they

---

14   An adult would be a person over 18. The proposed maximum sentence would be life where the child is under 13, and 10 years if the child is under 16, but over 13. Where the child is, say, aged 15, the proposal is more generous to the defendant than the current law of buggery, which carries a maximum sentence of life imprisonment for buggery of a child under 16.

15   [1975] 1 All ER 620, p 622, *per* Lawton LJ.

must be weighed by the trial judge. Also, as a general rule, and in addition to any aggravating or mitigating features, courts will regard buggery more seriously in correlation to the age of the victim: the younger the boy, the more serious the offence.

2.4.1   Aggravating factors

The Court of Appeal stressed that the list of aggravating factors was not to be regarded as exhaustive, but typically may include the following features.

First, where physical injury was caused to the boy:

> This may come about as a direct result of penetration. The Wolfenden Report [at para 85] thought this was very rare ... but it does sometimes occur in boys under the age of 10; and when it does the victim may be left for life with an embarrassing disability. Much more common is the case in which the offender has used violence to overcome the boy's resistance. This is a dangerous form of violence as it is under the driving force of lust and may be maintained with fatal results ... Offenders who use violence should be discouraged from repetition by severe sentences.[16]

Secondly, there may be emotional and psychological damage to the victim, although these will not inevitably result from the physical act of buggery *per se*. Similarly, the court believed that there was no evidence to support the view that experiencing an act of buggery at a young age would necessarily cause the development of homosexuality later in life.

Thirdly, there is a risk of moral corruption. This, as previously stated, does not mean that the act of buggery will predispose a boy to homosexuality, but rather that:

> ... that which leads up to the act may do so as, for example, by gifts of money and clothes and the provision of attractive outings and material comforts.[17]

Finally, aggravation may consist of the abuse of authority and trust:

> Those who have boys in their charge must not abuse their positions for the sake of gratifying their deviant sexual urges. If they do so, they must expect to get severe sentences. The factor of deterrence comes in here. All who have charge of the young must be made to appreciate through the sentences passed by the courts that society will not tolerate abuses of trust in this respect.[18]

It is a sad truth that the final aggravating factor appears to be of increasing relevance to the courts. Child sexual abuse scandals, often involving buggery of young boys, occur frequently within the context of adults holding positions of trust, whether they be social workers, residential care workers or teachers. It is right that the abuse of such positions should carry the sanction of increased penalties in order to mark societal concern and, more importantly,

---

16   [1975] 1 All ER 620.

17   *Ibid*, p 623.

18   *Ibid*.

to offer at least the possibility of enhanced protection for future vulnerable groups.

2.4.2   Mitigating factors

The Court of Appeal in *Willis* sought also to outline the main mitigating factors, which list, again, should not be regarded as exhaustive.

First, the defendant's 'mental imbalance' may operate as some mitigation. The court agreed with the Wolfenden Committee's rejection of the theory that homosexuality was a disease, and thus that some of its physical manifestations (such as the act of buggery) should be regarded as symptoms of that disease and not subject to criminal sanctions. But the court then continued:

> The Wolfenden Report recognised, however, that in some cases homosexual offences do occur as symptoms in the course of recognised mental or physical illness and cited as an example senile dementia ... When such cases are identified by satisfactory medical evidence judges will want to pass sentences which do not result in immediate committal to prison.[19]

Secondly, the courts will give consideration to defendants who have 'personality disorders':

> The types of disorder may vary: at one end of the scale there is the mentally immature adult who is in the transitional stage of psycho-sexual development; he can be helped to grow up mentally. At the other end are those with severely damaged personalities, such as the obviously effeminate and flautingly exhibitionist individuals and the deeply resentful anti-social types ... Offenders with personality disorders do ... present a difficult sentencing problem ... If they cannot be managed, either because they do not want to be or are mentally incapable of accepting management, they may become a danger to boys when at large in society. In such cases, the public are entitled to expect the courts to keep this class of offender away from boys, in really bad cases for indefinite periods.[20]

This is an interesting 'mitigating factor', as it seems to indicate that the more extreme personality disorder may result in detention for an indefinite period, which can hardly be described as mitigation. If this is to be regarded in any sense as 'mitigation', then it would be preferable to view it as mitigation of treatment and attitude, but not mitigation of sentence vis-à-vis detention, because, demonstrably, it is not.

Finally, mitigation may exist in the form of 'emotional stress'. This consideration rests upon the, arguably questionable, assertion that 'latent homosexuals who have controlled their urges for years will give way under stress or unexpected and powerful temptation'.[21]

---

19   [1975] 1 All ER 620.

20   *Ibid.*

21   *Ibid*, p 624.

The Court of Appeal continued:

> The unexpected and powerful temptation may come from a depraved homosexual who sets out to seduce someone whom he recognises as having the same urges as he himself has. It is a saddening and disturbing experience for judges to find ... that the wicked seducer was an adolescent boy. When an accused who has kept his homosexuality under control for a long time begins committing offences either because of some precipitatory stress or exceptional temptation, the case may call for a measure of leniency.[22]

As a matter of public policy, it is debatable whether the 'act of seduction' of the victim should be regarded as mitigation on behalf of the defendant. Whilst there may be instances in the wider criminal law of defendants receiving mitigation as a result of being enticed or led into the crime by another person (whether that person is the victim or not), we suggest that this is not appropriate in offences of a sexual nature, especially in relation to young victims, where such boys are more deserving of protection, not censure, as the 'instigators' of the acts.

3   GROSS INDECENCY BETWEEN MEN

A second offence which, traditionally, has been used by the law as a means to regulate physical expressions of homosexuality is that of gross indecency.

Section 13 of the Sexual Offences Act 1956 provides:

> It is an offence for a man to commit an act of gross indecency with another man, whether in public or private, or to be a party to the commission by a man of an act of gross indecency with another man, or to procure the commission by a man of an act of gross indecency with another man.

By s 1 of the Sexual Offences Act 1967 (as amended by s 145 of the Criminal Justice and Public Order Act 1994), the offence of gross indecency is subject to the same decriminalising 'exception' as buggery, that is, conduct which otherwise would be an act of gross indecency will not be so if it was committed in private by two consenting male adults aged 18 or over.

Similarly, s 144 of the Criminal Justice and Public Order Act 1994 amended Sched 2 to the Sexual Offences Act 1956, thereby altering the penalties available for the offence. Under the new Sched 2, there is a maximum sentence of five years' imprisonment where a man of or over the age of 21 commits an act of gross indecency with a man under the age of 18. In all other instances of gross indecency, the maximum sentence is two years' imprisonment. This would include such situations as where the parties are aged 19 and 17; or where both parties are of exempted age (for example, both 19), but the act does not take place in private.

---

22   [1975] 1 All ER 620.

3.1 Parties

Section 13 is an offence which can only be committed by males as principal offenders. Despite the use of the word 'man' in the section, it is clear that boys can be principal offenders, and although the vast majority of defendants will be adult males, a boy aged between 10 and 13 could commit the offence if a mischievous discretion is proven against him.

3.2 *Actus reus*

The purpose of an offence of gross indecency would appear to be to set down objective standards of conduct, and thus to enable the law to regulate particular types of behaviour which may be viewed as 'unacceptable'. However, there are difficulties with such a rationale. First, it must be remembered that this offence may be committed in private (unless the 'exception' can be established), so that gross indecency, like buggery, falls foul of the general argument that the law is being used solely to control a particular manifestation of sexuality, where no harm (even in its widest definition) could be said to exist.

Secondly, even if it could be argued that the law of gross indecency had a stronger rationale when used in respect of overtly public acts, it is clear that the very wide scope that the offence enjoys means that it is capable of being used in ways which discriminate against homosexuals, as compared with heterosexuals engaging in similar displays of affection.

3.2.1 *Gross indecency*

In common with many jurisdictions, most notably, Canada, there has been a marked reluctance on the part of the English judiciary to define the term 'gross indecency'. The prevalent view seems to be that it is both unnecessary and unwise to attempt a rigid definition. Indeed, in Canada, the courts have argued that 'gross' and 'indecency' constitute an ordinary English phrase, and, therefore, it is safe to leave the meaning of the words to be determined by the average juror in all the circumstances of each case. Thus, in *Quesnel v Quesnel* ((1979) 51 CCC (2d) 270), the Ontario Court of Appeal held that the jury should be instructed that 'gross indecency' was a marked departure from decent conduct expected of the average Canadian in the circumstances that existed. It was emphasised that a 'fair objective standard' was required, against which the conduct (allegations of, *inter alia*, oral sex in the present case) could be tested. This was to be preferred to a subjective approach which, inevitably, must vary according to the individual jurors' 'personal taste and predilections'.

Notwithstanding the reluctance to formulate a rigid test, there is limited English authority which provides at least guidance to the meaning of the phrase.

In *Hunt v Badsey* ([1950] 2 All ER 291), a case on the interpretation of s 11 of the Criminal Law Amendment Act 1885, two men who were discovered together in a shed were said to be making a 'grossly indecent exhibition' to each other. There, even though there was no physical contact between them, it was held to be sufficient for the offence to be committed that 'they were making filthy exhibitions the one to the other'.[23] Once again, this approach is consistent with the view taken in other jurisdictions. In *Pinard v Maltais* ((1983) 5 CCC (3d) 460), the Quebec Court of Appeal upheld convictions for gross indecency where the defendants, whilst at a homosexual bathhouse, were seen touching their own genitals in the presence of each other. It was held that, for gross indecency to exist, the parties did not have to touch each other.

An interesting perspective may also be gleaned from a number of comments in the Wolfenden Committee Report. It was suggested that 'gross indecency' would normally be constituted by three forms of conduct: mutual masturbation; intercrural contact; and oral-genital contact. However, it was emphasised that, given the variety of human sexual techniques, this was not an exhaustive list. The flexibility inherent in the phrase 'gross indecency' may be taken as a genuine attempt to leave open to juries the decision as to whether certain conduct is deserving of censure; or it may be viewed merely as another instance of the law unfairly proscribing homosexual conduct in circumstances where it would never do so in relation to similar heterosexual acts.

3.2.2   With another man

This criterion has been interpreted by the courts to mean that the willing participation of two (or more) men is required before either can be convicted of an offence under s 13. In addition, it seems that 'with' no longer means 'against' or 'directed towards' another man. This view was justified by Scarman LJ in *Preece v Howells* ([1976] Crim LR 392) on the basis that to hold otherwise, and thus to make one man only guilty, would be to cause distress and embarrassment to the other non-consenting man. In *Preece v Howells*, the two defendants were observed by police officers to be masturbating in adjacent cubicles of a public lavatory. There was a hole in the wall between the cubicles, but the evidence was inconclusive as to whether the men had watched each other. The trial judge directed the jury that they could convict if they were satisfied that the defendants had been 'acting in concert', that is, that 'they were each simultaneously and intentionally displaying sexual activity to the other by tacit or express agreement'. These directions were approved by the Court of Appeal in upholding the convictions.[24]

---

23   [1950] 2 All ER 291, p 301, *per* Lord Goddard.
24   [1976] Crim LR 392, *per* Scarman LJ.

3.3   *Mens rea*

Although there is little direct authority on the *mens rea* required for s 13, it seems that intention is required on the part of both men. The need for intention would appear to be consistent with the requirement of 'acting in concert'. Thus, if two men are observed masturbating in adjoining cubicles in a public lavatory, it seems right in principle that they should only be convicted if both are intending to display their sexual acts to the other. If they were acting independently, without knowledge of the other, then the requisite intention, by definition, would be absent (although satisfying the jury of this fact would, admittedly, prove very difficult in reality). An alternative scenario is where one man is acting in an indecent manner towards another, where that other is either an innocent, non-consenting party or simply unaware of the acts that are taking place. In such unlikely circumstances, a potential charge of attempting to commit an offence under s 13 may succeed, or (if the facts were appropriate) an indecent assault may be substantiated (see Chapter 6).

3.4   Sentencing gross indecency

An offence under s 13 is triable either way. Where a defendant is convicted on indictment, the maximum penalty is five years' imprisonment in those cases where he is 21 or over and the other man is under 18. In all other cases, the maximum penalty is two years' imprisonment. Where a defendant is convicted summarily, the maximum penalty is six months' imprisonment and/or a fine of £5,000.

One interesting aspect to sentencing for offences of gross indecency is the law's attitude towards first offenders. In *Morgan v Dockerty* ([1979] Crim LR 60), the defendants were convicted of committing acts of gross indecency in a public convenience. Morgan (aged 61) was sentenced to three months' imprisonment and Dockerty (aged 39) was sentenced to six weeks' imprisonment. On appeal, the Court of Appeal substituted fines of £100 and £50 respectively, stating that, although, until recently, such conduct would almost invariably have attracted a custodial sentence, sentencing policy with regard to first offenders had changed. Whilst such types of act were regarded as a nuisance to the public and sentences did have to try to deter such behaviour, nevertheless, experience showed that for the majority of first offenders a court appearance plus a fine stopped a repetition, at least in public conveniences.

3.5   Alternative offences to gross indecency

Where the criteria for a s 13 offence are unlikely to be established, for example, where the alleged behaviour is at the 'moderate' end of the scale of 'gross indecency' judged by modern, objective moral standards, then the law has not been slow in utilising alternative offences in order to regulate homosexual activity in public.

In *Masterson and Another v Holden* ([1986] 1 WLR 1017), the two defendants were kissing, cuddling and fondling near a bus stop in central London at 2 am. They were seen by two heterosexual couples, from which one male partner shouted to the defendants: 'You filthy sods.' The defendants were cautioned by police officers who happened to be nearby, after which Masterson said: 'We can cuddle, can't we? What's up with you?' The defendants were charged with and convicted of insulting behaviour under s 54(13) of the Metropolitan Police Act 1839, after the magistrates decided that their behaviour was insulting. On appeal, on the basis that such behaviour was not insulting, it was held that it was irrelevant that the defendants did not know anyone was present in the vicinity at the time. Rather, it was sufficient that the conduct was insulting and may have caused a breach of the peace. It is almost inconceivable that similar actions engaged in by a male and a female would have resulted in a successful prosecution. This proposition lends some support to the view that there remains an element of bias against homosexuals in the criminal process.

There is a body of opinion which suggests that there is an increasing tendency to use both local bylaws and public order offences as a further mechanism for controlling homosexual intimacy in public places. Tatchell,[25] for example, notes the use of s 4 of the Public Order Act 1986 against two men who were kissing in the street, which behaviour was regarded as likely to cause 'public alarm or distress'. It is the use of such wide ranging offences as these which lends very strong support to the belief that male homosexuals are being discriminated against in terms of their public displays of affection.

3.6   Reform

The Criminal Law Revision Committee recommended the retention of an offence essentially in accordance with the present s 13, provided that at least one of the parties was under the age of 18. The proposals were incorporated into cll 100 and 101 of the draft Criminal Code Bill as follows:

100   A man aged 18 or above is guilty of an offence if he commits an act of gross indecency with a boy under the age of 18, unless he believes the boy to be aged 18 or above.

101   A man is guilty of an offence if he commits an act of gross indecency with another man where either man is, or both are, under the age of 18, unless he is aged 18 or above and he believes the other to be aged 18 or above.

---

25   Tatchell, P, *Out in Europe*, 1990, Channel 4 Television, p 30.

It should be noted that the draft Bill, in line with the Criminal Law Revision Committee's recommendations, makes no attempt to define gross indecency. This was not supported by all members of the Law Commission, some of whom felt that a definition would be useful. However, as was noted a considerable time ago by the Wolfenden Committee, the range of potential human sexual conduct may be such that a definition of 'gross indecency' is not feasible and, in any case, the present position, whereby the phrase is determined by the reasonable juror, seems to cause few difficulties in practice.

As with the law relating to buggery, the offence of gross indecency will be subject to radical changes if recent reform proposals are implemented.

First, cl 1 of the Sexual Offences (Amendment) Bill 2000 would lower the age of consent to 16. It provides that an act of gross indecency, or procuring such an act or being a party to the commission of such an act, will not be an offence, provided the act is in private, that both parties have consented and that they have attained the age of 16 (rather than 18, as at present).

More radical proposals are contained in *Setting the Boundaries*. Recommendation 45, as noted above, would repeal the present offence of gross indecency. Once gross indecency *per se* ceases to be a crime, there will be no need for an offence of procuring others to commit homosexual acts, which relies upon those acts being defined as criminal. Consequently, Recommendation 46 proposes repeal of the offence of procuring others to commit homosexual acts.

4   SOLICITATION BY MEN FOR IMMORAL PURPOSES

Section 32 of the Sexual Offences Act 1956 provides:

> It is an offence for a man persistently to solicit or importune in a public place for immoral purposes.

This is not an offence which is limited to controlling the activities of male homosexuals. Indeed, its original purpose was to control specific heterosexual conduct, namely to prohibit and punish soliciting by men of female prostitutes. However, as will be seen below, due to a lack of precision in the drafting of the section, it has not been limited to heterosexual activities, and its primary purpose today may in fact be taken as being an overt method of regulating certain conduct of male homosexuals.

4.1   *Actus reus*

4.1.1   *Persistently*

To be guilty of this offence a defendant must have acted 'persistently'. This criterion raises a number of different issues.

In *Dale v Smith* ([1967] 2 All ER 1133), on the day specified in the charge, the defendant allegedly importuned a small boy and later said 'hello' in a public lavatory to a youth who was unknown to him. The defendant claimed that this was just a pleasantry, but the Divisional Court, in upholding the conviction, said that the justices were entitled to interpret this behaviour differently, especially as, on a previous day, the defendant had said 'hello' to another stranger and had shown him 'sexy photographs'. In coming to this conclusion, the Divisional Court emphasised that the word 'persistent' should be taken as connoting some 'degree of repetition, of either more than one invitation to one person or a series of invitations to different people'.[26]

Whilst this in itself may be regarded as a somewhat broad definition, indicative of the judiciary's willingness to interpret certain offences against the interests of homosexual defendants, the courts have considered also whether 'persistence' may be satisfied by a single but continuing act.

In *Burge* ([1961] Crim LR 412) (although not a case directly in point), the court had to consider, *inter alia*, whether the display of a card in a shop window amounted to 'persistent soliciting', despite there being no direct evidence of how long the card had actually been in place. At trial, it was held that the display was persistent even if the card had only been in place for half an hour, although it was inferred from the evidence in any case that it had been there for a longer period. On appeal to the Divisional Court, the defendant's conviction was quashed, but it was quashed on the basis that there was nothing capable of amounting to soliciting. The specific question of persistence was not decided by the Divisional Court.

However, the issue of 'persistence' was considered in some detail by the Court of Appeal, within the context of s 32, in *Tuck* ([1994] Crim LR 375). Here, the defendant was seen to enter a cubicle in a public lavatory where he left the door ajar and watched several other men using the urinals. He then went to a washbasin and continued to watch other men, including a police officer in plain clothes. The defendant then left the lavatory, but returned a short time later, whereupon he stood at a urinal masturbating, whilst still watching others. At one time, he turned towards and looked at the police officer. On appeal against his conviction, the defendant argued that there was nothing to satisfy the requirement of persistence. The Court of Appeal accepted that, on his first visit to the lavatory, the defendant had only looked at other men, but that on his later visit, especially when he turned towards the police officer, there was evidence of 'importuning'. But was that importuning 'persistent'? In agreeing with the trial judge, the Court of Appeal held that there was persistence on the facts, evidenced by persistence 'in a course of conduct'.[27] The decision has been supported by Professor Smith, who has argued[28] that evidence of masturbation for approximately seven minutes does and should

---

26 [1967] 2 All ER 1133, *per* Lord Parker CJ.
27 [1994] Crim LR 375, *per* Glidewell LJ.
28 *Ibid*, pp 375–76.

satisfy the requirement of persistence! We submit, with respect to both the Court of Appeal and Professor Smith, that the decision extends too far the meaning of persistence. In particular, it is inconsistent with the generally accepted definition in *Dale v Smith*, that is, that there must be some 'degree of repetition' evidenced by either 'more than one invitation to one person' or by a 'series of invitations to different people'. The decision seems to suggest that one continuous act is capable of amounting to 'more than one invitation' or 'a series of invitations'. This is stretching the language to unacceptable limits, arguably for no other reason than to regulate a piece of behaviour which the court found morally unacceptable. Whilst the defendant's behaviour may have been morally reprehensible in the eyes of some people, it is not acceptable to manipulate statutory wording beyond its legitimate bounds merely to uphold the desired conviction.

4.1.2   Solicit

In general terms the requirement of 'soliciting' may be taken as a need to show that the defendant has 'made an invitation to another person to engage in' certain acts. But, as with the requirement of acting 'persistently', the courts have long been willing to allow a very generous interpretation of the need for the defendant to 'solicit'.

In *Horton v Mead* ([1913] 1 KB 154), the defendant was seen by police officers to enter a number of public lavatories, in each of which he remained for a few minutes. Both inside the lavatories and on the streets outside, the defendant smiled at various men, pursed his lips and wriggled his body. It was accepted that he did not speak to or touch anybody and there were no complaints from members of the public. It was held that this conduct was capable of amounting to 'soliciting'. Although the spoken word often is used when soliciting, it is not a legal requirement and, therefore, physical movements alone can suffice. It was held also to be irrelevant that the defendant's 'invitations' failed to 'reach the minds' of the intended recipients or, that if they did, the 'recipients' did not realise their significance.

In the context of male homosexuals 'cruising' specific areas with a view to meeting like-minded men, this decision seems extreme and unjustified. Where there are no 'victims' (the complainants in such cases invariably being the police), it is difficult to see which of the perceived purposes of the criminal law is being upheld. Instead, this may be viewed as yet another instance of the 'immorality' of the defendant's actions being punished.

4.1.3   Importune

As Parliament has proscribed two alternative actions (to solicit or to importune), there is a strong case for expecting the two verbs to possess distinctive meanings. Again, however, this has not proven to be the attitude of the courts.

In *Field v Chapman* ([1953] CLY 787), the defendant had stood next to and in front of various young men in lavatories and had smiled at them. The indictment specifically referred to the defendant 'importuning', not 'soliciting', and it was argued on his behalf that whilst the latter may exist, the former did not. This argument was rejected by the Divisional Court in upholding the defendant's conviction, and no significant distinction was recognised between the two terms. Again, this is puzzling. If Parliament had not intended there to be a difference between the two verbs, why were alternative words incorporated into the offence? There is much to be said for the argument propounded on behalf of the defendant in *Field v Chapman* that 'importune' suggests a more physical act than does 'solicit', or that, at least, it is a more difficult criterion to prove, in the sense of being a more narrow activity. Up to the present, the courts have refused to accept these distinctions.

4.1.4 Immoral purposes

As has been noted previously, the original purpose of s 32 was to prohibit and punish the soliciting by men of female prostitutes, but because the phrase 'immoral purposes' was not defined within the statute, it left open the possibility of the section being interpreted more widely, including its extension to cover men who solicited for homosexual purposes.

In *Crook v Edmondson* ([1966] 2 QB 81), one of the earliest cases on the interpretation of s 32, the central question was whether a man solicited for immoral purposes by kerb-crawling and soliciting women for the purpose of sexual intercourse. The justices held that, whilst the defendant clearly had 'solicited', he had not done so for 'immoral purposes'. This ruling was approved by the Divisional Court, where Winn LJ held that 'immoral purposes' meant 'such immoral purposes as are referred to in this part of this Act'.[29] This is taken as meaning that the subsequent act, that is, the act for which the defendant was soliciting must involve an offence *per se* under the statute. Clearly, this was not the case, as requesting consensual sexual intercourse is a request for an act which is not a crime in itself.

Crook v Edmondson was distinguished in *Dodd* ((1978) 66 Cr App R 87), where the defendant on several occasions drove past three girls, all aged 14 years, and, by the use of phrases such as 'I want to screw you', made it clear that he wished to have sexual intercourse with them. He appealed against his conviction under s 32 by arguing, relying upon the decision in *Crook v Edmondson*, that kerb-crawling did not amount to immoral purposes within the section. The Divisional Court rejected that argument and upheld the conviction. Cusack J interpreted *Crook v Edmondson* as saying that not all things which are immoral, are also necessarily criminal (for example, sexual intercourse *per se*). Here, however, there was little doubt that the defendant's

---

29   [1966] 2 QB 81, p 88.

purpose, that is, to have sexual intercourse with girls aged 14, was 'in itself immoral'. This last phrase would tend to indicate that Cusack J was suggesting that 'immoral purposes' do not necessarily have to be at one and the same time a crime within the Act. But he added that if there did also have to be a criminal offence *per se* in order to uphold a defendant's conviction under s 32, then that requirement was satisfied anyway because sexual intercourse with girls aged 14 was (and is still) an offence under s 6 of the Sexual Offences Act 1956.

The question whether it was possible to convict a defendant under s 32 where the act which he was soliciting was itself undoubtedly lawful, was considered by the Divisional Court in *Ford* ([1978] 1 All ER 1129). The defendant appealed against his conviction under s 32, arguing that, as the man whom he had approached and importuned was over the age of 21, and the intended sexual acts would have taken place in private, then any eventual homosexual activities would have been lawful. Importuning for a 'lawful act', it was argued, could not amount to importuning for 'immoral purposes'. On appeal, this argument was rejected: although the stigma of criminality had been removed from (some) homosexual acts, this did not prevent them from being 'immoral' for the purposes of this offence. Whether or not the acts solicited amounted to immoral purposes, added the court, was a question of fact for the jury.

This approach to the determination of immoral purposes was given approval by the Court of Appeal in *Gray* ((1982) 74 Cr App R 324), where it was held that the trial judge had been wrong to rule that homosexual activity was, as a matter of law, immoral. Instead, such activities were *capable* of amounting to 'immoral purposes', but the question as to whether they did or not was ultimately one for the jury.

Notwithstanding such guidance, the actual meaning of 'immoral purposes' and, more importantly, the respective roles of the trial judge and the jury in determining the question, remained obscure. Further guidance was needed, and ultimately provided, by the Court of Appeal in two cases, although neither of them has resolved all the problems in this area.

In *Goddard* ([1991] Crim LR 299), the defendant had spoken to a female cyclist (aged 28) on three occasions, making comments, *inter alia*, about her 'sexy legs', and asking her to go to bed. A short while after these events, he had also asked a 14 year old paper girl if she would like to earn £10 by going to a field 'for some fun'. On behalf of the defendant, it was submitted that, whilst the (single) incident with the 14 year old could amount to importuning for immoral purposes, the incident with the 28 year old could not, as it involved merely a request to an adult to have consensual sexual intercourse. In effect, the defendant was admitting one act of importuning, but thereby denying the requisite 'persistence'. The trial judge rejected the defence submission and the defendant was convicted. The Court of Appeal, in upholding the conviction, sought to explain the relevant law. First, the trial judge must decide if the defendant's conduct is capable of amounting to importuning for immoral purposes, but then the jury must decide whether, in fact, it did so. Secondly, it was confirmed that 'immoral purposes' must mean 'sexually immoral', but the activity solicited need not amount to a criminal offence. Thirdly, the offence was not intended to capture 'innocuous invitations to sexual intercourse', but rather should be aimed at 'persistent conduct which was unpleasant, disturbing and offensive, and in a public place'.[30] The defendant's behaviour satisfied these criteria and thus the conviction would be confirmed.

Many of these issues were reconsidered within a homosexual context in *Kirkup* ([1993] 2 All ER 802). There it was alleged that the defendant's behaviour in a public lavatory amounted to a tacit invitation to other men to engage in homosexual acts, although there was no suggestion that those acts would take place otherwise than in private. The trial judge directed the jury that 'immoral purposes' meant 'for the purposes of sexual activity'.[31] The defendant was convicted and he appealed. The Court of Appeal confirmed that, as a matter of law, 'immoral purposes' must relate to some form of sexual activity. It was confirmed further, following *Goddard*, that the trial judge decides if the particular purpose is capable of being immoral, and the jury then decides if in fact it was so. On the present facts, the trial judge had been wrong to rule that any form of sexual contact or activity was immoral, as by doing so he had failed to let the jury decide if that particular activity was in fact an immoral purpose. However, despite this misdirection, the Court of Appeal upheld the conviction on the basis that any properly directed jury would have viewed the intended conduct as an 'immoral purpose'.

There are clear difficulties with the law as it stands following *Goddard* and *Kirkup*.[32] First, the criminalisation of sexual behaviour (and, even more so, actions preliminary to sexual acts) is a serious matter, and it is wrong in principle to leave a key issue, namely the meaning of 'immoral purposes', to the jury. The criminal law requires certainty, but this approach will result in inconsistent jury verdicts based upon widely differing moral views. Secondly, and conversely, if the meaning of 'immoral purposes' is left to the judge as a matter of law, there exists a danger that a definition may emerge which is regarded as 'out of touch' with contemporary views. Paradoxically, this was one of the reasons why the meaning of the phrase was given over to juries in cases like *Ford* and *Gray*. Thirdly, and perhaps most importantly, there remains a perception that the application of s 32 continues to operate in a discriminatory fashion as between homosexual and heterosexual activities. Although the Court of Appeal in *Goddard*, above, expressed the view that s 32

---

30   [1991] Crim LR 299, *per* Watkins LJ.

31   [1993] 2 All ER 802.

32   See Birch, D, 'Commentary on *Kirkup*' [1993] Crim LR 777.

should not be used to capture merely 'innocuous invitations to consensual sexual intercourse', the authorities may suggest that this restriction upon the use of the offence is applied less liberally in respect of homosexuals than heterosexuals. Behaviour whereby young heterosexual males 'chat up' females is taken for granted. Similar (or even less overt) behaviour in a homosexual context, often with no complainant, frequently will not be tolerated by the law.

4.2   Mens rea

The wording of s 32 discloses no overt *mens rea*. However, it is clear that the offence is not one of strict liability and that it is incumbent upon the prosecution to prove a mental element against the defendant. It is our view that the section should be interpreted so as to involve a purposive element. Thus, it must be proven that the defendant *intended* to either solicit or importune, that is, to make an invitation to another person to engage in certain acts *for immoral purposes*. Therefore, a defendant who smiled at and spoke to other men, and claimed that he had done so merely to pass pleasantries, may seek to argue that he did not act with the requisite immoral purposes, although, of course, as was noted in *Dale v Smith*, above, it is always open to the court to interpret the evidence differently and to infer that the defendant had been soliciting with the necessary purposes.

4.3   Reform

The Criminal Law Revision Committee has proposed[33] the replacement of s 32 with two distinct offences of male solicitation: one of persistent soliciting of women for the purposes of prostitution; the other of persistent soliciting for homosexual purposes. The latter offence was incorporated into the draft Criminal Code Bill as cl 138:

> A man is guilty of an offence if in a street or public place he persistently solicits another man or men for sexual purposes.

This proposal does deal with some of the difficulties outlined above, but does not solve all the problems. The move from 'immoral purposes' to 'sexual purposes' would be welcome, as it would remove much of the uncertainty of the former phrase, although, at the same time, the proposal could give rise to additional interesting problems. In *Brown*, for instance, it will be recalled that the majority of their Lordships were keen to stress that homosexual sado-masochistic acts were violent in nature, *not sexual* (that being one reason why consent was not permitted as a defence on the facts). Thus, if a defendant were persistently to solicit men to engage in sado-masochistic acts, could he, under

---

33   *Op cit*, fn 12.

this proposal, argue that these were 'violent purposes', rather than 'sexual' and hence fell outside the scope of the offence? It seems most unlikely that the courts would accept such an argument, illustrating again that homosexual conduct is likely to be defined as violent or sexual according to the definition which the court wishes to adopt on a particular occasion. However, the more fundamental question remains: is it appropriate at all to criminalise homosexual soliciting, when equivalent soliciting for heterosexual purposes (unless it be for prostitution) would not be an offence? The most radical solution would be to decriminalise soliciting for homosexual purposes, on the basis that it is outdated, discriminatory and very often serves no useful purpose. An alternative, less radical proposal, might be to enact legislation much along the lines recommended in the draft Criminal Code Bill, but to incorporate a requirement that some person must be shown to have suffered distress or nuisance as a result of the soliciting. This would ensure that the offence is no longer used in circumstances where, even taking the prosecution's case at its highest, it cannot be said that anybody was aware of, let alone affected by, the defendant's activities.

These, and other, arguments were considered in *Setting the Boundaries*. The Report's conclusion clearly supported the view that the current law was inequitable and uncertain:

> The offence of soliciting by men is so broadly drawn that it does not provide certainty as to its meaning or intention ... Its lack of clarity and certainty are problematic and make it open to inconsistency across the country. The role of the criminal law in this field is to deal with real nuisance, and to do so in a way that is readily understood ... We are not persuaded that chatting up a person of the same sex in public should be criminal – such approaches to women are not criminal.[34]

Consequently, Recommendation 47 proposes the repeal of s 32. The Report recognises that some soliciting by men may involve nuisance aspects, which are the legitimate concerns of the criminal law, in the same way that unwanted soliciting by prostitutes is capable of causing harassment and distress. Recommendation 48 therefore proposes consideration of regulating soliciting by men on the same basis as soliciting by women.

---

34 Home Office Consultation Paper, *Setting the Boundaries*, July 2000, para 6.6.16.

CHAPTER 3

RAPE

1 INTRODUCTION

The crime of rape is regarded by many people, both within and outside the legal profession, as the most serious sexual offence, and indeed as one of the most serious of all offences. The very personal nature of the requisite physical act, together with the almost inevitable violation of the victim, makes rape one of the most feared and controversial crimes. The controversy surrounding rape is exacerbated in the eyes of many commentators by the commonly held view that the law itself – in terms of the legal definition *per se*, procedure, evidence, attitude of the relevant authorities, etc – is biased in favour of the male defendant, and against the victim who is virtually always female (and, prior to the Criminal Justice and Public Order Act 1994, was always female).

The purpose of this chapter will be to consider not merely the many issues and difficulties pertaining to the legal definition of rape, but also the wider perspectives relating to how rape is perceived and, where reforms are needed, how they could be implemented.

2 AN OVERVIEW OF SOCIAL AND THEORETICAL ISSUES

2.1 Classifying rape

Is it possible or desirable to categorise rape solely as a crime of violence, or specifically as a sexual offence? Whilst it might be easy to classify rape as nothing but a crime of (male) violence, to do so runs the risk, as Lacey *et al* have suggested,[1] of overlooking the important connection between rape and 'cultural images of male and female sexuality'. In other words, the particular acts and circumstances which constitute the legal definition of rape, together with the judicial interpretation of those definitions, are linked inexorably to more widely held attitudes (social and cultural, as well as legal or judicial) concerning the sexual relationship between males and females. It would be better, therefore, to regard rape as neither solely 'sexual' (as many rapes involve other acts of violence and sexual degradation over and above the act of intercourse itself), nor as merely 'violent' (because the act may often

---

1   Lacey, N and Wells, C, *Reconstructing Criminal Law*, 1998, Butterworths, p 352.

amount to the man exercising (or imposing?) his 'right' of sexual domination upon the victim).

2.2 Rape and patriarchy: the feminist perspective

2.2.1 Rape and the family

Traditionally, it can be argued that both attitudes concerning the act of rape and the law relating to rape were created and interpreted with the purpose of maintaining the family structure and hence the economic and social significance of the family. To this end, the content and procedure of rape law liked to emphasise the paradigmatic rape as an act of violence committed by a stranger. If the law were to recognise that 'other forms' of rape (acquaintance rape, date rape, and especially rape within the family environment) were more common than traditionally accepted, then the central role of the family unit would be threatened. In particular, the comfortable male, authoritative view of rape as a 'violence-by-stranger' offence would be subjected to challenge:

> [W]e can begin to understand how it is that, though the sexual offence of rape formally penalises men, the enforcement of rape law often reinforces male domination over women, to the extent that one recent empirical study of rape cases concludes that the criminal process in fact 'condones' rape ... By focusing on rape as a crime committed by strangers who are deviant, the reality of 'intimate' rape is obscured.[2]

2.2.2 Control

Insofar as there has ever existed a common explanation for the occurrence of rape, traditional theory has viewed the offence from a purely legal and/or psychiatric perspective. Here, rape is seen as a violent sexual offence, and/or an offence resulting from the individual deviance of the defendant in question. However, an alternative, and more radical explanation has been proposed by a number of feminist theorists[3] who argue that patriarchy – as a system of social relations – serves to maintain men's power over, *inter alia*, women. All patriarchal societies are seen as utilising sexual violence as a form of gender control. According to this perspective, sexual violence is used by men (irrespective of race, class or status) and is often 'condoned' by the State in terms of the legal criteria adopted for offences (for example, in traditional views on rape in marriage), and in sentencing policy. The purpose of sexual violence, and its official 'condonation', is perceived often to involve the punishment and control of women in order to maintain male dominance and female subordination.

---

2   *Op cit*, Lacey and Wells, fn 1, p 366.

3   See, eg, Kelly, L and Radford, J, 'The problem of men: feminist perspectives on sexual violence', in Scraton, P (ed), *Law, Order and the Authoritarian State*, 1987, Oxford: OUP, pp 237–79.

Similarly, Lacey argues that 'law' and the criminal justice system are neither neutral nor isolated, that is, autonomous. Rather, they exist within the context of behaviour, social structures and ideologies, all of which operate essentially to reinforce the general patriarchal view of male/female relationships.

As a direct corollary to the patriarchal model (viewing sexual violence, including rape, as an instrument of male repression over women), it is argued further that such violence is not controlled by the police, the 'law' or any other relevant State agency: in a patriarchal, capitalist society, law is constructed and interpreted in a framework which protects and enforces dominant male interests. According to Kelly and Radford,[4] such protection of the male defendant's interests are clearly visible at several stages of the entire rape process. At the very outset of the process, for instance, the actual legal definition of rape itself is perceived as overly narrow, by being limited to penile penetration of the anus or vagina to the exclusion of acts such as forced oral sex or penetration with inanimate objects. Further, some legal criteria, as will be seen in relation to the absence of consent, are arguably difficult to prove. Secondly, there are major difficulties in relation to social stereotyping within rape, that is, there is a certain 'type' of woman who is raped and a particular 'type' of man who commits rape. Thirdly, negative perceptions (particularly where they are held by victims) about the likelihood of a prosecution and/or conviction often lead to a great reluctance to report incidents of rape or, where reported, to see the case through to its conclusion. Finally, judicial attitudes surrounding the sentencing of defendants convicted of rape are seen as supporting the general patriarchal model of contemporary society.

The latter three points identified above may all be taken, in their broadest sense, as being concerned with the issues of attitude and response, that is, how a variety of agencies within the broad legal spectrum, as well as lay persons generally, both view and respond to the phenomenon of rape. It will be useful to identify briefly these issues before the law of rape itself is analysed.

2.3   Rape: attitudes and responses

2.3.1   The incidence of rape

A number of studies[5] support clearly the general consensus of opinion that all sexual offences, and especially rape, are greatly under-reported. There are several obvious, but nonetheless important, explanations for such under-

---

4   *Op cit*, Kelly and Radford, fn 3, pp 237–49.

5   See references in *op cit*, Lacey and Wells, fn 1; Temkin, J, *Rape and the Legal Process*, 1987, Sweet & Maxwell; and Edwards, S, *Sex and Gender in the Legal Process*, 1996, Blackstone.

reporting, including, for example: unsympathetic treatment of the complainant ('she asked for it'); the trauma of the trial (where many victims describe the ordeal of giving testimony as like being raped again); the likelihood of eventual acquittal ('why bother?'); shame and embarrassment (of, say, physical examination or the thought of being required to provide numerous statements); and inversion of guilt ('it must have been my fault'/'I could have put up more resistance'), etc.

Whilst these issues raise difficult problems, they are not insurmountable. A legal definition of rape which was more generous to the complainant/prosecution, a less antagonistic set of evidential provisions and, perhaps most importantly, a general change in attitudes about the occurrence and meaning of rape, would all be ways in which victims could be encouraged to report more willingly the offence.

2.3.2   The 'seriousness' of rape

If it is accepted that rape is one of the most (if not *the* most) serious non-fatal criminal offences, there remains the fundamental question as to why, in many instances, there exists a perception that it is not treated as being so serious. The answer to this question, according to many commentators, may be found again within the realms of the feminist perspective on patriarchal society. Kelly and Radford, for example, have argued[6] that one major way of affecting change in patriarchal societies is to have all sexual violence taken seriously, that is to 'de-trivialise' it. In particular, this may be achieved within the context of rape by viewing the offence from the woman's perspective (not, as is traditional, from that of the male defendant). This could be achieved by, for instance, furthering the development of 'feminist services' (such as rape crisis lines and battered wife refuges), by pursuing specific campaigns of law reform, and by reconsidering relevant terminological issues (such as the use of 'survivor', not 'victim', because of the latter's inference of blame and passivity). By contrast, the entire legal process at present is seen to possess an over-emphasis on the male perspective. There exists 'an over-understanding' of the man's (that is the defendant's) view, in order to explain or even excuse his actions, and thus to 'rationalise' the conduct. Such 'over-understanding' is evidenced by a whole range of commonly held 'explanations' for the man's actions – they had both been drinking, he's never done it before, she led him on, etc – culminating, *in extremis*, in judicial statements at sentencing about the 'contributory negligence' of the victim (see below, sections 4.1.1 and 4.1.3.1).

According to the feminist perspective, many of the agencies (social services, medical and legal professions, the police, etc) which currently deal with rape processes, all fail women victims because, due to their essentially patriarchal nature, they fail to take seriously the extent, severity and impact of rape.

---

6   *Op cit*, Kelly and Radford, fn 3, p 54.

Similarly, even those programmes which have been developed by the State to alleviate some of these problems are criticised. Rape examination suites, diversion programmes (to keep defendants 'out of the system') and treatment programmes (to 'cure' men) are all condemned as ineffective 'window-dressing', and, in any case, processes which remain subservient to the general patriarchal system.

2.3.3   The police

The police have long been regarded as an obvious target for those writers and commentators who view official agencies concerned with rape processes as representative of typical patriarchal bias. They were seen as unsympathetic towards rape victims and cynical of rape complaints. Police attitudes were condemned frequently as sexist, and even formal police procedures possessed an element of bias. As Lacey has noted, for example, there was a tendency for the police to record many alleged incidents of rape as 'no crime', a process which, in particular, failed to distinguish between 'unsubstantiated' and 'false' complaints. To some extent, several of these issues have been addressed: the Home Office Circular 69/1986 recommended that a clearer distinction be drawn between 'unsubstantiated' and 'false' complaints, and that only an instance of the latter should be recorded formally as 'no crime'. There exists also a generally more sympathetic police attitude, exemplified by the creation and continuing development of rape examination suites, and the use of specially trained (female) officers in interviewing and evidence gathering.

2.3.4   Statistics

Government statistics, Home Office research projects and independent studies all suggest that not only is the incidence of sexual violence, including rape, increasing, but that the 'clear-up' rate, especially for rape, is dropping.[7] Whilst this is a worrying trend in its own right, analysis of statistical data is significant also in terms of what it says about the type of man who commits rape, the type of woman who is the victim of rape and the context within which rape occurs. As was noted above, there appears to exist a comfortable, if stereotypical view of the paradigm rape as an offence committed by a stranger upon a woman, often in a public place. But evidence from studies as long ago as the 1970s[8] suggests that this is far from necessarily the case. Figures from Smith's Home Office research study in 1989 suggest that the traditional view of rape as involving a single sexual act, committed in public between strangers, is doubtful. That research found that 69% of cases involved

---

7   See, eg, Lloyd, C and Walmsley, R, Home Office Research Study No 105, *Changes in Rape Offences and Sentencing*, 1989, HMSO; Smith, L, Home Office Research Study No 106, *Concerns About Rape*, 1989, HMSO.

8   Amir's 1971 study of rape in Philadelphia suggested that many of the myths relating to the 'stereotypical' rape were without foundation: Amir, M, *Patterns in Forcible Rape*, 1971, University of Chicago. See, also, Davidson, RN, *Crime and Environment*, 1981, Croom Helm, pp 27, 33.

vaginal intercourse only, but that 31% involved other offences or sexual violations, such as forced oral sex or buggery. In 53% of cases, the man threatened or used actual violence, that is, over and above that involved in the act of intercourse *per se*. Perhaps even more significantly, 31% of rapes occurred in the victim's home and 27% of rapes occurred in the offender's home. As far as the relationship between the parties was concerned, in 39% of cases the man was 'well known' to the victim and, of that figure, 37% involved current or former boyfriends, cohabitees or husbands; 29% of cases involved 'brief acquaintances' (for instance, parties who had met earlier in a pub) and only 32% of cases involved 'strangers', that is, parties with no previous acquaintanceship. Such statistics serve to cast serious doubt upon traditional views of rape as an offence-by-stranger, and lend some support to the assertion that a rape mythology has developed which those in authority may have been willing to perpetuate.

3 RAPE: THE OFFENCE

3.1   The legislative background

Prior to 1976, there was no statutory definition of rape. Section 1(1) of the Sexual Offences Act 1956 provided merely: 'It is an offence for a man to rape a woman', and it was further provided, by s 1(2): 'A man who induces a married woman to have sexual intercourse with him by impersonating her husband commits rape.'

Instead the definition of rape at the time remained that developed through the common law, namely 'unlawful sexual intercourse with a woman without her consent, by force, fear or fraud'. It was widely argued that the requirement of 'force, fear or fraud' was restrictive and misleading, as it distracted attention from the very essence of rape – absence of the woman's consent – which can clearly exist, irrespective of whether force, etc, is present.

3.1.1   DPP v Morgan [1975] 2 All ER 347

In this landmark decision, the defendant, Morgan, and three of his friends had sexual intercourse with the victim, Mrs Morgan. Morgan had told his friends that his wife would struggle and protest, but that she was 'kinky' and that it was her way of heightening her sexual enjoyment. The central question concerned the *mens rea* of the three friends and, in particular, whether that may be negatived by any mistaken belief in consent which they held. Although the House of Lords upheld the convictions of the three men by applying the proviso to s 2 of the Criminal Appeal Act 1968 (as amended), they did hold that, on a charge of rape, a defendant's belief that the woman was consenting, even if that belief was unreasonably held, could negate *mens rea* and thus provide a defence:

If the effect of the evidence as a whole is that the defendant believed, or may have believed, that the woman was consenting, then the Crown has not discharged the onus of proving commission of the offence as fully defined and, as it seems to me, no question can arise as to whether the belief was reasonable or not. Of course, the reasonableness or otherwise of the belief will be important as evidence tending to show whether it was truly held by the defendant, but that is all.[9]

At the time, the decision was criticised widely as amounting to a 'rapists' charter'. It was feared that a defendant need only state that he believed (however unreasonably) that the woman was consenting in order to gain an acquittal. The controversy surrounding the decision resulted in the Home Secretary appointing an Advisory Committee to consider the whole law of rape.

3.1.2 Report of the Advisory Group on the Law of Rape [the Heilbron Committee], Cmnd 6352, 1975

The Committee's report argued strongly that there was a need to declare the definition of rape in statutory form in order to:

... provide the opportunity to clarify the existing law and in particular to bring out the importance of recklessness as a mental element in the crime.

Such a definition would also emphasise that lack of consent (and not violence) is the crux of the matter.[10]

The Heilbron Committee's recommendations were accepted and subsequently enacted. Section 1(1) of the Sexual Offences (Amendment) Act 1976 provided:

A man commits rape if–

(a) he has unlawful sexual intercourse with a woman who at the time of the intercourse does not consent to it; and

(b) at the time he knows that she does not consent to the intercourse or he is reckless as to whether she consents to it.

This provision, in effect, amounted to express approval of the decision in *Morgan*, insofar as the defendant who failed to think about the risk of the woman not consenting, or who had made an unreasonable mistake as to her consent, would lack the requisite *mens rea* for the offence. Partly due to the widespread disquiet surrounding *Morgan*, and the (probably misplaced) belief that defendants would easily be able to claim that they thought the woman was consenting, Parliament also enacted s 1(2) in order to allay some of those fears. Section 1(2) provided that where a jury hearing a rape offence has to consider whether the defendant believed the woman was consenting to sexual intercourse, then 'the presence or absence of reasonable grounds for such a

---

9   [1975] 2 All ER 347, *per* Lord Fraser, p 380.

10 Heilbron, Committee, *Report of the Advisory Group on the Law of Rape*, Cmnd 6352, 1975, HMSO. VIII Summary of Recommendations, para 1 (p 36).

belief is a matter to which the jury is to have regard, in conjunction with any other relevant matters, in considering whether he so believed'. In many respects, this sub-section was unnecessary (even though, as will be seen below, it has been expressly retained in subsequent amending legislation), because a jury in any case (rape or otherwise) can consider the fact that a reasonable person would have known the fact or foreseen the consequence in question, as evidence tending to show that a particular defendant did so know or foresee. Section 1(2) rather unnecessarily enacted what was already sensibly permitted in law. It may be wise to regard the sub-section as no more than a 'public relations provision'[11] in the aftermath of *Morgan*.

3.2 The current law  old law now

The Criminal Justice and Public Order Act 1994 (the 1994 Act) significantly redefined rape by replacing the 1976 Act and introducing a new s 1 of the Sexual Offences Act 1956. The amended s 1 now provides:

    (1) It is an offence for a man to rape a woman or another man.

    (2) A man commits rape if–

        (a) he has sexual intercourse with a person (whether vaginal or anal) who at the time of the intercourse does not consent to it; and

        (b) at the time he knows that the person does not consent to the intercourse or is reckless as to whether that person consents to it.

3.2.1 Parties

Rape remains a sex-specific offence in relation to the person who can commit the crime as a principal offender. Section 1(1) clearly limits the principal offender to being 'a man', although it would be more accurate to refer to the offence as being committable by 'a male', as in certain circumstances (see below, section 3.2.1.1), a boy may undoubtedly commit rape.

In *Saunders* ((1990) unreported), the defendant, a pre-operative female-to-male transsexual, was charged with indecent assault after having 'intercourse' with two women. Saunders had effected intercourse by the use of an artificial, attachable penis. Although the two complainants believed that sexual intercourse had taken place, it was accepted by the court that as Saunders had been born female, she remained female in law. Consequently, the gender specific offence of rape could not be charged, as Saunders was not male. Whilst English law continues to determine one's sex at birth, and the crime of rape continues to require the perpetrator to be a man, it seems that a female-to-male transsexual (even post-operative) cannot be convicted as a principal offender to the offence of rape. Rather, the charge must be one indecent assault, with its significantly lower maximum penalty of 10 years.

---

11 Smith, J and Hogan, B, *Criminal Law*, 1999, Butterworths, p 456.

The decision in *Saunders*, in so far as it relates to rape, would not be affected by the proposals in *Setting the Boundaries*. The Report emphasises (at para 2.8) that rape should be retained as an offence that can be committed only by men as principal offenders and, further, that it should continue to be limited to penile penetration. However, it is worth noting that Saunders' behaviour would be covered by the proposed new offence of 'sexual assault by penetration' (see Recommendation 3 at para 2.9), to be discussed further in Chapter 6.

There is no gender restriction in terms of who may be a secondary party to rape. This means that it is legally quite possible to charge a female with, for example, aiding and abetting the principal offender's act of rape where the woman gave assistance by holding the victim down.

3.2.1.1 Boys under 14

Until recently, there existed an irrebuttable presumption that boys under the age of 14 were incapable of sexual intercourse. This fiction was removed by s 1 of the Sexual Offences Act 1993, which abolished the presumption of incapacity to have sexual intercourse, for acts done after 20 September 1993.

Of course, the removal of the fiction at that time did not alter the position in relation to the general rebuttable presumption of *doli incapax*. For a period after 1993, the prosecution was required still to prove that the boy of, say, 13 knew that his act of intercourse was 'seriously wrong'; more than just mere childish naughtiness. As with any instance of *doli incapax*, the presumption was not rebuttable on a charge of rape merely by adducing evidence of the heinous circumstances of the offence. However, the operation of the rebuttable presumption had been heavily criticised,[12] and it was abolished by s 34 of the Crime and Disorder Act 1998. If s 34 does no more than abolish the previous presumption, then, logically, it may still remain open to a child under 14 to adduce appropriate evidence showing that he did not know that his act was seriously wrong (rather than relying upon a presumption to that effect). In that case, the prosecution must then show that he did know that fact.[13] Although this is a plausible interpretation of the effect of abolition of the presumption, the likely purpose of s 34 is to remove the presumption and give children aged 10 and above the same moral and legal culpability as adults.

3.3 *Actus reus*

The law of rape stated, traditionally, that sexual intercourse had to be 'unlawful'. This was taken to mean 'outside marriage' and effectively

---

12 See, eg, *C (A Minor) v DPP* [1996] AC 1, *per* Mann LJ and Laws J in the Divisional Court, and (despite reversing that decision) Lord Lowry in the House of Lords: [1995] 2 All ER 43, p 64.

13 See Walker, N, 'The end of an old song' (1999) 149 NLJ 64.

amounted to a marital exemption, whereby a husband could not be guilty of raping his wife. This common law rule derived from the time of Sir Matthew Hale and was based upon the outdated notion that a woman had given irrevocable consent to sexual intercourse at the time of marriage. Although the courts had striven to develop a number of exceptions to this exemption,[14] the first statutory definition (in the 1976 Act) retained the rule and it continued to operate thereafter. However, in R ([1991] 4 All ER 481), the House of Lords ruled boldly that the word 'unlawful' was mere 'surplusage' and that no exemption existed for a husband in respect of a charge of rape against his wife. From a purely social perspective, the decision was widely applauded, although some doubts were raised as to the strict legality of the ruling.[15] These issues have now been resolved as the decision in R was confirmed by Parliament when the word 'unlawful' was removed from the new definition of rape contained in the 1994 Act. The entire question of the marital exemption to rape can now be left where it belongs: in history.

Following the developments in R and the 1994 Act, it is now the case that the *actus reus* of rape is reduced to just two elements: sexual intercourse and absence of consent.

3.3.1   Sexual intercourse

The requisite physical act necessary to constitute the *actus reus* of rape is that the man has sexual intercourse with another person. A partial definition of sexual intercourse, which, since the 1994 Act, applies equally to anal as well as vaginal intercourse, is provided in s 44 of the Sexual Offences Act 1956:

> Where ... it is necessary to prove sexual intercourse (whether natural or unnatural) it shall not be necessary to prove the completion of the intercourse by the emission of seed, but the intercourse shall be deemed complete upon proof of penetration only.

It is clear that, under this definition, the law permits the slightest degree of penetration by the penis to be sufficient. There is no requirement that the man should ejaculate, nor is it necessary, in the case of vaginal intercourse, to prove that the hymen was ruptured by that act of intercourse.[16] The purpose of s 44 seems to have been to provide for the minimum act necessary on the part of the defendant, thus preventing even the possibility of spurious arguments along the lines that the penetration was 'not proper', or that it lasted for only a minimal length of time.

---

14 See *Clarke* [1949] 2 All ER 448 (where consent was deemed to be revoked by the presence of a Separation Order); *O'Brien* [1974] 3 All ER 663 (where, between the *decree nisi* and the *decree absolute*, the marriage was regarded as 'a mere technicality'); and *Steele* (1977) 65 Cr App R 22 (where a formal undertaking in lieu of an injunction was held to be as good as an injunction in revoking consent).

15 See, eg, Giles, M, 'Judicial law-making in the criminal courts: the case of marital rape' [1992] Crim LR 40.

16 *Lines* (1844) 1 C & K 393.

The fact that rape is limited to the act of penile penetration is not approved of universally. Prior to the 1994 Act, it was argued that rape's limitation to one specific act (penetration of the vagina by the penis) was indicative of a male dominated society, with its male-fixated view of rape as being restricted to one form of intercourse. Even since the 1994 Act, the law is restricted to penetration by the penis, albeit now extended to penetration of the anus. Such a definition automatically narrows the scope of the offence by excluding other acts, some of which may be regarded as equally degrading, if not more so, to the victim. In addition, although other offences exist to cover such circumstances (notably indecent assault – see Chapter 6), the maximum sentence is often lower than rape. It seemed that the consensus of opinion followed the views expressed by the Criminal Law Revision Committee in 1984,[17] namely that rape should not be extended to cover other forms of penetration, such as forced oral sex, digital penetration or penetration with inanimate objects.

Although, at present, English law has not extended further the definition of the *actus reus* of rape, the courts themselves do, on occasion, equate some indecent assaults with rape in terms of their seriousness, even though the maximum sentences available are significantly different. In *McClone* ([2000] WL 544163), the defendant was sentenced to four years' imprisonment for indecent assault on a male youth, aged 15. He had forced the youth to perform oral sex on him by threatening to kill the young child for whom the youth was babysitting at the time. The trial judge, in sentencing the appellant, described the indecent assault as 'oral rape', commented on the likely long term effect of the act on the complainant and described the offence as at the 'top end of indecent assault'. These comments, and the sentence, were approved by the Court of Appeal, where Butterfield J stated:

> So far as sentence is concerned … this was, as the judge said, very close to male rape, and the sentence passed upon you was a perfectly proper one.[18]

In light of the offence being likened to 'oral rape' and being described as a serious example 'very close to male rape', the sentence of four years (in relation to a maximum of 10 years) was upheld. However, in the context of the relatively serious circumstances of the case, it is arguable that if the conviction had been for anal rape (rather than indecent assault), the initial sentence may have been more than four years. Perhaps the more important issue from *McClone* is the overt recognition by the judiciary that, in some instances, the nature of the indecent assault and, in particular, its potential effect upon the

---

17 Criminal Law Revision Committee, *Fifteenth Report, Sexual Offences*, Cmnd 9213, 1984, HMSO, para 2.47. For a further discussion of the arguments, see, also, Leng, R, 'The Fifteenth Report of the Criminal Law Revision Committee: Sexual Offences (1) The Scope of Rape' [1985] Crim LR 416.

18 Court of Appeal, 19 April 2000, Westlaw Transcript, [2000] WL 544163.

complainant, can make the offence comparable to rape. This is an important point for the judiciary to have recognised.

Although, traditionally, there has been a reluctance to extend further the *actus reus* of rape (particularly, for instance, to cover non-consensual oral sex, as in *McClone* itself), there appears to have been a significant shift in attitude on this point in recent times. Recommendation 1 in *Setting the Boundaries* (at para 2.8.5) proposes a radical redefinition of rape to include penetration of the mouth (see, further, below).

The current legal requirement that the *actus reus* of rape is limited to penile penetration of either the anus or the vagina, gives rise to an important potential loophole, namely the extent to which the law affords adequate protection to a transsexual who has undergone surgery to create an artificial vagina. The issue was discussed in detail in *Matthews* ((1996) unreported).[19] The defendant was charged with the rape of 'C', a post-operative male-to-female transsexual. The central question for the trial judge, Hooper J, was whether it was rape in law for the defendant to penetrate C's artificial vagina. It was argued on behalf of the defendant that 'natural sexual intercourse' was limited to intercourse *per vaginam*, and that both the penis and the vagina had to be those provided by nature. It was argued further that 'unnatural sexual intercourse' meant buggery, that is, anal intercourse or bestiality. Consequently, the act of 'vaginal intercourse' on the present facts, it was contended, fell within neither definition. Hooper J rejected those arguments, ruling that there could be rape in respect of C's artificial vagina. Having noted that s 44 refers to 'mere penetration whether natural or unnatural', Hooper J ruled that there was no reason to limit the phrase 'sexual intercourse' only to heterosexual vaginal intercourse ('natural sexual intercourse'), and heterosexual or homosexual anal intercourse and bestiality ('unnatural sexual intercourse'). In addition, if the law required a vagina to be 'wholly natural', then a woman with an entirely or partially artificial vagina would not be afforded the protection of the law of rape. Consequently, C's artificial vagina was an 'intimate orifice' for the purpose of rape. After Hooper J's ruling, the defendant was acquitted on the facts. A number of potentially important issues remain. It is arguable that there is a difference between a woman's (wholly or partly) artificial vagina and that of C, who remains a man in English law. Secondly, Parliament re-defined rape as recently as 1994 and, despite having the benefit of comparative jurisdictions upon which to draw (for example, the state of Victoria in Australia), chose not to extend the law in the way interpreted by Hooper J. It is possible that Parliament did not intend to extend rape to include transsexuals as victims. Consequently, the first instance decision in *Matthews* leaves the law in a potentially uncertain state. Without a definitive judgment from the Divisional Court, Hooper J's ruling

---

19 See, especially, Hicks, M and Branston, G, 'Transsexual rape – a loophole closed?' [1997] Crim LR 565.

remains of persuasive authority only. In order to avoid any possible ambiguity and to provide the protection of the law to transsexuals (or indeed to women with artificially constructed vaginas), Parliament should state expressly that the law of rape does extend to such intimate orifices.

The reference in s 44 to the sexual intercourse being 'complete' means that the act of sexual intercourse must have commenced, not that it is required to have finished. This has significant implications for the view that the *actus reus* of rape can be constituted by a continuing act: sexual intercourse begins at the time of initial penetration and continues until the man withdraws. In *Kaitamaki* ([1985] AC 147), the defendant did not dispute that he had had sexual intercourse twice with the complainant, but he claimed that she had consented. The defendant admitted that, after the second penetration, he had become aware that she was not consenting, but that he did not withdraw. He appealed against his conviction for rape, arguing that, as rape was 'penetration without consent', once penetration was complete, sexual intercourse for the purposes of rape was concluded. This argument was rejected by the Privy Council, where it was held, in construing the corresponding provision to s 44 (in s 127 of the New Zealand Crimes Act 1961), that 'sexual intercourse is a continuing act which only ends with withdrawal'.[20] The word 'complete' was interpreted as meaning 'having come into existence', not 'being at an end'.[21]

This interpretation has not met with unanimous approval. It has been argued that the decision means that rape, in effect, can be committed by omission. Furthermore, whilst rape clearly is not an 'instantaneous' act, penetration without consent is an essential part of the *actus reus* which should be accompanied by *mens rea*: the decision in *Kaitamaki* stretches this requirement almost to breaking point.[22]

In spite of these reservations, the English courts have now approved the *Kaitamaki* principle. In *Brookes* ((1993) 14 Cr App R(S) 496), the Court of Appeal upheld a sentence of three years for rape where the defendant had pleaded guilty, having admitted that he became aware the victim was not consenting after sexual intercourse had commenced. Perhaps of equal significance was the court's acknowledgment that the defendant's initial belief that the victim was consenting was a 'mitigating factor'. But as the trial judge had already reflected this fact in his sentence, there was no basis for varying the three year term.

It was accepted expressly by the Court of Appeal in *Greaves* ([1999] 1 Cr App R(S) 319) that where a man is convicted of rape as a result of the

---

20 [1985] AC 147, *per* Lord Scarman, pp 151–52.

21 *Ibid*, p 151.

22 See, eg, the dissenting judgment of Woodhouse J in the New Zealand Court of Appeal [1980] 1 NZLR 59; and commentary by Professor Smith [1984] Crim LR 565.

application of the *Kaitamaki* principle, then that should operate as some mitigation of the sentence. In *Greaves*, the defendant was convicted of rape when he had commenced sexual intercourse with a young woman with her consent, but then refused to withdraw when she changed her mind and asked him to withdraw. He was sentenced to 42 months' imprisonment and appealed against the sentence. In reducing the sentence to 18 months' imprisonment, Sir Patrick Russell stated that 'the facts, whilst not entirely unique, are certainly unusual and ... undoubtedly afford substantial mitigation to this appellant'.[23]

The principle was given fuller consideration by the Court of Appeal in *Cooper and Schaub* ([1994] Crim LR 531). In response to a question from the jury, the trial judge had ruled that:

> ... if after vaginal penetration a man becomes aware that the woman is no longer consenting, he is guilty of rape if he nonetheless continues to have intercourse ... [and he] knew that she was no longer consenting ... or was reckless ...[24]

Although the convictions were quashed on other grounds, the Court of Appeal approved the above direction, albeit with some apparent reservation:

> The practical question that arises is: how long would it be necessary for him to take before the withdrawal was complete? Indeed it is a salutary thought ... that a man who is unable to restrain himself at such a moment ... commits the very serious offence of rape ... Notwithstanding these considerations ... penetration in this context must be a continuing act ...[25]

So it is now confirmed that rape is a continuing act, but it has yet to be determined exactly how immediate, upon realisation, withdrawal has to be if the man is to be acquitted. Whilst this is not likely to prove a frequent problem for the courts, it does, nevertheless, raise some interesting and serious issues. The requirement that the man should withdraw when he becomes aware of the removal of consent, does not, as yet, clarify whether that withdrawal should be instantaneous, immediate, or within some reasonable time. These matters are likely to cause immense difficulties for trial judges faced with the task of directing juries.

3.3.2   Consent

The key element in the *actus reus* of rape is the absence of consent. The prosecution must prove that the victim did not consent to sexual intercourse (whether anal or vaginal) at the time of that intercourse. Non-consensual anal intercourse must be charged, since 1994, as rape (albeit with buggery as an alternative charge if appropriate). It is clearly not appropriate to charge a man

---

23   [1999] 1 Cr App R(S) 319, p 320.

24   [1994] Crim LR 531. Quoted from Court of Appeal hearing, 29 November 1993, *per* Farquharson LJ (LEXIS transcript).

25   *Ibid*.

with buggery and then sentence him on the basis that the other party had not consented. Where this occurs, the Court of Appeal will uphold an appeal against sentence, on the basis that the appellant has been sentenced for a crime (rape) with which he was not charged.[26] Although many cases of rape will involve the use of force by the man upon the victim, this is no longer a legal requirement: it is the absence of consent on the part of the victim which is the crux of the matter. Unfortunately, the notion of consent is a difficult one to define and, in rape, the concept gives rise to a number of different issues.

3.3.2.1   Ability to consent

However 'consent' is subsequently defined, it may be taken as read that the victim must be capable of giving valid consent which the law, at least *prima facie*, is prepared to recognise. In *Larter v Castleton* ([1995] Crim LR 75), the two defendants were charged with rape of a girl aged 14 whilst she was insensible, probably through drink, at a party. The trial judge directed the jury on consent in part as follows: 'The question is, did she at the material time understand her situation and was she then capable of exercising a rational judgment?'[27] This direction was approved by the Court of Appeal in upholding the convictions.

Similarly, in *Malone* ([1998] Crim LR 834), the defendant was charged with raping an acquaintance, a girl of 16, in her house. She claimed that, due to her intoxicated state, she was unable to prevent the defendant from having intercourse with her. The defendant argued first that the prosecution had failed to prove that she had physically resisted and, secondly, that they had failed to prove that she was in no position to decide whether to consent or not. The Court of Appeal, in upholding the conviction, rejected these submissions. On behalf of the Court, Roch LJ held that there was no requirement in rape that absence of consent has to be communicated to the defendant in order for the *actus reus* to be established. Rather, the prosecution must prove that the victim did not consent and that fact must be evidenced in some way. The decision provides clear confirmation that the victim does not necessarily have to communicate the fact of non-consent to the defendant, although, doubtless, evidence of such communication will strengthen the prosecution's case evidentially. Although the point was not discussed expressly in the case, it is also clearly the law that, even in cases where the victim is unable to give consent, the defendant must be shown to have *mens rea*: he must know that, or be reckless to the fact that, the other party was not consenting.

It is submitted that this is correct in principle, and should apply equally to cases where, for instance, the victim is unconscious due to medical reasons, or insensible following the application of proscribed drugs, etc.

---

26   See *Davies (Tarian John)* (1997) *The Times*, 22 October; [1998] Crim LR 75.

27   [1995] Crim LR 75. Quoted from Court of Appeal hearing, 1 July 1994, *per* Hobhouse LJ (LEXIS transcript).

Difficulties about the capability of giving consent arise also in respect of victims who are mentally impaired and/or of a very young age. In the old case of *Fletcher* ((1859) Bell CC 63), the defendant had intercourse with a girl aged 13 who was described to the court as having a 'weak intellect'. It was held to be correct to direct the jury that the defendant was guilty if she was incapable of giving consent or exercising any judgment on the matter.

It is equally clearly rape to have intercourse with very young children. There must be an age when a child is incapable of understanding the nature of the act to which it is claimed she consented. However, as a strict matter of law there is no age limit below which a child may not consent. Rather, it is a question of fact in each case. The prosecution must prove absence of consent, although this becomes correspondingly easier the younger the child victim, as was stated by Humphreys J in *Harling* [1938] 1 All ER 307:

> It may well be that in many cases the prosecution would not want much evidence beyond the age of the girl to prove non-consent, but in every charge of rape the fact of non-consent must be proved to the satisfaction of the jury.[28]

In such cases where the victim has a low mental awareness or is very young, there is a general consensus of opinion that she (or he) must be able to give an informed and intelligent consent as to the nature of the act itself in order for that consent to be valid in law.

3.3.2.2 Consent v submission

Many of the present difficulties relating to consent appear to have arisen as a result of the courts' attempts to distinguish between 'consent' and 'submission'. The leading authority is the Court of Appeal decision in *Olugboja* ([1981] 3 All ER 443), the facts of which are useful for illustrating some of the problems inherent in many rape cases. The victim (V) and her friend (K) were driven by Olugboja and the second defendant (D2), to D2's house. On the way, V had already been raped once by D2. On arrival at the house, D2 dragged K into a bedroom, leaving V alone with O. O told V that he was going to 'fuck her', and, despite her plea to be left alone, O told her to remove her trousers. This she did because, she said, she was frightened. O then pushed her on to the sofa and sexual intercourse took place. V accepted that, at this stage, she did not struggle, resist or scream or cry for help, but that she finally struggled when she feared O was about to ejaculate inside her, whereupon O withdrew. Had V legally 'consented' in these circumstances? According to Dunn LJ, the notion of 'consent' covers a wide spectrum, from 'actual desire on the one hand to reluctant acquiescence on the other'.[29] Because of this wide range, it was important, on occasion, to provide further direction to a jury. In cases where sexual intercourse has been induced by

---

28   [1938] 1 All ER 307, p 308, *per* Humphreys J.

29   [1981] 3 All ER 443, p 444, *per* Dunn LJ.

force or the fear of force, then a 'simple' direction may well suffice. In this 'simple direction', the trial judge should tell the jury that:

> Consent, or the absence of it, is to be given its ordinary meaning and if need be ... [it should be said that] there is a difference between consent and submission.[30]

Of course, not all cases are so straightforward:

> In the less common type of case ... not involving violence or the fear of it ... an appropriate direction ... will have to be fuller. They [the jury] should be directed to concentrate on the state of mind of the victim immediately before the act of sexual intercourse, having regard to all the relevant circumstances, and in particular the events leading up to the act, and her reaction to them, showing their impact on her mind.[31]

Unfortunately, the Court of Appeal did not try to distinguish those threats or pressures which would vitiate consent from those which would not. It is not easy, for instance, to categorise economic pressure in this context, such as the threat to dismiss (or prevent the promotion of) an employee, if she refused to have intercourse with her employer. Without making such fine distinctions, the Court of Appeal believed that a jury should be reminded of the difficulty of 'drawing the dividing line in such circumstances between real consent ... and mere submission',[32] but rather should be encouraged to use their 'good sense' and general experience and knowledge of human nature and modern behaviour, in deciding whether the victim consented. In principle the decision in *Olugboja* is to be welcomed: it appears to allow a rape complainant to argue that she did not consent, in law or fact, despite the absence, for example, of force or threats of violence. However, it has been argued that in cases where the victim is merely 'intimidated' and there is no violence or threat of violence by the man, or no evidence of a struggle or resistance on the part of the victim, then the CPS is most unlikely to proceed.[33]

Undoubtedly, the parameters surrounding the notions of consent and submission are vague and difficult to define precisely, and cases are likely to occur where even reasonable people are unable to reach agreement on their application. Thus, in *Olugboja* itself, the court referred to the unreported case of *Kirby* ((1961) *The Times*, 19 December, p 7). There, Winn J had ruled that the defendant, a police constable, was not guilty of rape where he had induced the complainant (a girl aged 15) to engage in sexual intercourse by threatening to report the fact that he had discovered her having intercourse with a youth. In dismissing the rape charge, Winn J told the jury: 'I have considered matters of law and if the facts of this case were fully established it could not constitute

---

30   [1981] 3 All ER 443, p 445.

31   *Ibid*, pp 448–49.

32   *Ibid*, p 448.

33   *Op cit*, Edwards, fn 5, p 340.

rape.'[34] Conversely, in *Wellard* ((1978) 67 Cr App R 364), the court noted that the defendant had a previous conviction for rape, committed after he had posed as a security officer and induced a girl to have sexual intercourse with him by threatening to report to her parents and the police the fact that she had been seen having intercourse in a public place. No comment was made about the incorrectness of Wellard's earlier conviction, and it may, therefore, be inferred that the court viewed such a threat as sufficient to vitiate consent in those circumstances.

There remain a number of other criticisms of, and problems relating to, the decision in *Olugboja*. First, it leaves the notion of consent, in this context, undefined and vague. Whether or not certain types of pressure should suffice to negate consent raises a central question of public policy and it is arguable that this should be determined by clear legal rules. Secondly, in the absence of a clear definition, the issue of consent is, essentially, to be determined by the jury. The uncertainty and obvious potential for inconsistency which this will produce cannot be supported. Thirdly, and partly as a result of such criticisms, the CLRC, which also believed that uncertainty would result from the decision, proposed a much tighter definition of consent.[35] Under this proposal, a woman (or, today, a man) would be deemed to have consented unless there existed explicit or implicit threats of immediate violence by the man; any 'lesser' threats would not serve to remove consent:

> The offence of rape should arise where consent to sexual intercourse is obtained by threats of force, explicit or implicit, against the woman or another person, for example, her child: but that it should not be rape if, taking a reasonable view, the threats were not capable of being carried out immediately. If, for example, a woman is confined by a man for the purpose of sexual intercourse, there may well be an express or implied threat of force to be used against her should she try to escape. If so, the man should be open to conviction for rape should sexual intercourse occur under such duress. In other cases the threats may be capable of being carried out only at some time in the future, and that should not lead to liability for rape.[36]

This proposal, in turn, has been heavily criticised. In particular, the Criminal Law Revision Committee definition, if ever implemented, would significantly limit the scope of rape: in an attempt to clarify the undoubted vagueness of *Olugboja*, the proposal would, in fact, make the law narrower and less fair than it was prior to 1981. Notwithstanding such forceful criticisms, the Criminal Law Revision Committee proposal was accepted by the Law Commission and incorporated, as cl 89(2)(a), into the draft Criminal Code Bill. Furthermore, alternative proposals for reform are not without their difficulties. In its 1995 Consultation Paper, the Law Commission proposed

---

34 (1961) *The Times*, 19 December, at p 7.

35 Criminal Law Revision Committee, *Fifteenth Report, Sexual Offences*, Cmnd 9213, 1984, HMSO.

36 *Ibid*, paras 2.26–2.29.

that there should be a new offence, distinguishable from rape, where sexual intercourse is induced by non-violent threats.[37] Whilst this impliedly recognises that many victims may allow sexual intercourse to occur as a result of a wide range of pressures, it is unfortunate that, by distinguishing such acts from rape, what is normally accepted as being the very essence of the offence, namely non-consent, loses some of its central importance. If non-consent is the crux of the *actus reus* (and it is submitted that it is), then the reason why the victim did not consent should be irrelevant. However, it is submitted further that this should be subject to a test of reasonableness. If D, for example, were to induce an act of sexual intercourse with his girlfriend, V, by telling her that otherwise he would refuse to take her to a party the following night, then, even if it is accepted that V would not have had intercourse on that occasion without D's statement, it cannot be argued that there is anything other than a valid consent in those circumstances.

3.3.2.3   Consent: deception and mistake

Where consent is alleged to exist, thus removing an essential element of the *actus reus*, it is accepted that that consent must be valid. Here, a particular issue concerns the situation where consent is obtained as the result of a deception on the part of the defendant and/or as a result of a mistake by the complainant. The question which arises is: what type of deception or mistake is sufficient to render the complainant's otherwise valid consent invalid? The generally accepted view is that only a mistake (whether resulting from a deliberate deception on the part of the man or not) which relates to the identity of the man or to the very nature of the physical act, is sufficient to negate consent.

The general rule on this point was confirmed recently by the Court of Appeal in *Linekar* ([1995] 3 All ER 70). The defendant, aged 17 at the time of the incident, had intercourse with the complainant, who worked occasionally as a prostitute in order to supplement her social security benefit, after agreeing to pay the sum of £25. After the act of intercourse, the defendant left the complainant without making payment. The trial judge (Coombe J) directed the jury that, if they accepted one version of events – namely that he had obtained her consent by pretending falsely that he was going to pay – then that was a consent vitiated by fraud and the Crown would have proven lack of consent. On appeal, the Court of Appeal quashed the conviction and Morland J reiterated: 'An essential ingredient of the offence of rape is the proof that the woman did not consent to the actual act of sexual intercourse with the particular man who penetrated her.'[38] Thus, where a complainant consents to sexual intercourse in return for a promise of payment, fraud on the part of the man does not remove consent *to the act* on her part:

---

37   Law Commission, *Consent and the Criminal Law*, Law Com No 139, 1995, para 6.45.

38   [1995] 3 All ER 70, p 73.

[H]ere there was consent by the prostitute to sexual intercourse – *consensus quoad hoc*. There was consent by the prostitute to sexual intercourse with this particular appellant – *consensus quoad hanc personam.*[39]

His Lordship referred, with approval, to the decision of the High Court of Australia in *Papadimitropolous* ((1957) 98 CLR 249), where the 'central point', in the view of the court, was emphasised:

Rape is carnal knowledge of a woman without her consent: carnal knowledge is the physical act of penetration; it is the consent to that which is in question; such a consent demands a perception as to what is about to take place, as to the identity of the man and the character of what he is doing.[40]

Applying this *dictum* to the present case, Morland J concluded (rightly, it is submitted) that the prostitute had consented to sexual intercourse with this specific man, and the reality of that consent was not destroyed by his false representation that he intended to pay subsequently for her services. It is worth noting that Linekar would, almost certainly, have been guilty of an offence under s 3 of the Sexual Offences Act 1956 (see Chapter 4, section 2.2), but this was not put as an alternative to the jury.

The decision in *Linekar* appears to be consistent with the law as it has developed in some Commonwealth jurisdictions. For example, until a recent and potentially wide ranging decision of the Supreme Court in Canada, the law in Canada had developed along similar lines to that in England. Under the Canadian Criminal Code of 1983, consent would only be vitiated if the complainant's consent had been obtained by 'fraud'. Prior to 1983, the common law requirement had been that for fraud to vitiate consent, it must have related to the 'nature and quality of the act'. In *Cuerrier* ((1996) 111 CCC 3d 261), the defendant was charged with aggravated assault contrary to s 268(2) of the Criminal Code of Canada (in which lack of consent is one of the constituent elements) after he had had sexual intercourse with two complainants on a number of occasions, without disclosing to them the fact that he was HIV positive. On appeal to the Court of Appeal for British Columbia, the Crown submitted that the trial judge (Drost J) had erred in law by deciding that there was no evidence to support any of the following findings:

(1) that the complainants' apparent consent was vitiated by fraud;

(2) that the respondent's behaviour exceeded the scope of the complainants' consent;

(3) that the apparent consent given by the complainants was ineffective because it was not informed consent;

(4) that the apparent consent was vitiated by reasons of public policy.

---

39 [1995] 3 All ER 70, p 74.
40 (1957) 98 CLR 249, p 261.

The Court of Appeal rejected these submissions and dismissed the Crown's appeal:

> The invitation extended to us to enlarge the common law of assault by creating another category of conduct which will vitiate consent is one which I respectfully decline to accept ... We are here concerned with the most intimate and private of human behaviour, the sexual act, which, as far as these individuals were concerned at the time, was consensual ... I am not persuaded that this is a case ... where it is clear that the law should vitiate consent as a matter of public policy ...
>
> I am also reluctant to create a further category of conduct which would vitiate consent in these circumstances, since to do so would come perilously close to creating a new offence ... One of the purposes of the criminal law and its codification is to warn the public in advance of the type of behaviour which will subject them to criminal sanction ... It is contrary to basic criminal law principles to brand behaviour criminal ... after the fact.[41]

In coming to this conclusion, Prowse J cited with approval the decision of the Supreme Court of Canada in *Bolduc and Bird v The Queen* ([1967] SCR 677). There, the Supreme Court quashed convictions for indecent assault, after Bolduc, a medical doctor, had falsely represented to the complainant (his female patient) that his friend, Bird, was a medical intern who needed to gain further experience by being present at her gynaecological examination. On the basis of this representation, the woman allowed Bird to be present during the examination. According to Prowse J, the Supreme Court had been correct to quash these convictions:

> The complainant here knew what Bolduc was proposing to do to her, for this was one in a series of such treatments. Her consent to the examination and treatment was real and comprehending and it cannot, therefore, be said that her consent was obtained by false or fraudulent representations *as to the nature and quality of the act to be done*, for that was not the fraud practised on her.[42]

However, the decision of the Court of Appeal for British Columbia was reversed by the Supreme Court in *Cuerrier* ([1998] 2 SCR 371). Although all seven judges concurred in upholding the appeal and ordering a retrial, the individual judgments illustrate a wide range of views on the question of how and in what circumstances consent should be vitiated by fraud. The broadest view, representing the widest extension to the law, was advocated by L'Heureux-Dube J:

> In my view ... fraud is simply about whether the dishonest act in question induced another to consent to the ensuing physical act, whether or not that act was particularly risky and dangerous ... Where fraud is in issue, the Crown

---

41 (1996) 111 CCC 3d 261, paras 83, 84, *per* Prowse J.

42 *Ibid*, para 34 (emphasis added).

would be required to prove ... that the accused acted dishonestly in a manner designed to induce the complainant to submit to a specific activity, and that absent the dishonesty, the complainant would not have submitted to the particular activity, thus considering the impugned act to be a non-consensual application of force.[43]

The potential danger in such a test is that it could result in an unacceptably wide application. This was recognised by L'Heureux-Dube J, who proposed a 'safeguard', in that, in cases of fraud, the Crown must prove that 'the accused acted dishonestly in a manner *designed* to induce the complainant to submit to a specific activity'.[44] Such dishonesty would be judged on the objective standard of the reasonable person.

A much narrower extension to the law was proposed by McLachlin J, namely that vitiation should be 'limited to failure to disclose venereal disease' (para 145). It is clear that McLachlin J held concerns that broad changes to the law whereby any deception or dishonesty inducing consent served to vitiate that consent, could result in uncertainty, complexity and trivialisation. He was prepared for the law to allow for vitiation of consent where the deception went to the presence of a sexually transmitted disease which gave rise to a serious risk or probability of infecting the complainant:

> This rule is clear and contained. It would catch the conduct here at issue, without permitting people to be convicted of assault for inducements like false promises of marriage or fur coats. The test for deception would be objective, focussing on whether the accused falsely represented to the complainant that he ... was disease-free when he knew or ought to have known that there was a high risk of infecting his partner. The test for inducement would be subjective, in the sense that the judge or jury must be satisfied ... that the fraud actually induced the consent.[45]

The judgment of Cory J represents a midway approach between those of L'Heureux-Dube and McLachlin JJ. Cory J sought to develop a concept of consent in assault based upon analogous principles from commercial fraud, namely dishonesty (including non-disclosure of important facts) and deprivation or risk of deprivation:

> The first requirement of fraud is proof of dishonesty ... [T]he dishonest action or behaviour must be related to the obtaining of consent to engage in sexual intercourse ... The actions of the accused must be assessed objectively to determine whether a reasonable person would find them to be dishonest.
>
> The second requirement ... is that the dishonesty result in deprivation, which may consist of actual harm or simply a risk of harm ... [T]he Crown will have to establish that the dishonest act (either falsehoods or failure to disclose) had

---

43   [1998] 2 SCR 371, para 136.

44   *Ibid*. The application of the *de minimis* principle was stated to be a further safeguard (para 140).

45   *Ibid*, para 189.

the effect of exposing the person consenting to a significant risk of serious bodily harm.[46]

By limiting the factors which can operate to vitiate consent to only 'fraud as to the nature and quality of the act', the law ignores obviously pertinent surrounding circumstances (such as the existence of the HIV virus or the presence of a non-doctor during an intimate medical examination).

It is interesting to note, however, that despite the somewhat restrictive nature of this rule, it is possible to establish that a fraud perpetrated by a defendant was of such a fundamental character that it did indeed go to the nature and quality of the act so as to vitiate consent. In *R v Maurantonio* ([1968] 2 CCC 115, Court of Appeal of Ontario), the defendant had falsely represented himself as being a doctor licensed to practice medicine. A number of complainants 'consented' to examinations and treatment by him on the basis of his statements. The Court of Appeal upheld his convictions for six indecent assaults, the majority holding that the examinations of the complainants by the accused were something entirely different from that to which they had consented. The representation by the defendant that he was a doctor went to the very nature and quality of the act, so that the complainants' consent was vitiated. This decision is correct in principle, as an intimate examination by a qualified doctor is fundamentally different in its very nature to the same examination carried out by a fraudulent non-doctor.

This specific issue, albeit in the context of indecent assault rather than rape, was considered by the Court of Appeal in *R v Tabassum* ([2000] Crim LR 687; [2000] WL 571330). The appellant, who had no medical qualifications or relevant training, was convicted of three counts of indecent assault. He had asked several women to take part in what he described as a breast cancer survey, so that he could prepare a database software package for sale to doctors. Three separate complainants had agreed to the appellant showing them how to examine their breasts. The appellant himself had felt the breasts of two of the woman and he had used a stethoscope under the bra of the third woman. Each of the women stated that they would not have consented to the acts if they had known at the time that he had neither medical qualifications nor relevant training. The trial judge (HH Judge Livesey QC) had rejected a submission from defence counsel that the defendant's lack of medical qualifications did not change the nature and quality of the act, which was exactly what the complainants had consented to. On behalf of the Court of Appeal, Rose LJ dismissed the appeal, holding that the trial judge's ruling had been consistent with previous authority:

> The wife in *Clarence*, and the prostitute in *Linekar*, each consented to sexual intercourse knowing both the nature and the quality of that act. The additional unexpected consequences, of infection in the one case and non-payment in the

---

46   [1998] 2 SCR 371, paras 245, 247.

other, were irrelevant to and did not detract from the woman's consent to sexual intercourse.[47]

The Court of Appeal emphasised the importance of the complainants' mistaken belief, that is, the belief that the appellant was medically qualified or, in one case, that he had been appropriately trained:

> As this was not so, there was no true consent. They were consenting to touching for medical purposes not to indecent behaviour, that is, *there was consent to the nature of the act but not its quality.*[48]

Clearly, the Court of Appeal has drawn a distinction between the nature of the defendant's act and its quality. The women were aware of the physical nature: the touching of their breasts by the appellant. But they had not consented to the *quality* of that same act: touching by an unqualified person for non-medical reasons is different in quality to the same touching by a medically qualified person for genuine medical reasons.

If the courts in future do pursue a distinction between consent to the *nature* of an act and consent to the *quality* of an act, there could be very significant consequences. Let it be supposed that Miss X refuses to have sexual intercourse with D unless he uses a condom, because she has a fear of becoming pregnant. D is aware of X's fear, but tells her not to worry and states, falsely, that he has had a vasectomy. As a result of D's false statement, X engages in intercourse with D, but would not have done so in the absence of the falsehood. In this situation, we submit, there is a strong possibility that a charge of rape could be substantiated. X may have consented to the nature of the act, that is sexual intercourse with D. But, she has not consented to the *quality of the act*, because an act of sexual intercourse that could never result in pregnancy (X's belief) is different in quality to the same act which could so result.[49]

Nevertheless, the distinction between, say, *Maurantonio* and *Bolduc and Bird* remains a very fine one, and the complainant in the latter case may rightly feel that her consent was just as fraudulently obtained as was that of the complainants in the former case. A remedy to this unsatisfactory state of affairs would be to re-define and broaden the circumstances in which fraud vitiates consent, in a manner which does not divorce the act (whether that be the act of sexual intercourse for the purpose of rape, or other sexual acts for the purpose of indecent assault) from the surrounding circumstances.

This general rule, as was noted above, is subject to two categories of exception. The first is where the victim makes a mistake as to the identity of the man who penetrates her. Following a series of inconclusive 19th century

---

47 Court of Appeal, 11 May 2000, Westlaw Transcript, [2000] WL 571330, *per* Rose LJ.

48 *Ibid* (emphasis added).

49 For other criticisms of the decision, see Professor Smith's Commentary [2000] Crim LR 687, pp 688–89.

cases in which there was held to be consent where defendants impersonated the complainants' husbands,[50] it was enacted, first in the Criminal Law Amendment Act 1885, and later in the 1956 Act that 'a man also commits rape if he induces a married woman to have sexual intercourse with him by impersonating her husband'. This provision was re-enacted when it was included as s 142(3) of the Criminal Justice and Public Order Act 1994. But once again it was restricted to impersonations within marriage, leaving open the question of whether impersonations of other 'types' of person would vitiate consent. This question was considered in *Elbekkay* [1995] Crim LR 163, which adopted, *prima facie*, a much broader approach. The defendant was staying overnight with the victim and her boyfriend. The victim had gone to bed alone and, later that night, felt someone get into bed with her. She assumed it was her boyfriend, but when shortly afterwards she felt a penis enter her, she realised it was not her boyfriend, but was, in fact, the defendant, whom she pushed away. On appeal against his conviction for rape, the defendant argued that, under the common law, sexual intercourse obtained by impersonation was not rape and that the only statutory exception was limited to impersonation of a complainant's husband. This was rejected by the Court of Appeal, where it was stated that the relevant statutory provision was no more than declaratory of the common law and was not intended to create an exception limited to the impersonation of husbands. Rather, the key question, which had been rightly stressed by the trial judge, was whether the victim had consented to intercourse with that particular man. It would be 'extraordinary' to say that a defendant commits rape where he impersonates the victim's husband (just because a specific statutory provision so says), but not where another man impersonates the victim's cohabitee or partner. In principle the decision seems correct: there was no *consensus quoad hanc personam* and it may be distinguished clearly from, say, *Linekar* on that basis. However, the subsequent re-enactment of the 'impersonation-of-husband' rule in the 1994 Act causes some difficulty. It is at least arguable that, by re-enacting that provision, Parliament did intend to limit the exception to the impersonation of husbands (so that no 'lesser' impersonation would suffice), and thus that *Elbekkay* is impliedly overruled. The alternative (and, it is submitted, better) view, is that *Elbekkay* is sound in principle, and that if the occasion arises, the courts will take the opportunity of ignoring s 143 as an unnecessary aberration which does not alter the common law rule.

The second category of exception whereby an otherwise valid consent may be negated, is (as already noted in the wider context of *Cuerrier*, above) where the complainant makes a mistake as to the nature of the act, such that she does not realise that she is submitting to sexual intercourse. In *Flattery* ((1877) 1 QBD 410, CCCR), the defendant induced the victim, a young woman of 19, to have sexual intercourse with him after pretending to her that this would

---

50   *Jackson* (1822) Russ & Ry 487; *Barrow* (1868) 11 Cox CC 191.

amount to the performance of a surgical operation. This was held to be an invalid consent and the defendant was guilty of rape. Similarly, in *Williams* ([1923] 1 KB 340 CCA), the defendant was found guilty of rape after inducing a girl of 16 to have sexual intercourse by telling her that the act was an operation designed to improve her breathing as part of her singing lessons. Both of these cases were approved in *Linekar*, above, where it was emphasised that 'it is the non-consent to sexual intercourse rather than the fraud of the doctor or choir master that makes the offence rape'.[51] Whilst this seems instinctively right in principle, it is interesting to note that the decision in *Williams* has not met with universal approval. Thus, Glanville Williams has argued[52] that there was evidence to suggest that the victim was deceived only as to the effect of the act, but not to its essential nature. If this were so, she did know the physical act to which she was consenting, and the defendant should not have been guilty. Notwithstanding such doubts, the central question seems to be whether the victim mistook the fundamental nature of the act of intercourse. But, interestingly, this test may be viewed as overly restrictive. Lacey *et al* have argued[53] that such a test is too narrow and unfair, as it wrongly separates the act of sexual intercourse from its particular circumstances. There is some merit to this argument. The prostitute in *Linekar* knew the nature of sexual intercourse, that is, the act to which she was consenting. It is also possible to envisage a situation whereby a girl, in circumstances only slightly different to those in *Williams*, fully appreciated the nature of the act, but genuinely believed that it would improve her voice. But whether they still would have consented had they known, in each respective case, that the defendant was not going to pay and that the act would not improve the voice, is very doubtful. Undoubtedly, there would be a deception in each case, but, as the law stands at present, they would not be deceptions which are sufficient to vitiate consent. The law may be viewed as unsatisfactory in this area, as it places an undue emphasis upon the nature of the act to which the victim is consenting, rather than the circumstances surrounding the act. In many instances, the circumstances are crucial to understanding whether a truly valid consent was given. Thus, the prostitute who agrees to sexual intercourse following a man's explicit statement that he will pay for her services, may have consented to the physical act, but cannot in reality be said fairly to have consented to the act within the relevant circumstances, namely that she expected and believed payment to be made. Although in this scenario other offences will almost certainly be committed (see Chapter 4), the law at present is unfairly narrow in relation to the woman who consents to sexual intercourse knowing of its nature, but is deceived as to some other fundamental issue.

---

51   [1995] Crim LR 163, p 164, *per* McCowan LJ.
52   Williams, G, *Textbook of Criminal Law*, 1983, Stevens, pp 561–62.
53   *Op cit*, Lacey and Wells, fn 1, pp 388–89.

3.4 Mens rea

3.4.1 Definition

The *mens rea* for rape consists of two elements. The man must:

(a) intend to have sexual intercourse with another person; and

(b) at the time, either know that the other person was not consenting to the sexual intercourse or be reckless as to whether she or he was so consenting.

The first of these elements – an intent to have sexual intercourse – appears to cause little difficulty in reality, although, as a strict matter of law, the prosecution must prove that the defendant intended to penetrate the victim. Since the broadening of the definition of rape in the 1994 Act to include anal and vaginal intercourse, it is at least feasible to envisage a situation where the defendant 'accidentally' penetrates the victim's anus whilst attempting to effect vaginal penetration (see discussion of *Watson* in Chapter 2). As an intent to penetrate the vagina is clearly not an intent to penetrate the anus, it would seem that the requisite intention does not exist in such a situation.

The considerably more important mental element relates to the defendant's state of mind in respect of the victim's consent. The prosecution must prove that the defendant knew the victim was not consenting or that he was reckless as to that fact.

3.4.2 Reckless rape

The decision in *Morgan*, the recommendations of the Heilbron Committee and the subsequent enactment in s 1 of the 1976 Act, all confirm that the law's view of reckless rape in the 1970s was that it involved subjective *Cunningham* recklessness. The defendant would be reckless to the fact that the woman was not consenting only if he had thought about the possibility that she might not be so consenting and continued to have intercourse in any case. This position was explained by Lord Fraser in *Morgan* as follows:

> If the effect of the evidence as a whole is that the defendant believed, or may have believed, that the woman was consenting, then the Crown has not discharged the onus of proving commission of the offence as fully defined and ... no question can arise as to whether the belief was reasonable or not. Of course, the reasonableness or otherwise of the belief will be important as evidence tending to show whether it was truly held by the defendant, but that is all.[54]

It is clear that the Heilbron Committee was in agreement with the principle underlying *Morgan*, and this was confirmed by the enactment of the Committee's proposals in the 1976 Act. The effect of that Act was to allow a defendant to argue that he had held a genuine, but mistaken belief that the

---

54 Heilbron, Committee, *Report of the Advisory Group on the Law of Rape*, Cmnd 6352, 1975, HMSO, p 380.

victim had been consenting and, where the jury found that there was evidence that he may have had such a belief, then they should be directed to acquit. As has been noted, the Act also sought to allay widespread fears about a 'rapists' charter' by enacting s 1(2), which merely emphasised to juries their right to consider the reasonableness of the defendant's belief and all other relevant matters when deciding if he did in fact hold such a belief.

The question of recklessness in rape, as with recklessness in criminal law generally, was thrown into confusion by the decision of the House of Lords in *Caldwell* ([1982] AC 341). In the years immediately following the decision, it seemed that the courts were prepared to apply Lord Diplock's objective test to the offence of rape where the question arose as to whether the defendant had been reckless to the victim's consent. This clearly caused a tension with what hitherto had been regarded as a subjective test. In *Pigg* ((1982) 74 Cr App R 352), Lane LCJ purported to apply Lord Diplock's objective test, with modifications, to the crime of rape:

> [S]o far as rape is concerned, a man is reckless if either he was indifferent and gave no thought to the possibility that the woman might not be consenting in circumstances where, if any thought had been given to the matter, it would have been obvious there was a risk she was not, or that he was aware of the possibility that she might not be consenting but nevertheless persisted regardless of whether she consented or not.[55]

The *Pigg* direction suffered from a number of ambiguities. In particular, the reference to 'obvious' did not make clear whether this should be obvious to the reasonable man or the defendant himself. Also, the notion of being 'indifferent' is difficult to reconcile with 'giving no thought to the possibility'. Can a man be indifferent at the same time as giving no thought to something? If this was meant to refer to indifference on the part of the defendant *if he had* given any thought, then it would involve the jury in very complex hypothetical reasoning.

Most of the uncertainties inherent in *Pigg* have now been resolved by the Court of Appeal. In *Satnam and Kewal* ((1984) 78 Cr App R 149), the court agreed that the direction in *Pigg* had been ambiguous, but, in any case, felt themselves free to review the situation as the references to recklessness had been *obiter*. Bristow J emphasised that the court wished to acknowledge the applicability of the subjective test in rape:

> Any direction as to the definition of rape should ... be based upon s 1 ... and ... *Morgan* without regard to *Caldwell* or *Lawrence*, which were concerned with recklessness in a different context and under a different statute.

> The word 'reckless' in respect of rape involves a different concept to its use in relation to malicious damage or ... offences against the person. In the latter

---

55 (1982) 74 Cr App R 352, p 355.

cases the foreseeability, or possible foreseeability, is as to the consequences ... In the case of rape the foreseeability is as to the state of mind of the victim.[56]

The return to subjectivity in reckless rape has been confirmed by the Court of Appeal in a number of cases. In *Taylor* ((1985) 80 Cr App R 327), Lane LCJ, in giving the judgment of the court, stated:

> Another way of putting it ... is: Was the defendant's attitude one of 'I could not care less whether she is consenting or not, I am going to have intercourse with her regardless'? Finally ... in rape the defendant is reckless if he does not believe that the woman is consenting and could not care less whether she is consenting or not but presses on regardless.[57]

Of course, a man cannot 'not care less' unless he has first, at least, considered the risk that the woman may not consent, that is, that he has been subjectively reckless to her consent. As always when a subjective *mens rea* prevails, there may be fears that it is easy for a defendant to say 'I did not think that she was not consenting', but, as has been noted, the common sense provision in s 1(2) of the 1976 Act enables a jury to disbelieve the more spurious of such assertions. Thus, in *McFall* ([1994] Crim LR 226), the defendant was charged with the kidnapping and rape of the victim – a woman with whom he had been cohabiting. She claimed that she was terrified of the defendant and that, out of fear, she pretended to consent to intercourse and faked enjoyment of the act. This, she said, was necessary to save her life. The defendant appealed against his conviction for rape, arguing that he believed she had been consenting. The Court of Appeal upheld the jury's conviction. This case is of some importance, as it indicates not only that a woman may often appear to be consenting for an ulterior purpose (that is, self-preservation), but also that juries are capable of seeing through the less believable defendants who claim that they thought the woman was consenting.

It is important also to recognise that it is not necessarily incumbent upon a trial judge to give a direction as to honest belief in every case of rape where consent is in issue. Whether a trial judge should give such a direction or not will depend upon the precise factual circumstances of the case in question. In many cases, the defendant will either have known that the victim was not consenting, or will have been reckless as to that fact (whilst proceeding with intercourse, for instance, whilst 'not caring less' whether she consented or not). Here, the question as to holding a mistaken belief as to consent simply will not arise. This point was emphasised by Roch LJ on behalf of the Court of Appeal in *R v Adkins* ([2000] 2 All ER 185):

> Such a direction need only be given when the evidence in the case is such that there is room for the possibility of a genuine mistaken belief that the victim was consenting. In our view this accords with the basic principle that the jury

---

56   (1984) 78 Cr App R 149, p 154.
57   (1985) 80 Cr App R 327, p 332.

should not be subjected to unnecessary and irrelevant directions. Similarly, it is only when the issue of honesty arises on the evidence that the requirements of s 1(2) of the 1976 Act apply ... The question of honest belief does not necessarily arise where reckless rape is in issue.[58]

3.4.2.1 Intoxication and reckless rape

As rape is a crime of basic intent it follows that the principles established in *DPP v Majewski* ([1977] AC 443) are applicable, and the defendant's self-induced intoxication cannot be used as evidence that his *mens rea* was negatived at the time of the sexual intercourse. In *Woods (W)* ((1981) 74 Cr App R 312), the defendant was charged with rape, but claimed that he was so drunk at the time that he did not realise that the victim was not consenting. It was argued on the defendant's behalf that s 1(2) of the Sexual Offences (Amendment) Act 1976, above, entitled the jury to consider 'any other relevant matters' when determining whether he had reasonable grounds for his belief that the woman was consenting, and that his drunken state was such a relevant matter. This argument was rejected by the court, and it was held that a defendant's self-induced intoxication is not a legally relevant matter for a jury to consider when deciding if there were reasonable grounds for his belief. In effect, 'reasonable grounds' become 'reasonable sober grounds' and the jury must consider whether the defendant would have realised the victim was not consenting *if* he had been sober.

3.4.2.2 Reckless attempted rape

Whilst it is now clear that the substantive offence of rape may be committed (subjectively) recklessly, the position was not as straightforward in respect of attempted rape. Insofar as the law proscribed a particular consequence (the death of the victim, for example, in murder), it seemed that it was necessary to prove that the defendant intended that result before he could be guilty of attempting the offence in question. But in relation to circumstances, there appears to have been a tacit assumption that recklessness on the part of the defendant would suffice. This assumption was challenged by the Law Commission in the first version of the draft Criminal Code (Law Com No 143, 1985, para 14.30), but the contrary view was subsequently adopted in cl 49(2) of the draft Criminal Code Bill:

> For the purposes of sub-section (1) [an attempt to commit an offence], an intention to commit an offence is an intention with respect to all the elements of the offence other than fault elements, except that recklessness with respect to circumstances suffices where it suffices for the offence itself.

The question of whether a defendant could be guilty of attempting to commit rape recklessly, was not considered directly by the Court of Appeal until the decision in *Khan et al* ([1990] 2 All ER 783). It had been assumed at common

---

58   [2000] 2 All ER 185, p 191.

law, following the decision in *Mohan* ([1976] QB 1), that nothing less than a specific intent was required before a defendant could be convicted of an attempt to commit an offence. In *Khan*, it was argued on behalf of the appellants that the phrase 'with intent to commit an offence' (in s 1(1) of the 1981 Act) required an intention in respect of every element of the crime, and thus that recklessness as to lack of consent was not sufficient *mens rea* for attempted rape. The Court of Appeal rejected this argument and confirmed that the mental element necessary for attempted rape is the same as for the completed offence, that is, intent to have sexual intercourse and knowledge of or at least recklessness towards the absence of consent. Of course, a defendant charged with attempted rape must be proven to have intended to engage in sexual intercourse, but it is sufficient to establish recklessness vis-à-vis the circumstance, namely the victim's consent. The principle was summarised by Russell LJ:

> [T]he words 'with intent to commit an offence' ... mean, when applied to rape, 'with intent to have sexual intercourse with a woman in circumstances where she does not consent and the defendant knows or could not care less about her absence of consent'. The only 'intent' ... of the rapist is to have sexual intercourse. He commits the offence because of the circumstances in which he manifests that intent – that is, when the woman is not consenting and he either knows it or could not care less about the absence of consent.[59]

The rationale of *Khan* in respect of *mens rea* in attempts seems to rest upon the distinction between the acts (or omissions) of the defendant on the one hand, and the circumstances on the other. In the context of rape this is a distinction which is relatively easy to draw, that is, between the act (sexual intercourse) which must be intended and the circumstance (non-consent) to which the man may be reckless. This distinction appears also now to have the approval of the Law Commission (with the adoption of cl 49(2)), and for the present it may be taken as representing the law on attempted rape.[60]

4 SENTENCING RAPE

4.1 Sentencing policy

The maximum sentence that may be imposed upon a defendant who is convicted of rape (or attempted rape) is life imprisonment. But, because of the very fact that this is a maximum, not a mandatory, penalty, inevitably tensions and disagreements will arise about the precise level at which rape sentences ought to be set.

---

59   [1990] 2 All ER 783, p 788.

60   In *Attorney General's Reference (No 3 of 1992)* (1993) 98 Cr App R 383, the Court of Appeal approved and extended the principle in *Khan* by stating that on a charge of attempted arson, reckless whether life would thereby be endangered, a defendant could be guilty if he intended the act, but was merely reckless in relation to the result.

There may well be a general consensus of opinion that a certain level of conformity in sentencing is desirable as a matter of social justice and equality. And, without moving into the wealth of literature on theories of punishment, there may even be broad agreement that legal justice can be upheld partially by 'making the punishment fit the crime'. However, such a popular notion of 'just desserts' immediately runs into difficulties. In particular, whilst an individual crime (for instance, rape) must always satisfy the specific criteria set down in the definition of the offence, it is equally true that no two examples of rape will be absolutely identical. Conversely, there exists an almost natural desire to 'treat like cases alike', which desire for parity of treatment may lead to calls for, at least, approximate equality in sentencing.

The law may respond to these tensions in two broad ways. It may, rarely, impose a fixed penalty for a particular offence. Alternatively, there will be no fixed penalty but rather a statutory maximum (or perhaps maxima, as in buggery, depending upon the precise factual ingredients), together with detailed judicial guidelines to accompany that maximum. The perceived advantage of the fixed penalty is the certainty which it provides, but this is far outweighed by its inflexibility and thus, on occasion, harshness.[61] The advantage of the statutory maximum is that it does allow for flexibility and fairness of treatment depending upon the individual circumstances of each case, via the exercise of judicial discretion. This, however, must be balanced against a common perception that the judiciary is often 'out of touch' with reality and that sentences, especially in rape, are imposed which are far too lenient. Nevertheless, in rape at present English law provides for the discretionary model of sentencing, within the statutory maximum of life imprisonment and subject to a number of judicial guidelines.

4.1.1   Social disquiet

Throughout the late 1970s and early 1980s, there appeared to be a growing number of instances of defendants convicted of sexual offences, especially rape, receiving very lenient sentences. The sentences often were coupled with controversial and unpopular judicial statements.

In an unreported case heard at Ipswich Crown Court in 1982, the defendant was convicted of the rape of a woman who had been hitchhiking late at night. In sentencing the defendant to a fine of £2,000, the trial judge stated: 'I am not saying that a girl hitching home late at night should not be protected by the law, but she was guilty of a great deal of contributory negligence!'

---

61   Similarly, controversial debates take place in other areas, most noticeably in relation to the continuing debates surrounding the compulsory penalty in murder. See, eg, Criminal Law Revision Committee, *Fourteenth Report, Offences Against the Person*, Cmnd 7844, 1980, paras 19–31; Select Committee of the House of Lords on Murder and Life Imprisonment (the Nathan Committee), HL Paper 78–I (Session 1988–89) (especially paras 66–71, 118).

Similarly, in an unreported decision, also in 1982 (*The Guardian*, 16 December), Argyle J imposed a suspended sentence upon a man convicted of attempted rape, and stated:

> You have been all over the world and you are an experienced man. You have never seriously been across the law before ... For goodness sake make this the last time. Once you put your hands around a woman's neck in drink anything can happen ... You come from Derby which is my part of the world. Now off you go and don't come back to this court.

Such judicial statements, coupled with the very low sentences imposed, were bound to bring the whole question of rape sentencing under scrutiny, if not into contempt in certain quarters. The response of the judiciary was to formulate a series of guidelines vis-à-vis the approach to be taken in sentencing rape.

4.1.2   The guidelines

Even as early as 1982, the Court of Appeal had sought to allay some of the concerns surrounding rape sentences. In *Roberts (H)* ([1982] 1 All ER 609), the court had stressed that, as a general rule, rape was always a serious crime which deserved an immediate custodial sentence other than in wholly exceptional circumstances.

In *Billam* ([1986] 1 All ER 985), appeals against sentences for rape and attempted rape were listed jointly, in order to give the Court of Appeal the opportunity to reformulate and stress the principles appropriate to guide trial judges in sentencing such offences. Lord Lane CJ began by citing with approval a passage from the Criminal Law Revision Committee's Report on *Sexual Offences* (Cmnd 9213, 1984), where the severe degree of emotional stress and psychological trauma suffered by rape victims had been noted. The court reconfirmed also the general comments made in *Roberts* concerning the seriousness of rape, and it was noted that most trial judges did appear to be following the need for the imposition of custodial sentences: in 1984, for example, 95% of all defendants sentenced at Crown Court for a rape offence received some form of custodial sentence. It was arguable, however, that it was the brevity of and inconsistency between some of those sentences which need to be addressed urgently.

Lord Lane CJ recognised that variable factors existed (and still exist) in rape cases which make it difficult to use strict guidelines for the imposition of 'proper sentences'. Nevertheless, an analysis of the reported decisions suggested that a current practice could be determined. In particular, Lord Lane CJ identified four 'starting points' for sentencing particular categories of rape depending upon specific factual ingredients.

First, where rape is 'committed by an adult without any aggravating or mitigating features, a figure of five years should be taken as the starting point in a contested case'.[62]

Secondly, a starting point of eight years should be adopted where one or more of the following features is present: two or more men act together; the offence takes place in the premises where the victim is living; the defendant is in a position of responsibility towards the victim; the victim is abducted or held captive.

Thirdly, a sentence of 15 years or more might be regarded as 'appropriate' where the defendant has carried out a 'campaign of rape', by committing rape on a number of different women. This sentence is justified because the defendant represents 'a more than ordinary danger'.[63]

Finally, where the defendant's acts represent 'perverted or psychopathic tendencies or gross personality disorder, and where he is likely, if at large, to remain a danger to women for an indefinite time, a life sentence will not be inappropriate'.[64]

However, it is worth emphasising that these categories do represent 'starting points', and that the court was keen to stress that there will often exist also aggravating or mitigating factors which will serve to increase or decrease the sentence as appropriate.

The court identified eight aggravating factors, namely where:

(1) violence is used over and above the force necessary to commit the rape;

(2) a weapon is used to frighten or wound the victim;

(3) the rape is repeated;

(4) the rape has been carefully planned;

(5) the defendant has previous convictions for rape or other serious offences of a violent or sexual kind;

(6) the victim is subjected to further sexual indignities or perversions;

(7) the victim is either very old or very young;

(8) the effect on the victim, whether physical or mental, is of special seriousness.

Where any one or more of these aggravating features are present, the sentence should be substantially higher than the figure suggested as the starting point.[65]

By contrast, the court identified three specific factors which may operate to mitigate the defendant's sentence: where the defendant has pleaded guilty, thus removing the extra distress upon the victim which giving testimony

---

62 [1986] 1 All ER 985, p 987.

63 *Ibid.*

64 *Ibid*, p 988.

65 *Ibid.*

would involve (which is perhaps more acute in rape cases than in many other types of offence); if the victim has 'behaved in a manner which was calculated to lead the defendant to believe that she would consent to sexual intercourse'; and the previous good character of the defendant, although this was emphasised to be of minor relevance only.

Interestingly, the court gave two explicit instances of factors which cannot amount to mitigation, namely where the victim exposes herself to danger by acting imprudently (and the court used the specific example of accepting a lift in a car from a stranger), and the victim's previous sexual experience.

Whilst the *Billam* guidelines constituted an admirable attempt by the Court of Appeal to tackle the problems of brevity and inconsistency in rape sentencing, it is clear that they did not solve all the difficulties. In particular, the guidelines have been seen as lacking precision in relation to a specific 'tariff' for mitigation and aggravation (that is, exactly how far above or below the starting point the sentence should be set), as well as not being specifically directed towards rapes other than by strangers or where violence is used.[66]

4.1.3   Post-Billam

An analysis of sentencing statistics pre and post-*Billam* would tend to suggest that the guidelines did have a considerable impact on the general length of rape sentences. In the early 1980s, a large majority of defendants receiving custodial sentences received terms of imprisonment of under five years. In 1980, for instance, of 339 men imprisoned for rape, 287 (85%) were sentenced to less than five years. In 1981 and 1982, the figures were 204 from a total of 247 (83%), and 229 from 309 (74%) respectively. In the same three year period, there were only 10 sentences of over 10 years' imprisonment in total (3, 2 and 5 respectively), and only 27 life sentences (4, 9 and 14 respectively).[67] By contrast, a glance at a random selection of years post-*Billam* shows a considerably different picture. In 1988, of 378 men imprisoned for rape, 175 (only 46%) received a term of less than five years. By 1992, this had dropped further to 41% (162 out of 394). The same two years saw a total of 54 sentences of over 10 years' imprisonment (27 each year), and a total of 21 life sentences (11 and 10 respectively). Such data suggests clearly that there was a general increase in the length of rape sentences in the years following the *Billam* guidelines. In particular, the 'five-year starting point' for contested rapes, without aggravation or mitigation, seems to have had a noticeable impact on sentencing practice. The general adherence to the guidelines, and the subsequent overall increase in rape sentences, will be welcomed by many. However it should not be supposed that all the sentencing difficulties have dissipated post-1986. There are still instances of perceived lenient sentences, as well as instances where even the application of the guidelines may not

---

66   For these and other concerns see, eg, *op cit*, Edwards, fn 5, pp 361–62.

67   Criminal Statistics Supplementary Tables, Vol 2, 1980–94.

provide adequate protection for the public. In addition, the courts may deem it necessary, and on occasion have already deemed it necessary, to develop further the instances of 'aggravating factors' identified in *Billam*. Conversely, there will be instances where the courts are prepared to expand upon the categories of 'mitigating factors' for the benefit of defendants. These four issues deserve further analysis.

4.1.3.1 Additional aggravation and mitigation

In *Malcolm* ((1987) 9 Cr App R(S) 487), the victim stated that she feared she had contracted the AIDS virus as a result of being raped by the defendant. It was held that a trial judge could consider the victim's fear of having contracted a sexually transmitted disease from the defendant, provided it could be shown that the victim had a valid reason for her fear, or that her blood did, in fact, contain the AIDS virus as a result of the rape. A mere fear of contracting AIDS, without such evidence, would seem to be insufficient for increasing the sentence. The effect of the decision seems to be that where a defendant says to his victim, falsely, that he is HIV positive in order to terrify her, then (providing there is evidence to this fact) his statement and the victim's resulting fear would suffice to act as an aggravating factor.

The courts have also given useful guidance on sentencing rape where the parties had been, at one time, cohabitees. The existence of a previous relationship between the victim and the defendant is not mentioned in the *Billam* guidelines, but it was considered by the Court of Appeal in *Attorney General's Reference (No 7 of 1989)* [1990] Crim LR 437. There, Lord Lane CJ stated that the fact that the defendant and the victim had cohabited for over two years and that intercourse had occurred throughout that period did not give the man licence, once the cohabitation and intercourse had stopped, to have sexual intercourse with the woman 'willy nilly'. The fact of past cohabitation was a factor to which the sentencer could give weight (presumably on the basis, although this was not articulated clearly, that this may afford some mitigation), albeit in the circumstances of the case itself (particularly the physical injury caused to the victim and the defendant's plea of not guilty), the sentence was raised from two years' imprisonment to four and a half years. It may be wiser to regard this factor not so much as a mitigating feature *per se*, but rather as an issue not amounting to aggravation. However, the authorities on this point to date are not entirely consistent and there certainly are some cases where past cohabitation appears to have been treated as relevant to limited mitigation. Thus, in both *Maskell* ((1991) 12 Cr App R(S) 638), where the defendant was convicted of the rape of a former partner, and in *Collier* ((1992) 13 Cr App R(S) 33), where the defendant was convicted of raping his current partner, sentences of four years were reduced to three years. In *Maskell*, the Court of Appeal quoted with approval from the judgment of Mustill LJ in *Berry* ((1988) 10 Cr App R(S) 13):

The relevance of a previous settled sexual relationship was made plain by the decision of this court in *Cox* (1985) 7 Cr App R(S) 422. The rape of a former wife or mistress may have exceptional features which make it a less serious offence than otherwise it would be ... To our mind these cases show that in some instances the violation of the person and defilement that are inevitable features where a stranger rapes a woman are not always present to the same degree when the offender and the victim had previously had a long standing sexual relationship.[68]

Nevertheless, it is not easy to deduce from all such cases a clear reasoning that the sentences were reduced *because of* the existence of a previous sexual relationship. In *Collier* in particular, the court placed some significance on other factors, especially the defendant's plea of guilty and evidence of a reconciliation between the parties subsequent to the offence. By contrast, in *R v W* ([1992] Crim LR 490), a sentence of five years (following a plea of not guilty) was upheld. The Court of Appeal stated that, whilst the fact of cohabitation was a relevant factor, where, as here, there had been threats of serious violence with a knife and two forcible rapes, the facts of marriage, long cohabitation and consensual intercourse fairly recently prior to the offence were of very little significance in terms of sentencing. We would submit that both the decision and the reasoning in *W* are correct in principle: the central issue in rape is not the 'degree of defilement' suffered, but simply whether the victim consented to the intercourse. The absence of consent is the fundamental issue and the violation experienced by the victim where there is such an absence may be just as keenly felt, irrespective of the existence of any prior relationship with the defendant, and irrespective of the nature of that relationship. Of course, where further 'aggravating' or 'mitigating' features exist, it is only correct that these should be considered as relevant to the level of sentence, but the existence of a relationship (whether prior or current) between the victim and the defendant, should be regarded as an irrelevant consideration in all but the most exceptional of circumstances.

Nevertheless, in spite of this view it seems beyond doubt that the courts continue to find rape of a wife to be a less serious offence, and the grounds for some mitigation at the point of sentence. In *R v M* ([1995] Crim LR 344), the Court of Appeal reduced M's sentence for rape of his wife from three years to 18 months' imprisonment and stated:

While the existence of such a relationship did not necessarily mean that a lower scale of penalties should be applied than in normal cases, in a case where the parties were cohabiting normally at the time and the husband insisted on intercourse against the wife's wishes but without threats or violence, *the previous relationship would be an important factor in reducing the length of the sentence.*[69]

---

68 (1991) 12 Cr App R(S) 638, p 640.

69 [1995] Crim LR 344, pp 344–45 (emphasis added).

Similarly, in *R v H* ([1997] 2 Cr App R(S) 339), although a sentence of five years imprisonment against H was upheld for a series of rapes and indecent assaults on his wife, the Court of Appeal stated that 'the consequences of rape, grave though they are likely to be ... may not be as grave as when a woman is raped by a stranger'.[70]

It is clear that decisions such as these support the view that rape of a wife or partner, whether in relation to previous or continuing cohabitation (and in circumstances where all other factors are equal), is somehow less serious than rape of a stranger. Such comments and sentence reductions are likely to make wives and partners, who have been the victims of rape, even less inclined to complain about the offence. However, it is equally clear (from the cases referred to above) that prior or current cohabitation between the defendant and the complainant continues to be viewed by some in the legal profession as an important factor in mitigation.

One development which may be regarded as raising significant concerns, relates to the law's attitude to the sentencing of defendants convicted of raping prostitutes. In *Cole and Barik* ((1993) 14 Cr App R(S) 764), the defendants were convicted of, *inter alia*, the rape of a prostitute. The Court of Appeal reduced the sentences of nine years' imprisonment, imposed by the trial judge, to ones of seven years. In doing so, Tucker J stated:

> It is of course true that a prostitute is entitled to refuse to have sexual intercourse. She can say 'no' and the law will uphold that right. But it is submitted – and with some effect, as we think, that a factor which the court can take into account is that the prostitute is, in the nature of her trade, prepared to have intercourse with any man who pays for it and that her situation and the hurt that she may suffer as a result of the rape is to some extent different from that of another woman who would only be prepared to have sexual intercourse with a man whom she knows and respects. To some extent the hurt in cases such as this is not simply the act of intercourse but the fact that no payment has been made for it. That being said, it is repeated that a prostitute is fully entitled to the protection of the law and if she says 'no' and means it then the law will protect her by sentencing those who take advantage of her.[71]

The undeniable implication of this statement is that, whilst 'the law will protect her by sentencing those who take advantage of her', it will not protect her *as much* as any other rape victim, merely because of her status *qua* prostitute. There are also a number of assumptions implicit in the Court of Appeal's reasoning which are not supported by the available research evidence. For instance, it is clear that a prostitute is not necessarily 'prepared to have intercourse with any man who pays for it', but rather that many prostitutes are selective in terms of their clients.[72] It is equally clear that a

---

70   [1997] 2 Cr App R(S) 339, p 340, *per* Swinton Thomas LJ.

71   (1993) 14 Cr App R(S) 764, p 765.

72   See, eg, Jarvinen, M, *Of Vice and Women: Shades of Prostitution*, 1992, OUP, p 25.

prostitute as victim can suffer the same trauma from being raped as a non-prostitute.[73]

Finally, a potentially worrying development may be seen in the view occasionally expressed in some courts that the attitude of the victim herself may amount to a form of mitigation. This was recognised overtly in *Attorney General's Reference (No 36 of 1995) (Dawson)* ([1996] 2 Cr App R(S) 50) where the defendant was sentenced originally to three years' imprisonment for, *inter alia*, raping his 11 year old niece. Although this was increased to five years on the basis of its being unduly lenient, the Court of Appeal nevertheless noted:

> If, by reason of having been corrupted or being precocious (or both), the victim instigates offences against herself, that is another aspect which the judge is entitled to take into account. It is a matter of mitigation only in a negative sense that the child has not been treated in a way which she personally was resisting or found repugnant at the time. It does not, however, redound to the credit of the offender that he succumbed to provocation or teasing or tempting from a girl aged 11. The important point which is central to the sentencing exercise in cases of this kind is that young girls are to be protected from themselves as much as from anybody else. If a girl is precocious or for whatever reason provocative, then the adult has a duty not to succumb but to dissuade the child from that kind of conduct.[74]

Although, on the facts, it was accepted by all parties that the child was of such an age that she could not have given an informed and sensible consent to the acts in question, the decision is important for recognising in principle that an element of 'precociousness' by the victim, even if she is of a particularly young age, may amount to some mitigation of sentence. This has the potential to be dangerous, in the sense that a sentencer may regard a 'precocious' teenager or child as having 'led on' the defendant, which sits uncomfortably with the need to protect young and vulnerable victims.

4.1.3.2 Unduly lenient sentences

Prior to the passage of the Criminal Justice Act 1988, there existed no procedure whereby the Court of Appeal was empowered to state that a sentence imposed at the Crown Court was too light and thus that it should be increased. But such a power was introduced by ss 35 and 36 of the Criminal Justice Act 1988. The sections state that where a defendant has been sentenced in the Crown Court for an indictable offence, or for certain specified either-way offences, and the Attorney General considers that the defendant was sentenced unduly leniently, then he may refer the sentence to the Court of Appeal for them to review. The Court of Appeal must grant leave in order for such a reference to be made but, once that is granted, the court has the power to vary the sentence, replacing it with one which it considers to be

---

73   See, eg, West, D, *Male Prostitution*, 1992, Duckworth, pp 103–11.
74   [1996] 2 Cr App R(S) 50, p 52, *per* Lord Taylor CJ.

appropriate. The general principles upon which the Court of Appeal will operate in reviewing sentences have been laid down in a number of References.

In *Attorney General's Reference (No 4 of 1989)* ([1990] 1 WLR 41), the court emphasised the following general principle:

> The first thing to be observed is that it is implicit in the section that this court may only increase sentences which it concludes were *unduly* lenient. It cannot ... have been the intention of Parliament to subject defendants to the risk of having their sentences increased – with all the anxiety that this naturally gives rise to – merely because in the opinion of this court the sentence was less than this court would have imposed. A sentence is unduly lenient ... where it falls outside the range of sentences which the judge, applying his mind to all the relevant factors, could reasonably consider appropriate. In that connection regard must of course be had to reported cases, and in particular to the guidance given by this court from time to time in the so called guideline cases.[75]

The impact upon the defendant of increasing a sentence was reiterated in *Attorney General's Reference (No 1 of 1991)* ([1991] Crim LR 725). The Court of Appeal emphasised that the element of 'double jeopardy', whereby the defendant will face the hardship of being sentenced twice over, may act as some mitigation for not increasing the sentence by as much as might otherwise have been the case.[76]

It is also worth mentioning that the powers contained within ss 35 and 36 are, of course, discretionary. Even where the Court of Appeal accepts that the sentence imposed by the trial judge was lenient, it does not follow that there will inevitably be an increase in that sentence. There may be, for example, specific reasons for not increasing a sentence, such as the subsequent circumstances of the defendant or the impact any increase may have on persons dependant upon the defendant.

Finally, in *Attorney General's Reference (No 5 of 1989)* ((1990) 90 Cr App R 358), the Court of Appeal commented specifically on wider public policy considerations, namely that intervention by the Court should occur only where there had been an error of principle in the Crown Court sentence so that public confidence would be undermined if the sentence were not altered.

Notwithstanding the consensus of opinion that the *Billam* guidelines have produced more consistent as well as, generally, higher rape sentences, it is equally clear that there remain several instances of trial judges imposing upon defendants convicted of rape sentences which arguably are unduly lenient, even though, *prima facie*, there has been adherence to the guidelines. It is in

---

75 [1990] 1 WLR 41, pp 45–46.

76 See, also, the specific comments to this effect by Lord Taylor CJ in *Attorney General's Reference (No 19 of 1992)* [1993] Crim LR 82 (offences of non-consensual buggery by a husband on his wife).

these cases that ss 35 and 36 may serve the valuable purpose of empowering the Court of Appeal to act as a check upon undue leniency, and thus reassure the public that unacceptably low sentences in rape can and will be reviewed.

Thus instances of where sentences have been increased include: where the rape of a prostitute occurred at knifepoint (from two to three years in *Attorney General's Reference (No 12 of 1992)* (1993) 14 Cr App R(S) 233); and where the defendant tricked his way into the home of the victim, an elderly bereavement counsellor (from five to seven years in *Attorney General's Reference (No 1 of 1991)* ((1992) 13 Cr App R(S) 134). In *Attorney General's Reference (No 28 of 1993)* ((1995) 16 Cr App R(S) 103), the sentence was raised from six and a half to eight years. On first consideration, this seems somewhat on the harsh side. However, it was justified, rightly, by the Court of Appeal on the basis of several factors. The defendant has a previous conviction for rape and the present offence had involved gratuitous violence and a breach of trust in obtaining a key to the victim's residence, and there was also evidence of the careful planning of the offence. In the light of these several aggravating features, the original sentence of six and a half years was felt to be unduly lenient.

4.1.3.3 Longer than normal sentences

Even where a trial judge properly considers and applies the *Billam* guidelines, there may well remain cases where the particular circumstances may be seen as warranting a sentence above that indicated by the 'starting point' (including those cases where any aggravating features have also rightly been taken into account). Particular difficulties have occurred, not exclusive to rape, where sentencers wish to impose a sentence which will contribute to the future protection of the public, whilst at the same time not forgetting that the sentence imposed should bear some proportionality to the convicted person's present crime.

The difficult balancing act between the desire for proportionality and the desire to protect the public, was first addressed by Parliament in the Criminal Justice Act 1991 (now contained in the Powers of Criminal Courts (Sentencing) Act 2000). Section 2(2) of the Criminal Justice Act 1991 states:

The custodial sentence shall be–

(a) for such term (not exceeding the permitted maximum) as in the opinion of the court is commensurate with the seriousness of the offence, or the combination of the offence and other offences associated with it; or

(b) where the offence is a violent or sexual offence, for such longer term (not exceeding that maximum) as in the opinion of the court is necessary to protect the public from serious harm from the offender.

It is clear that s 2(2)(a) prioritises the principle of proportionality. The sentence imposed must, essentially, be commensurate with, that is proportionate to, the seriousness of the defendant's offence. Of course, the embodiment of this principle in s 2(2)(a) does not affect the sentencer's power to consider either aggravating or mitigating factors in determining the seriousness of the offence itself, nor does it prevent the sentencer from considering more general 'mitigation' (irrespective of its relationship to the seriousness of the offence) such as a plea of guilty, co-operation with the police, good character or the potential impact upon dependant persons.

Notwithstanding the primacy of proportionality, the sentencer may decide that a term which is longer than that which is commensurate with the seriousness of the offence must be imposed. This may be done where the criteria in s 2(2)(b) are satisfied. Clearly, rape is one of those offences which falls within the term 'sexual offence'. In addition, the court must be satisfied that a 'longer term ... is necessary to protect the public from serious harm from the offender'. This criterion means that a longer sentence may be imposed in order to prevent this particular offender from reoffending, which will thus give protection to the public. It cannot be used as a deterrent, even where a sentencer may believe genuinely that a longer term may serve to deter similar defendants from committing similar crimes. Nor may it be used to protect the defendant from himself or from harm from the public.

It has not proved easy to balance the two paragraphs in s 2(2). In particular, the sentencer must be aware that, whilst the sentence must be long enough to protect the public, it must still possess a reasonable relationship to the offence for which it was imposed. In *Kennan* ([1995] Crim LR 578), the defendant was convicted of the rape and assault occasioning actual bodily harm of a 16 year old prostitute. The defendant had threatened the victim with a knife, had struck her, forced her to strip and then have sexual intercourse. He had many previous convictions for a wide range of offences including robbery, actual bodily harm, indecent assault, rape and buggery (of males and females). The trial judge sentenced the defendant to 14 years' imprisonment, passed as a longer than normal sentence under s 2(2)(b). This sentence was confirmed by the Court of Appeal, where the defendant's 'appalling' record of violent sexual crime was noted, as was the absence of any evidence of psychiatric or mental illness. Whilst the Court of Appeal stressed that the sentence must not be 'out of all proportion to the nature of the offending on the instant occasion',[77] there was clear evidence that the defendant did pose a threat of serious harm to the public. Furthermore, specific factors such as the age of the victim, the use of a knife, the use of additional violence and the effect of the offence upon the victim, all contributed to the court's conclusion that the sentence was correct.

However, the propriety of this decision has been challenged by Professor Smith,[78] who had argued that, in these circumstances, a 'commensurate sentence' would have been probably seven to eight years. Therefore, he argues:

---

77 [1995] Crim LR 578, p 579, *per* Lord Taylor CJ.
78 In 'Commentary on *Kennan*', *ibid*, pp 579–80.

... it would be difficult to see how a sentence which was more than double (*sic*) the commensurate sentence could be considered to bear a 'reasonable relationship' to the seriousness of the offence, and this length of sentence must come near to the outer limit of sentences permitted under s 2(2)(b) for this type of case.

4.1.3.4   Extended sentences

Section 58 of the Crime and Disorder Act 1998[79] gave sentencers the power, in certain circumstances and subject to specified criteria, to impose an 'extended sentence'. The essence of s 58 is that it allows a judge passing a custodial sentence to add to the 'custodial period' an 'extension period' of supervision and, potentially, recall to custody at any time within the duration of the extension. Under s 58(1), the sentencer must consider that the period for which the offender would be subject to a licence 'would not be adequate for the purpose of preventing the commission by him of further offences and securing his rehabilitation'. An 'extended sentence' thus comprises two parts: the 'custodial term' and the 'extension period'. The custodial term itself may be either a commensurate sentence or a longer than commensurate sentence, within s 2(2)(a) and (b) respectively, above.[80]

For an extended sentence to be imposed, the custodial term must be for a violent offence (provided the custodial term was not less than four years) or for a sexual offence. Where it is imposed for a sexual offence, the extension period must not exceed 10 years. In addition, under s 58(5), it must also not exceed the maximum sentence allowed for the offence. If, for example, a defendant were convicted of indecent assault and sentenced to six years imprisonment (the custodial term), the sentencer (provided the necessary conditions existed) could impose an extension period of four years.

It is clear that sentencers may face the difficult decision, in some cases, of whether it is more appropriate to impose a longer than commensurate sentence (under s 2(2)(b)) or an extended sentence (under s 58). In *Thornton* ([2000] Crim LR 312), the appellant pleaded guilty to indecent assault on a woman, after grabbing her arm, placing his hand under her skirt and pulling down her tights. He was sentenced to five years' imprisonment. The trial judge stated specifically that this had been passed as a longer than commensurate sentence, that a period of two years was commensurate and that the additional three years were needed for the protection of the public. The Court of Appeal substituted a s 58 extended sentence for the longer than commensurate sentence. The substituted extended sentence of five years

---

79   Section 58 was repealed by the Powers of Criminal Courts (Sentencing) Act 2000. It was replaced by an identical provision, contained in the 2000 Act, s 85. See, for the general operation of the provisions, the decision in *Ajaib* [2000] Crim LR 770.

80   See, eg, in the context of a 'violent offence' (wounding with intent to cause GBH, contrary to the Offences Against the Person Act 1861, s 18), the decision of the Court of Appeal in *Gould* [2000] Crim LR 311.

comprised a custodial term of two years imprisonment and an extension period of three years.

The practical consequences of using s 58 rather than s 2(2)(b), as typified by *Thornton*, could be significant. A defendant may be entitled to an earlier date of release where s 58 is used, but at the risk of a longer period in custody if subsequently he were to be recalled by the Parole Board.[81]

In addition to the length-of-sentence implications, the trial judge should consider the differences in the criteria which need to be established. The conditions necessary for the imposition of s 58 (that the normal licence would not be adequate to prevent the commission of 'further offences' and for 'securing his rehabilitation') are less onerous than those in s 2(2)(b), where the court must be of the opinion that a longer term is 'necessary to protect the public from serious harm from the offender'.

4.2 Male rape and anal rape of females

As has already been noted above, one consequence of the Criminal Justice and Public Order Act 1994 is that the old (pre-1994) offence of non-consensual buggery is now incorporated into the new definition of rape. As a result, non-consensual anal intercourse, whether the victim is a male or a female, is rape, and the convicted defendant is liable to a maximum penalty of life imprisonment. In some respects it may seem that these changes will cause few, if any, difficulties: instances of non-consensual vaginal intercourse and non-consensual anal intercourse (of a male or female) are all now merely different ways of committing the same offence, and presumably will be subject to a consistent judicial approach vis-à-vis sentencing. However, a closer analysis of the pre-1994 authorities indicates that judicial attitudes towards both male and female victims of non-consensual buggery (as it then was) may not lead necessarily to such a fair and consistent approach.

4.2.1 Sentencing non-consensual buggery

4.2.1.1 Maximum sentences

Prior to 1994, maximum sentences for buggery varied according to a variety of factors: consent or absence of consent; the sex of the parties; and the ages of the participants.

One particular anomaly arose where the male victim was over the age of 16 and the male defendant was over the age of 21, in which case, the maximum penalty was 10 years. This contrasted starkly with the position of a defendant who committed buggery with a female where, by virtue of s 13 of the Sexual Offences Act 1967, the maximum penalty in all cases was life imprisonment, regardless of whether or not the female victim was consenting.

---

81   See the Commentary on *Gould* and *Thornton* by Thomas, DA: [2000] Crim LR 313.

It seems clear that even the judiciary found difficulties in reconciling such differences, and in dealing with the wider issue of principle as to whether non-consensual buggery was, in fact, a 'less serious offence' than vaginal rape. Although views on the latter issue were not unanimous, there appeared to be some consensus that non-consensual buggery was not as serious as rape.

In *Wall* ((1989) 11 Cr App R(S) 111), it was stated by Lloyd LJ on behalf of the Court of Appeal that:

[I]n the 15th Report of the Criminal Law Revision Committee, the Committee accepted the view of the Policy Advisory Committee that rape should be regarded as the most serious of all sexual offences ... If other sexual offences, however serious in themselves, were equated with rape, then there is obviously a risk that we should be appearing to diminish rape as the most serious of all sexual offences ... By enacting the Sexual Offences Act 1967 s 3 Parliament had made clear its view that non-consensual buggery is a less serious crime than rape.[82]

A different attitude was adopted by the trial judge in *Stanford* ([1990] Crim LR 526), where the defendant had pleaded guilty to buggery, without consent, of a male aged under 21. The victim, then aged 19, had met the defendant when they were both living in a hostel, and they had stayed together on several occasions. On one occasion, the defendant, in addition to making the victim engage in oral sex, had forced him to kneel and had buggered him over a period of about 15 minutes. The defendant had numerous convictions for similar offences committed over 20 years. The trial judge initially imposed a life sentence but, when he realised that the 1967 Act had reduced the maximum available in these circumstances, he reduced the sentence to eight years. However, this in turn was reduced by the Court of Appeal to five years. The court noted the general view, as expressed in *Wall* and in *Jackson* ((1988) 10 Cr App R(S) 297) that rape was a more serious offence than non-consensual buggery. In addition, the court noted specifically that there had been no excessive violence, no use of a weapon, no serious physical injury, no abuse of a position of trust or authority, no evidence of careful planning by the defendant and that the victim was not as young as some victims of such offences. In effect, the Court of Appeal was recognising that the main guidelines on buggery – the *Willis* guidelines – applied only in cases where the victim was a boy under the age of 16, so that, instead, the *Billam* guidelines on rape would be applied, albeit subject to a general reduction in the length of the sentence due to the perceived 'less serious nature' of buggery.

The sentencing situation was confused further by the fact that there existed numerous instances of the judiciary seemingly ignoring the principle of sentencing defendants at the appropriate level within the respective maxima (that is, life for buggery of a female and 10 years for buggery of a

---

82   (1989) 11 Cr App R(S) 111, p 112.

male over 16), and instead imposing sentences which approached some degree of equality. Indeed, it is arguable that the eventual sentence in *Stanford* was disproportionately high when compared with the likely sentence if the offence, in similar circumstances, had been vaginal rape and the *Billam* guidelines had been applied.[83]

The move towards a greater degree of equality in the sentencing of defendants convicted of non-consensual buggery, regardless of the victim's sex, may be seen in *Attorney General's Reference (No 19 of 1992) (R v S)* ([1993] Crim LR 82). The defendant had pleaded guilty to five specimen counts of buggery of his wife over a period of six years, although he claimed that she had consented. The trial judge accepted the wife's evidence, given in a *Newton* hearing, that she had not consented to any of the acts of buggery. Some of the offences had involved the use of violence and others had involved very distressing circumstances, including, for instance, the victim being tied to a bed, buggery whilst she was unwell and vomiting, and buggery during the later stages of pregnancy. The Attorney General asked the Court of Appeal to review the sentence – nine months' imprisonment, suspended for 18 months – on the basis that it was unduly lenient.

The Court of Appeal noted that there were few mitigating factors: the defendant had pleaded guilty, but, as the victim had still been required to give evidence, the benefit of that had been diminished. Also, there were no relevant previous convictions. By contrast, there were considerable aggravating features, including the facts of repeated buggery over a lengthy period of time, violence, the repugnant circumstances and the victim's general fear of her husband. Accordingly, the Court substituted a sentence of four years' imprisonment.

These types of cases may be taken as indicative of a possible trend, on the part of some sentencers, to equalise the sentences imposed upon defendants convicted of buggery, irrespective of the sex of the victim and irrespective of the fact that there was a considerable difference between the maximum sentences available to be imposed on a defendant vis-à-vis male and female complainants. But, as with sentencing trends within any specific offence, or type of offence, it is impossible to impose a precise formula as that runs the risk of ignoring the particular circumstances of each case and thus removing a valuable judicial discretion. Thus, in *Ball* ((1982) 4 Cr App R(S) 351), the Court of Appeal accepted that a sentence of two years' imprisonment for the non-consensual buggery of a female partner was appropriate, but still reduced it to 12 months because of the absence of any great violence and, perhaps more significantly, the fact that the parties were now reconciled and had stated their intention to be married.

---

83   See, eg, 'Commentary on *Stanford*' [1990] Crim LR 526, pp 526–27.

4.2.1.2   Offence seriousness

It is, perhaps, worth re-emphasising that, even prior to the amendments brought about by the 1994 Act, and irrespective of the predominant view of the seriousness of rape expressed in cases such as *Wall*, there were an increasing number of instances, pre-1994, where the judiciary was willing to comment upon the very nature of buggery (usually in cases of buggery of females) and its relationship with rape.

In *Mendez* ((1992) 13 Cr App R(S) 94), where the defendant was sentenced to five years' imprisonment for the buggery of an adult female, Glidewell LJ stated: 'In our view, forcible buggery of a woman is equable to rape, but worse than normal vaginal rape.'[84] Whilst the reasoning behind this statement may be understandable, it nevertheless appeared to conflict with the view expressed by the legislature who, by enacting different penalties for certain categories of buggery, had clearly intended vaginal rape to be the more serious offence. Admittedly, the maximum penalties for rape and buggery of a female, prior to 1994, were identical (life imprisonment), and the Court of Appeal in *Mendez* expressly adopted the *Billam* guidelines in upholding the sentence, but, nevertheless, *Mendez* may still be taken as being out of line with the general consensus at the time, insofar as rape was regarded as the 'uniquely serious' offence.

Clearly, the sentencing structures pre-1994 were inequitable and open to potentially unfair and discriminatory application. Whilst it may be argued that the judiciary's (occasional) attempts to equate the seriousness of vaginal rape with that of non-consensual buggery of females were laudable, such a course of action was not open in respect of defendants who committed acts of non-consensual buggery upon males over the age of 16. In the latter cases, the maximum sentence had been limited by Parliament to 10 years' imprisonment, so that no equalisation of the seriousness of vaginal rape and (male-to-male) non-consensual buggery was possible, however much the judiciary may have wished to pursue such a course.

4.2.2   Sentencing anal rape: post-1994

The first English case in which a man was convicted of a rape offence against a male victim is *Richards (Andrew Gestyn)* ([1996] 2 Cr App R(S) 167). The defendant was convicted of, *inter alia*, the attempted rape of a male youth (aged 18), for which he was sentenced to life imprisonment, with a recommendation that he should serve a minimum of 10 years, as provided by ss 34 and 35 of the Criminal Justice Act 1991. The facts giving rise to this sentence were as follows. The defendant had forced his penis into the victim's mouth and then ejaculated, and had then attempted to perform fellatio on the victim. 'Eventually he forced the victim to turn over and attempted to bugger

---

84   (1992) 13 Cr App R(S) 94, p 95.

him. The only thing that can be said about that in mitigation is that he did not prolong the attempt ...'[85] The defendant had several previous convictions for offences including rape and indecent assault, and was described as having a 'psychopathic personality disorder' which was exacerbated by his addiction to drink and drugs. The Court of Appeal upheld the life sentence, saying that that in itself could not be criticised, given the defendant's record and the opportunity that the trial judge had had to observe his demeanour and personality. However, insofar as the offence of attempted rape *per se* was concerned (that is, regardless of the additional aggravating factors), the court felt that a sentence of nine years would have been appropriate and, accordingly, the correct period to specify for the purpose of s 34 would be six years.

On first consideration, it is possible to view *Richards* as an example of the law treating attempted rape of a male as more serious than the completed rape of a female. However, this perhaps misses a significant point, namely that, by applying the *Billam* guidelines, the Court of Appeal has firmly set out its stall by stressing that rape offences post-1994 will be treated consistently, irrespective of the victim's sex. Several of the 'aggravating features' identified in *Billam* existed in the present case: the defendant's past record of sexual offences; the further sexual indignities imposed on the victim; the likelihood of the defendant remaining a threat to other persons; the defendant's personality disorder; and the need for the victim to give evidence. Bearing in mind these factors, the sentence is supportable in principle and consistent with authority,[86] and it is to be hoped that it will lead the way to an equitable treatment of defendants convicted of rape regardless of the sex of the victim or the form of penetration. Indeed, the proposition that, in principle, all 'types' of rape should be treated equitably in terms of sentencing, receives some support from a consideration of the debates during the passage of the Criminal Justice and Public Order Bill itself.

In particular, Alan Howarth MP commented upon some of the discrepancies which existed as a result of the sentences then available for buggery and rape:

> Buggery without consent carries a maximum of 10 years' imprisonment compared with the maximum of life for rape. This implies that, even if we do not condone it, we take a more indulgent view of it. All the evidence shows that male victims of rape experience a trauma that should be understood as comparable to that suffered by female victims.[87]

In support of these claims, Mr Howarth quoted[88] from Dr Michael King: 'The rape trauma syndrome, and the traumatic effect and the possible behaviour

85 [1996] 2 Cr App R(S) 167, *per* Waterhouse J, p 168.
86 In addition to *Billam* itself, see, also, *Fenton* (1992) 12 Cr App R(S) 85.
87 *Hansard*, 3 April 1994, HC Debs, Vol 242, Cols 174–76.
88 *Ibid*, Col 177.

changes following from such an assault, occurs in both men and women.' He referred also to an unreported decision from Doncaster Crown Court in 1992, where Crabtree J expressed the opinion: 'When it comes to punishment I do not see that it makes any difference whether it was a man or a woman who has been violated and degraded.'[89]

Views such as these clearly played a role in persuading some Members of Parliament that the time had come to effect a radical change and bring into line the maximum sentences for rape and non-consensual buggery.

However, it should not be supposed that there will be no problems to face in the future when sentencing defendants convicted of anal rape, especially where the victim is male. Three general areas may prove to be of particular interest.

First, sentencers will need to consider what impact, if any, the fact that the victim was a male prostitute should have on sentence. By analogy with the attitude of the Court of Appeal in *Cole and Barik* in relation to female prostitutes, it may be that the fact of the victim's prostitution will be taken as some mitigation leading to a reduction in the defendant's sentence. If this were to happen, it would be regrettable, especially in the light of the particularly vulnerable position of many (young) male prostitutes, who are in need of extra protection from the law, not an implicit criticism of their activities.

Secondly, the issue of rape within prisons, where male victims face almost unique difficulties, will need to be considered. In *Wall*, the victim, a remand prisoner, was threatened with a razor blade and buggered by one of the men sharing his cell. The Court of Appeal reduced the sentence imposed by the trial judge from six years' imprisonment to four years, whilst commenting that 'the fact that the act of buggery was committed in prison should not be regarded either as an aggravating factor or as a mitigating factor'.[90]

It is difficult to support this contention. The inevitable factor of confinement, often with the perpetrator of the offence, together with the general lack of support and counselling which may be available to victims 'on the outside', would tend to amount to clear aggravation of an already traumatic experience. Only time will tell whether the courts will regard future rapes in such circumstances as possessing aggravating features.

Thirdly, as again with 'traditional' rape, sentencers will have to come to terms with the difficulties caused by the precise relationship between the parties and the behaviour of the victim. Thus, *Billam* itself allows the sentencer to consider, as some mitigation, the behaviour of the victim if that would have led the defendant into believing that she would consent to intercourse.

---

89 *Hansard*, 3 April 1994, HC Debs, Vol 242, Col 178.
90 (1989) 11 Cr App R(S) 111, p 112.

Similarly, it has already been noted (in *Maskell* and *Collier*, above) that vaginal rape of former or existing partners has resulted on occasion in a reduction of sentence on appeal, and it is unlikely that the courts would adopt a different attitude in the context of homosexual relationships.

5   REFORM OF RAPE LAW

In recent years, the first major proposals for reform in the law of rape may be found in the recommendations of the Criminal Law Revision Committee in 1984. Subsequently, these were adopted by and incorporated into the draft Criminal Code Bill. Several of the Bill's clauses must now be read in the light of later changes in the law, especially, for example, in relation to the marital rape exemption, rape by boys aged 10–13 inclusive and anal rape. The most recent proposals are contained in the 2000 Home Office Paper, *Setting the Boundaries*.

5.1   Interpretation

Clause 87 of the draft Bill deals with issues of interpretation, although much of that clause is either now law or has been rendered redundant by subsequent legislation. Thus, the reference to 'men' including 'boy' 'whether under the age of 14 or not' has already been implemented by the change brought about by the Sexual Offences Act 1993. Likewise, the 1994 Act has extended the definition of rape so as to include anal intercourse, not just vaginal intercourse as stated in cl 87.

One issue within cl 87 which remains of significance is the explicit definition of 'sexual intercourse' as being an act which 'continues until the man's penis is withdrawn'. This part of cl 87 would have the effect of confirming the Privy Council's decision in *Kaitamaki*, and thus removing any possible argument that a defendant, in order to be guilty, must possess *mens rea* at the initial point of penetration, rather that when he later becomes aware of the victim's absence of consent.

5.2   *Actus reus*

The current law of rape, as noted above, limits the proscribed physical act to penile penetration of the vagina or anus. Recommendation 1 in *Setting the Boundaries* proposes a radical extension of the *actus reus* by including oral penetration in the definition:

Forced oral sex is as horrible, as demeaning and as traumatising as other forms of forced penile penetration, and we saw no reason why rape should not be defined as penile penetration of the anus, vagina or mouth without consent.[91]

The same Recommendation confirms that (as with the current law) penetration needs only be 'to the slightest extent', but proposes also that 'for the avoidance of doubt, surgically reconstructed male or female genitalia should be included in the definition in law'. This proposal would confirm, in effect, the first instance ruling of Hooper J in *Matthews*, above. It would make clear that persons with wholly or partially constructed genitalia do fall within the legal definition of rape, thus extending the law's protection to, for example, transsexuals or a woman with a surgically reconstructed vagina. It would make clear also, if the issue should ever arise, that a man with an artificially constructed penis is capable of committing the offence of rape. These are welcome proposals that would add consistency and certainty to the law.

Setting the Boundaries does not propose extending the *actus reus* of rape beyond penetration by the penis. Penetration by any other object (whether by another part of the body, such as the tongue or fingers, or by an inanimate object, such as a bottle) would fall within the proposed new offence of sexual assault by penetration, which will be considered in Chapter 6.

5.3 *Mens rea*

Clause 89 of the draft Bill proposes a significant amendment to the definition of the *mens rea* for rape. The clause states:

(1) A man is guilty of rape if he has sexual intercourse with a woman without her consent and–

   (a) he knows that she is not consenting; or

   (b) he is aware that she may not be, or does not believe that she is, consenting.

Paragraph (b) has been worded widely, and has avoided deliberately use of the word 'reckless'. The effect of the clause is that a man will possess the *mens rea* for rape if he *knows* that the woman was not consenting (para (a)), or if he, subjectively, either was *aware* that she might not be consenting or *did not believe* that she was consenting (para (b)). By differentiating clearly between the two paragraphs, a sentencing judge would know, in appropriate cases, the precise basis upon which the defendant was convicted, that is, 'intentional rape', or what would under the current law be described as 'reckless rape'. The clear implication of this division is that sentencers may sentence intentional rape more severely than 'reckless rape'.

---

91 Home Office Consultation Paper, *Setting the Boundaries*, July 2000, para 2.8.5.

In terms of *mens rea*, *Setting the Boundaries* is broadly in agreement with the current law, whereby a man will be guilty of rape if he intentionally had intercourse without consent, or was reckless as to consent. However, the Report emphasises that the law should reflect clearly the full extent of recklessness as to consent, and that this is best encapsulated by the 'could not care less' attitude of the defendant:

> A person who could not care less about consent is rightly regarded as reckless. A person who fails to take all the steps which are reasonable in the circumstances to find out if there is free agreement on the occasion in question could not care less about the other person's consent and is therefore reckless. We consider that this should be considered in any definition in law.[92]

5.4   Consent

The second part of cl 89 deals with 'Consent and threat or deception', and states:

> (2) For the purposes of this section a woman shall be treated as not consenting to sexual intercourse if she consents to it–
>
>   (a) because a threat, express or implied, has been made to use force against her or another if she does not consent, and she believes that, if she does not consent, the threat will be carried out immediately or before she can free herself from it; or
>
>   (b) because she has been deceived as to–
>
>   (i) the nature of the act; or
>
>   (ii) the identity of the man ...

The purpose of cl 89(2)(a) is to seek to clarify the meaning of consent, especially in the wake of uncertainties following *Olugboja* (in relation to situations where sexual intercourse is obtained by threats), where juries are required to grapple with the difficult question of whether the victim consented.

Clause 89(2)(a) states clearly that a man commits rape if he obtains the woman's consent 'because a threat, express or implied, has been made to use force against her or another if she does not consent, and she believes that, if she does not consent, the threat will be carried out immediately or before she can free herself from it'. But as has already been noted in the discussion of *Olugboja*, the requirement of the threat being carried out 'immediately' may be seen as unfairly narrowing the scope of rape. If a defendant, for example, were to demand sexual intercourse with the victim on the basis that otherwise he will harm her young child on some undefined occasion in the future as the child leaves school, it is difficult to see how this very real threat would satisfy the immediacy requirement. It would appear not to be rape, even though there is no genuine consent on the part of the victim.

---

92 Home Office Consultation Paper, *Setting the Boundaries*, July 2000, para 2.12.16, and see Recommendation 8.

Similarly, although it is accepted generally that force (or the threat of force) should be construed widely, so as to include not only violence, but also other acts such as unlawful detention or abduction, this criterion also appears to have its limitations. Thus, an employer who tells an employee that she will be placed on a forthcoming redundancy list unless she consents to sexual intercourse, would appear not to be guilty of rape on this definition, albeit the 'economic threat' posed by the demand may be of huge and real significance to the woman concerned.

Clause 89(2)(b) would clarify the law where consent is obtained by 'deception'. The clause would preserve expressly the present law whereby rape exists if the woman is deceived as to the very nature of the act. In addition the clause would extend the 'impersonation' rule, so that it would be rape not merely where a man impersonates the victim's husband, but also expressly where he deceives her as to the identity of any man. This extension has already been suggested by the Court of Appeal in *Elbekkay*, above, but it would remove any lingering doubts as to the validity of that decision.

The most radical proposals in relation to the reform of consent are to be found in *Setting the Boundaries*. The Report recognises the centrality of the concept of consent, as a notion governing both the parameters of private sexual relationships and the extent to which the criminal law can and should restrict those parameters. It was accepted that the current law is unclear and uncertain:

> In an area of human behaviour where there are debates within society about what is and is not appropriate, it is more than ever important that the law is clear and well understood, particularly about what behaviour is criminal.[93]

Consequently, Recommendation 4 proposes that 'consent should be defined in law as "free agreement"'. This was seen as having the advantages of being simple and clear, and of emphasising that 'free agreement' must necessarily be 'voluntary and genuine'.

In an even more innovative move the Report proposes (in Recommendation 5) that the 'law should set out a non-exhaustive list of circumstances where consent [that is, free agreement] was not present'. The Report emphasises that it is not a complete list, but rather sets out instances of non-consent that are well established, and often 'obvious', from case law. It is intended to provide a list of examples of when a person does not give consent to sexual activity. The following summary of Recommendation 6 lists those examples, whereby consent is not given if a person:

- submits or is unable to resist because of fear or force;
- submits because of threats or fear of serious harm or serious detriment of any type to themselves or another person;

---

93 Home Office Consultation Paper, *Setting the Boundaries*, July 2000, para. 2.10.2.

- was asleep, unconscious, or too affected by alcohol or drugs to give free agreement;
- did not understand the purpose of the act, whether because they lacked the capacity to understand, or were deceived as to the purpose of the act;
- was mistaken or deceived as to the identity of the person or the nature of the act;
- submits or is unable to resist because they are abducted or unlawfully detained;
- has agreement given for them by a third party.

Finally, the Report considers in detail the question of the defendant's honest, albeit mistaken, belief in consent, and whether such a mistake should be reasonable. The Report notes (at para 2.13) that this is a highly controversial issue, and that many of the submissions to the review were in favour of reversing the decision in *Morgan*, above, and returning to a requirement of reasonableness. After a detailed consideration of the options, the review did not propose a completely objective requirement of reasonableness, but rather a defence of honest belief in free agreement, but with limitations on its use. Recommendation 9 states:

> A defence of honest belief in free agreement should not be available where there was self induced intoxication, recklessness as to consent, or if the accused did not take all reasonable steps in the circumstances to ascertain the free agreement at the time.

CHAPTER 4

OFFENCES RELATED TO SEXUAL INTERCOURSE

1 INTRODUCTION

In a number of situations it may be impossible legally, or very difficult factually, for the prosecution to establish all the elements necessary for a charge of rape to succeed. Frequently, this may be due to the fact that an absence of consent (as defined in and required by the law of rape) cannot be established or, even more fundamentally, that the victim did give *de facto* consent, but, nevertheless, the law regards it as having been given in circumstances which merit criminalisation, albeit of a 'lesser' crime than rape.

In this chapter, therefore, we shall consider briefly a few of the offences which possess or relate to an element of sexual intercourse, and which may be charged as alternatives to more serious crimes, in particular, s 1 rape.

2 PROCURING SEXUAL INTERCOURSE WITH A WOMAN

The very great difficulties in both defining consent and subsequently establishing the absence of consent were considered in Chapter 3. Particular problems may occur in two general situations, namely where the defendant puts pressure upon the victim in circumstances where that pressure is insufficient to vitiate consent for the purpose of rape, and, secondly, where false pretences or representations are made by the defendant, again other than in the limited circumstances recognised as vitiating consent. Where consent for the purpose of rape is not vitiated, then the 'wider' offences contained in ss 2 and 3 of the Sexual Offences Act 1956 should be considered as potential alternatives.

2.1 Procuring a woman by threats or intimidation

Section 2(1) of the 1956 Act (as amended) provides:

> It is an offence for a person to procure a woman, by threats or intimidation, to have sexual intercourse in any part of the world.

2.1.1 Parties

The origins of s 2 may be traced back to s 3(1) of the Criminal Law Amendment Act 1885, which was designed essentially to protect young girls by punishing men who forced those girls into the white slave trade.

Whilst the purpose of the original offence may have been to criminalise the man who procured sexual intercourse between the victim and another man, the wording of s 2 does not necessarily limit the offence in such a way. Therefore, the defendant will be guilty if he procures sexual intercourse either with a different man or with himself. As the offence can be committed by a 'person' it is equally clear that a female may be guilty as a principal offender. Of course, the female defendant cannot be guilty by procuring another woman to commit an act of sexual intercourse with herself, but she will be guilty where, by her threats, she procures the victim to have sexual intercourse with a man.

Prior to 1993, a boy under 14 (provided he was aged at least 10) could have been guilty as a principal to an offence under s 2 in circumstances where he procured a woman to have sexual intercourse with another man, but would not have been guilty by procuring a woman to commit the same act with himself, as he was deemed to be incapable of sexual intercourse. However, this fiction was removed by the Sexual Offences Act 1993 so that, providing mischievous discretion is proved, a boy aged 10–13 would now be guilty in the latter circumstances as well.

Finally, it should be noted that the word 'unlawful' was deleted from the definition in s 2 by the Criminal Justice and Public Order Act 1994, thus removing any possible difficulties in respect of charging a husband with the offence where he procures his wife to have sexual intercourse by threats.

2.1.2   Procure

There is no direct authority on the meaning of the word 'procure' as used in s 2, although it is a word frequently used in the criminal law, and it would seem sensible to define the word consistently with its use in analogous provisions. The most useful general guidance as to the meaning of the word can be found in the judgment of Lord Widgery CJ in *Attorney General's Reference (No 1 of 1975)* ([1975] QB 773):

> To procure means to produce by endeavour. You procure a thing by setting out to see that it happens and taking the appropriate steps to produce that happening.[1]

The essence of procuring is the need to establish an element of causation. It is not the existence *per se* of threats or intimidation which will make the defendant guilty, unless those threats, etc caused the act of sexual intercourse. If the victim would have engaged in the act irrespective of the threats, then their mere existence will not make the defendant liable. This view is supported by analogy with the decision in the old case of *Christian and Another* ((1913) 23 Cox CC 541) where the defendants were charged with, *inter alia*,

---

1   [1975] QB 773, p 779.

procuring a girl to become a common prostitute. In directing the jury to acquit, the Common Serjeant, Sir FA Bosanquet, stated:

> The girl wanted no procuring at all. It must be real procuration ... This girl says she went of her own free will. The Act is not aimed at brothel-keepers who give girls an opportunity ... of carrying on that trade. It is aimed at people who get girls by some fraud or persuasion ...[2]

Similarly, in *Broadfoot* ([1976] 3 All ER 753), on a charge of attempting to procure a woman to become a prostitute, under s 22(1)(a) of the 1956 Act, the Court of Appeal held that procuring:

> ... could perhaps be regarded as bringing about a course of conduct which the girl in question would not have embarked on spontaneously or of her own volition.[3]

From such cases, it follows that if the woman would not have engaged in the act of sexual intercourse but for the existence of the threats or intimidation, then the defendant may be regarded as having procured the intercourse. However, this deals only with the issue of causation and thus still leaves open the more fundamental question of which type or degree of threat will suffice to impose liability.

2.1.3   Threats or intimidation

The words 'threats' and 'intimidation' are not defined in the 1956 Act, although it is clear that the offence in s 2 is designed to be considerably broader than rape, in the sense that it will cover circumstances where the consent of the victim has been induced by threats, etc, but those threats were insufficiently serious to negative consent for the purpose of rape.

'Intimidation', which is a wider concept than 'threats', would appear to be designed to cover the defendant whose actions or words instil fear in the mind of the victim, irrespective of whether there is a threat of violence. Furthermore, threats in this context are given a considerably broader interpretation than in, say, the defence of duress *per minas*, where the concept is regularly limited to threats of death or really serious bodily harm.[4] For the purpose of s 2, threats of consequences other than violence amounting to death or really serious harm will suffice. In *Harold* ((1984) 6 Cr App R(S) 30), the defendant had pleaded guilty to attempting to procure a woman, by threats, to have sexual intercourse, after he had threatened to disclose to the victim's employers the fact that she had once worked as a prostitute, unless she gave him a 'freebie', that is, had sexual intercourse with him without payment. Although the appeal was one against sentence, it is clear by

---

2   (1913) 23 Cox CC 541, p 542.

3   [1976] 3 All ER 753, p 756, *per* Cusack J.

4   See, eg, *Hudson and Taylor* [1971] 2 QB 202; *Graham* [1982] 1 All ER 801. 'Lesser' threats will not suffice: *Valderrama-Vega* [1985] Crim LR 220.

implication that the demand issued in this case was accepted by the court as being more than sufficient to satisfy the threat criterion.

It is clear also that where the threats are ones of physical harm or injury, they do not necessarily have to be levelled at the woman herself. In *Wilson (T)* ((1973) 58 Cr App R 304), the defendant was convicted of several offences in respect of his daughter, including the offence of attempting to procure sexual intercourse with her by threats. The threats included a specific threat that the girl's mother would be stabbed unless she had sexual intercourse:

> We respectfully concur with the direction given by the learned judge that, were that established, it would none the less be attempted procurement of the girl by threats because these threats were to harm someone other than herself.[5]

With regard to other types of threats or intimidation the position is less clear. Whilst it may be clear that some threats ('I won't buy you another drink unless you have intercourse with me') are insufficient to amount to an offence under s 2, there will inevitably be other borderline cases where even two reasonable people may genuinely disagree as to the scope of the offence. It seems likely that this will be held to be an issue to be determined by the jury, but, in reaching their decision, they must take account of the characteristics of the woman concerned.[6] If this should prove to be so then we submit that some element of objectivity must be retained. A woman's extreme timidity or excessive susceptibility to suggestion, for example, are incompatible with an essentially objective test, and are not characteristics which should be considered by the jury.

2.1.4 Sexual intercourse

Although the issue has not been determined by the courts, it seems likely that this phrase has not been affected by the Criminal Justice and Public Order Act 1994, and so will be limited to vaginal intercourse and not extended to cover anal intercourse. Thus, a man commits no offence under s 2 by making threats to a woman whereby she permits anal intercourse to take place, unless the threats are of such a serious nature that there is a negation of consent, in which case, the offence of (anal) rape would occur. In other respects, the phrase 'sexual intercourse' has the same meaning as in rape, so that the merest degree of penetration by the man's penis suffices for liability.

The offence is only complete once it is proved that the act of sexual intercourse has taken place. Where that act did not occur, or cannot satisfactorily be established, then, as noted above, a charge of attempting to procure sexual intercourse by threats may be made in appropriate circumstances.

---

5   (1973) 58 Cr App R 304, p 307, *per* Edmund Davies LJ.
6   See Smith, J and Hogan, B, *Criminal Law*, 1996, Butterworths, pp 463–64.

2.1.5 Mens rea

The prosecution must establish a specific intent on the part of the defendant, namely that he intended to procure the woman to have sexual intercourse with either himself or another man.

2.2 Procuring a woman by false pretences or representations

Section 3(1) of the 1956 Act (as amended) provides:

> It is an offence for a person to procure a woman, by false pretences or false representations, to have sexual intercourse in any part of the world.

The majority of the criteria necessary to establish this offence (such as the meaning of 'procure' and the parties to the offence) are common to the offence under s 2. The main element of distinction between ss 2 and 3 is the method whereby the woman is procured.

2.2.1 False pretences or false representations

As with s 2, the wording of s 3 is designed to encompass a wider range of circumstances than those covered in rape, and thus criminalise behaviour which would not involve a negation of consent for the purpose of rape. It was seen in Chapter 3 that sexual intercourse obtained by fraud on the part of the defendant is only rape in very limited circumstances, namely where there is fraud as to the nature of the physical act itself, or where there is impersonation of the woman's husband.[7] Section 3, by contrast, has the potential for a wide interpretation, thereby criminalising other 'lesser' types of fraud. Although the section is little used in practice, its scope should be sufficiently broad to capture the defendant who states, falsely, to a woman that he is a rich and famous film star, as a result of which falsehood, the woman is induced to have sexual intercourse with him.

One remaining uncertainty about the scope of the offence is whether the words false pretences or representations will be limited to a misrepresentation as to present fact, or whether they will extend to a misrepresentation as to future facts. If a man were to state, falsely, to a young woman that the act of sexual intercourse improves the voice (in circumstances where she knows the nature of the act *per se*, but genuinely, albeit mistakenly, believes this consequence will result), this must be a misrepresentation as to a future fact, as opposed to a present one. Nonetheless, where sexual intercourse is induced, this should be the kind of false statement against which the section was designed to afford protection.

---

7   Although this itself was extended to the impersonation of the victim's boyfriend in *Elbekkay* [1995] Crim LR 163 – see Chapter 3.

A similar uncertainty exists in relation to false statements of (future) intention as, in many areas of criminal law, such false statements do not amount to 'false pretences'. Thus a false promise of a future intention to marry a woman may not be regarded as amounting to the requisite false pretences. However it is interesting that many commentators appear to accept that the false statement by the defendant in *Linekar* (see Chapter 3), to the effect that he would pay the prostitute for her services after the act of intercourse, could have amounted to an offence under s 3.[8] Once again, this seems to be a clear misrepresentation as to future intention and, on that basis, might fall outside the scope of the offence. However, it would be contrary to the objective of the section if this type of false statement were to be held not to be a 'false pretence'. In this respect, it is important to note that the Criminal Law Revision Committee has recommended replacing the words 'false pretences or false representations' with the word 'deception'. This proposed change, which is incorporated in cl 91 of the draft Criminal Code Bill (procuring a woman 'by deception' to have sexual intercourse) would broaden the scope of the offence (by clearly encompassing false statements of future intent) and remove any possible doubts as to its application in circumstances such as those of, say, *Linekar*.

2.2.2 Mens rea

As with s 2, for a charge under s 3 to succeed, it is incumbent upon the prosecution to prove that the defendant intended to procure a woman to have the act of sexual intercourse with himself or another man.

2.3 Administering drugs, etc, to obtain or facilitate sexual intercourse

Section 4(1) of the 1956 Act provides:

> It is an offence for a person to apply or administer to, or cause to be taken by, a woman any drug, matter or thing with intent to stupefy or overpower her so as thereby to enable any man to have unlawful sexual intercourse with her.

2.3.1 Parties

The offence may be committed by either males or females as principal offenders. The person with whom it is intended the woman should have sexual intercourse must, of course, be male, and, since the Sexual Offences Act 1993, this would include a boy aged 10 or above.

The victim of the offence must be a woman, and the act which the defendant intends to facilitate is limited to vaginal sexual intercourse. This

---

8   See, eg, 'Commentary on *Linekar*' [1995] Crim LR 321; and Reed, A, '*Contra bonos mores*: fraud affecting consent in rape' (1995) 145 NLJ 174, p 176.

naturally imposes a restriction on the offence, as it does not cover, for instance, the defendant who applies a drug for the purpose of enabling a man to commit an act of gross indecency or anal intercourse. The present law therefore provides inadequate protection in two senses: it fails to protect males by excluding them from the definition and it fails to protect females in some circumstances by limiting the nature of the sexual act intended. These deficiencies were recognised by the Criminal Law Revision Committee, which has recommended an extension of the offence currently contained in s 4. This recommendation was adopted by the Law Commission and incorporated in to the draft Criminal Code Bill as cl 92:

> A person is guilty of an offence if he applies or administers to, or causes to be taken by, another any article or substance, intending to stupefy or overpower that other in order to enable himself or a third person to have sexual intercourse with, or to commit buggery with, or to commit an act of gross indecency with, that other.

If it were ever enacted, cl 92 would extend the offence to cover not only the person who applied a drug, etc, for the purpose of enabling (vaginal) sexual intercourse, but also to cover a person whose actions were aimed at enabling acts of buggery and gross indecency, irrespective of the sex of the victim.

2.3.2 Actus reus

2.3.2.1 Any drug, matter or thing

Parliament has used a particularly wide phrase in relation to the items which can be administered by the defendant to the woman. The word 'drug' is included specifically, and, in the absence of any direct authority, the remainder of the phrase should be given a common sense meaning and would certainly cover items such as gas and alcohol. Clause 92, above, would substitute the simpler phrase 'article or substance' for the present words 'drug, matter or thing'. The retention, and indeed extension, of the offence was justified by the Law Commission on the basis that it would constitute a specifically sexual offence and would appear as such on the record of the defendant.

2.3.2.2 To apply or administer to or cause to be taken by ...

Section 4 stipulates three alternative modes of action whereby the defendant can cause the woman to be affected by the item in question. The phrase is wide and would cover not only the 'normal' situation whereby a woman takes a drug orally, or by inhalation or injection, but also where the item is left to be consumed directly by the victim herself, or is applied to the victim through the actions of an innocent third party. It is questionable whether the word 'administer' would extend to the defendant's action of squirting something at the victim, but, in the context of s 4, this is of little significance, as such an act would clearly amount to 'applying'.

2.3.2.3 Consent

It is implicit from the context of s 4 that the words 'apply, administer and cause to be taken' should all be interpreted as indicating that something has been done to the victim without her consent. Thus a defendant has not 'caused a drug to be taken' if the woman knows the nature of the substance which she is taking and, furthermore, takes it voluntarily. This will be so even if the defendant, at the time of causing the woman to take the drug, intends sexual intercourse to take place once she has become stupefied. Of course, if the woman becomes so affected by the drug or substance that, subsequently, she lacks an understanding and knowledge of the acts that are taking place and is unable to give a valid consent, then the defendant may be guilty of other offences, such as rape itself, or indecent assault if no sexual intercourse occurs.

A difficulty may also arise if the woman takes a substance voluntarily, knowing its nature, but has been misled by the defendant about the volume or strength of the substance. We submit that this should not be regarded as a consensual taking. In this context, consent must mean consent whilst being aware of all the relevant circumstances, and to hold otherwise would be to defeat the purpose of the section.

2.3.2.4 'Unlawful sexual intercourse' and the completion of the *actus reus*

The offence under s 4 is complete as soon as the drug, etc, has been applied, administered or taken. It is not a necessary element of the offence that the act of sexual intercourse itself should take place. Because the essence of the *actus reus* is 'the administration', it follows that there must be one act of administration for each offence. This is so even if a single act of administration was intended to facilitate more than one act of sexual intercourse. In *Shillingford and Vanderwall* ([1968] 2 All ER 200), the defendant, Shillingford, was convicted of two offences under s 4, having administered a barbiturate drug to the victim, a French *au pair*, in order to enable both himself (count 1) and Vanderwall (count 2) to have sexual intercourse with her. The Court of Appeal quashed the conviction in respect of count 2 on the basis that, as there had been only a single 'administration', there could only be one offence. Whilst this may be correct in principle, it could cause considerable practical difficulties. If a defendant were to place several sleeping tablets into the drink of the victim over a short period of, say, 10 minutes, with the purpose of facilitating sexual intercourse between the woman and both himself and a friend, is this just a single administration or more than one? It looks like more than one, but if that is so, it is a fine distinction between that scenario and the situation where the defendant places several tablets into the victim's drink at one time, albeit with the same purpose as above.

Although the act of sexual intercourse *per se* does not have to take place for an offence under s 4 to exist, it must be proved that the defendant acted in order to enable such an act. But it is important to note that s 4 (unlike, for example, ss 2 and 3, above) has retained the word 'unlawful' as a qualification to 'sexual intercourse'. As Parliament, as recently as 1994, decided not to remove the word 'unlawful' from this section, it must be assumed that it retains the traditional meaning of 'outside marriage'. Consequently, a limited marital immunity still exists in circumstances where the drug, etc, is administered in order to facilitate a man to have sexual intercourse with that man's own wife. In that case, there appears to be no *unlawful* sexual intercourse. Such haphazard law reform causes confusion and inconsistency, and is not to be welcomed. Reform along the lines of cl 92, above, where the word 'unlawful' is omitted, is needed urgently.

2.3.3   Mens rea

The prosecution must establish two distinct elements in respect of the defendant's *mens rea*.

First, he must intend to 'stupefy or overpower her'. The words 'stupefy or overpower' are given their ordinary dictionary definition, and thus would include an intention to make the woman insensible, to cause her to lose feeling, or to place her asleep or in an unconscious condition.

Secondly, the defendant must be proven to have an ulterior intent, namely that he intended, as a result of the administration, that some person would be enabled to have sexual intercourse with the victim.

Although the point has never been decided by the courts, it seems logical to assume that a certain contemporaneity must exist between the *actus reus* and the two aspects of the *mens rea*. Thus, the defendant who, without question, administers a drug to a woman with the admitted purpose of making her insensible, does not commit the offence unless it is proven that, at that precise time of administration, he possessed also the requisite ulterior intent. Where the defendant makes the woman insensible for any reason other than to enable a later act of sexual intercourse, he commits no offence under s 4. This is so even where, shortly after she becomes insensible, a man decides to take advantage of the situation and have sexual intercourse with her. Of course, it has long been recognised as the law that where a man has sexual intercourse with a female who is insensible through drink and thereby incapable of consenting (whether that insensibility was a result of his instigation or not), that this is capable of amounting to rape.[9]

2.4   Reform

Each of the three preceding offences is considered in *Setting the Boundaries*. The offences currently contained in ss 2 and 3 may be justified as serving

---

9   See *Camplin* (1845) 1 Den 45, applied in *Lang* (1975) 62 Cr App R 50.

useful functions in circumstances where the threats/intimidation (s 2) or false pretences/representations (s 3) are insufficient to vitiate consent for the purpose of rape. The Review agreed that the current offences served such a useful purpose and, in fact, has proposed replacing them with an extended offence. Recommendation 14 states:

> There should be an offence of obtaining sexual penetration by threats or deception in any part of the world.

This proposal represents an extension to the present law in several ways. First, it is gender neutral, giving protection to male and female victims. Secondly, it extends the type of act covered by the offence, by referring to 'sexual penetration' rather than sexual intercourse. Thirdly, the word 'deception' would replace the current phrase 'false pretences or representations'. This is in line with the proposal contained in cl 91 of the draft Criminal Code Bill, and would remove any potential uncertainty as to the meaning of the current phrase, as discussed above.

The Review gave strong support also to the offence contained currently in s 4 of the 1956 Act. In line with its recommendations pertaining to ss 2 and 3, the proposal here is to retain and indeed enhance the offence. Recommendation 15 states:

> An offence of administering drugs (etc) with intent to stupefy a victim in order that they are sexually penetrated should be retained.

Under this proposal, the new offence would be gender neutral, thus giving protection both to men and women. Although the recommendation is not explicit, it is likely that the reference to a person being 'sexually penetrated' means penile penetration of the vagina, anus or mouth (that is, to make it analogous to rape).

Finally, the Review identified a range of potential activities related to the above offences, where a person compels others to carry out sexual acts against their will. This type of compulsion can relate to various forms of behaviour. The person acting as compellor may wish the other person to perform sexual acts on him or herself (that is, upon the compellor), they may wish the other to masturbate in front of them or they may compel the other to engage in sexual acts with a third party or even an animal. It is the element of compulsion which removes consent and makes such activity potentially serious. There exist already offences which are capable of criminalising these actions (see, for example, indecent assault, below), but the law is not always clear in its scope or application. Consequently, Recommendation 16 proposes that 'there should be new offences of compelling another to perform sexual acts, with several levels of seriousness depending on the nature of the compelled acts'. The most serious level would involve, for instance, compelling sexual penetration of a person or an animal, whilst the less serious level would involve compelling other sexual acts.

3 SEXUAL OFFENCES AGAINST THE MENTALLY HANDICAPPED

A number of sexual offences exist whose purpose is to afford protection to persons identified as suffering from mental handicap or mental illness. Such offences seemingly satisfy society's paternalistic desire to provide a degree of protection to vulnerable and susceptible persons, but, at the same time, the potential justifications for those offences do give rise to several competing interests.

On one hand, there are many instances of a defendant abusing a position of trust and authority, and obtaining sexual gratification from a women whose level of mental impairment is such that she deserves fully the protection of the law. This type of case, which is not difficult to rationalise or justify, was summarised forcefully by Keene J in *Phillips* ([1996] 1 Cr App R(S) 339):

> [Y]oung adult women who are mentally retarded do need protection. There has to be a deterrent in order to deter men from taking advantage of the unhappy combination of the physical maturity but mental immaturity of such women, and that seems ... to be one of the reasons why the law provides that consent in fact by a woman with severe impairment of intelligence provides no defence ...[10]

A similar rationale was identified by the Criminal Law Revision Committee in its *Fifteenth Report on Sexual Offences* in 1984, where it was noted that severely mentally handicapped persons require protection from sexual abuse and sexual exploitation.[11] In addition, and notwithstanding the element of potential exploitation, there will frequently be circumstances where a woman's mental handicap is such that she is unaware of the true nature of the sexual act and thus unable to give a genuine consent.

All these concerns have to be contrasted with the view that persons with mental handicaps are just as entitled to enjoy a fulfilling sex life as people who have no mental impairment. Any laws which seek to curtail one's basic human desire for sexual fulfilment, where it exists, are oppressive and an unnecessary restraint on individual autonomy. However, in this respect, it may be useful to distinguish between two situations: the first, where two persons, both with mental handicaps, engage in sexual activity together; and the second, where the male party, who has no mental impairment, engages in sexual acts with a mentally handicapped woman. There is undoubtedly a much greater risk of corruption and exploitation in the latter case than in the former. Indeed, cl 106 of the draft Criminal Code Bill would specifically

---

10 (1996) 1 Cr App R(S) 339, p 341.

11 Cmnd 9213, 1984. See, especially, para 9.1.

provide a defence, on a charge of sexual intercourse with a woman who has a severe mental handicap, to a man who himself is severely mentally handicapped.

In this section, we shall consider a few of the major offences which exist in relation to victims with some degree of mental impairment.[12] Those offences are contained, predominantly, in several sections of the Sexual Offences Act 1956, as well as in s 128 of the Mental Health Act 1959.

3.1 The common elements

The 'mental handicap' offences contained within the 1956 Act possess a number of common elements, two of which are of central importance in understanding the scope and operation of the sections.

3.1.1 Defective

The relevant offences under the 1956 Act can only be committed against a female who falls within the statutory definition of a 'defective'. Section 45 of the 1956 Act provides:

> In this Act 'defective' means a person suffering from a state of arrested or incomplete development of mind which includes severe impairment of intelligence and social functioning.

The reference in the section to 'severe impairment of intelligence and social functioning' is clearly not intended to amount to an example of arrested or incomplete development of mind. Rather, the phrase amounts to the two minimum criteria which must exist in all cases for any person to satisfy the definition of a defective. It is equally clear that the courts view the words of the phrase as ordinary English words to be determined by the jury. In *Hall* ((1988) 86 Cr App R 159), the defendant, the principal of a residential college run for the education of profoundly mentally handicapped young people, was charged with indecent assault on a defective girl. The victim, who was aged 16–17 at the time of the acts, had the mental age of a girl aged about seven. Parker LJ emphasised that 'severe impairment' had to be judged against the standard of a 'normal person', and not against the standard of another mental defective. This approach must be correct, because to hold otherwise would run the risk of a finding that a victim was only moderately impaired when compared to another mental defective, as opposed to severely impaired when compared to a mentally normal person, and thus defeat the protective objective of the statute.

In determining whether or not the victim is a 'defective' within the terms of s 45, it is normal to adduce expert medical evidence for the purpose of

---

12 For a comprehensive and detailed analysis of the issues, see, especially, the excellent account in Rook, P and Ward, R, *Sexual Offences*, 1997, Sweet & Maxwell, Chapter 7.

quantifying the level of 'intelligence and social functioning'. However, such evidence is not essential. Moreover, where expert testimony on the issue is adduced, the jury are not bound to follow it, but are quite entitled to reject the expert's opinion and reach their own conclusion on the basis of all the evidence. This again was emphasised in *Hall*:

> [I]t is clear that such [expert] evidence is admissible to establish the extent of the victim's intelligence, but we are unable to accept that a medical expert's opinion that a woman of, say, 30, with the intelligence of a girl of five, is not severely impaired is of any real weight, if indeed admissible at all. If, having heard such evidence, the jury observe the victim happily playing with toys suitable for a child of five, unable to cope with toys for slightly older girls, and only able to converse like a child of five, the doctor's opinion cannot be regarded as preferable to the observation of the jury.[13]

3.1.2   The common defence

Where an offence under the Sexual Offences Act 1956 can be committed only in respect of a 'defective', the defendant will have a total defence if he 'does not know and has no reason to suspect' or suppose that the person involved is a defective.

Despite the use of the word 'reason' in the phrase 'has no reason to suspect', which might be taken as indicating an objective test on the basis of the reasonable man's knowledge of the circumstances, it is clear that the courts apply a subjective test to the question of the defendant's belief. This approach may be justified from the wording of the defence itself, which unquestionably refers to a man being not guilty 'if *he* does not know and has no reason to suspect', etc. The subjective nature of the test was confirmed in *Hudson* ([1966] 1 QB 448), although the court emphasised that the jury must be made aware of all the relevant facts of the case, and that the defence should not be available to the defendant who deliberately shut his eyes to the obvious fact that the woman was a defective:

> [I]f an accused man succeeds in establishing [on] the balance of probabilities ... that he, himself, did not know and that he, himself, had no reason to suspect the woman to be a defective, then he succeeds in his defence. It is, of course, right to say ... that in considering whether he knew or whether he had cause to suspect, the jury are obviously entitled to look at the whole of the evidence regarding the girl's condition, appearance, conversation and the like. It is true also to say that a man is not entitled to take advantage of the defence by ... shutting his eyes to the obvious ...[14]

---

13   (1988) 86 Cr App R 159, pp 162–63.
14   *Hudson* [1966] 1 QB 448, p 455, *per* Ashworth J.

3.2   Unlawful sexual intercourse with a female defective

Section 7(1) of the Sexual Offences Act 1956, as amended, provides:

> It is an offence, subject to the exception mentioned in this section, for a man to have unlawful sexual intercourse with a woman who is a defective.

The exception referred to in s 7(1) is contained in s 7(2) which provides:

> A man is not guilty of an offence under this section because he has unlawful sexual intercourse with a woman if he does not know and has no reason to suppose her to be a defective.

Section 7(2) provides one specific example of the 'common exception' pertaining to offences where the victim must be a defective, and its scope and meaning are as discussed above. However, one specific issue deserves particular mention. The offence can be committed only in respect of a 'defective', who is defined as a person who is suffering from a *severe* mental impairment of intelligence (see above). It follows from this that a woman who is suffering a 'mere' mental impairment (that is, one which is not 'severe') is not afforded protection. Furthermore, this fine distinction will have implications for the defendant's defence under s 7(2), as it must be open to the defendant to argue that, whilst he was aware that the woman was suffering from a mental impairment, he had no reason to suspect that it was a severe mental impairment:

> [A]lthough the doctors were of opinion that this girl suffered from severe subnormality, it is at least open to question whether the defendant or, indeed, a casual observer would have known that she was suffering from severe subnormality as opposed to subnormality ... It is not for this court to enquire why an offence under s 7 is limited to a person who is suffering from severe subnormality ... but in view of the distinction between that condition and mere subnormality it is important ... that ... the jury should be told specifically what it is that is involved, not only in the offence itself but in the defence which is provided ...[15]

The offence under s 7(1) can be committed as a principal offence only by a male person. This normally would be an adult, but now also includes a boy aged at least 10. A female cannot be a principal offender, but could be charged as a secondary party to the offence. The offence must be committed against a female.

Unlike a number of other sexual offences, s 7(1) has retained the word 'unlawful' in respect of the act of sexual intercourse. This means that the act of sexual intercourse must occur outside marriage, and consequently a man will commit no offence under s 7 where he has intercourse with his wife in circumstances where he is aware that she has become a defective.

---

15 *Hudson* [1966] 1 QB 448, p 456. In *Hudson*, the distinction was that which then existed between 'subnormality' and 'severe subnormality', although there seems no reason to expect that a similar fine distinction will not exist between mental impairment and severe mental impairment.

3.3 Procuring a female defective to have unlawful sexual intercourse

Section 9 of the Sexual Offences Act 1956 provides:

(1) It is an offence, subject to the exception mentioned in this section, for a person to procure a woman who is a defective to have unlawful sexual intercourse in any part of the world.

(2) A person is not guilty of an offence under this section because he procures a defective to have unlawful sexual intercourse, if he does not know and has no reason to suspect her to be a defective.

The majority of the criteria which need to be established for an offence under s 9 to exist are the same as in other sexual offences. Thus, 'procure', 'defective', 'unlawful sexual intercourse' and the scope of the defence are all as previously discussed.

There is potential for a certain overlap to exist between the offences in ss 7 and 9. Where a man has sexual intercourse with a female defective and he was instrumental in bringing about that act by some form of persuasion (thus satisfying the requirement of procuring), then the conditions necessary for both offences may exist.

However, there are, of course, differences between the two sections. In s 9, the element of procuration must be established. If there is insufficient evidence of the defendant having brought about the act of sexual intercourse, then the charge cannot be substantiated.[16]

Secondly, s 9 is broader than s 7 in the sense that it may be committed by any person, not necessarily a man as principal offender. A woman will be guilty as a principal where she procures X (a female defective) to commit an act of sexual intercourse with a man. In this situation, the defence in s 9(2) is as equally available to the female defendant as it is to the male.

3.4 Indecent assault on a defective

There is no separate offence as such of indecent assault on a defective. Rather, the relevant offences are the generally applicable ones of indecent assault on a woman and indecent assault on a man, contained within ss 14(1) and 15(1) respectively of the Sexual Offences Act 1956, and discussed in detail in Chapter 6. However, there is specific provision within the 1956 Act dealing with a defective's ability to give a valid consent and these provisions, in effect, create distinct offences where the victim is a defective.

It is true also that where an indecent assault is committed on a defective, the offence, almost without exception, does not involve or relate to the act of

---

16   *Christian and Another* (1913) 23 Cox CC 541. See, also, *Cook* [1954] 1 All ER 60, *per* Stable J.

sexual intercourse *per se*. However, as the offence can only be committed against a defective it is sensible to discuss it within the present chapter.

3.4.1   Defectives and consent

In cases of indecent assault where the victim is a defective, the 1956 Act states expressly that such a person cannot consent. Section 14(4) provides:

> A woman who is a defective cannot in law give any consent which would prevent an act being an assault for the purposes of this section, but a person is only to be treated as guilty of an indecent assault on a defective by reason of that incapacity to consent, if that person knew or had reason to suspect her to be a defective.

The effect of this provision is that a woman cannot consent to an act which would amount to an indecent assault, and the defendant will be guilty of that offence on the basis of her inability to consent, but only if he knew or had reason to suspect that she was a defective. A similar provision relating to male defectives is contained in s 15(3). Of course, irrespective of the provisions in ss 14(4) and 15(3), if a defective (male or female) does not give a valid consent, as defined for any other person, then the defendant cannot rely on the fact that he did not know nor had reason to suspect that the victim was a defective for the purpose of excusing his liability.

3.4.2   Sentencing indecent assaults on defectives

The maximum sentence following conviction for an indecent assault on a woman was raised from two years' imprisonment to 10 years' imprisonment by the Sexual Offences Act 1985, but the maximum sentence of two years' imprisonment for an offence of unlawful sexual intercourse with a female defective (under s 7 of the 1956 Act, above) was not altered. The existence of different maximum sentences for these two offences could give rise to rather anomalous results in certain circumstances: the defendant who succeeds in having sexual intercourse with a defective is liable to a potential maximum sentence of two years' imprisonment, whereas the defendant who does not complete the act of intercourse, but commits other sexual acts amounting to an indecent assault is subject to a potential maximum of 10 years' imprisonment. These issues were considered specifically by the Court of Appeal in *Blair* ([1996] 1 Cr App R(S) 336). The defendant was convicted of indecently assaulting the victim, a woman aged 22, but with a mental age of about nine, after he had given her a lift in his car, taken her to his flat and inserted his fingers into her vagina. Medical evidence confirmed that the woman had been a virgin, that her hymen had been ruptured by the assault and that, afterwards, she was found by her mother to be bleeding. In allowing the appeal against a sentence of four years' imprisonment and substituting a sentence of 21 months' imprisonment, the court made clear that insufficient attention had been given to the different maximum sentences relating to ss 7 and 14, namely two years and 10 years respectively:

This gives rise to the to the situation which might be thought by some to be anomalous, whereby a defendant who has been convicted of an indecent assault but falls short of sexual intercourse with a defective is liable to a greater penalty than that which may be imposed for actual intercourse with a defective victim.[17]

It is therefore correct in principle to remain mindful of the maximum sentence available for an offence under s 7 when sentencing a defendant for the offence of indecent assault of a defective. Such reasoning has long been recognised by the courts in respect of other offences where widely differing maximum sentences exist. In *Quayle* ((1993) 14 Cr App R(S) 726), a similar point was noted in relation to the offences of indecent assault and unlawful sexual intercourse with a girl aged under 16:

> In principle, it may sound odd that the technical maximum for the touching of a girl's breast between the ages of 13 and 16 is 10 years, whereas the maximum for unlawful sexual intercourse with her is two years' imprisonment. It is submitted that the right approach for the court, in respect of something which is, in truth, no more than unlawful sexual intercourse, is not to award more than two years if she is between the ages of 13 and 16.[18]

Undoubtedly, therefore, an anomaly exists, but it would be wrong to exacerbate any discrepancy by imposing unduly long sentences on those convicted of indecent assault in circumstances similar to those of *Blair*. A more rational solution would be to increase the maximum sentence available following conviction under s 7, thus reducing the level of sentencing discrepancy between the two offences.

3.5   Unlawful sexual intercourse, etc, with a mental patient

In addition to the provisions protecting 'defectives' in the Sexual Offences Act 1956, the Mental Health Act 1959 imposes a very broad restriction upon carers of mentally disordered persons, where those carers abuse their positions of trust by committing certain sexual offences.

Section 128(1) of the Mental Health Act 1959, as amended, provides:

> Without prejudice to s 7 of the Sexual Offences Act 1956 it shall be an offence, subject to the exception mentioned in this section–
>
> (a) for a man who is an officer on the staff of or is otherwise employed in, or is one of the managers of, a hospital or mental nursing home to have unlawful sexual intercourse with a woman who is for the time being receiving treatment for mental disorder in that hospital or home, or to have such intercourse on the premises of which the hospital or home forms part with a woman who is for the time being receiving such treatment there as an outpatient;

---

17   [1996] 1 Cr App R(S) 336, p 338, *per* Keene J.

18   (1993) 14 Cr App R(S) 726, p 728, *per* Schiemann J.

(b) for a man to have unlawful sexual intercourse with a woman who is a mentally disordered patient and who is subject to his guardianship under the Mental Health Act 1983 or ... in his custody or care under the Mental Health Act 1983 or ... [pursuant to] Pt III of the National Assistance Act 1948 ... or the National Health Service Act 1977, or as a resident in a residential care home ...

Although s 128(1) was limited to the offence of unlawful sexual intercourse committed by a man against a mentally disordered *female*, the scope of the offence has now been broadened, by s 1(4) of the Sexual Offences Act 1967, so as to include acts of buggery and gross indecency committed with another man.

3.5.1   Mental disorder

The phrase 'mental disorder' is defined in s 1(2) of the Mental Health Act 1983 as 'mental illness, arrested or incomplete development of mind, psychopathic disorder and any other disorder or disability of mind'. It is a particularly broad definition and highlights one of the key distinctions between this offence and that under s 7 of the 1956 Act, where the word 'defective' is given a much more restrictive interpretation. Thus, even more so than in relation to s 7, s 128 must tread a fine line between prohibiting persons in authority from abusing their positions of trust and responsibility, and allowing people with mental disorders to have fulfilling and sometimes therapeutically beneficial sexual relationships. In this respect, it is worth emphasising that proceedings for an offence under s 128 may only be instituted by or with the leave of the DPP. This may be expected to provide an important safeguard in relation to certain cases where a genuine sexual relationship exists, and a criminal prosecution would clearly not be in the public interest.

3.5.2   The exception

The offence under s 128(1) is subject to an exception which is similar in terms to the general exception pertaining to defectives throughout the 1956 Act. Section 128(2) provides:

It shall not be an offence under this section for a man to have sexual intercourse with a woman if he does not know and has no reason to suspect her to be a mentally disordered patient.

It is, of course, inevitably more difficult to establish the defence in relation to s 128 than for, say, s 7. If a man is the guardian of, or has custody of a mentally disordered woman, it will be very difficult for him to satisfy the court that he did not know of her mental state. Similarly, where the man is employed in a mental hospital, it will be difficult for him to argue that he was unaware of the nature of the patients (whether in-patients or out-patients) who attended there.

As the definition of 'mental disorder' is so wide, especially when compared to that of 'defective', it also will not be open to a defendant to argue that he was unaware of the level of impairment. Consequently, whereas a man charged under s 7 may argue that he was aware that the woman was mentally impaired, but not severely mentally impaired, such an argument is not available to a man charged under s 128(1), where mental disorder is not defined in terms of its severity.

3.5.3   Sentencing: s 128

The maximum sentence available following conviction for an offence under s 128(1) is two years' imprisonment. In *Goodwin* ((1995) 16 Cr App R(S) 144), the defendant was found guilty on, *inter alia*, two counts under s 128 and was sentenced to the maximum term of imprisonment. The defendant was a State-enrolled psychiatric nurse at a hospital where the victim, a woman aged 39, was an in-patient. She was suffering from severe depression and was addicted to valium at the time of her admission to hospital. The Court of Appeal upheld, and strongly approved of, the sentence of two years' imprisonment in the specific circumstances:

> The case was, as the learned judge remarked in passing sentence, a gross and deliberate and wicked ... breach of trust by a nurse to a patient ...[19]

Goodwin provides the perfect illustration of the courts' paternalistic attitude towards women who, due to their particular mental circumstances, are at an especially vulnerable time. Such patients deserve the protection of the law, and defendants should be aware that abuses of the special positions of responsibility and care into which they have been placed will be dealt with severely.

3.6   Reform

There is overt recognition in *Setting the Boundaries* (at para 4.5.13) that the issue of vulnerable people's capacity to consent 'is an area that is fraught with difficulty'. Before proposing any offence based upon a person's mental disability, it seemed sensible to tackle first the complex issue of capacity *per se*. There are highly sensitive personal and social issues to be considered:

> There is a very real tension between the right to a private life and the need to protect people who are susceptible and easily taken advantage of. We concluded that any test of capacity should apply to the most severely disabled, rather as the definition of 'defective' in the present law does.[20]

Consequently, two related recommendations should be noted. First, Recommendation 30 proposes that 'there should be a statutory definition of

---

19   (1995) 16 Cr App R(S) 144, p 146, *per* Ian Kennedy J.
20   Home Office Consultation Paper, *Setting the Boundaries*, July 2000, para 4.5.2.

capacity to consent which reflects both knowledge and understanding of sex and its broad implications'.[21]

Secondly, Recommendation 31 proposes that 'there should be a specific offence relating to sexual activity with a person with severe mental disability who would not have the capacity to consent to sexual relations'. It would have to be proven that the defendant knew, or ought to have known, that the victim was a person with severe disability. This offence would replace those existing offences which are currently defined in terms of the 'defective' victim. Because the proposed offence refers to 'sexual activity', there would be no need to distinguish between the separate offences of sexual intercourse with a defective and indecent assault on a defective.

Finally, the offence which is contained currently in s 128 of the Mental Health Act 1959 would be replaced and considerably extended by the proposal in Recommendation 32 to create new offences of a breach of relationship of care. This would prohibit: sexual relationships between a patient with a mental disorder, whether inpatient or outpatient, and any member of staff, whether paid or unpaid; sexual relationships between a person in residential care and a member of staff, whether paid or unpaid; sexual relationships between a person receiving certain care services in the community and designated care providers whether paid or unpaid; sexual relationships between doctors and their patients, and therapists and clients.

---

21 The Report cited with approval the definition of capacity proposed by the Law Commission in its policy paper, *Consent in Sex Offences*, February 2000. The definition is set out in para. 4.5.8 of *Setting the Boundaries*.

CHAPTER 5

SEXUAL OFFENCES AGAINST THE YOUNG

1 INTRODUCTION

Offences committed against children and young persons are portrayed frequently as producing considerable feelings of repugnance and anger in the minds of reasonable people. These feelings are exacerbated when the offences in question are of a sexual nature. Whilst all sexual offences (or at least those where the absence of consent is an element) are viewed with revulsion, that revulsion is heightened where the victim is a child. Indeed, the last decade has witnessed a number of high profile child abuse scandals (in Rochdale, Cleveland, South Wales and Orkney, for example), to such an extent that a moral panic about the incidence of paedophile activities seems to have seized the general population. Whilst it is undoubtedly true that such moral panics are not unique to the late 20th century, it is also clear that the incidence of sexual offences, including those committed against children, is on the increase. If it is accepted, also, that the number of reported crimes is often considerably lower than the actual number of offences committed, then the phenomenon does become of huge social and legal significance.[1]

It is of course true that a large number of sexual offences are not in any way delimited by an age criterion. Thus, the offence of rape (see Chapter 3) may be committed against a child just as much as against an adult victim. Similarly, an indecent assault (see Chapter 6) may be committed against a person of any age. Consequently, a range of offences exists already which serves to provide protection to child victims, just as those offences seek to protect adult victims.

In this chapter, therefore, we shall concentrate discussion upon those offences which are limited specifically to the situation where the age of the victim is a relevant factor. It is worth noting that there is no uniformity in English law in respect of the age below which the law seeks to offer protection. Rather, the ages will vary from crime to crime, although the most frequently significant ages are 16, 14 and 13. It should also be noted that we adopt the use of the word 'victim' throughout this chapter, for the sake of convenience, as a way of referring to the person in respect of whom the defendant has been charged. This may be important in those cases where the other person has consented *de facto* to the defendant's act (and, indeed, she

---

1   For an excellent discussion of these general issues, see Sampson, A, *Acts of Abuse*, 1994, Routledge, especially 'Introduction' and Chapter 1.

may not regard herself at all as the 'victim' in any common sense of that word), but, nevertheless, the law does not recognise her as being capable of giving a valid consent and thus defines her as the victim. This situation may arise most commonly in relation to offences of unlawful sexual intercourse with girls under the age of 16 (discussed below).

Finally, it is worth considering briefly at this stage the rationale for creating offences specifically aimed at the protection of young persons. This may seem a rather unnecessary question, in that surely it is axiomatic that children and young persons require and deserve the protection of the criminal law from sexual acts committed by adults. However, the position is not as simple as it first appears, and a number of competing interests and rationales may be seen to exist when consideration is given as to why sexual offences against the young are created.

One obvious rationale revolves around the issue of consent, and the age at which it may objectively be said that a child can give a genuine and informed consent to acts of a sexual nature. Here, society deems it appropriate to set certain minimum ages, below which particular acts are proscribed as against the defendant. The offence of unlawful sexual intercourse with a girl under the age of 13 (s 5 of the Sexual Offences Act 1956, discussed below) would fall clearly into this category. Such acts are socially and ethically unacceptable, run the clear risk of being exploitative and corrupting, and, especially where the victim is particularly young, may sometimes involve doubts as to whether the girl was in a position to give a genuinely informed consent.[2] But, even here, it is worth noting that there is not total unanimity of opinion and some groups, such as the Paedophile Information Exchange, have advocated the abolition of the age of consent as a legal concept.[3]

A second potential rationale would appear to involve a relationship between consent and the implementation of a paternalistic attitude by the state. The perfect example of this relationship is the law's imposition of the age of 16 as the age at which girls can consent legally to (most) sexual activity. Clearly girls of, say, 14 and 15 years of age can and do give genuine and informed *de facto* consent to sexual acts, but nevertheless such consent is not recognised in law.[4] The offence of unlawful sexual intercourse with a girl under the age of 16, contrary to s 6 of the Sexual Offences Act 1956, causes some difficulties here. In this situation, it is much more difficult to argue convincingly that a girl of the age of 14 or 15 does not know the nature of the act so that she cannot give an

2   Where the girl is of such tender years that she does not understand the very nature of the act of sexual intercourse to which she is purportedly consenting, then a charge of rape may be entirely appropriate (see Chapter 2). But s 5 remains useful where it would be difficult to prove either absence of consent or the requisite *mens rea*.

3   See *op cit*, Sampson, fn 1, pp 4–5, where Britain's age of consent in respect of other European countries and the view of the European Commission are also discussed.

4   See discussion of unlawful sexual intercourse with girls under the age of 16, below, and indecent assault on minors, discussed in Chapter 6.

informed consent, nor indeed in many cases that there is an element of corruption or exploitation. Instead, the key rationale would appear to be that society regards sexual intercourse with girls of a certain age as socially, morally and possibly medically undesirable, and that the age of 16 presently represents the arbitrary age at which the limit has been set.

Finally, issues of consent and the protection of specific child victims, cannot be viewed as the rationale for the existence of certain sexual offences. In relation to offences pertaining to indecent photographs, for example, there may not be an identifiable child victim or, as will be discussed below, given recent developments in technology, there need not even be a 'real child' depicted in the photograph. Nevertheless, the defendant, rightly, may be committing an offence, and a number of potential justifications may be advanced, including: where a real child has been involved there is an obvious risk of exploitation and corruption; even where, for instance, the photograph is one that has been 'created', the inherently objective wrongfulness of child pornography is such that the behaviour *per se* merits proscription; and there exists also the risk that defendants (usually men) who possess indecent photographs may progress to other more serious offences, and thus criminalising the possession of such photographs can operate as a preventative measure.

2   UNLAWFUL SEXUAL INTERCOURSE WITH GIRLS

The criminal law's involvement in regulating acts of sexual intercourse between men and young girls has a long history, and may be traced back to the Offences Against the Person Acts of 1828, 1861 and 1875, when Parliament's primary concern was to take action in respect of the growing tendency of girls of very young ages to resort to prostitution. Today, child prostitution may not represent a problem on the same scale as it did in 19th century England, but child sexual abuse, brought to prominence in a number of recent highly publicised scandals, remains an emotive and topical issue. Where there is no consent (neither *de facto* nor *de jure*), then a range of potential offences may be used against the defendant. But where the girl has given *de facto* consent – thus removing, for example, the possibility of a successful charge of rape – then the two related, but distinct, offences of unlawful sexual intercourse may be utilised.

2.1   Unlawful sexual intercourse with a girl under the age of 13

Section 5 of the Sexual Offences Act 1956 provides:

> It is a felony for a man to have unlawful sexual intercourse with a girl under the age of 13.

2.1.1 Parties

An offence under s 5 can be committed, as a principal offence, only by a male. In the overwhelming majority of cases, the defendant will be an adult (frequently considerably older than the girl herself), although 'man' clearly includes 'boy' and, since the passage of the Sexual Offences Act 1993, this must be taken as including boys aged 10–13 inclusive.

There is no reason in principle why a female may not be charged as an accessory to an offence under s 5, although this clearly does not extend to the girl against whom the offence is committed: she is regarded as the victim of the offence and, under the rule in *Tyrell* (above), she would face no criminal liability. Although the wording of s 5 (and indeed s 6, below) would appear to be affording more overt protection to young girls as opposed to young boys, this is not in fact the case. Where sexual acts are committed against young boys, a range of potential offences exist. These would include indecent assault, acts of gross indecency and (where penetration occurs) buggery or rape, depending on the question of consent.

2.1.2 Consent

The fact that the victim consented to the act of sexual intercourse is irrelevant to a charge under s 5 and will not provide a defence to the defendant. However, as will be seen below, if the girl takes a more active role beyond merely consenting, then that fact may be taken into consideration in respect of sentencing. Of course, if the girl did not give a valid consent, including those circumstances where she was too young to understand the nature of the act to which she was 'consenting', then a charge of rape is entirely appropriate.

2.1.3 Mens rea

The issue of the *mens rea* required for s 5 has rarely troubled the English courts, but the general consensus of opinion is that strict liability will be imposed in respect of the age of the girl. Therefore, the defendant who claims, however reasonably, that he thought the girl was over the age of 16, will not be able to rely upon that belief in his defence. Similarly, the defendant who says he thought the girl was 15 (whereas, in fact, she was aged 12) will commit the more serious s 5 offence, not that under s 6 below.

It must also be proved, in common with other offences requiring sexual intercourse, that the defendant intended to penetrate the girl's vagina with his penis. Whilst 'accidental' penetration in the course of other sexual acts may be most unlikely in reality (and would give rise to other offences in any case), it nevertheless is a legal requirement that intentional penetration be proven.[5]

---

5   See, eg, the discussion of *Watson* in Chapter 2.

2.1.4   Sentencing: s 5

The maximum punishment that may be imposed on a man convicted of an offence under s 5 is life imprisonment. As always, however, to talk in terms of a mere maximum sentence fails to take account of a wide range of potential aggravating and mitigating factors, as well as other specific factual considerations, such as the precise age of the girl in question. Despite the possible existence of 'mitigating features', it is arguable, in the light of both social and legal concerns about sexual abuse of the young, that sentences for offences under s 5 are somewhat generous to defendants.

The main guidelines for sentencers in respect of the offence of incest were set down by the Court of Appeal in *Attorney General's Reference (No 1 of 1989)* ((1989) 11 Cr App R(S) 409). Insofar as the act of incest occurs with a girl under the age of 13, it is accepted that the incest guidelines are equally applicable to offences under s 5:

> If the girl is not far short of her 13th birthday and there are no particularly adverse or favourable features on a not guilty plea, a term of about six years on the authorities would seem to be appropriate. It scarcely needs to be stated that the younger the girl when the sexual approach is started, the more likely it will be that the girl's will was overborne and accordingly the more serious would be the crime.[6]

In the context of incest, Lord Lane then identified a number of further aggravating features. These would include, but were not intended to be limited to: evidence that the girl suffered physically or psychologically; continuation of the acts at frequent intervals over a long period of time; where the girl was threatened, treated violently by or was terrified of the father; other accompanying sexual perversions (for instance, buggery or fellatio); a resulting pregnancy; or other similar offences by the man.

In *Vaughan* ((1991) 12 Cr App R(S) 731), it was accepted expressly by the Court of Appeal that the incest guidelines were applicable to a case where the defendant was convicted under s 5 of having unlawful sexual intercourse with his stepdaughter (S). The defendant was convicted of a number of offences against his stepdaughter, including the offence under s 5 for which he was sentenced to seven years' imprisonment. The offences were committed over a period of about four years, whilst the girl was aged between 10 and 14. The court considered the aggravating features identified above, noting in particular the duration of the incidents and the fact that the defendant had made threats to S, namely that he would cause her mother to be taken away from her if she told anybody about the acts between them. Conversely, the court accepted that there had been no evidence of S being caused physical suffering (albeit she had lost her virginity), there had been no specific sexual

---

6   (1989) 11 Cr App R(S) 409, p 414, *per* Lord Lane CJ.

perversions (the trial judge having explicitly rejected a claim that fellatio had occurred) and no pregnancy resulted. In addition, the defendant's plea of guilty was regarded as a considerable mitigating feature. In the light of all these circumstances, the Court of Appeal held that the original sentence was a little too long and a sentence of five years' imprisonment was substituted.

In *Brown* ((1994) 15 Cr App R(S) 495), the defendant (aged 56) was sentenced to eight years' imprisonment following conviction on two counts of unlawful sexual intercourse with a girl aged 11. In reducing the sentence to six years' imprisonment, the Court of Appeal noted several differences between the present case and that of, for instance, *Vaughan*. In particular, there had been no breach of trust, no incestuous relationship, no abuse of a stepfather/stepdaughter relationship, no perverted practices and the incidents had occurred over a much shorter period than in some comparable cases. However, there had not been a plea of guilty, which had necessitated the victim giving traumatic and embarrassing testimony, but, notwithstanding that fact, the court felt a reduction in sentence was appropriate for the reasons given.

It might be thought that, as the purpose of s 5 is to afford protection to girls of particularly young ages, little attention would be paid by the courts to the alleged 'precociousness' of the victim. However, in certain circumstances, it is clear that this may be a factor. In *Polley* ([1997] 1 Cr App R(S) 144), the defendant's sentence of three and a half years' imprisonment, for an offence of unlawful sexual intercourse with a girl aged 12, was reduced on appeal to two and a half years. A number of mitigating factors existed, but the role of the girl herself was undoubtedly a prime consideration:

> In this case it is true that the girl instigated and encouraged the one act. It is recognised that she was precocious and sexually experienced.[7]

An interesting comparison can be found in *Attorney General's Reference (No 20 of 1994)* ((1995) 16 Cr App R(S) 578). The defendant pleaded guilty to, *inter alia*, three counts under s 5, in respect of a girl aged 12 who was a member of a school majorette troupe for which he was responsible. The defendant was sentenced to two years' probation and an order requiring psychiatric treatment was made. A reference was made to the Court of Appeal by the Attorney General, pursuant to s 36 of the Criminal Justice Act 1988, asking the Court to review the sentence on the basis that it was unduly lenient. This was accepted by the Court of Appeal, where a number of serious features were noted. These included the emotional vulnerability of the girl, a considerable age discrepancy, the abuse of a position of trust by the defendant as a family friend, a range of other explicit sexual acts (including oral sex) and thus an

---

7 [1997] 1 Cr App R(S) 144, p 146, *per* Astill J. There must be some doubts as to how far the 'precociousness' of a girl aged 12 should operate as mitigation in such a case. It may be that the defendant's admittedly low intelligence was an important contributory factor, and partially explains why he should not have been expected to show greater restraint.

element of corruption, and the fact that the defendant had used no contraception. These features did need to be balanced against his early admissions, plea of guilty and previous good character, but, notwithstanding this mitigation, the original sentence was unduly lenient and a sentence of three years' imprisonment was substituted. The court noted expressly that probation orders, coupled with psychiatric treatment, may be appropriate in relation to such offences, but only where the defendant effectively has a low criminal responsibility, and the present case was not one such rare instance.

2.2 Unlawful sexual intercourse with a girl under the age of 16

Section 6(1) of the Sexual Offences Act 1956 provides:

> It is an offence, subject to the exceptions [below] ... for a man to have unlawful sexual intercourse with a girl under the age of 16.

2.2.1 Parties

The majority of the issues relating to the parties to an offence under s 6 are identical to those discussed in s 5, above. Thus, the principal offender must be male (including, now, boys between 10 and 13); and a woman (although not the girl against whom the offence is committed) can be an accessory to the offence. Where a girl is below the age of 13, the defendant may, in fact, be charged with a s 6 offence (such a girl is, after all, under the age of 16). In effect, therefore, where a girl is under 13, there exists a total overlap between the two offences. In practice, where the girl is under the age of 13, a charge under s 5 should be preferred.

One specific issue in relation to parties concerns the extent to which a doctor (or, presumably, any other healthcare professional, such as, for example, an employee in a family planning clinic) can be liable as an accessory to an offence under s 6. This was one of the issues discussed by the House of Lords in *Gillick v West Norfolk and Wisbech Area Health Authority* ([1986] AC 112), where their Lordships considered whether a general practitioner who provided contraceptive advice or treatment to a female patient known to be under the age of 16 could be liable as an accessory to any subsequent offence under s 6 committed against that girl. A majority of their Lordships held that the doctor would not be guilty as the exercise of his 'clinical judgment', in the best interests of his patient's physical, mental and emotional well being, would amount to a complete negation of the requisite *mens rea*. In terms of public policy, this decision is correct: it allows doctors (and, it should be expected, other healthcare professionals) to provide practical advice and treatment, often necessary to prevent the risk of unwanted teenage pregnancies, with all their associated social and medical difficulties. However, it must be recognised that the decision conflicts with the generally accepted rule in criminal law that a defendant's 'good motive' should be irrelevant in determining the question of liability. It is difficult to avoid the conclusion that the doctor's 'clinical judgment' is no more than a good motive in disguise and that, in reality, considerations of public policy heavily influenced the decision.

2.2.2   Actus reus

2.2.2.1   Unlawful

It was noted in Chapter 2 that the House of Lords held in *R v R* ([1992] AC 599) that the word 'unlawful' in the context of rape was 'mere surplusage', thus opening up the way for the removal of the marital exemption in rape. That decision was subsequently confirmed when Parliament omitted the word 'unlawful' from the statutory revision of rape in 1994. However, s 6 was not one of the consequential amendments contained in Sched 10 to the 1994 Act. Thus, the word was not removed from that section and it can be assumed that it retains a relevant meaning, namely that the offence under s 6 is limited to *unlawful* sexual intercourse – that is, sexual intercourse outside marriage – so that where a man is married validly, under foreign law recognised in England, to a girl under the age of 16, he commits no offence by having sexual intercourse with her in this country. This issue was considered in *Alhaji Mohamed v Knott* ([1969] 1 QB 1), where the husband, a Nigerian citizen, was cohabiting in England with a girl aged 13 to whom he was married validly under Nigerian law. Although the case centred upon the question of whether the girl should be committed to the care of a local authority, the Divisional Court commented expressly on the possibility of an offence under s 6 existing in such circumstances, and concluded firmly that it would not:

> There is one other point which has given me some trouble, and that is the suggestion that every time this husband in England has intercourse with his wife, he is committing a criminal offence [that is, s 6] ... It is a point which was apparently not before the justices; they certainly do not base their decision on any such consideration. Nor ... do I think that the police could ever properly prosecute in a case such as that if the marriage is a marriage recognised by this country.[8]

2.2.2.2   Sexual intercourse

For the purpose of s 6, 'sexual intercourse' is limited to vaginal intercourse and is not given the extended definition within the 1994 Act so as to cover anal intercourse. Such an extension was not necessary as anal intercourse with a girl under the age of 16 (even where consensual) was, and remains, the offence of buggery carrying a maximum sentence of life imprisonment (see Chapter 2). The law on this point seems to be clear, if not exactly free from a potential anomaly. Thus, a man, who is married validly under foreign law to a girl under the age of 16, may have vaginal intercourse with his wife and commit no offence within s 6 (the act not being unlawful as defined). But a

---

8   [1969] 1 QB 1, p 16, *per* Lord Parker CJ.

consensual act of buggery in the same circumstances would be an offence, as the definition of buggery contains no criterion of unlawfulness.

In other respects, 'sexual intercourse' in s 6 is defined as in rape. In particular, the slightest degree of penetration by the man's penis will suffice, and there need not be ejaculation or a rupturing of the girl's hymen.

2.2.2.3 Consent

Absence of consent is not part of the definition of s 6(1), and thus the fact that the girl consented to, or even played the major part in instigating, the act of intercourse will not provide a defence to the defendant.

Of course, if there is no consent, then the defendant could face a charge of rape. Where a defendant has faced a charge under s 6 then the question of consent *may* become relevant to the level of sentence, but this can cause procedural difficulties for the trial judge and should not be used by the prosecution as a way of avoiding the burden of establishing an absence of consent. In *Druce* ((1993) 14 Cr App R(S) 691), the defendant (aged 46 at the time of the offences) pleaded guilty to unlawful sexual intercourse with, and indecent assault on, a girl aged 14. The defendant claimed the girl had consented to the acts, whilst she denied this and stated that the acts had occurred against her will. The trial judge held a *Newton* hearing[9] to determine the issue of consent for the purpose of sentence and, in that hearing, the prosecution alleged that there had been no consent. On appeal, it was stated by the Court of Appeal that it was not appropriate for the prosecution, at trial, to present an argument that there had been no consent. Rather, if that had been their contention, then a charge of rape should have been made in the first place. Furthermore, it was not right in principle to ask a trial judge, within a *Newton* hearing, to consider finding a man guilty of a more serious offence than that with which he had been charged.

2.2.3 Defences to s 6(1)

In addition to any of the standard defences available to a defendant under the general criminal law, there are two specific defences contained within s 6 itself.

2.2.3.1 Belief that girl was the defendant's wife

Section 6(2), which contains a defence little used in practice, provides:

> Where a marriage is invalid under s 2 of the Marriage Act 1949, or s 1 of the Age of Marriage Act 1929 (the wife being a girl under the age of 16), the invalidity does not make the husband guilty of an offence under this section because he has sexual intercourse with her, if he believes her to be his wife and has reasonable cause for the belief.

---

9   A hearing in which the trial judge, faced with conflicting views of the facts from the prosecution and defence, may hear evidence from both sides in order to determine the issue and sentence the defendant accordingly: *Newton* (1982) 77 Cr App R 13.

It is clear from the wording of the sub-section that the defendant (who has the burden of proving the exception) must establish two distinct elements: he must both actually believe that the girl was his wife, and that he possessed reasonable grounds for such a belief.

2.2.3.2 The 'young man's defence'

The more frequent defence to a charge under s 6(1) is that contained in sub-s (3), which provides:

> A man is not guilty of an offence under this section because he has unlawful sexual intercourse with a girl under the age of 16, if he is under the age of 24 and has not previously been charged with a like offence, and he believes her to be of the age of 16 or over and has reasonable cause for the belief.

> In this subsection, 'a like offence' means an offence under this section or an attempt to commit one ...

The defendant has the burden of proving a number of elements in order to establish successfully his defence.

An offence under this section

The defence in s 6(3) is applicable to 'an offence under this section', but the meaning of this phrase is not without some ambiguity. In particular, some doubts have been raised as to whether the defence should be limited to the full, substantive offence under s 6(1), or whether it should extend also to attempts to commit such an offence. This specific issue was considered by Streatfeild J in *Collier* ([1960] Crim LR 204), where it was held, rightly, we submit, that the defence was available to both the full offence and attempts to commit the offence. To hold otherwise would be to produce the absurd position that a defendant who completed the act of sexual intercourse with a girl of, say, 14 might be able to avail himself of the defence, whereas a defendant who attempted to have intercourse, but failed, would automatically be excluded from raising the defence.

Under the age of 24

The defence is available only to a man who is under the age of 24, an age which he attains at the commencement of the 24th anniversary of his birth.

The age limit itself is somewhat arbitrary, but presumably has its origins in the historical development of the offence. Thus a defence was introduced under the Criminal Law Amendment Act 1885, available to all men (irrespective of age) charged with the then lesser offence of having carnal knowledge with a girl aged between 13 and 16. This defence (with its broad scope and potential for misuse) proved unpopular and an amendment followed in s 2 of the Criminal Law Amendment Act 1922, which restricted the age of the man to whom the defence was available, and which is now essentially contained in s 6(3). If a rationale for an age limit of 24 is to be found at all, it may be seen as providing a partial excuse to men of a younger (and thus more immature) age, who may be more likely to make a genuine mistake about the age of the girl and where, because of the relative closeness of the ages of the man and the girl, there is less scope for exploitation and corruption. These factors will be less likely to exist in the case of 'older men' and thus a threshold (albeit still an arbitrary compromise) of 24 was accepted. This 'explanation' may be viewed as making certain assumptions about both male and female sexuality. It is arguable that men beyond a particular age do not deserve to be given the opportunity of raising the defence as a matter of law on the basis that the greater the age disparity between the man and the girl, the greater the need for protection from exploitation and corruption. Conversely, where a lesser disparity in age exists, the law's desire to balance the protection of girls against the right of the defendant to raise his mistake as to age, errs on the side of the man.

Charged

A defendant will not be able to rely upon s 6(3) if he has 'previously been charged' with a like offence. There is little direct authority on the interpretation of this phrase within s 6(3) itself, but a useful analogy may be found in *Rider* ((1954) 37 Cr App R 209), where Streatfeild J considered the meaning of s 2 of the Criminal Law Amendment Act 1922, the forerunner of the present law. Section 2 allowed a defendant to rely upon a mistake of age, but only 'on the first occasion on which he is charged with an offence under this section'. It was held:

> [T]here is a charge before a court which has jurisdiction to determine the matter in question. That may well be the justices, if they refuse to commit for trial ... and if they refuse to commit, there clearly would be a charge before a court having jurisdiction to determine it. But if the justices ... commit for trial they are not adjudicating upon it at all; the only thing they have determined is whether there is a *prima facie* case to answer ... The man is then brought before the assizes on indictment, and it seems to me that then, for the first time, he is before a court having jurisdiction to determine the matter.[10]

Assuming that the decision in *Rider* is applicable, by analogy, to s 6(3), it would seem to follow that a defendant who attends a magistrates' court and is subsequently transferred for trial, by the justices, to the Crown Court, has not yet been 'charged', because he has not appeared before a court having jurisdiction to determine the matter. He will be charged as soon as he appears on indictment at the Crown Court.

With a like offence

The phrase 'like offence' is defined in s 6(3) itself, above, as meaning either an offence under s 6(1), or an attempt to commit such an offence. This unambiguous, yet somewhat restrictive definition could lead to anomalous outcomes. Thus, a man who previously has been charged with, and indeed

---

10   (1954) 37 Cr App R 209, pp 212–13.

convicted of, the offences of rape of a girl aged 14, and unlawful sexual intercourse with a girl aged 11 (that is, s 5) may still, nevertheless, raise a defence under s 6(3) if he were subsequently to be charged with an offence under s 6(1), as he has not been charged with a 'like offence' as defined. Conversely, a man who has been charged on a previous occasion with an offence under s 6(1) cannot subsequently use the s 6(3) defence, even if, for example, he had been acquitted on the first charge. The assumption in the latter instance would seem to be that the man has 'had his one chance' at the defence and, being now aware of it by definition, he cannot avail himself of it again. There would exist an even greater absurdity if, having raised the defence on the first occasion, the defendant were then to be acquitted for an entirely separate reason (that is, distinct from his mistake as to age). It remains to be seen whether, in this scenario, a subsequent s 6(3) defence would be precluded.

Belief

As a result of doubts as to whether s 2 of the Criminal Law Amendment Act 1922 required the defendant to hold actual belief (as opposed to having merely a 'reasonable cause to believe'), the 1956 Act states expressly that the defendant himself must actually believe that the girl was aged 16 or above. Consequently, the fact that a reasonable person may believe the girl to be over that age will not avail the defendant if the evidence establishes either that he knew her not to be, or even that he had never given any consideration to the fact: a man cannot hold a belief (even a mistaken one) about a girl's age, unless, at the very least, he has given some thought to it.

Reasonable cause

In addition to holding, subjectively, such a belief, the defendant must have reasonable cause for so holding. This matter is determined by the jury and, in deciding the issue, they are not limited to considering evidence from the defendant himself. Instead, the jury may look at all relevant surrounding circumstances,[11] including the physical appearance of the girl herself. Although the latter point has received little direct consideration in English courts, we submit that the New Zealand Court of Appeal in *Perry v Pledger* ([1920] NZLR 21) has provided a very clear and accurate statement of how the issue should be approached:

> One of the material pieces of evidence ... is the personal appearance of the girl herself. If in the eyes of the jury she might well be taken by an ordinary person to be of the age of 16 that would be evidence – we do not say proof – of a reasonable cause for the belief that she was of that age.[12]

---

11 In *Re Roberts* [1967] 1 WLR 474, it was held that the justices (in considering the reasonableness of the defendant's belief) were entitled to take note of the fact that some girls at the school attended by the complainant stayed on at school until they were 17 or 18 years of age, and that the defendant was aware of this. It follows that this type of specific evidence could be considered by the jury in appropriate circumstances.

12 [1920] NZLR 21, p 23.

2.2.4   Mens rea

In respect of the age of the complainant, s 6(1) creates an offence of strict liability although, as has been seen, this is subject to the availability of the limited young man's defence. Where the defence, for whatever reason, is not available (for instance, the man is not aged under 24), then the defendant's belief, however reasonably and honestly held by him, that the girl was over the age of 16, will not provide him with a defence.

In addition, it should be noted briefly that the prosecution must prove that the defendant intended to commit the act of sexual intercourse. As was noted in the discussion of s 5, above, this requirement provides few, if any, difficulties in practice, but, nevertheless, it remains a criterion which formally must exist.

2.2.5   *Sentencing: s 6*

An offence under s 6 is triable either way. The maximum sentence for a conviction on indictment is two years' imprisonment. For a conviction following summary trial, the maximum is six months' imprisonment, or a fine not exceeding £5,000, or both. Following the *Practice Note: National Mode of Trial Guidelines*,[13] offences which are triable either way should, generally, be tried summarily, unless one or more of the specified features exists in the case, and the court considers its sentencing powers to be insufficient. In respect of unlawful sexual intercourse with a girl under 16, those specified features are: where there is a wide disparity between the ages of the man and the girl; where there has been a breach of a position of trust; and where the victim was particularly vulnerable. Of course, as the Practice Note itself makes clear, the guidelines on unlawful sexual intercourse apply only to the offence under s 6 (girls under 16), because the s 5 offence is triable only on indictment.

The primary rationale for the offence is to provide protection for young girls at a period of time when they may be viewed as particularly emotionally and sexually vulnerable. This point was reiterated forcibly by Blofeld J in *Doolan* ((1991) 12 Cr App R(S) 634), when he stated:

> It must never be forgotten that the purpose of this Act is clearly to protect young girls at an age when they are emotionally vulnerable and particularly vulnerable to older men ... who can have an influence over them.[14]

Notwithstanding the logical and powerful argument that girls of a certain age require the protection of the law in this respect, it may be questioned whether the present age limit itself is at the correct level. It is unrealistic to suppose that a moderate lowering of the age of consent (to, say, 15 or even 14 for acts of vaginal intercourse) would have a major impact upon the incidence of 'under-

---

13   (1991) 92 Cr App R 142.

14   (1991) 12 Cr App R(S) 634, p 635.

age sex'. Rather, such acts which undoubtedly now occur *de facto*, would be usefully decriminalised, and it is unlikely that girls of 15 or 14 would be under any greater pressure to engage in sexual activity merely because the acts in question have ceased to be criminal. It is arguable that a lowering of the age of consent, coupled with a more efficient programme of sex and health education, would produce a sexually more healthy young population and achieve a reduction in the incidence of teenage pregnancies in Britain, which currently has one of the highest rates in Europe.

Notwithstanding such arguments, the courts must impose sentences within the terms of the present legislation. The leading guideline case in terms of sentencing within the statutory maximum is that of the Court of Appeal in *Taylor et al* ((1977) 64 Cr App R 182). There, three defendants – S (aged 28), T (aged 26) and R (aged 22) – all pleaded guilty to offences of unlawful sexual intercourse committed against the same girl, who was aged 14 at the time of the acts. It was accepted that the girl was sexually experienced prior to meeting the three defendants, and that she kept a diary in which she recorded her sexual activities. The defendants appealed against their sentences of imprisonment (of four months, four months and two months respectively). The Court of Appeal noted that s 6 covers a 'wide spectrum of guilt' from, at one end of the scale, an initially virtuous relationship between a youth of 17 or 18 and a girl of 15 which ends in sexual intercourse, to, at the other end, a man in a supervisory capacity, such as a head teacher or social worker, who deliberately seduces a girl in his care:

> Nowadays, most judges would ... rightly take the view, that when there is a virtuous friendship which ends in sexual intercourse, it is inappropriate to pass sentence of a punitive nature ... At the other end, a man in a supervisory capacity who abuses a position of trust for sexual gratification, ought to get a sentence somewhere near the maximum ... In between there come many degrees of guilt ...[15]

Having considered the diverse range of circumstances which may exist and the particular facts of the instant case, the Court of Appeal confirmed that the sentences imposed on S, R and T were appropriate. The court accepted that the girl was already a 'wanton', and that the men had not corrupted her, but, nevertheless, they had 'confirmed her in her wantonness', and thus an immediate custodial sentence was correct.

In common with sentencing practice in all sexual offences, a wide range of potential aggravating and mitigating factors may exist which the sentencer may take into consideration. As far as aggravating factors are concerned, the courts will consider largely the same range of features as when sentencing for

---

15 (1977) 64 Cr App R 182, p 185, *per* Lawton LJ.

rape (Chapter 3) and indecent assault (Chapter 6).[16] A similar approach will also be adopted in respect of mitigating features, although a number of specific points are worthy of brief mention. In *O'Grady* ((1978) 66 Cr App R 279), the defendant, a youth of unspecified age, but about 16, received 'suggestive letters' from the complainant, who was aged 14. It was noted by the Court of Appeal that she had made 'all the advances', including the making of certain vague threats against the youth if no sexual intercourse took place. Eventually, he succumbed to the pressure and sexual intercourse occurred. In allowing the appellant's appeal against a detention order of three months (of which he had already served one month), the court noted the behaviour of the girl and the fact that the parties were in the same age group, and, importantly, took specific regard to current standards of sexual behaviour. In light of all these features, it had been wrong to impose an immediate custodial sentence. *O'Grady* is a good illustration of an attempt by the judiciary to take note of, and reflect in the sentence, their perception of common social attitudes about sexual activities, especially between the young. It is easy to be critical of the judiciary in general terms as being out of touch and unresponsive to social, especially sexual, mores. Therefore, decisions which recognise social attitudes and seek to represent current standards should be welcomed.

In *R v B (James Walter)* ((1993) 14 Cr App R 482), the Court of Appeal allowed an appeal against sentence following conviction for, *inter alia*, unlawful sexual intercourse.[17] In substituting a probation order for the original sentence of two years' imprisonment, the court noted a psychiatric report on B (aged 40) which described him as having significant impairment in his intellectual, social and emotional skills, to the extent that he was unable to live without supervision. Such limited emotional and intellectual development meant that he could not be equated with an adult of normal intelligence. It is clear, therefore, from *R v B* that impairment of a defendant's mental faculties may operate as a mitigating factor.

Finally, it is worth noting that, *prima facie*, there exists an odd discrepancy in terms of the maximum sentence available following a conviction under s 6(1), namely two years' imprisonment, and that available in respect of indecent assault, namely 10 years' imprisonment (see Chapter 6). As every act

---

16 For examples of aggravating features in s 6, see *Doolan* (1991) 12 Cr App R(S) 634 (abuse of positions of authority and trust as a school teacher and family friend); *Palmer* (1995) 16 Cr App R(S) 642 (causing pregnancy and having a previous conviction for a like offence); and *Asher* (1995) 16 Cr App R(S) 708 (considerable age difference between the parties and the girl was a virgin).

17 Although the victim here was aged only 10 (and the charge was, in fact, one under s 5), the court's reasoning in respect of the defendant's mitigation should, we submit, be equally applicable where the girl is aged between 13 and 15. Given the particularly young age of the girl in *B* and the large age discrepancy between her and the defendant, it must be assumed that especially strong consideration was given to his mental condition as being a mitigating factor.

of sexual intercourse with a girl under the age of 16 necessarily involves an indecent assault, it would be possible in principle to avoid the lower maximum sentence by charging a man with indecent assault. However, in practice, this course of action is not adopted by the prosecuting authorities where that would be done merely in order to seek to attain a higher sentence. Of course, if a man commits other sexual acts with a girl under 16 prior to, during or after the act of sexual intercourse *per se*, then an indecent assault in its own right will almost certainly have been committed and a charge of such may be entirely appropriate.

3 GROSS INDECENCY WITH OR TOWARDS A CHILD UNDER 14

Section 1(1) of the Indecency with Children Act 1960 makes it an offence where:

... any person ... commits an act of gross indecency with or towards a child under the age of 14, or ... incites a child under that age to such an act with him or another ...

There is clear potential for some overlap between this offence and the offence of indecent assault (see Chapter 6), where the indecent assault is committed against a child under 14. Prior to a change effected by the Crime (Sentences) Act 1997 (see below), where such overlap existed, there seemed to be no reason in principle or practice why a charge of indecent assault should not have been preferred in order to take account of the considerably higher maximum penalty (10 years' imprisonment for indecent assault, as opposed to two years' imprisonment, on indictment, under s 1(1)). That sentencing anomaly, and thus the need to consider charging a defendant with indecent assault in circumstances which were better suited to a charge of indecency with a child, was resolved by s 52 of the Crime (Sentences) Act 1997, which increased the maximum sentence for an offence under s 1(1) to 10 years' imprisonment.

However, the s 1 offence remains of particular importance where, for whatever reason, the necessary elements of assault or battery cannot be established. Thus, where a defendant makes an invitation to a child, requesting, for example, that the child touch his (the defendant's) penis, in circumstances where the child is in no fear or apprehension, it is difficult to substantiate a charge of indecent assault (see Chapter 6), and s 1 may provide a much more appropriate alternative.

3.1   Parties

Section 1(1) may be committed, as a principal offence, by both males and females. It can only be committed against a child, whether male or female, who is under the age of 14 at the time of the act in question. In common with other sexual offences, the child's age is determined by reference to the commencement of the anniversary (in this case, the 14th anniversary) of his or her birth.

Where there is doubt as to whether the child was or was not aged 14 at the time of the act, it is quite permissible to charge indecent assault as an alternative in order to avoid the practical problems of proving the requisite age.[18]

3.2   *Actus reus*

Section 1 effectively creates two offences, namely *committing* an act of gross indecency with or towards a child under the age of 14 and *inciting* a child under that age to commit such an act.

3.2.1   *Act of gross indecency*

The essence of committing an act of gross indecency is that the defendant must act in a grossly indecent manner in the presence of a child. Clearly, it is not a condition that the defendant must touch the child, or vice versa, although, of course, touching may, and frequently does, take place. The meaning of 'act' within the definition of the offence was given the widest possible interpretation in *Speck* ([1977] 2 All ER 859). There, the complainant (a young girl aged eight) approached the defendant, who was sitting in a chair watching some children play. The girl placed her hand on the defendant's penis outside his trousers, leaving it there for about five minutes. As a result of the pressure of her hand, the defendant had an erection. It was accepted that he remained inactive at all times and that he did nothing to encourage the girl, but that equally he did not attempt to prevent her action. He appealed against his conviction under s 1, arguing that his mere inactivity could not amount to the requisite 'act of gross indecency' within the terms of the section. This argument was rejected by the Court of Appeal, where it was held that the defendant's inactivity was capable of amounting to an invitation to the child to act, or to continue to act, in a certain way. Thus, inactivity on the part of the defendant is equated with an 'invitation to continue', which, in turn, becomes capable of being viewed by a jury as an 'act'. It is difficult to avoid the conclusion that, in their understandable desire to uphold the conviction and thus to highlight their disapprobation of the defendant's *inactivity*, the Court

---

18   See *Goss and Goss* (1990) 90 Cr App R 400.

of Appeal has stretched the literal words of s 1 to an almost unacceptable breaking point.

The decision in *Speck* was distinguished by the Court of Appeal in *R v B* ([1999] Crim LR 594). The defendant, B, was convicted of gross indecency against P, a youth aged 13. B, a homosexual, was a friend of P's family. B and P had spoken about homosexual practices, and P disclosed that he might be homosexual. On the night in question, they had shared a bed, with a duvet between them. On B's evidence, he later felt P's erect penis pushing into his back and buttocks, and P seemed to be rocking to and fro. B immediately told P to 'cut it out'. The trial judge directed the jury that the prosecution must prove indecency 'with or towards' a child, as well as intention. B was convicted and appealed. The Court of Appeal quashed the conviction. It was held that the trial judge should have emphasised that B needed to have invited P to have participated in an indecent act. It is worth noting that if B had not immediately stopped P's actions, then that itself may have amounted to an invitation, by allowing P to continue, and thus have constituted an act as in *Speck* itself.

There is little direct authority on the meaning of 'gross indecency' specifically within s 1. However, there seems no reason to suppose that, in common with other offences where the phrase is used (see, for example, the discussion of s 32 of the Sexual Offences Act 1956 in Chapter 2), the courts will do anything other than regard it as a normal English phrase to be determined by the jury.

3.2.2   With or towards

There is no requirement that the defendant and the child(ren) need to come into physical contact with each other. In *Francis* ((1989) 88 Cr App R 127), the defendant was seen by two boys to be masturbating in the changing rooms of a public swimming pool, although there was no suggestion that he had spoken to them or tried to touch them. It was held by the Court of Appeal that a man could be guilty under s 1(1) in such circumstances if he knew the children were watching him and he gained some satisfaction from that fact, albeit he had not deliberately attracted their attention. He would not be guilty if he believed that the children were not watching him. The reasoning in *Francis* was given a different interpretation in *R v R (J)* ([1993] Crim LR 971), where the Court of Appeal held that it was not necessary for the defendant actually to derive satisfaction from his conduct (although, presumably, he often will), provided he intended to derive such satisfaction.

3.2.3   Incites

A defendant does not necessarily have to commit an act of gross indecency. In the alternative it is equally an offence to *incite* such an act, the mere incitement *per se* being proscribed. Incitement is a broad concept and covers a wide range of activities. These activities would include persuading and encouraging a child to an act of gross indecency, as well as using threats or other forms of pressure. It is irrelevant that the act incited does not subsequently take place and, equally, the defendant need not intend that the act of gross indecency should take place with him. Thus, the defendant commits an offence if he seeks to force two boys aged 13 to masturbate in his presence, irrespective of whether or not they subsequently do so. Incitement, in whatever form, is only complete when it comes to the attention of the person incited. Prior to that time, it may be possible to substantiate a charge of attempting to incite an act of gross indecency, because incitement within the terms of s 1(1) is a substantive offence in its own right, not an inchoate offence. In *Rowley* ((1992) 94 Cr App R 95), the defendant left a series of notes in public places offering money to boys if they would act as his 'pretended son' or deliver secret messages. Although the conviction was quashed on appeal, the Court of Appeal expressly recognised that a charge of attempting to incite a child under the age of 14 to commit an act of gross indecency could exist in appropriate circumstances:

> Incitement to commit gross indecency would require a proposition to be made for this specific purpose. A letter sent by an accused inviting a boy to commit gross indecency which did not reach him would be an attempted incitement ... Here ... the note went no further than to seek to engineer a preliminary meeting. No proposition or incitement to the offence had emanated from the appellant. At most he was preparing the ground for an attempt.[19]

3.3 Mens rea

Although the wording of s 1(1) discloses no overt *mens rea*, it seems that the offence requires intention on the part of the defendant. Thus, a defendant will be guilty if, *inter alia*, he intended to commit an act of gross indecency with or towards a child, or intended to incite such an act. The much more controversial issue in respect of *mens rea*, as with most age based sexual offences, relates to the position of the defendant who makes a mistake about the age of the child in question. Does the law impose strict liability in respect of the defendant's mistake of age? Or can he rely upon his mistake to remove criminal responsibility? Until the recent landmark decision of the House of Lords in *B (A Minor) v DPP* ([2000] 1 All ER 833), the general consensus of academic opinion was that the old decision in *Prince*, above, operated to impose strict liability on defendants in sex offences, so that a defendant could not rely upon his mistaken belief that the complainant was older than the age specified in the relevant offence.

In *B*, the defendant (a youth aged 15) was convicted under s 1(1) with inciting a girl aged 13 to commit an act of gross indecency with him, after he had asked her on several occasions to perform oral sex on him. B claimed that

---

19 (1992) 94 Cr App R 95, p 100, *per* Taylor LJ.

he thought the girl was older than 13. His appeal to the Divisional Court was rejected, albeit with strong concerns being expressed about, specifically, the rationale of *Prince*, and, more generally, the position of age based criteria in sexual offences.[20] Subsequently, the House of Lords unanimously quashed B's conviction, holding that a defendant was entitled to be acquitted of an offence under s 1(1) if he held, or may have held, an honest belief that the child in question was aged 14 or over. In reaching this conclusion, their Lordships emphasised strongly the general presumption in favour of *mens rea*, and, equally strongly, cast major doubts on whether *Prince* should continue to be regarded as providing a special principle in respect of age based criteria in sexual offences:

> I would reject the contention that there is a special rule of construction in respect of age based sexual offences which is untouched by the presumption as explained in *Sweet v Parsley*. Moreover, *R v Prince* is out of line with the modern trend in criminal law which is that a defendant should be judged on the facts as he believed them to be ... It is no longer possible to extract from *R v Prince* a special principle ... applicable only to age-based sexual offences.[21]

Their Lordships emphasised the primacy of the presumption in favour of *mens rea* as stated in Lord Reid's famous speech in *Sweet v Parsley* ([1970] AC 132, pp 148–49). Consequently, *mens rea* must be taken to be required unless Parliament, either expressly or by necessary implication, has provided to the contrary. As with any case where the court must consider a potential finding of strict liability, the decision in *B* emphasises that such a finding should only be made where that is the 'necessary implication'. This suggests a high standard, that is, not merely that Parliament may have intended strict liability to be imposed, or that the court feels the circumstances are such that the implication is possible. In deciding whether the presumption for *mens rea* has been removed by necessary implication, their Lordships reiterated a number of factors to be taken into account. In terms of the instant case, the more important factors are the following.

First, courts will consider the statutory background and language. The Indecency with Children Act 1960 was recognised as an appendix to the Sexual Offences Act 1956. It was designed, in particular, to fill the gap created by decisions such as those in *Fairclough v Whipp*, above, whereby no indecent assault was committed by the defendant who merely invited a child to commit an act of indecency, without that invitation amounting to, say, an indecent assault. If the 1960 Act was, therefore, no more than an 'appendix' to the 1956 Act, the earlier Act becomes important in terms of any patterns of *mens rea* or strict liability. Unfortunately, the 1956 Act was regarded as a 'motley collection of offences, of diverse origins ... [which] displays no

---

20 See, eg, the judgment of Brooke LJ [1999] 3 WLR 116, pp 129–32.
21 [2000] 1 All ER 833, p 850, *per* Lord Steyn. See, also, Lord Nicholls at pp 839–41.

satisfactorily clear or coherent pattern'.[22] The statutory background and language therefore provided no assistance.

Secondly, the court must consider the 'seriousness' of the offence. They will often ask themselves whether the behaviour prohibited is 'truly criminal'. This criterion frequently covers a range of issues. Here, it is useful to note that the maximum sentence for an offence under s 1(1) is 10 years' imprisonment, and that a person convicted of such an offence is required to register under the registration requirements of the Sex Offenders Act 1997. Irrespective of these purely legal consequences, there is a high stigma attached to any person convicted of an offence under s 1(1).

Thirdly, consideration must be given to the scope of the offence. It is essential to recognise that there may be a considerable difference between the public's perception of the 'type' of person who normally commits such an offence – often perceived as a mature or older male paedophile – and the actual factual circumstances of B. This issue was recognised expressly by their Lordships:

> The [offence] is apt to cover acts of paedophilia and all responsible citizens will welcome effective legislation in respect of such a great social evil. But it also covers any heterosexual or homosexual conduct between teenagers if one of them is under 14. And the actus reus extends to incitement of a child under 14: words are enough. [It] therefore extends to any verbal sexual overtures between teenagers if one of them is under 14 ... For the law to criminalise such conduct of teenagers *by offences of strict liability* would be far reaching and controversial.[23]

Fourthly, the court should address the mischief to be prevented. If the imposition of strict liability would serve to act as a deterrent and, therefore, more effectively operate to protect children, then that would be a strong factor for displacing the presumption in favour of *mens rea*. On the facts, the House of Lords believed that the other factors noted above outweighed this consideration.

The decision in B has potentially far reaching implications for most sexual offences where an age based criterion exists, and the defendant seeks to rely upon his mistaken belief as to the complainant's age. However, it is unlikely that it will have any effect on ss 5 and 6 of the Sex Offences Act 1956. Parliament has already been explicit in providing the 'young man's defence' in respect of s 6 (see above), and the necessary implication from that specific defence is that Parliament intended s 5 to impose strict liability as to age. By contrast, in relation to other offences, B gives rise to huge implications. The courts will now be required to consider in detail whether Parliament did intend to remove the presumption, bearing in mind the House of Lords'

---

22 [2000] 1 All ER 833, *per* Lord Nicholls, pp 839–40.

23 *Ibid, per* Lord Steyn, pp 845–46.

strong criticisms of the decision in *Prince* and their equally strong approval of the reasoning in *Sweet v Parsley*.[24] If Parliament is unhappy with the courts' new approach to this issue then, as Lord Hutton, for example, made clear (at pp 854–55), it must act to change the law.

One final practical issue deserves specific mention. Their Lordships have confirmed that the defendant's belief (as to age) needs only be honest and genuine, not necessarily reasonable. This was to be expected in the light of the criminal law's recent move away from objectivism and back towards subjectivism. This could allow a defendant to abuse the defence by claiming that he honestly thought the complainant was older than her or his actual age. This potential danger was recognised by the House of Lords. As is often the case in such circumstances, the jury was seen as the 'safeguard', that is, where there are no reasonable grounds for such a belief to be held, the jury will conclude, only in exceptional circumstances, that the belief was, in fact, held by the defendant.

3.4   Sentencing: s 1(1)

As noted above, the maximum sentence following a conviction on indictment under s 1 was two years' imprisonment. Given that the offence must be committed in respect of children under the age of 14, and compared with the maximum of 10 years' imprisonment for indecent assault, the s 1 penalty may have appeared somewhat low.

The sentencer will take note of the usual aggravating and mitigating factors as appropriate. Thus aggravation will include: large age discrepancy between the parties; the precise age of the child; abuse of a position of trust or authority; effect on the child; the seriousness of the actual act, etc. Mitigation may include: a plea of guilty; the mental state of the defendant; the effect that imprisoning the defendant may have on other persons or dependants; good character; remorse, etc.

For the purpose of illustrating the courts' attitude to sentencing s 1(1) offences prior to 1997, one example will suffice. In *Aston* ((1993) 14 Cr App R(S) 779), the defendant pleaded guilty to two counts of gross indecency with a child, but only after the child had given evidence and been cross-examined. The defendant had persuaded the complainant K, a girl of 12, to touch his penis and he had later masturbated in front of K and her friend F, also 12. On a separate occasion, he had persuaded K to masturbate him and later had forced F to place her hand on his penis and masturbate him. In

---

24 It is clear that the courts will still impose strict liability in appropriate cases, even after the decision in B. In *Harrow London Borough Council v Shah* [2000] 1 WLR 83, the Court of Appeal confirmed that selling a lottery ticket to a youth under the age of 16, contrary to the National Lottery Act 1993, s 13 and the National Lottery Regulations 1994, reg 3, was a crime of strict liability, despite the employee's genuine and reasonable belief that the youth was aged over 16.

upholding sentences of 12 months' imprisonment consecutively on each count, the Court of Appeal stated that elements of both planning and compulsion were aggravating features and, specifically, that there would be no mitigation for the plea of guilty, as it had been made too late to prevent the trauma of giving testimony.

4   INDECENT PHOTOGRAPHS OF CHILDREN

Some of the greatest concerns in recent decades about sexual offences which are committed against the young have centred around the creation, possession and distribution of indecent photographs of children. An increasing public awareness of, and concern about, individuals with paedophile tendencies, as well as organised paedophile rings (consisting usually, though not exclusively, of mature adult males) have led to a number of legislative steps to deal with the problem of child pornography and, in particular, indecent photographs of children.

Although it by no means follows that a person's possession or distribution of an indecent photograph of a child will inevitably lead that person to commit further offences of a sexual nature, it is clear that a risk of such escalating behaviour exists, and that that is a risk which is unacceptable to society. Even if it could be proved (which seems unlikely) that there was no link between mere possession, etc, of indecent photographs and subsequent offending of a sexual nature, the activities themselves are identified by society as *mala in se*. There may, in addition, be an obvious fear of corruption and exploitation, but even where that fear is not necessarily present, the very existence of such indecent photographs (whether of, or depicting, children) deserves to be legally proscribed.

The arguments in respect of the criminalisation of indecent photographs may be seen as typically representative of the wider debate surrounding the rationale for criminalising a broad range of activities. Thus, to a very large extent, the question whether the taking, or even mere possession, of indecent photographs *should* be criminalised will depend upon one's view about notions of harm, morality and paternalism. According to Gross, for example, there are four main groups of 'harms' with which the criminal law should be concerned. One of these harms concerns 'offences to sensibility':

> Such concern is reflected in penal provisions that deal with punishing pornography, publicly uttering an obscenity ... and the like.[25]

On this basis, it would be possible to construct an argument for the criminalisation of indecent photographs, because the existence of such articles amounts to an offence against, or a harming of, our sensibilities.

---

25   Gross, H, *A Theory of Criminal Justice*, 1979, OUP, pp 115–16.

An even more elaborate categorisation has been made by Kaplan,[26] who distinguishes between 'primary harms' (that is, those which involve direct harm to others) and 'secondary harms' (that is, those which involve indirect harm to others). Applying this distinction to indecent photographs of children, it is arguable that the taking and possession of such photographs are activities which are capable of constituting both primary harm (corruption and exploitation of the children, for example), as well as secondary harm. The latter is considerably more difficult to define and quantify in the present context, but may include, for instance, the *potential risk* of the defendant's behaviour escalating into further and more serious offences.

Finally, even where 'harm to others', however defined, is not established, it may be possible to identify other, wider, justifications for criminalisation. These justifications, whilst not exhaustive, may include: the 'offence principle', whereby prohibition is necessary to prevent hurt or offence (in the sense of insult, as opposed to harm) to others; or the notion of 'legal moralism' whereby certain behaviour is inherently immoral and thus must be prevented, irrespective of whether or not it is 'harmful' or 'offensive' to others.[27]

In the light of such potential rationales, there are two major provisions which deal with indecent photographs of children, namely the offences contained in s 1(1) of the Protection of Children Act 1978 and s 160(1) of the Criminal Justice Act 1988. Both of these offences were subjected to important modifications as a result of the Criminal Justice and Public Order Act 1994 (see below), especially in relation to so called 'computer pornography' and the creation of 'pseudo-photographs'.

4.1 Taking, etc, an indecent photograph of a child

Section 1(1) of the Protection of Children Act 1978 (as amended by s 84 of the 1994 Act) provides:

It is an offence for a person–

(a) to take, or permit to be taken, or to make an indecent photograph or pseudo-photograph of a child; or

(b) to distribute or show such indecent photographs or pseudo-photographs; or

---

26 Kaplan, J, 'The role of the law in drug control' [1971] Duke LJ 1065.

27 Amongst a mass of literature dealing with the concept of harm as the basis for criminalisation, see, especially, Feinberg, J, *Harmless Wrongdoing (The Moral Limits of the Criminal Law*, Vol 4), 1988, OUP. For a further representative cross-section of arguments, see: Mitchell, B, *Law, Morality and Religion in a Secular Society*, 1967, OUP, especially pp 252–69; Dworkin, R, 'Lord Devlin and the enforcement of morals' (1966) 75 Yale LJ 986; Hughes, G, 'Morals and the criminal law' (1962) 71 Yale LJ 662; Reynolds, N, 'The enforcement of morals and the rule of law' (1977) 11 Georgia Law Rev 1325; and Sartorius, R, 'The enforcement of morality' (1972) 81 Yale LJ 891.

(c) to have in his possession such indecent photographs or pseudo-photographs, with a view to their being distributed or shown by himself or others; or

(d) to publish or cause to be published any advertisement likely to be understood as conveying that the advertiser distributes or shows such indecent photographs or pseudo-photographs or intends to do so.

4.1.1 Parties

The offences under the 1978 Act may be committed, as principal offences, by either males or females. Further, it is expressly provided by s 3 of the Act that the offences may be committed by corporations.

4.1.2 Actus reus

It is clear from the four distinct paragraphs within s 1(1) that Parliament intended to proscribe as wide a range of activities as possible in respect of indecent photographs. The offence therefore can be committed not only by the more obvious 'taking' of indecent photographs (para (a)), but also, for example, by the distribution or showing of such photographs (para (b)), the possession of them, with a view to them being distributed or shown (para (c)) and, most broadly, the publishing of any advertisement conveying that the advertiser distributes or shows such photographs.

The requirement (found in both paras (b) and (c)) that the defendant must 'show' the photograph has been interpreted as meaning 'shown to another person', not to the defendant himself. Although this may seem an obvious point, it can occasionally cause the courts difficulties. In *R v ET* ([1999] Crim LR 749), the defendant was charged under s 1(1)(c). The prosecution relied on his admission that he had the film in question and intended to show it to himself, but did not seek to prove that he intended to show it to others. The trial judge ruled that this was sufficient to satisfy the requirement of showing within para (c). The Court of Appeal, however, disagreed and quashed the conviction. It was held that 'showing' in s 1(1)(b) clearly meant 'showing to others', and thus it should be given the same meaning within para (c). Perhaps more importantly, if showing were to be interpreted widely so as to include showing to oneself, the offences in s 1 would in effect have covered mere possession by the defendant. This was evidently not the case as, otherwise, Parliament would not have needed specifically to criminalise 'simple possession' by the later enactment of s 160 of the Criminal Justice Act 1988 (see below).

The reference in s 1(1)(a) to 'making' an indecent photograph was the result of the amendments introduced by the 1994 Act. The original wording of s 1(1)(a) contained only the verb 'take'. This was first extended by s 160 of the Criminal Justice Act 1988, which introduced the new and separate offence of 'possession' and, subsequently, by the 1994 Act itself. The requirement that the defendant should 'make' an indecent photograph or pseudo-photograph has given rise to a number of interesting questions of interpretation in several recent judgments.

In *Bowden* ([2000] 2 WLR 1083), the appellant was convicted, on a plea of guilty following a ruling from the trial judge, to the making of indecent photographs of children contrary to s 1(1)(a) of the 1978 Act. The appellant had downloaded onto his hard disk from the Internet indecent images of boys. He had himself printed out some of the images, whilst he had stored others on his computer discs. It was accepted that the photographs were indecent and that they involved children under the age of 16. It was argued on the appellant's behalf that, whilst he was in possession of the photographs, his behaviour did not amount to 'making' them within the terms of the section. The trial judge rejected this submission and ruled that the appellant's actions did amount to taking or making such photographs. This ruling was approved by the Court of Appeal, where it was held that the addition of the verb 'make' had 'merely complemented' the original offence:

> In our judgment, s 1 as amended is clear and unambiguous ... Quite simply, it renders unlawful the making of a photograph or a pseudo-photograph. There is no definition section. Accordingly the words 'to make' must be given their natural and ordinary meaning. In this context this is 'to cause to exist; to produce by action, to bring about'.[28]

The Court emphasised that s 1 was neither ambiguous nor obscure, and did not believe that a natural interpretation would lead to absurdity. In terms of the rationale behind s 1, strong approval was given to the following submission, made by counsel for the Crown:

> A person who either downloads images on to disc or who prints them off is making them. The Act is not only concerned with the original creation of images, but also their proliferation. Photographs or pseudo-photographs found on the Internet may have originated from outside the United Kingdom; to download or print within the jurisdiction is to create new material which hitherto may not have existed therein.[29]

The joined appeals in *Atkins v DPP; Goodland v DPP* ([2000] 2 All ER 425), raise several important issues of interpretation in respect of indecent photograph provisions generally. In the present context, the decision of the Divisional Court in *Atkins* is most significant.

The appellant, Dr Atkins, was charged with offences under s 1(1)(a) of the 1978 Act and s 160 of the Criminal Justice Act 1988 (see below). He had downloaded from the Internet indecent photographs of children. Some of the photographs had been stored deliberately on his computer's 'J directory'. Other photographs were found to be on the computer's 'cache': a temporary store created automatically by an Internet browser programme when

---

28 [2000] 2 WLR 1083, p 1089, *per* Otton LJ.
29 *Ibid*.

accessing an Internet site. The charges of 'making indecent photographs' under s 1(1)(a) related both to the J directory photographs and the cache photographs. The possession charges under s 160 related solely to the photographs in the cache.

Atkins was convicted of the possession offences after the stipendiary magistrate held (irrespective of not being sure that Atkins was aware of the operation of the cache) that s 160(1) created an offence of strict liability. However, he held further that there was no case to answer in respect of the making charges under s 1(1)(a), as 'making' required an act of 'creation' which was not satisfied by the mere storing or copying of a document. Atkins appealed against his conviction on the 'possession' charges, and the Crown appealed against his acquittal on the 'making' charges.

The Divisional Court held that the offence under s 1(1)(a) was not one of strict liability. Rather, a defendant would be guilty where there had been an *intentional* copying of indecent photographs. Consequently, Atkins had been properly acquitted on the charge of making the photographs in the cache, the magistrate having found that there was no evidence of Atkins being aware of the operation of that system. However, he should have been convicted of making the photographs stored by him in his J directory. In this respect, the decision in *Bowden*, above, was applied. The copying of indecent photographs onto a computer's directory is an offence provided, as here, it was done *knowingly*.

4.1.2.1 Indecent

The question of whether a photograph or pseudo-photograph is indecent is essentially one to be determined by the jury, but it is incumbent upon the trial judge to give some guidance as to the meaning of the word 'indecent'. The standard test, albeit in relation to the offence of sending certain articles by post contrary to s 11 of the Post Office Act 1953, is that adopted in *Stanley* ([1965] 2 QB 327), where Lord Parker CJ said that the words 'indecent or obscene' 'convey one idea, namely offending against the recognised standards of propriety, indecent being at the lower end of the scale and obscene at the upper end of the scale'.[30]

In *Owen* ([1988] 1 WLR 134), the defendant, a professional photographer, was charged with an offence under s 1(1)(a) after taking photographs of a girl, aged 14, who wished to become a model. In some of the photographs, the girl had bare breasts and wore little clothing. The Court of Appeal stressed that the epithet 'indecent' related to the phrase 'photograph of a child'. Thus, it is not the defendant or his behaviour which must be indecent, but rather the consequence of his behaviour, that is the photograph of a child. In addition, it is quite permissible, said the court, for the jury to consider not just the girl's

---

30   [1965] 2 QB 327, p 333.

appearance, but also her age. After all, it is inevitable that the jury will be aware of the child's general age, as it is a requirement of the offence that she or he is aged under 16 at the time the photograph was taken.

Although the issue was not considered specifically in *Owen* itself, it is now clear that the jury must limit their consideration to the child's age and appearance in the photograph, rather than all other surrounding circumstances, in determining the question of indecency. This was confirmed by the Court of Appeal in *Graham-Kerr* ([1988] 1 WLR 1098), where, in quashing the appellant's conviction, it was held that the only relevant evidence (on the question of indecency) was 'the photographs themselves'. This would exclude consideration of the surrounding circumstances, including the motives of the defendant in taking the photographs, and in reaching this decision it is clear that the court was keen not to extend the reasoning adopted by the House of Lords in *Court* (see Chapter 6), in relation to indecent assault:

> [W]hether or not a photograph is indecent cannot be related to the question whether or not an assault is indecent. An assault is an ephemeral matter, the *mens rea* of the offence being that of the person committing the assault. A photograph is a permanent matter. The question ... is whether the photograph itself is indecent.[31]

4.1.2.2 Photograph

As with any legislation dealing with technology, the 1978 Act faces the challenge of keeping pace with continuing and developing technological advances. The Act itself made some attempt to deal with these issues by providing a broad definition of the word 'photograph' as used in the phrase 'indecent photograph', although, as will be seen below, further amendments subsequently became necessary.

Section 7(2) of the 1978 Act provides that references to 'indecent photograph' include an indecent film, a copy of an indecent photograph or film and an indecent photograph comprised in a film. Furthermore, 'film' is taken as covering any form of video recording. Perhaps even more importantly, given advances in computer technology, s 7(4) provides that references to 'photograph' include the negative as well as positive version, and data stored on a computer disk or by other electronic means which is capable of conversion into a photograph. All material stored on and moved between computers is represented in digital form, and is stored on computer disk (whether hard, floppy or CD-ROM). Thus, a photograph can be converted into digital form, distributed electronically and even printed as a hardcopy, but doubts still existed as to whether this was sufficient to make

---

31 [1988] 1 WLR 1098, p 1104, *per* Stocker LJ. It is, however, quite permissible for the jury to look at the surrounding circumstances in determining issues other than that of indecency; in considering, for example, the defendant's defence that the photographs were taken accidentally.

such material into a 'photograph' or even a 'copy of a photograph'. The scope of this latter phrase was considered in detail by the Court of Appeal in *Fellows and Arnold* ([1997] 1 Cr App R 244) (although it should be noted that the amending provisions introduced by the 1994 Act were not in force at the time of the alleged offences, and thus were not considered in the appeal). The first appellant, Fellows, used his employers' computer to store data which enabled it to produce indecent pictures of children onto a computer screen and to produce hardcopies in print. He made this data available on the Internet, but access was limited by a password which was provided only to persons vouched for by existing password-holders, or to persons who provided similar data, by which means he could increase his database. The second appellant, Arnold, was one person who provided additional data. Although the Court of Appeal held strong doubts as to whether such data could constitute a 'photograph' for the purpose of the Act, there was no such restriction in respect of the phrase 'copy of a photograph', to which a very broad definition was applied:

> If not a 'photograph', is the computer disk nevertheless a 'copy of an indecent photograph' within s 7(2)? It contains data, not visible to the eye, which can be converted by appropriate technical means into a screen image and into a print which exactly reproduces the original photograph from which it was derived. It ... makes the original photograph, or a copy of it, available for viewing by a person who has access to the disk. There is nothing in the Act which makes it necessary that the copy should itself be a photograph within the dictionary or the statutory definition, and if there was, it would make the inclusion of the reference to a copy unnecessary. *So we conclude that there is no restriction on the nature of a copy, and that the data represents the original photographs in another form.*[32]

4.1.2.3   Pseudo-photograph

Advances in computer technology have led to a considerable increase in both the creation and distribution of digital images resembling photographs, and, as a result, the photograph provisions of the 1978 Act became increasingly difficult to apply to 'computer pornography'. Particular problems arose in relation to the increasing existence of composite and created or manipulated photographic images. This would cover the situation, for example, where two (or more) photographs, with or without additional modifications, are converted into digital form and then amalgamated to create a single composite photographic image. Thus, a child's head could be superimposed upon the body of an adult, or a photograph of a child could be manipulated to produce an image where certain features only (such as the breasts or genitalia) were represented physically as those of an adult. Prior to the introduction of

---

32   [1997] 1 Cr App R 244, p 254, *per* Evans LJ (emphasis added). For a further discussion of these general issues, see the excellent analysis in Manchester, C, 'Criminal Justice and Public Order Act 1994: obscenity, pornography and videos' [1995] Crim LR 123; and Manchester, C, 'More about computer pornography' [1996] Crim LR 645.

the concept of a 'pseudo-photograph', this type of image created several potential difficulties for the law as it then stood. First, it was not clear whether such a composite image would be interpreted as a 'photograph' (or copy of a photograph) at all. Secondly, that part of the image which was undoubtedly indecent (that is, the body of an adult) was not that of a child; conversely, that part of the image which was that of a child (for instance, the head) may not necessarily have been held to be indecent.

The amendments introduced by the 1994 Act sought to deal with these potential difficulties. Thus, s 1(1) now covers 'pseudo-photographs', which, by the new s 7(7), means 'an image, whether made by computer graphics or otherwise howsoever, which *appears to be* a photograph'. Furthermore, s 7(9)(b), as amended, provides that references to an indecent pseudo-photograph include 'data stored on a computer disk or by other electronic means which is capable of conversion into a pseudo-photograph'.

Most significantly in the context of manipulated photographic images, s 7(8), as amended, now provides:

> If the *impression conveyed* by a pseudo-photograph is that the person shown is a child, the pseudo-photograph shall be treated for all purposes of this Act as showing a child and so shall a pseudo-photograph where the *predominant impression conveyed is a child notwithstanding that some of the physical characteristics shown are those of an adult* [emphasis added].

However, it is clear from early authority that the interpretation of the phrase 'pseudo-photograph' will not be without interest and difficulty. In *Goodland v DPP*, above, the appellant was found in possession of an indecent item, namely two individual photographs sellotaped together. It was accepted that the person pictured in the item was a child and that it was indecent. The item was unusual, in that it had been created by the appellant. The main photograph was that of a girl aged about 10, dressed in a gymnastic outfit. The second photograph (a cutting from a larger photograph) showed the naked abdomen, genital area and upper thighs of a girl or young woman. The second photograph had been sellotaped in one corner to the main photograph so that it could be turned away from or superimposed upon the lower section of the girl in the first photograph. The magistrates held that this was an item which 'appears to be a photograph', rejecting the defence submission that an item consisting of two photographs sellotaped together was a collage, not a photograph. Consequently, the magistrates held that the item amounted to a pseudo-photograph for the purpose of s 7(7).

The Divisional Court upheld Goodland's appeal and quashed the conviction. The Court rejected the Crown's argument that the item was a pseudo-photograph, because it amounted to 'a product of photography' or was 'photographic in nature'. Rather, the item did not amount to an image which appears to be a photograph:

> In my judgment an image made by an exhibit which obviously consists, as this
> one does, of parts of two different photographs sellotaped together cannot be
> said to appear to be 'a photograph'.[33]

The Divisional Court accepted that if the item, consisting of its two individual components, were itself to be photocopied (or, presumably, photographed in the traditional sense), then the resulting product *could* amount to a pseudo-photograph.[34] This appears to be correct, given the meaning of pseudo-photograph in s 7(8), but, undoubtedly, is capable of producing an absurd result. If D1 possesses a composite 'item' similar to that in *Goodland*, no offence is committed. But if D2 possessed a photocopy or photograph of that same item, he could be guilty on the basis that it amounts to a pseudo-photograph. The image depicted in each case is identical. The mischief sought to be prevented (namely the representation of children through indecent images) is the same. Consequently, such an anomalous result is insupportable. A simple remedy would be for Parliament to extend the definition of pseudo-photograph so that, for example, it means 'an image, *or composite image comprising more than one part,* ... which appears to be a photograph'.

4.1.2.4 Child

The offences can only be committed in respect of a 'child', which, for the purposes of the 1978 Act, means a person under the age of 16. Where a defendant is charged under s 1(1)(a) – but not under paras (b)–(d) – the court may infer from the victim's present appearance a rebuttable presumption that he or she was under the age of 16 at the time of the alleged offence.

Of course, given the nature of the offences under the 1978 Act, it is frequently the case that the identity of the child in the photograph cannot be ascertained, so that age cannot be established by any normal methods (such as the production of a birth certificate). Without specific provision to deal with this issue, almost insuperable problems of proof would arise. Consequently, s 2(3) provides:

> In proceedings under this Act relating to indecent photographs of children, a
> person is to be taken as having been a child at any material time if it appears
> from the evidence as a whole that he was then under the age of 16.

In most cases, it will be the physical appearance itself of the subject of the photograph which will provide the evidence from which the court may infer that the person was a child. This was confirmed recently by the Court of Appeal in *Land (Michael)* ((1997) *The Times*, 4 November; [1998] Crim LR 70), where the appellant was convicted of, *inter alia*, two offences of possessing an indecent photograph of a child, with a view to its being distributed or shown by himself or others, contrary to s 1(1)(c) of the 1978 Act. On behalf of the

---

33 [2000] 2 All ER 425, p 439, *per* Simon Brown LJ.
34 *Ibid.*

Court of Appeal, Judge LJ rejected the appellant's claim that paediatric or other expert evidence was admissible to help the jury assess the question of whether the person depicted in the photograph was under the age of 16. Furthermore, it was held that the purpose of s 2(3) was to avoid the obvious difficulties frequently involved in identifying an unknown person in a photograph, and thus in ascertaining his or her age. Rather, for the purpose of this offence, the question whether an unknown person depicted in a photograph was a child (that is, under the age of 16) was one of fact and could be inferred by the jury from all of the circumstances. Whilst this interpretation of s 2(3) seems correct in principle (as, without it, establishing the requisite age would often be impossible), it is not without interest. Let it be assumed that a defendant has in his possession a photograph of a female aged *in fact* 16, but whose significant lack of physical development gives her the appearance of being considerably younger. The defendant may or may not know of her real age, but, in any case, the girl is unidentifiable and he has no way of proving that she is 16. In the light of these circumstances, including the girl's physical appearance, the jury infer that she was under the age of 16. The decision in *Land* clearly allows such an inference to be made, although its obvious impact is that the offence can be committed not only in respect of children who are under 16 *de facto*, but also in respect of young persons who appear to be such in the eyes of the jury.

Finally, it is clear that, in relation to pseudo-photographs, there does not have to be, in fact, a child as defined. Rather, as s 7(8), above, provides, the defendant will be guilty if the image which is created or produced conveys the predominant impression that the person is a child, that is, under the age of 16.

4.1.3   Mens rea

The *mens rea* required for s 1(1) is made more complicated by the fact there are four quite separate offences contained within paras (a)–(d).

In respect of s 1(1)(a), the Court of Appeal in *Graham-Kerr* held that it was necessary for the prosecution to prove that the defendant took the photograph(s) deliberately and intentionally. This was explained by the court as requiring an intention to take the photograph 'of the subject as ultimately disclosed by the photograph produced'.[35] Consequently, it must remain open to a defendant to argue that the photograph ultimately produced contains a different image from that which he saw when he looked through the viewfinder of the camera and depressed the shutter, due, for instance, to the fact that the child moved suddenly and unexpectedly. This possibility was expressly recognised in *Graham-Kerr*,[36] although it will not avail the defendant who was aware of the possibility of the child moving, or who was hoping that the child may move in such a way that an indecent photograph would be

---

35   [1998] 1 WLR 1098.
36   *Ibid*, p 1104.

produced. Where the charge under s 1(1)(a) refers specifically to 'making', it is clear from the Divisional Court in *Atkins*, above, that there must be knowledge on the part of the defendant.[37]

Insofar as s 1(1)(a) also proscribes the 'permitting' of an indecent photograph to be taken, it seems likely that permission will be interpreted as requiring an element of knowledge on the part of the defendant.

The two offences in s 1(1)(b) and (d) would also appear to require an element of intention. Thus, a defendant will only be guilty of distributing or showing indecent photographs if it is established that he acted intentionally vis-à-vis the distribution or showing. Likewise, the defendant must be shown to have published an advertisement intentionally.

The mental element required for s 1(1)(c) is inexorably linked to the concept of possession. This is discussed more fully in relation to the following offence.

4.1.4   Sentencing s 1(1) offences

The maximum sentence that can be imposed on a person convicted of an offence under s 1(1) is three years' imprisonment. Given the problems and concerns associated with the increasing incidence of child pornography, and especially its availability on the Internet, this may be seen as a low maximum (or at least in relation to more serious instances, such as those involving very young children or widespread exploitation), which lacks the necessary deterrent effect. These issues were addressed in *Caley* ([1999] 2 Cr App R(S) 154). The defendant was convicted under s 1(1)(b) of distributing indecent photographs of children and under s 1(1)(c) of possession, with a view to distribution. In all instances, he had downloaded photographs from the Internet onto floppy disks. He was sentenced to 30 months' imprisonment after the trial judge, Watling J, had commented specifically that this was a case for very nearly the maximum as a deterrent to others who may be minded to engage in similar activities. In dismissing the appeal against sentence, the Court of Appeal approved both the level of sentence and the deterrence rationale:

> The penalties provided by the 1978 Act, 20 years old as it now is, may be thought to be somewhat inadequate to cope with the commercial potential which access to the Internet now provides for those who wish to download and exploit material of this nature. The judge ... was right to pass a deterrent sentence.[38]

However, it is equally clear that no two offences under s 1 are identical, and the courts will consider the precise factual circumstances of each case in determining the appropriate sentence. In this respect, the decision in *Bowden* (discussed above) provides an interesting contrast with the 'deterrence

---

37   [2000] 2 All ER 425, p 437.
38   [1999] 2 Cr App R(S) 154, p 156, *per* Mitchell J.

argument' propounded in *Caley*. Although the Court of Appeal upheld Bowden's convictions, all of the original sentences (four months' imprisonment concurrent for each of the s 1 offences) were quashed. A conditional discharge for 12 months in respect of each count was imposed. The Court emphasised a number of specific factors in reaching that decision:

> There was no evidence of risk to the public. Although he was a schoolteacher there was a total absence of any evidence or history of inappropriate behaviour towards children. There was no breach of trust. Mr Bowden's position in the chain of production of indecent material was as low as could be consistent with the commission of the offences. There was no further dissemination of the material. Above all he had no previous convictions of any sort.[39]

Although Bowden may be taken as possessing a number of general mitigating factors, it is arguable that the courts will attach considerable significance to the presence, or otherwise, of exploitation and gain. Bowden's indecent images were constantly referred to as being for 'his own use'. Caley, by contrast, was acting with a view to wider distribution and gain. It seems that deterrence will be a weightier consideration in the latter circumstances.

4.2 Possession of an indecent photograph of a child

The 1978 Act did not proscribe the mere possession *per se* of an indecent photograph of a child. Even the offence in para (c), which came closest to criminalising possession, required the additional element that the defendant had possession of photographs *with a view to their being distributed*, etc.

It was not until 1988 that the mere fact of possession alone was criminalised. Section 160(1) of the Criminal Justice Act 1988 (again, as amended by the 1994 Act) provides:

> It is an offence for a person to have any indecent photograph or pseudo-photograph of a child in his possession.

As the majority of the criteria needed to establish liability under s 160(1) are common to the offences in s 1(1) of the 1978 Act, it is important to concentrate upon the distinctive elements. By far the most significant element is that of 'possession', which connotes both physical and mental requirements. There is little direct authority on the meaning of possession within s 1(1), but the notion of 'possession' is a common one in criminal law, and a number of useful analogies exist.

4.2.1 'Physical' possession

In order to be in physical possession of the indecent photograph, it must be proven that the defendant had some degree of control over it. In *Bellerby v*

---

39 [2000] 2 WLR 1083, p 1090, *per* Otton LJ.

Carle ([1983] 2 AC 101), the House of Lords considered the meaning of possession within the context of s 16(1) of the Weights and Measures Act 1963. Lord Brandon, whilst stating that he was not prepared to set down an exhaustive definition of the phrase 'has in his possession', did nevertheless state that:

> A person cannot 'have in his possession' weighing or measuring equipment ... unless he has at least some degree of control over it.[40]

It is possible to envisage a situation arising whereby a defendant was in possession lawfully of indecent photographs, but that possession subsequently became unlawful. In the old case of *Burns v Nowell* ((1880) 5 QBD 444), the court had to consider the meaning of the word 'carrying' within s 3 of the Kidnapping Act 1872:

> It may ... be suggested that the carrying, though not unlawful in its commencement, became so ... But before a continuous act or proceeding, not originally unlawful, can be treated as unlawful ... a reasonable time must be allowed for its discontinuance.[41]

Thus, if a man were to find, in an envelope in the street, a number of indecent photographs of children, and he picked them up in order to take them to the police, he would at that precise time appear to be in lawful possession of them. But if, subsequently, he decided to keep the photographs for two days in order to show them to his friends, then, notwithstanding that he intended genuinely to hand them to the police in 48 hours, he would be in unlawful possession by failing to discontinue the original lawful possession.

4.2.2   'Mental' possession

It must be established that the defendant knew that he had the photographs in his possession. For these purposes, where the photographs are in a container of some description, the defendant knew he was in control of the container, and knew that something (albeit not necessarily indecent photographs) was in the container, then he will be deemed to have the requisite knowledge. This seemingly harsh rule may be justified on the basis that, without it, the very objective of the legislation would be defeated.

Of course, the above rule does not negate the requirement imposed upon the prosecution of proving that the defendant knew he was in possession of something. But, once initial possession with knowledge is established, the defendant cannot evade liability by saying that he had forgotten about the items. In *Martindale* ([1986] 1 WLR 1042), the defendant admitted that he had been given a small quantity of cannabis two years previously, but claimed that he had forgotten about it subsequently. This argument was rejected forcibly by Lord Lane CJ:

---

40 [1983] 2 AC 101, p 108.

41 (1880) 5 QBD 444, p 454, *per* Baggallay LJ.

> It is true that a man does not necessarily possess every article which he may have in his pocket. If for example some evil-minded person secretly slips a portion of cannabis resin into the pocket of another without the other's knowledge, the other is not in law in possession of the cannabis ...

> But ... here the appellant himself put the cannabis in his wallet knowing what it was and put the wallet into his pocket. In our judgment ... he remained in possession, even though his memory of the presence of the drug had faded or disappeared altogether. Possession does not depend upon the alleged possessor's powers of memory.[42]

It was emphasised by the Divisional Court in *Atkins*, above, that possession requires a mental element before liability can be established:

> [K]nowledge is an essential element in the offence of possession under s 160 ... so that an accused cannot be convicted where, as here, he cannot be shown to be aware of the existence of a cache of photographs in the first place.[43]

It is arguable that Atkins did not have 'knowledge of possession', because he was unaware of the cache itself. However, if he had been aware of the cache but was arguing that he did not know it contained any photographs, the position may have been indistinguishable from the situation where a person who knows he has a container is deemed to have knowledge of its contents.

4.2.3 Defences to s 160 'possession'

In addition to arguing lack of physical or mental possession, a defendant charged under s 160 may also seek to rely on a related, but specific, statutory defence.

Section 160(2) of the 1988 Act, as amended, provides:

> Where a person is charged with an offence under sub-s (1) above, it shall be a defence for him to prove: (a) that he had a legitimate reason for having the photograph or pseudo-photograph in his possession; or (b) that he had not himself seen the photograph or pseudo-photograph and did not know, nor had any cause to suspect, it to be indecent; or (c) that the photograph or pseudo-photograph was sent to him without any prior request made by him or on his behalf and that he did not keep it for an unreasonable time.

Dr Atkins, above, had sought also to rely on the 'legitimate reason' defence contained specifically in s 160(2)(a). The magistrates had held that the defence was not available, as it was limited to specific persons – anti-pornography campaigners, defined medical researchers and persons in the criminal justice system – but not to those researching into child pornography, even if they were 'honest and straightforward'. The Divisional Court accepted the finding of the magistrates that Dr Atkins had not been conducting honest and straightforward research, but also gave useful guidance on the potential scope of the defence. The Court's *dictum* is potentially wider than the view expressed by the magistrates:

---

42 [1986] 1 WLR 1042, p 1044. See, also, *Buswell* [1972] 1 WLR 64, p 67, *per* Phillimore LJ.
43 [2000] 2 All ER 425, p 437, *per* Simon Brown LJ.

The question of what constitutes 'a legitimate reason'... is a pure question of fact (for the magistrate or jury) in each case. The central question where the defence is legitimate research will be whether the defendant is essentially a person of unhealthy interests in possession of indecent photographs in the pretence of undertaking research, or by contrast a genuine researcher with no alternative but to have this sort of unpleasant material in his possession. In other cases there will be other categories of 'legitimate reason' advanced. They will each have to be considered on their own facts. Courts are plainly entitled to bring a measure of scepticism to bear on such an inquiry: they should not too readily conclude that the defence has been made out.[44]

5   CONTROLLING SEX OFFENDERS: THE SEX OFFENDERS ACT 1997 AND THE CRIME AND DISORDER ACT 1998

The Sex Offenders Act 1997 received Royal Assent on 21 March 1997 and came into force on 1 September 1997.[45] The Act is relatively short (containing only 10 sections and two schedules) and has two main objectives: to extend jurisdiction beyond the UK in respect of certain sexual offences, and, centrally, to impose a notification requirement upon persons who have committed certain sexual offences.

The Bill went through Parliament with, if not undue haste, a certain degree of alacrity. It was, perhaps understandably, driven by a desire for some action to be seen to be taken in respect of increasing alarms about activities of paedophiles and a perception amongst many people (both in the popular press and in local communities) that convicted sex offenders were being released back into the community with few, if any, safeguards for the residents concerned. These concerns were frequently fuelled by disclosures that some sex offences were being committed by men only recently released from sentences relating to previous offences, in circumstances where the local residents were unaware of their backgrounds.

5.1   Notification requirements for sex offenders

Section 1 of the 1997 Act imposes a notification requirement upon a person who commits certain sexual offences. The requirement applies equally to persons who have been convicted, or found not guilty by reason of insanity or to be under a disability, or who have been cautioned (where the offence is admitted at the time of the caution). The Act applies to three categories of person: those convicted, etc, after the commencement of the Act (s 1(1)); those already convicted, but not yet dealt with in respect of the offence (s 1(2)); and

---

44   [2000] 2 All ER 425, pp 432–33.

45   Sex Offenders Act 1997 (Commencement) Order (SI 1997/1920 (C 78)).

those who, at commencement, are serving a sentence of imprisonment, are subject to supervision or are detained in hospital, in respect of a relevant offence (s 1(3)).

Under s 2, any person subject to the notification requirements must inform the police, within a specified period, of, *inter alia*, his name (or names if more than one is used, as is frequently so in the case of many paedophiles), his address, and any subsequent changes of name(s) or address.

The Act sets down the minimum periods for which a person must register. These periods relate to the type and length of sentence imposed. Where a person has received a caution or non-custodial sentence, the period of registration is for a minimum of five years. Where a custodial sentence of less than six months has been imposed, the minimum registration period is seven years. Where a custodial sentence is between six and 30 months, the minimum registration period is 10 years. Finally, where the custodial sentence is more than 30 months, then registration is for an 'indefinite period'. Initial authority suggests that, even where an error is made in identifying the correct registration period, a successful appeal will not automatically follow. In *Rawlinson* ((1999) *The Times*, 27 October), the defendant was convicted of two offences of indecent assault on a male and two offences of gross indecency with a child. He was sentenced to two years' imprisonment, and the trial judge, after being wrongly advised of the notification periods, then inaccurately informed him that he should register for five years. On appeal against sentence, the Court of Appeal dismissed the appeal, holding that the court was not under a legal duty to inform a defendant as to the length of time he was required to be registered under the Act. The correct period on the facts was identified as 10 years (the defendant having received a custodial sentence of between six and 30 months). In addition, the Court of Appeal suggested that it would be appropriate for Rawlinson to be informed of the correct period either by the relevant prison authorities or by his legal advisers.

Section 3(1) creates a summary offence where any person: (a) fails to provide, without reasonable excuse, the details required within the terms of the notification requirements; or (b) where he notifies to the police any information pursuant to the notification requirement which he knows to be false.

Schedule 1 to the Act provides a list of the sexual offences to which the notification requirements apply. The offences include (subject to several minor exceptions based upon the ages of the parties – see para 1(2) to Sched 1): rape; unlawful sexual intercourse contrary to ss 5 and 6 of the 1956 Act; indecent assault on males and females; an offence of indecency with or towards a child under s 1(1) of the 1960 Act; and indecent photographs offences under s 1(1) of the 1978 Act. It is clear, therefore, that, although the notification requirement is not limited to persons who have committed offences against the young,[46] most of the major sexual offences against the young are included, and it is likely that the 'register' will come to be viewed as a paedophile register.

It is, as yet, far too early to evaluate the potential operation and effectiveness of the register, but what is clear is that strong differences of opinion exist as to whether such a scheme is the most efficient method of dealing with the issue of sex offenders generally and paedophiles in particular. These differences have been exacerbated by Home Office guidelines issued on 11 August 1997, in respect of the operation of the registration scheme. Under the guidelines, there should exist a 'general policy of confidentiality' and the police will only disclose personal information about sex offenders in exceptional circumstances where disclosure is 'justified on the basis of the likelihood of the harm which non-disclosure might otherwise cause'. There is no doubt that fears of vigilante violence are partly responsible for the authorities' reluctance to make disclosure of information more widespread. In a number of well documented cases, several people (convicted paedophiles and innocent victims of mistaken identity) have been the victims of vigilante attacks by concerned local residents.[47] Such incidents must give rise to grave concerns about both public order and individuals' civil liberties. Perhaps even more significantly, the creation of a register (with or without widespread disclosure of information) and the fears of a vigilante response may result in many sex offenders becoming even more secretive in their movements. Paradoxically, therefore, at a time when supervision and rehabilitation are seen by many expert psychiatrists and psychologists as effective methods of treating some sex offenders, those same offenders may be tempted to avoid such treatment out of fear of the consequences of publicity. Furthermore, one specific criticism of the Act is that the creation of the offence in s 3, relating to non-disclosure of the relevant details or the provision of false information, will have very little practical impact in the majority of cases: the possibility of being convicted of a summary offence may prove to have little influence upon a convicted sex offender who gives thought to the potential consequences of correct registration.

In addition, the Act does not apply retrospectively. Initial government predictions therefore estimated that only about 6,000–7,000 names would be placed on to the register at the commencement of its operation, although it was further estimated that approximately 3,500 names a year will be added thereafter. According to Home Office statistics, there are approximately 110,000 convicted paedophiles in England and Wales, but, unless they commit, and are convicted of, further offences in the future, the vast majority

---

46 Sub-paragraph 1(1)(a)(i) to Sched 1, eg, refers to the offence of rape, which is not subsequently delimited by any age criterion.

47 See, eg, (1997) *The Daily Telegraph*, 12 August, p 2.

of them will not appear on the register. However, even these initial estimates appeared to be optimistic. The National Association of Probation Officers (NAPO) identified approximately 2,200 offenders who should be on the list but, at the deadline for registration (midnight on 14 September 1997), only about 700–800 had registered. The reasons for the apparently low registration figure are not difficult to find, as Harry Fletcher, assistant general secretary of NAPO, has noted:

> This is a group of people who are devious, difficult and dangerous and spend their lives avoiding the police. So it is not surprising that some have not registered. At most, 2–3% of them will have absconded. Some will be keeping a low profile and hoping it goes away. Others will be frightened of coming forward because they don't know what will happen to the information they are required to give.[48]

The latest figures (March 2000) show that a total of 12,076 persons were required to have registered under the Act. In fact, by March, 11,773 persons had registered, leaving a shortfall of 303.[49]

In respect of non-registering offenders who are regarded as the most serious, the police may exercise their right to publish the names of those offenders on the Internet. Whilst this might be an understandable attempt to trace the most dangerous offenders, it could give rise to further fears about vigilantism and certainly may have the effect of driving such offenders even further underground.

Whilst low numbers of registrations from those persons who should have registered may in itself be a problem, there was perceived also to be an issue of concern in relation to the non-retrospective operation of the Act. A loophole was identified where, for example, a sex offender had committed an offence several years ago, had served a custodial sentence and had been released prior to the enactment of the Act. Concerns were often exacerbated where the offender returned to local communities who saw themselves as having no adequate safeguards against potential re-offending. This loophole was addressed by Parliament via the introduction of Sex Offender Orders under s 2 of the Crime and Disorder Act 1998 (see below).

Notwithstanding these concerns and potential difficulties, the philosophy behind Pt I of the 1997 Act is clear and laudable, namely to provide a mechanism whereby the authorities are in a better position to supervise sex offenders and thus ultimately to protect the public. The impetus behind the Act may have been a wave of public concern, but, nevertheless, it should provide the police, and any other persons to whom, exceptionally, information is disclosed, with at least some data which can be used in the control and monitoring of sex offenders.

---

48 (1997) *The Daily Telegraph*, 15 September, p 2.
49 Home Office figures provided to the authors in September 2000.

5.2 Sexual offences committed outside the UK

Part II of the 1997 Act makes provision for the extension of jurisdiction in respect of certain sexual offences committed outside the UK. Section 7 provides:

(1) Subject to sub-s (2), any act done by a person in a country or territory outside the United Kingdom which–

    (a) constituted an offence under the law in force in that country or territory; and

    (b) would constitute a sexual offence to which this section applies if it had been done in England and Wales, or in Northern Ireland,

shall constitute that sexual offence under the law of that part of the United Kingdom.

(2) No proceedings shall by virtue of this section be brought against any person unless he was at the commencement of this section, or has subsequently become, a British citizen or resident in the United Kingdom.

(3) An act punishable under the law in force in any country or territory constitutes an offence under that law for the purposes of this section, however it is described in that law.

Schedule 2 to the 1997 Act lists nine sexual offences which apply in relation to s 7. This Schedule provides a less comprehensive list of offences than Sched 1 (in relation to s 1), as s 7 is clearly aimed at extending jurisdiction in respect of child victims. This is made clear from the wording of the Schedule itself. In sub-para (1)(a), two offences (ss 5 and 6 of the Sexual Offences Act 1956) are already delimited by an age criterion, as are the offences in paras (b) and (c), namely offences under s 1 of the Indecency with Children Act 1960 and s 1 of the Protection of Children Act 1978 respectively. But the remaining offences in sub-para (1)(a) are then expressly stated to 'not apply where the victim of the offence was 16 or over at the time of the offence'.

The purpose of s 7, despite its necessarily complex wording, is to allow English courts to take proceedings against a British citizen or resident who does an act abroad, where that act constituted an offence abroad, and that same act would constitute a sexual offence against a young person as listed in Sched 2.

5.3 Sex Offender Orders

A loophole was identified, above, whereby some sex offenders were not required to register under the 1997 Act because, for example, their offence(s) and period(s) in custody had occurred prior to the registration requirements becoming operative. This was so even if there existed a real and reasonable risk of that person re-offending in the near future. As a result, Parliament sought to fill that gap by the creation of Sex Offender Orders. Under s 2 of the Crime and Disorder Act 1998, a chief officer of police may apply to the magistrates' court for a Sex Offender Order to be made. The two conditions specified in s 2(1) are: '(a) that the person is a sex offender; and (b) that the person has acted ... in such a way as to give reasonable cause to believe that an order ... is necessary to protect the public from serious harm from him ...'

If those two conditions are fulfilled, the magistrates' court may make an order which 'prohibits the defendant from doing anything described in the order' (s 2(3)). The potential scope of such an order is very wide. It appears to be limited only by the condition stipulated in sub-s (4): 'The prohibitions that may be imposed by a sex offender order are those necessary for the purpose of protecting the public from serious harm from the defendant.' Consequently, an order cannot be made in order to protect the defendant himself from, say, sections of the community (even if he should want this), or to act as a deterrent (whether as a deterrent specifically to the defendant or, more generally, to other persons in similar circumstances). Rather, the magistrates must believe not only that the order is necessary to protect the public, but also that they need to be protected from '*serious* harm' from the defendant. It follows that an order should not be imposed merely because the court feels that the defendant is likely to re-offend, unless it is believed that the risk of 'serious harm' can be proven. The types of conditions which may be expected to be imposed under a Sex Offender Order include: night-time curfews; restrictions on movements (such as not going within specified distances of schools or playgrounds); and restrictions on behaviour (such as talking to or approaching children).

The consequences of a Sex Offender Order being imposed are twofold. First, under sub-s (8), a triable-either-way offence is committed if 'without reasonable excuse a person does anything which he is prohibited from doing by a sex offender order'. Secondly, under sub-s (5), the Order shall be effective for the period stated therein, but it shall be for at least five years. Furthermore, whilst it is in force, the defendant is subject to the notification requirements of the 1997 Act. Thus, a person who was not originally within the scope of the registration requirements may be brought within those requirements by the imposition of a Sex Offender Order.

The Orders may be seen as controversial, as they have the potential for restricting individual liberty in circumstances where the person concerned has committed no criminal offence on the occasion in question. The courts will need to be very careful to be seen to balance the public's right to be protected (in the sense of preventing serious harm before it has occurred), against the individual's right to not have severe restrictions imposed upon his liberty of movement and behaviour.

The need for a balance to be struck is well illustrated by the decision of the magistrates' court in *Gordon* ((1998) unreported).[50] The Chief Constable of Greater Manchester Police had sought a Sex Offender Order against Gordon, who had been released after serving a custodial sentence for several rapes in Manchester's student bedsit land. After release, Gordon had been seen by several police officers near university premises and looking into windows of student accommodation late at night. In addition, he was found to be in possession of audiotapes containing sexually explicit material. However, no specific substantive or inchoate offences had been committed. The magistrates granted the Order, which contained the following conditions: a night-time curfew; a requirement to stay away from a specified area of Manchester; and a ban on entering the grounds and premises of Manchester's three universities. In addition, once the Order was imposed, Gordon became subject to the registration requirements of the 1997 Act, and a registration period of seven years was imposed on the facts.

5.4   Disclosure

Under both the 1997 Act (registration requirement) and the 1998 Act (imposition of the Sex Offender Order), there exists a general policy of confidentiality. As noted above, the police will only disclose personal information of which they are aware about sex offenders in 'exceptional circumstances'.

The issue of disclosure was discussed in detail by the Court of Appeal in *R v Chief Constable of North Wales ex p AB and CD* ([1998] 3 All ER 310). AB and CD had been released from prison following completion of their sentences for serious sexual offences committed against children. Northumbria Police had sent a report to North Wales Police (NWP), detailing the considerable risk which AB and CD posed to children and vulnerable adults. NWP decided it was in the public interest to disclose the identities of AB and CD, and to pass on other information, to the owners of a caravan site where they were staying. AB and CD sought judicial review of NWP's decision to disclose that information. In dismissing the application for judicial review, Lord Woolf MR on behalf of the Court of Appeal recognised the difficult and competing interests which the courts are required to balance:

> In determining what should be done the overriding priority must remain to protect the public, particularly children and other vulnerable people ... The information may be of a nature which means it would be undesirable for it to be disclosed because of its confidentiality or sensitivity or on the grounds of public interest immunity ... Each case must be judged on its own facts. However, in doing this, it must be remembered that the decision to which the police have come as to whether or not to disclose the identity of paedophiles to

---

50   See (1998) *The Daily Telegraph*, 24 December, p 7.

members of the public, is a highly sensitive one. Disclosure should only be made where there is a pressing need for that disclosure.[51]

In concluding that there was a 'pressing need' for disclosure on the present facts, Lord Woolf was keen to stress that the individual circumstances of each case would be of significance. In particular, it was felt that the police had acted fairly in the light of the imminence of the Easter holidays (and thus the likely increase in numbers of children at the site) and their attempts to find suitable alternative accommodation.

The question as to whether there should be a right of wider disclosure, for example, to local communities where paedophiles may be living, was propelled into the public arena by the 'name and shame' campaign conducted by the *News of the World* newspaper following the murder of schoolgirl Sarah Payne in July 2000. In its campaign, the names and addresses of a large number of paedophiles and alleged paedophiles were published. As a result, there were widespread civil disturbances, including attacks on the homes of paedophiles. In some instances, attacks took place on persons whose identities had been mistaken. Notwithstanding the public's understandable concerns in such matters, it is clear that the issue of disclosure must be dealt with sensitively and objectively. The widespread disorders, reported at length in the media throughout the summer of 2000, give rise to a number of concerns. First, many paedophiles may feel compelled to go underground. This removes them from the control of the Probation Services and makes it correspondingly more difficult to pursue effective treatment programmes. Secondly, the lack of effective control may, paradoxically, lead to a higher rate of re-offending. Thirdly, such campaigns can result in vigilantism. Vigilantism can result, and has, in fact, resulted, in innocent persons being the victims of mistaken identity, either because they physically resemble the photograph of a named paedophile, or even because they happen to share the name of a paedophile. Fourthly, there may be serious consequences for the innocent families of paedophiles subjected to such direct action. Finally, serious public disorder in itself has negative effects on the local community.

6 REFORM

The offences discussed in this chapter, and partly in the preceding chapter, that currently may be identified as seeking to offer protection to the young, possess little coherence or consistency. Protection is afforded at different ages, and some offences distinguish between the genders of the children. Reforms in this area, if implemented, would result in significant changes.

---

51 [1998] 3 All ER 310, p 320.

6.1 Sexual Offences (Amendment) Bill 2000

Clauses 3 and 4 of the 2000 Bill, as noted above in both Chapters 1 and 2, would create a new offence of abuse of position of trust. The clauses were introduced as a safeguard to allay the fears of those who believed that reducing the age of consent to 16 would increase the vulnerability of teenagers aged 16 and 17, especially from older 'predatory' persons.

Clause 3 states:

(1) Subject to sub-ss (2) and (3) below, it shall be an offence for a person aged 18 or over:

(a) to have sexual intercourse (whether vaginal or anal) with a person under that age; or

(b) to engage in any other sexual activity with or directed towards such a person,

if (in either case) he is in a position of trust in relation to that person.

Under sub-s (2), there will be no offence by the defendant ('A') in respect of the younger person ('B') in any of the following circumstances: (a) if A did not know, and could not reasonably have been expected to know, that B was under 18; (b) if A did not know, and could not reasonably have been expected to know, that B was a person in relation to whom he was in a position of trust; or (c) he was lawfully married to B.

The offence will not operate retrospectively. Sub-section (3) provides that A will commit no offence if, immediately before the commencement of this Act, A was in a position of trust in relation to B and a sexual relationship existed between them.

The offence will be committed in respect of sexual intercourse or any other sexual activity. Whether conduct amounts to sexual activity depends upon whether a reasonable person would in the circumstances regard it as sexual. The Explanatory Notes to the Sexual Offences (Amendment) Bill give the following useful example of how the determination of 'sexual activity' may be approached:

> So for instance, a normal gynaecological examination by a doctor is an activity which it is envisaged a reasonable person would not regard as 'sexual activity'. Behaviour which a reasonable person would only regard as sexual activity if he was aware of the parties' intentions, motives or feelings is specifically excluded. Thus, behaviour which is non-sexual in nature, for example, a sports trainer tackling a pupil on a rugby pitch, may not be challenged because of alleged hidden motives.[52]

The essence of the new offence is that the person aged 18 or over (A) must be in a 'position of trust' to the younger person (B). This criterion will be met if

---

52 House of Commons Explanatory Notes, 28 January 2000, para 15.

any one of four conditions (specified fully in cl 4) is established, namely where:

(a) the younger person (B) is detained in an institution pursuant to a court order or enactment, and the older person 'looks after' persons under 18, and B is so detained in that institution;

(b) the younger person (B) is resident in and provided with accommodation (or maintenance and accommodation) by a local authority or a voluntary organisation in a home or other place, and the older person (A) looks after persons under 18, and B is so resident in that place;

(c) the younger person (B) is accommodated and cared for in a hospital, a residential care home, nursing home, mental nursing home or private hospital, a community home, voluntary home, children's home, or residential establishment or a home provided under s 82 of the Children Act 1989. Again, this criterion is subject to the older person (A) looking after persons under 18 in that institution, and that B is accommodated and cared for in that institution;

(d) the younger person (B) is in full time education in an educational institution and the older person (A) looks after persons under 18 who are receiving full time education at an educational institution, and that B is receiving such education at that institution.

All of the above conditions require A to 'look after' persons under the age of 18. This is explained in cl 4(7) as meaning:

> A person looks after persons under 18 for the purposes of this section if he is regularly involved in caring for, training, supervising or being in sole charge of such persons.

It remains too early to say whether these detailed provisions will give the protection to young persons which the clause is intended to provide. However, it is important to note that each of the criteria possess some element of attendance at, or residence or accommodation in, an institution. In addition, all the criteria require the older person to be 'regularly' involved in caring etc. These conditions would seem to exclude a number of persons from the scope of the offence. Scout masters and staff in holiday camps, for example, would seem to be excluded, as would youth and community workers involved in daytime activities with no provision of accommodation. The conditions in para (d), in particular, may give rise to a number of loopholes. Many 16 and 17 year olds are in part time education, which excludes them from the protection of the clause. Similarly, any child who is receiving part time private tuition (for example, ballet or horseriding lessons) is outside the definition: it is neither full time nor in an educational establishment. The requirement of providing care 'regularly' may cause problems in respect of those older persons involved in any of the above activities only on an irregular basis.

If such loopholes were to appear, it should be noted that cl 4(1) empowers the Secretary of State by statutory instrument to add to the list of those circumstances amounting to positions of trust.

There exists a further potential anomaly due to the precise wording of cl 3(1) and its relationship with the 'position of trust' criterion in cl 4. The offence itself will be committed by a person aged 18 or over in respect of a person under that age, but only if he 'is in a position of trust *in relation to that person'*. This seems to require that the position of trust operates as a direct relationship between A and B. However, the four conditions in cl 4 defining 'position of trust' may prove to be ambiguous. In each case, B needs only to be resident or accommodated, etc, in the institution, etc, provided A looks after other persons in the institution in which B is resident, etc. Let it be supposed that A is a school teacher having a sexual relationship with B, a pupil aged 17, receiving full time education at the educational institution where A is employed. There would appear to be an offence by A, even though he may have no responsibility for looking after B herself, provided he 'looks after' other persons under 18. The offence is committed because A is in a position of trust: he meets the combined criteria of cll 4(5) and 4(7), namely by looking after (that is, regularly caring for, etc) persons under 18 at an educational institution where B receives such education. This harsh outcome seems to result from the wording of the proposed offence, whereby the concept of 'position of trust' appears to relate to A's *position*, rather than his direct relationship with B.

6.2   *Setting the Boundaries*

Those recommendations in *Setting the Boundaries* which relate to offences against the young are diverse and wide ranging. The following, most important, proposals should not be read in isolation, but rather as part of an overall package of reforms.

First, as noted in Chapter 2, the Review proposes (at para 3.5.7) that, as a matter of public policy, the age of legal consent should remain at 16. The Review's approach to reforming the law in the area of sexual offences against children was centred upon the overwhelming desire to remove current anomalies and to create gender neutral offences, whilst continuing to set standards of behaviour which provide fair and appropriate protection to children.

Secondly, a simple and effective offence should be created which would cover a wide range of sexual behaviour committed by adults with children. This would be in addition to the proposed serious sexual offences where the prosecution are required to prove lack of consent: the offences of rape, sexual assault by penetration and sexual assault would all be available against defendants in respect of the child-victim. Thus, Recommendation 19 states:

There should be an offence of adult (over 18) sexual abuse of a child (under 16). The offence would cover all sexual behaviour that was wrong *because* it involved a child; it would complement other serious non-consensual offences such as rape, sexual assault by penetration and sexual assault.

This offence would criminalise specifically only the adult. The child, however much she or he may have appeared to have consented to or encouraged the act in question, would not face criminal liability.

Thirdly, having proposed the above offence of adult sexual abuse, the Review wished to clarify the issue of consent. In a sensible move towards rationalisation, the review proposes (in Recommendation 18) that the age of 13 should be set, as the age below which a child cannot consent in law. It should be emphasised that this age applies only to the proposed specific offences against children. It is not intended, for example, to create a crime of statutory rape. In the consent-based offences (such as rape or sexual assault by penetration), it will remain incumbent upon the prosecution to prove absence of consent, irrespective of the age of the victim.

Finally, the Review considered the position where 'non-adults' are concerned, that is where one of the parties is under the age of consent and one is aged 16 or 17, as well as the situation where both parties are under the age of consent. The former scenario is covered by Recommendation 27, which states:

There should be an offence of sexual activity between minors to replace the existing offences of unlawful sexual intercourse, buggery, indecency with children and sexual activity prohibited for children. It should apply to children under the age 18 with those under the age of consent.

This proposal amounts to something of a compromise. It is a 'mirror' to the more serious adult sexual abuse offence (above), which continues to give protection to those under the age of consent, whilst providing a two year gap (for those aged 16 and 17) before the more serious offence becomes applicable.

As far as consenting acts between parties who are both under 16 are concerned, the Review proposes (in Recommendation 28) that 'further consideration should be given to appropriate, non-criminal, interventions for young people under 16 engaged in mutually-agreed under-age sex who are not now, and should not in future, normally be subject to prosecution'. The clear implication in this proposal is that there is no desire to prohibit, in law, the prosecution of persons under the age of 16. That would, in effect, reduce the age of consent below 16 in some circumstances. Instead, the law should continue to develop a policy of discretion, based on clear prosecution guidelines, recognising features such as imbalance of power, coercion and mental competence.

CHAPTER 6

INDECENT ASSAULT

1   INTRODUCTION

The origins of the modern law of indecent assault can be traced back to the middle of the 19th century, when the Offences Against the Person Act 1861 created an offence of indecent assault on a woman and a second offence of indecent assault on a man. These two offences are contained now in ss 14 and 15 respectively of the Sexual Offences Act 1956, which provide as follows:

> 14(1)   It is an offence, subject to the exception mentioned in sub-s (3) of this section, for a person to make an indecent assault on a woman.

> 15(1)   It is an offence for a person to make an indecent assault on a man.

These offences are best regarded as forms of 'aggravated assault', in that an assault (or battery) *per se* is a precondition for an indecent assault. Then, in addition, the aggravating feature of 'indecency' is required to be proven.

2   *ACTUS REUS*

2.1   Assault or battery

Despite the use of the phrase 'indecent assault' in both ss 14 and 15, it is clear that the offences cover actions which amount to either an assault or battery. In effect, therefore, the sections create two offences each, that is, indecent assault and indecent battery. This position was confirmed by both the Court of Appeal and the House of Lords in the leading decision in *Court* ([1988] 2 All ER 221). On this particular point, it was stated by Ralph Gibson LJ in the Court of Appeal:

> The offence of indecent assault included both a battery, or touching, and psychic assault without touching. If there was touching, it was not necessary to prove that the victim was aware of the assault or of the circumstances of indecency. If there was no touching, then to constitute an indecent assault, the victim must be shown to have been aware of the assault and of the circumstances of indecency.[1]

---

1   [1987] 1 All ER 120, p 122. See, also, Lord Ackner in the House of Lords: [1988] 2 All ER 221, p 229.

2.1.1   Battery

Most indecent assaults, in fact, will consist of a 'battery', whereby D must actually touch the victim. In such a situation, there is no requirement that the victim needs to be aware either of the indecency of the acts or circumstances, or indeed of the touching (that is, battery) itself. It is just as much an indecent battery to touch indecently a person who is asleep, unconscious or insensible, as it is to touch a sentient person. Furthermore, unlike the law of battery *per se*, there appears to be no application of the *de minimis* rule in indecent assault. This, it is submitted, is right in principle. It would be contrary to public policy and the rights of all victims, especially female victims, for the law to say that some indecent assaults were 'too trivial' to be the subject of legal control. This point was stated succinctly by Laws J in *Ananthanarayanan* ((1994) 98 Cr App R 1):

> His [defence counsel's] argument was that the evidence of indecent touching by the appellant disclosed such trivial acts as not, in law, to amount to indecent assault at all ... [H]e submitted that the jury should have been given a direction that if they felt that any particular incident was *'de minimis'* that would not amount to indecent assault.

> In our judgment that would have been a pernicious approach for the judge to take. It would amount to saying that, so far as the law is concerned, women have to put up with minor indecent assaults. Of course, there may be cases where the circumstances of an alleged indecent assault are such that a real question arises whether the public interest requires prosecution, but in principle there should be no doubt that under the modern law any deliberate and non-consensual touching accompanied by circumstances of indecency constitutes the criminal offence of indecent assault. There is no room in this area of the law for any *'de minimis'* exception.[2]

2.1.2   Assault

As the *actus reus* of assault involves the apprehension, by the victim, of immediate unlawful personal violence, it follows that this is a condition of indecent assault. In addition, and unlike indecent battery, the victim must also be aware of the act or circumstance of indecency.

In *Rolfe* ((1952) 36 Cr App R 4), the defendant had exposed himself and moved towards the victim, an adult woman, making indecent suggestions and inviting her to touch his penis. In fact, the woman did not touch the defendant, but it was nevertheless held, rightly, that the defendant had committed an indecent assault, as his act had put the victim in the requisite fear.

Similarly in *Beal v Kelly* ([1951] 2 All ER 763), the Divisional Court upheld the defendant's conviction after he had invited the victim, a boy of 14, to touch his exposed penis and had then, when the boy refused, grabbed his arm and

---

2   (1994) 98 Cr App R 1, p 5.

dragged him towards himself. It was clear that, whilst the touching itself was not indecent, there was a real likelihood of indecent contact and that was apprehended by the victim.

The reasoning in these cases was taken a step further in the recent decision in *Sargeant* ([1997] Crim LR 50). There, the defendant had grabbed the victim, a youth aged 16, had wielded a stick in a threatening manner, and had forced the youth to masturbate into a condom. The trial judge rejected the defence submission that, for indecent assault where there was no actual indecent touching, then at least the threat had to be of indecent touching, and the defendant was convicted of indecent assault under s 15 of the Sexual Offences Act 1956. The appeal was dismissed by the Court of Appeal, where it was held that there clearly was an assault and, by compelling somebody to masturbate in a public place, there were circumstances accompanying that assault which were capable of being considered by right-minded persons as indecent. The decision confirms that, for indecent assault, there does not have to be indecent touching (which has long been recognised as the law), but also that there does not even have to be the threat of indecent touching. Instead, it suffices to prove that there exists the coincidence of an assault and the necessary accompanying circumstances of indecency.

2.2 Indecency

'Indecency' is that extra aggravating factor which turns assault or battery into an indecent assault. The question whether an assault is indecent is one of fact to be determined by the jury. In *Court* (above) – the leading decision on indecent assault – the House of Lords gave detailed guidance on how the question of indecency should be left to the jury for their consideration. An awareness of the circumstances of *Court* will assist an understanding of the rather complex legal position. The defendant, a shop assistant, grabbed a young girl aged 12, threw her across his knee and spanked her a number of times on her bottom through her shorts. The defendant had asked the girl on a previous occasion whether she had ever been spanked. When asked by the police why he had done this, he replied: 'Don't know – buttock fetish.' The trial judge directed the jury that 'indecent' in this context meant 'overtly sexual'. Lord Ackner, in the House of Lords, accepted that this was a 'convenient shorthand expression, since most, but not necessarily all, indecent assaults will be clearly of a sexual nature'.[3] However, he continued by suggesting that matters might be clarified for the jury if they were to be asked whether they thought 'right-minded persons would consider the conduct indecent or not'.[4] It was in the context of this question that the House of Lords then went on to elaborate upon and distinguish between three possible scenarios within indecent assault.

3   [1988] 2 All ER 221, p 229.
4   *Ibid.*

2.2.1 Inherent indecency, or acts rendered indecent by accompanying circumstances

In deciding whether the assault committed by the defendant was indecent, it is important to identify two different situations, namely acts which are inherently indecent and those which are rendered so by the accompanying circumstances. An inherently indecent assault will occur where an objective observer would be sure that he was witnessing an act which was indecent. Some such instances will be straightforward, as where, for example, the defendant touches the victim's genitals without the consent of the victim. A further example of an inherently indecent act would be Lord Ackner's own illustration of a man who removed a woman's clothing, in public, against her will.[5] This is inherently indecent (and thus an indecent assault) regardless of the defendant's motive. He may have been acting for the purposes of sexual gratification, but need not have been. It will be equally indecent if his 'motive' was to embarrass, humiliate or to obtain a 'laugh' from his watching friends. This category of 'indecency' was confirmed in the subsequent case of *DPP v H* ([1992] COD 266), where the court held that the defendant was guilty of indecent assault where he had inserted his thumb into the anus of a young baby who had been crying. It was held, rightly, to be irrelevant that the defendant may have been acting for a reason other than sexual gratification, for instance, simply to hurt the child. Similarly, in *Leather* ((1993) 14 Cr App R(S) 736), in upholding a custodial sentence on the defendant (a female aged 17) after she had grabbed and squeezed the testicles of a police officer, Beldam LJ stated, *obiter*, that 'this attack was an indecent assault on this officer', even though her intention was to prevent the arrest by the officer of a third party. The sexual implications in this case are interesting. Admittedly, *Leather* was not charged with indecent assault and Lord Justice Beldam's statement was only a *dictum*. However, it must be doubted whether any useful purpose can be served by identifying this act as an indecent assault. If a young man had assaulted the officer in a like manner, it may be surmised that the case would have passed without comment. It seems that Leather's sex was a relevant factor in the court's recognition of this offence as a technical indecent assault.

Where an act is not inherently indecent, it may nonetheless be rendered so by the accompanying circumstances, provided the defendant was aware of those circumstances at the time of the assault. As an example, Lord Ackner cited with approval the decision in *Beal v Kelly*, above, the necessary element of indecency in that case clearly being established by the circumstances surrounding the assault.

2.2.1.1 Indecency and surrounding circumstances

A brief consideration of other authorities indicates that there are no closed categories in relation to when surrounding circumstances may operate to

---

5   [1988] 2 All ER 221, p 230.

render an assault indecent. Instead, and it is submitted that this is correct in principle bearing in mind the almost endless variety of human behaviour, each case deserves to be considered on its merits.

In *Leeson* ((1968) 52 Cr App R 185), the defendant had assaulted a girl by grabbing her and kissing her against her will. It was held that this should be rendered an indecent assault, due to his accompanying suggestions that she should submit also to sexual intercourse. Because, in *Leeson*, there existed also other accompanying circumstances, the case does not decide whether an unwanted kiss *per se* is to be regarded automatically as an indecent assault. It is submitted that, as a matter of common sense, one obvious criterion to be considered is whereabouts upon the victim's body the defendant places his unwanted kiss. Some kisses, for instance, those placed on or near the genitals or breasts of the victim, would seem clearly to fall within the 'inherently indecent' category. Other kisses would appear to depend on the precise factual circumstances of the case in question. Thus, in *Kallides* (unreported, but discussed at [1997] 1 WLR 1089), there was held to be an indecent assault where the defendant had stroked and kissed a small boy, even though there was no suggestion of genital contact. Similarly, there is Commonwealth authority which suggests that a kiss *per se* is capable of amounting to an indecent assault. In *Inglis v Police* ([1986] NZ Current Law 1152), the defendant kissed a girl, aged seven, on the lips. It was held that, although the girl had consented *de facto*, that was not a valid legal consent and the defendant was guilty of indecent assault.

The possibility that the acts or behaviour of the victim may be regarded as relevant to the 'surrounding circumstances' was considered expressly by the court in *Goss and Goss* ((1990) 90 Cr App R 400), where the defendants, Mr and Mrs Goss, were charged with, *inter alia*, indecent assault on a girl aged about 14 at the time of the incident. In relation to Mrs Goss, it was stated that whilst 'by itself a cuddle is not an indecent assault ... you must look at the circumstances, because the circumstances and the adult's intentions may again make it perfectly clear that what was happening was indecent'.[6] Thus, it was held to be correct for the trial judge to tell the jury to look at not merely Mrs Goss's act of cuddling the victim, but also at the wider circumstances, including what the girl herself was doing. The facts that the girl was sexually excited and that she was simultaneously touching the breasts and vagina of the defendant for the purpose of sexual gratification, were clearly capable of providing evidence of 'circumstances of indecency'.

However, it is not in all cases that surrounding circumstances will suffice to turn an assault into an indecent assault. In *Thomas* ((1985) 81 Cr App R 331), the defendant touched and rubbed the bottom of a girl's skirt. On a number of occasions some months before, he had asked the girl to kiss him. The Court of Appeal held that whilst there may have been an assault on the facts, it was

---

6   (1990) 90 Cr App R 400, p 407, *per* Saville J.

neither inherently indecent nor rendered so by the accompanying circumstances.

2.2.1.2   Indecent assault by words alone?

Until very recently, there was very little direct authority on the question whether words alone may constitute even assault *per se*, not to mention indecent assault, although the consensus of academic opinion was that words by themselves should be capable of constituting common assault.[7] Similarly, some judicial support, albeit *obiter*, could be found.[8] However, the particular point of assault by words appears now to have been settled by the courts, even though the case in question may have caused confusion in relation to a number of other issues. In *Ireland* ([1996] 1 WLR 650), the Court of Appeal approved the reasoning of Taylor J in *Barton v Armstrong*, and indeed extended it by holding that 'the making of a telephone call followed by silence, or a series of telephone calls, is capable of amounting to a relevant act for the purposes of s 47. The act consists in the making of the telephone call, and it does not matter whether words or silence ensue'.[9]

This was subsequently confirmed by the House of Lords, where it was held that nuisance telephone calls, whether involving words or silence, were capable of amounting to an assault. It does not follow that all such calls will, in future, be held to constitute assaults. This would appear to depend upon the precise facts of the case and the effect upon the complainant:

> The proposition that a gesture may amount to an assault, but that words can never suffice, is unrealistic and indefensible. There is no reason why something said should be incapable of causing an apprehension of immediate personal violence ...

> That brings me to the critical question whether a silent caller may be guilty of an assault. The answer ... seems to me to be 'Yes, depending on the facts'. It involves questions of fact within the province of the jury. ... He intends by his silence to cause fear and he is so understood. The victim is assailed by uncertainty about his intentions. Fear may dominate her emotions, and it may be the fear that the caller's arrival at her door may be imminent. She may fear the possibility of immediate personal violence. As a matter of law the caller may be guilty of an assault: whether he is or not will depend on the circumstances and in particular on the impact of the caller's potentially menacing call or calls on the victim.[10]

If it is accepted, therefore, in principle, that a common assault may be committed by words alone, then it follows as a matter of logic that an indecent

---

7   See Smith, J and Hogan, B, *Criminal Law*, 1999, Butterworths, p 404.

8   See *Wilson* [1955] 1 All ER 744, p 745, *per* Lord Goddard; and *Barton v Armstrong* [1969] 2 NSWR 451, a civil action in the Supreme Court of New South Wales, where Taylor J held that a threat made over the telephone was capable of constituting assault.

9   [1996] 3 WLR 650, p 656, *per* Swinton Thomas LJ.

10   [1997] 4 All ER 225, p 236, *per* Lord Steyn.

assault, whether inherently indecent or rendered so by accompanying circumstances, can be similarly constituted.

In *Coombes* ([1961] Crim LR 54), the defendant was convicted of indecent assault on an adult female. The complainant's evidence stated that he had followed her for some distance in the street, before catching up with her and asking her the time. It was alleged that he then touched her lightly on the back and said: 'Are you going to give me a bit?' The defendant's version of events was that he had touched her accidentally and then said: 'I'm sorry, I didn't mean it a bit.' The Court of Criminal Appeal quashed the conviction on the basis that the trial judge had wrongly allowed the defendant to be cross-examined about a previous conviction for indecent assault on a young girl. Having quashed the conviction for that reason, it appears that the court made no specific reference to the nature of the present indecent assault itself. Instead, it seemed to be assumed that the light touch on the back was an indecent assault. But if this is so, such an act is clearly not 'inherently indecent'. Rather, it can only be justified on the basis that the words spoken amounted to accompanying circumstances of indecency.

We submit that this decision is correct in principle and, indeed, that it could be extended to the situation where the victim is put in fear by the defendant's words alone, irrespective of the absence of any physical contact. Thus, if a defendant were to approach his victim from behind and, whilst unseen by that victim, he were to utter rude and threatening words which made her apprehend an immediate battery of an indecent nature, there seems no reason in either principle or logic why that should not amount to an indecent assault.

2.2.2   *Assaults objectively incapable of indecency*

If, viewed objectively, there is neither inherent indecency nor circumstances capable of rendering the defendant's act indecent, then the prosecution is not permitted to call evidence of the defendant's secret indecent motive in order to establish an indecent assault. An objectively innocent act cannot be rendered otherwise, merely because the defendant possesses a hidden, subjective indecent motive.

In this respect the House of Lords in *Court* cited with approval the decisions in both *Thomas* (above) and *George* ([1956] Crim LR 52). In the latter case, the defendant had tried on several occasions to remove a girl's shoe, which act he admitted was for his sexual gratification. The trial judge ruled that this was not an indecent assault; because there were no 'overt circumstances of indecency', the defendant's sexual motive could not make his act into an indecent assault.

2.2.3   *Ambiguous circumstances making assault capable of indecency*

It is this category of indecency which is potentially the most significant, and which certainly gives rise to the most interesting legal issues.

In the specific circumstances of *Court* (see above), the trial judge allowed the prosecution to adduce evidence of the defendant's 'explanation' for his act (namely his 'buttock fetish') for the purpose of establishing indecency. Therefore, where the defendant's act is, at most, *capable* of being regarded as indecent (as opposed to being either inherently indecent or objectively innocent), then evidence of motive may be admitted in order to prove indecency. According to Lord Griffiths, there are many actions, like spanking, which are equivocal. There might be an innocent explanation for those acts, or the defendant might have an indecent intent. At most, in such cases, the defendant's actions were capable of being indecent, but whether 'right-minded' people would consider them to be so depends upon various factors, including, for example, the relationship between the defendant and the victim, and the defendant's motive.

Lord Ackner provided a further example of the 'ambiguous circumstances' category. An intimate medical examination by a doctor on a young girl, if medically necessary, is not an indecent assault, as right-minded people would not regard it so (even if, coincidentally, the doctor were to receive some sexual pleasure from the act). But, if the examination were not necessary, then it could constitute an indecent assault: it was capable of so being and thus evidence of the doctor's motive (for example, sexual pleasure) was relevant to prove the fact of indecency.

The essence of *Court*, therefore, is that evidence of the defendant's secret motive is admissible to establish indecency, *provided* that right-minded people *might* regard the assault as indecent, but could not say so without knowing the defendant's reason for acting. This principle places trial judges in a difficult and unenviable position, for they must now decide whether a particular act might be indecent, or whether, viewed objectively, it is incapable of being so regarded. A trial judge, then, must be able to make a sensible distinction between a defendant who spanks the victim's bottom (capable of indecency in *Court*) and the defendant who rubs a girl's skirt or removes her shoe (not capable of indecency in *Thomas* and *George* respectively).

If this task were not difficult enough, the problem is exacerbated where the facts themselves are in dispute. Let it be supposed that a defendant is charged with indecent assault after allegedly smacking young girls. The prosecution claims that he spanked the girls on their buttocks, which acts are clearly capable of indecency. The defendant denies this, but admits that he smacked the girls on the backs of the girls' legs near to their ankles. The prosecution wish to adduce evidence of the defendant's secret motive in gaining sexual pleasure from the chastisement of young girls, irrespective of where on their bodies he in fact struck them. It is submitted that on such facts the trial judge would be likely to allow evidence of motive in the first scenario, but not in the second, as that, objectively, is not capable of indecency. This task involves not only a difficult qualitative evaluation, but also, effectively, requires a trial judge to usurp part of the jury's function by deciding if the prosecution have established one aspect of their case.

These potential difficulties could be overcome if Lord Goff's dissenting judgment in Court represented the law. Lord Goff was of the opinion that evidence of indecent motive should be irrelevant in determining the question of indecency. Instead, indecent assault should be proven only if the prosecution can establish that the assault was 'objectively indecent', that is, that it was indecent *per se* or in conjunction with the accompanying circumstances. In other instances, the prosecution should not be able to support its case by adducing evidence of the defendant's secret indecent intent. These much simpler principles do not, at present, represent the law.

We would submit that it is also true, of course, that an equally straightforward legal solution could be achieved if the complete reverse of Lord Goff's position were to be adopted, so that a defendant's indecent motive was always *admissible* in all 'categories' of indecent assault for the purpose of establishing indecent intent. This course of action, which, again, does not represent the current law, would have the effect of reversing decisions such as *Thomas* and *George*. Admittedly, there will always be difficulties of proof in such cases, although as the authorities themselves do indicate defendants occasionally make statements amounting to admissions of indecent intent. But, in any case, evidential problems should not dictate the content of the substantive law, and indecent motive should be admissible for the purpose of establishing the requisite indecency.

2.3   Consent

As absence of consent is an essential ingredient of assault *per se*, it follows that there is no indecent assault if a defendant touches X indecently, but X has consented to that touching. If, in such a situation, X's consent is to provide a defence to the defendant, it must be a consent which is recognised as valid in law. There are a number of limits to and issues surrounding consent in indecent assault.

2.3.1   Consent and victims under 16

It is clear that, *de facto*, children under the age of 16 can and do consent to sexual acts that would, without such consent, amount to indecent assaults. However, consent of a child is not recognised as valid in law, so that the person who perpetrates that act upon a child is unable to rely upon consent as a defence. This limitation to consent, based upon the paternalistic notion that children below a certain age are not yet able to exercise a mature judgment in terms of their sexual conduct, is found in statute. Section 14(2) of the Sexual Offences Act 1956 provides:

A girl under the age of 16 cannot in law give any consent which would prevent an act being an assault for the purposes of this section.[11]

It is, largely, a matter of opinion as to whether ss 14(2) and 15(2) have set the age at which a child can consent to sexual acts at the correct level. It is at least arguable that, at the present day, it is unrealistic not to recognise that young persons mature much more quickly than in previous generations, and that perhaps even legislation drafted in 1956 is now outdated, in the sense that many young people are sexually active at an age considerably below that of 16. Of course, children of a certain age need protection from acts about which they may not have a genuine understanding, but, conversely, it may be ignoring reality to suppose that a girl of, say, 14 cannot give a valid consent to sexual acts which would otherwise amount to an indecent assault.

2.3.2   Consent and hostility

The rule that a child under the age of 16 cannot give a legally valid consent seemed to be ignored in a series of cases which suggested that a defendant could not commit indecent assault unless there was a 'hostile act' on his part against the victim. This 'requirement' was first referred to in *Beal v Kelly* (above), where it was stated by Lord Goddard CJ, in upholding the conviction, that this was upheld because, *inter alia*, there was 'a hostile act ... against the boy's will'.[12]

The same issue was discussed in *Fairclough v Whipp* ([1951] 2 All ER 834), where the defendant had exposed his penis to the victim and then invited her to touch it, which she did. Although the Divisional Court quashed the conviction on the basis that a person who merely invites another to touch him commits no assault (indecent or otherwise), Lord Goddard did state, *obiter*, that the court may have upheld the conviction if the defendant had accompanied his invitation with 'a threatening gesture or a threat to use violence'. In two subsequent cases, Lord Goddard commented expressly that *Fairclough v Whipp* had been decided on the basis of an absence of a hostile act. Thus, in *Burrows* ((1951–52) 35 Cr App R 180), where the defendant had invited a boy to touch his penis, there was held to be no indecent assault, because he 'did not in any way threaten the boy or commit a hostile act towards him'.[13] Similar reasoning was adopted in *DPP v Rogers* ([1953] 1 WLR 1017), where the defendant had placed his arm around the shoulders of his victim, his daughter aged 11, and led her upstairs in order that she should masturbate him. The Divisional Court again held this to be no indecent assault, as there had been no threat or threatening gesture, nor had there been an element of hostility by the defendant.

---

11   Section 15(2) provides an equivalent limitation in respect of boys under the age of 16.
12   [1951] 2 All ER 763, p 764.
13   (1951) 35 Cr App R 180, p 183.

In *Mason* ((1968) 53 Cr App R 12), the central question for the court was whether the defendant had committed indecent assault by allowing boys under the age of 16 to have sexual intercourse with her. Veale J noted the need to establish an assault even before the requirement of indecency was considered, and he then discussed the 'hostility cases':

> What is the hostile act relied upon by the prosecution? What has this woman done towards the boys which by any fair use of language can be called compulsion? There was no threat, no gesture, no pulling of the boy, no reluctance on his part.[14]

In spite of commenting that to require hostility 'to some extent ignore[s] the statutory rule that the consent of a child under 16 is irrelevant',[15] Veale J nevertheless retained as correct in principle the 'hostile act' requirement for indecent assault.

As Veale J himself recognised, by developing the requirement of hostility, the courts seemingly had ignored the clear rule, set down by Parliament, that a child under the age of 16 was to be regarded as incapable of consenting. In addition to this obvious criticism, it was clear also that, even if a hostility requirement was sustainable in principle, it frequently was incompatible with the facts of such cases, that is, proving hostility *de facto* often was difficult, if not impossible, as many defendants displayed no overt hostility; indeed, frequently, they displayed excessive friendliness towards their victims.

Fortunately, the requirement of hostility has been challenged in a number of decisions since *Mason*. In *McCormack* ([1969] 2 QB 442), the defendant had inserted his finger into the vagina of a girl aged 15 with whom he had been sharing a bed. The defendant appealed against his conviction for indecent assault on the basis that there had been no hostility. In rejecting this argument, Fenton Atkinson LJ stated that the 'hostility cases' should be confined to those instances where the defendant invites the child to touch him, but there is no hostility or compulsion. By contrast, in the present case (due to the terms of s 14(2)), it was 'plain beyond argument that if a man inserts a finger into the vagina of a girl under 16 there is an indecent assault, in view of her age, and it is an indecent assault however willing and co-operative she may in fact be'.[16] In *Faulkner v Talbot* ([1981] 1 WLR 1528), the defendant was found guilty of indecent assault where she had held the penis of a boy of 14 immediately prior to having sexual intercourse with him. In upholding the conviction, Lord Lane CJ stated:

> An assault is any intentional touching of another person without the consent of that person and without lawful excuse. It need not necessarily be hostile, rude or aggressive, as some of the cases seem to indicate. If the touching is an

---

14   (1969) 53 Cr App R 12, p 18.

15   *Ibid*, p 19.

16   [1969] 2 QB 442, p 445.

intentional touching, as in this case, it plainly was because the appellant took hold of the boy's penis, then the provisions in s 15(2) ... come into play.[17]

The decisions in *McCormack* and *Faulkner v Talbot* go a considerable way in clarifying the hostility requirement, but they both remain difficult to reconcile with the decision of the Court of Appeal in *Sutton* ([1977] 1 WLR 1086). There, the defendant was convicted of indecent assault on the basis that he had touched the arms, legs and torsos of several naked boys in order to arrange poses for photographs. On appeal, he argued that there had been no assault, as his acts had been neither hostile nor threatening. The Court of Appeal quashed his conviction, Lord Widgery stating that where, as here, the defendant's act is not indecent *per se*, but rather is merely committed in indecent circumstances, then consent may be available as a defence. It is submitted that this is not a supportable distinction, as ss 14(2) and 15(2) make no distinction between assaults which are inherently indecent and those which are rendered so due to the accompanying circumstances. Thus, when Sutton touched the boys, he clearly was committing an assault. The accompanying circumstances were, equally clearly, capable of rendering the assault indecent. And, therefore, within the unambiguous terms of s 15(2), the boys' 'consent' was irrelevant.

It is difficult to avoid the view that *Sutton* was wrongly decided. The preferable view of the law is that it is represented by *McCormack* and *Faulkner v Talbot*, and that the hostility/consent issue can best be resolved by considering three distinct scenarios.

First, where the indecent assault takes the form of a battery, then any purported 'consent' of a child under the age of 16 is irrelevant due to the provisions in ss 14(2) and 15(2). In this category, 'hostility' should no longer be recognised as having a legal role.

Secondly, where the indecent assault takes the form of 'assault' (that is, non-battery), then 'hostility' may have a role to play, in the sense that it can provide very pertinent evidence of the child being placed in the fear necessary to establish an assault.

Thirdly, a situation may arise where a defendant is a 'hostile invitor', but his invitation to the victim is not sufficient to amount to an assault, because the child is not put in the requisite fear. Here, this would appear still not to be an indecent assault, and an appropriate alternative charge should be used. Such a charge would depend upon the precise factual circumstances of each case. Where both parties are male, then a charge of procuring or attempting to procure an act of gross indecency under s 13 of the Sexual Offences Act 1956 should be considered (above). Alternatively, where the child is under the age of 14, a defendant could be charged with committing 'an act of gross

17 [1981] 1 WLR 1528, p 1534.

indecency with or towards a child' or inciting a child to commit such an act, under s 1 of the Indecency with Children Act 1960 (see Chapter 5).

2.3.3 Scope of consent: public policy

It has long been recognised that the law has, on public policy grounds, a general role to play in restricting the right of an individual to consent to assault, whether indecent or otherwise. The general principle that a person cannot legally consent to the imposition upon himself of actual bodily harm can be traced back to the decision in *Donovan* ([1934] 2 KB 498), where the defendant was charged with indecent assault after he had persuaded a girl aged 17 to let him cane her. Evidence was adduced to establish that the defendant engaged in such acts for the purpose of sexual pleasure. Although the Divisional Court quashed the appellant's conviction on the basis of a misdirection by the trial judge on the question of the burden of proof, a detailed consideration was made on the scope of consent as a defence in these circumstances. The Divisional Court stated:

> As a general rule ... it is an unlawful act to beat another person with such a degree of violence that the infliction of bodily harm is a probable consequence, and when such an act is proved, consent is immaterial.[18]

Later, the court continued:

> [A]n act likely or intended to cause bodily harm is an unlawful act ... [S]uch hurt or injury need not be permanent, but it must be more than merely transient or trifling.[19]

In the opinion of the court, the defendant's 'corrupt motive' (that is, his sexual gratification) did not fall within any of the recognised exceptions, such as 'manly diversions' or 'rough and undisciplined horseplay', and, therefore, the victim's consent was not valid in law.

This principle was confirmed, in essence, by the Court of Appeal in *Attorney General's Reference (No 6 of 1980)* ([1981] QB 715), where the court was asked to give its opinion on the following point of law:

> Where two persons fight (otherwise than in the course of sport) in a public place can it be a defence for one of those persons to a charge of assault arising out of the fight that the other consented to fight?[20]

In giving the opinion of the court, Lane LCJ stated:

> We think that it can be taken as a starting point that it is an essential element of an assault that the act is done contrary to the will and without the consent of the victim ... Ordinarily, then, if the victim consents, the assailant is not guilty.

---

18 [1934] 2 KB 498, p 507, *per* Swift J.

19 *Ibid*, p 509.

20 [1981] QB 715, p 716.

But the cases show that the courts will make an exception to this principle where the public interest requires.[21]

Consequently, held Lord Lane, it is not in the public interest for people to cause or try to cause actual bodily harm for no good reason; fighting in order to sort out your differences (whether in a public place or not) is not a good reason which the law can recognise.

The leading authority now on the role of public policy in limiting the scope of consent as a defence is the House of Lords decision in *Brown et al* ([1993] 2 WLR 556). Here, a majority of their Lordships held that consent was not available as a defence to charges of assault and wounding under ss 47 and 20 Offences Against the Person Act 1861, where injuries were inflicted within the context of homosexual sado-masochistic encounters. Lord Templeman stated:

> The question whether the defence of consent should be extended to the consequences of sado-masochistic encounters can only be decided by consideration of policy and public interest.[22]

And he continued later:

> In my opinion sado-masochism is not only concerned with sex. Sado-masochism is also concerned with violence ... I am not prepared to invent a defence of consent for sado-masochistic encounters which breed and glorify cruelty.[23]

Similarly, Lord Jauncey expressed 'no doubt that it would not be in the public interest that deliberate infliction of actual bodily harm during the course of homosexual sado-masochistic activities should be held to be lawful'.[24] The majority judgments were keen to stress the correctness of the principle derived largely from *Attorney General's Reference (No 6 of 1980)*, namely that there had to be a 'good reason' for allowing consent, and thus for adding homosexual sado-masochistic activities to the generally accepted list of exceptions. In the majority's view, there was no such good reason to justify adding to activities like tattooing, body-piercing and most sports (including some deliberately violent ones, such as boxing).

In forceful dissenting judgments, Lords Mustill and Slynn rejected the often paternalistic approach of the majority and did not accept that many of the potential 'risks' which seemed to influence the reasoning of the majority (risk of corruption, risk of more serious harm, etc) were relevant

---

21 [1981] QB 715, p 718.

22 [1993] 2 WLR 556, p 563.

23 *Ibid*, p 564.

24 *Ibid*, p 574. It should be noted that three of the appellants in *Brown* subsequently complained to the European Commission of Human Rights that their convictions were in contravention of Art 8 of the Convention. The European Court of Human Rights upheld the right of the House of Lords to protect public health in the pursuance of a legitimate aim: see *Laskey, Jaggard and Brown v UK* [1997] 24 EHRR 39.

considerations when assessing consent in the present circumstances. It was argued by Lord Mustill, in particular, that, in this area of law, it would be wise to avoid trying to establish a general all-encompassing principle sufficient to cater for any eventuality:

> I cannot accept that the infliction of bodily harm, and especially the private infliction of it, is invariably criminal, absent some special factor which decrees otherwise. I prefer to address each individual category of consensual violence in the light of the situation as a whole. Sometimes the element of consent will make no difference and sometimes it will make all the difference. Circumstances must alter cases.[25]

Lord Mustill's approach has much to commend it. Whilst it is axiomatic that a degree of certainty is desirable in the law (and in criminal law in particular), it is equally true that the law should attempt, so far as is possible, to recognise and take account of ever-changing moral values. This is nowhere more significant than in the realm of purportedly consensual sexual acts within an increasingly pluralistic society.

A more flexible judicial attitude towards consent may also be seen in the Court of Appeal decision in *Wilson* ([1996] 3 WLR 125). The appellant had been convicted of assault occasioning actual bodily harm contrary to s 47 of the Offences Against the Person Act 1861. He admitted to the police that he had used a hot knife to burn his initials (AW) onto his wife's left buttock and right buttock respectively. He did this because of his wife's desire to have a tattoo of her husband's name on her body, whereas he did not know how to do a tattoo. At trial, Crabtree J ruled that he was bound by the decisions in *Donovan* and *Brown* and the jury convicted. In allowing the appeal and quashing the conviction, Russell LJ stated that all their Lordships were fully satisfied that no factual similarities existed between the present case and either *Donovan* or *Brown*. Mrs Wilson had not only consented to the appellant's acts, she had, in fact, instigated them. His desire was not to cause injury, but to assist his wife in obtaining what she regarded as a desirable physical adornment. In their Lordships' opinion, *Brown* had not decided that consent was never available as a defence to a charge under s 47 in cases where actual bodily harm was inflicted deliberately. Indeed, *Brown* could not be taken as extending any further than its own very specific (and extreme) circumstances.

If *Brown* did set down no more than a very general proposition, then, of necessity, exceptions to it must be available. But that would still leave open the broader question of whether, on the present facts, public policy and interest should demand that the appellant's conduct be criminalised. In their Lordships' view, public policy and interest were quite relevant considerations. Consequently, it was not in the public interest to criminalise such behaviour,

---

25   [1993] 2 WLR 556, p 597.

and the appellant's wife's consent was a defence to the charge. The potential importance of *Wilson* lies in its recognition that consent within the ambit of criminal assault has to deal with a continually changing set of circumstances and that in this area, perhaps more than any other, social attitudes and levels of acceptability are in a continual state of flux. It is perhaps of equal significance to consider whether any useful distinction may be drawn between *Brown* and *Wilson* in terms of the sexualities of the parties. Although the cases are not factually identical, and it is possible to read the majority judgments in *Brown* as refusing consent as a defence to violence (rather than it being a case concerned with sexual freedom),[26] it seems that the court in *Wilson* was more prepared to recognise the rights of a married (and, by definition, heterosexual) couple to inflict harm, than the House of Lords was prepared to recognise in respect of male homosexuals.

However, whilst it is possible to analyse the decisions in *Brown* and *Wilson* in terms of the parties' sexualities and the law's unfair treatment of homosexual males, such a critique must now be read in the light of the Court of Appeal decision in *Emmett* ((1999) *The Times*, 15 October). Emmett was convicted by the jury on one count of assault occasioning actual bodily harm (contrary to s 47 of the Offences Against the Person Act 1861) following a ruling by the trial judge that there was no defence of consent available, and, in the light of that ruling, he pleaded guilty to a second count. During the course of sexual activity between Emmett and his partner, Emmett had placed a plastic bag over her head and tied it around her neck. Some time in the course of the sexual act, Emmett realised that his partner had been partly asphyxiated, to the extent that she had probably lost consciousness. Later, she required medical treatment for haemorrhages to both eyes and bruising to her neck. This incident gave rise to count one on the indictment. On a later occasion, Emmett had set fire to his partner's breasts with lighter fuel, causing burns which required medical treatment. This gave rise to count two. The trial judge, relying upon the decision in *Brown*, ruled that the *de facto* consent of the complainant was not a defence. In upholding the convictions, Wright J (giving the judgment of the court) approved the reasoning of the majority of their Lordships in *Brown*, namely that the deliberate infliction of actual bodily harm in a sado-masochistic activity should be held to be unlawful, notwithstanding the victim's consent. The Court felt that there was 'no good reason' for permitting such acts, noting and approving the comments of the trial judge that 'on the first occasion, there was a very considerable degree of danger to life; on the second, there was a degree of injury to the body'.[27] In an even more significant comment, Wright J added that there was 'no reason in principle ... to draw any distinction between sado-masochistic activity on a heterosexual basis and that which is conducted in a homosexual context'.[28]

---

26   See, eg, Wilson, W, 'Is hurting people wrong?' [1992] Journal of Social Welfare & Family Law 388.

27   Court of Appeal hearing, 18 June 1999 (quoted from LEXIS transcript).

28   *Ibid.*

The decision seems to confirm that the level of harm, *including risks of potential harm or death*, is more important than the context in which the injuries occur. The paternalism of the courts now extends equally to injuries inflicted during the course of heterosexual and homosexual sadomasochistic activities.

2.3.4   Scope of consent: vitiation by force, fear or fraud

Under common law, the traditional view of the courts was that any purported consent to assault was vitiated by force, fear or fraud on the part of the defendant. If consent were to be vitiated, then fear had to be the fear of force, whilst fraud was only relevant if it related to the nature of the act or the identity of the actor. In *Case* ((1850) 1 Den 580), the defendant, a medical practitioner, had induced a young girl to have sexual intercourse with him after telling her that the act was a medical procedure. On upholding the conviction, Wilde CJ stated on behalf of the court:

> The prisoner disarmed [the girl] by his fraud. She acquiesced under a misrepresentation that what he was doing was with a view to a cure and that only; whereas it was done solely to gratify the passions of the prisoner ... She consented to one thing, he did another materially different, on which she had been prevented by his fraud from exercising her judgment and will.[29]

The entire question of the meaning of 'consent' in indecent assault, must now be read in the light of the decision in *Olugboja* (see Chapter 3). Although *Olugboja* was, of course, a decision on consent in rape, it is clear that the principle is now equally applicable to instances of indecent assault. In *McAllister* ([1997] Crim LR 233), the defendant was convicted of committing an indecent assault upon his wife, from whom he was separated. He had gone to the victim's house and a number of sexual acts occurred (although not sexual intercourse *per se*), which the defendant claimed were consensual, although this was denied by the complainant. In upholding the conviction, it was held by the Court of Appeal that the trial judge had directed the jury properly on the definitions of 'consent' and 'submission', and that it had rightly been left to the jury to decide whether there was or may have been consent in respect of sexual acts between adults. Indeed, in such cases, it may be wiser for the judge not to attempt an over-elaborate definition of consent and submission, but to leave it instead to the good sense and general experience of the jury in deciding whether the victim consented or not.

---

29   (1850) 1 Den 580, p 582.

3   MENS REA

3.1   Indecent intent

The leading decision on the *mens rea* required for indecent assault is, again, that of the House of Lords in *Court*. Lord Ackner, with whom the majority of their Lordships agreed, answered the certified question as follows:

> Whether it is correct that on a charge of indecent assault the prosecution must prove:
>
> (1) that the accused intentionally assaulted the victim;
>
> (2) that the assault, or the circumstances accompanying it, are capable of being considered by right-minded persons as indecent;
>
> (3) that the accused intended to commit such an assault as is referred to in (2) above.[30]

The effect of this statement is that the House of Lords has imposed a requirement upon the prosecution of proving an 'indecent intention' on the part of the defendant. Whilst assaults generally may be committed recklessly, this appears not to be the case, for the most part, in respect of indecent assaults. It is, therefore, incumbent upon the prosecution to prove either that the defendant intended his assault to be indecent or that he intended to commit an assault which right-minded persons would consider indecent.

3.1.1   Proving indecent intent

It has already been seen (above) how the House of Lords in *Court* distinguished at length between three situations for the purpose of establishing the necessary ingredient of indecency in indecent assault. The effect of the decision is to create a parallel three situations in respect of establishing the defendant's *mens rea*.

First, where the assault is either inherently indecent, or is rendered so by the accompanying circumstances, then, provided the defendant is aware of those circumstances at the time, he will possess the necessary *mens rea*. In this category, the defendant need not necessarily have a sexual motive (although, frequently, of course, there may be one). In Lord Ackner's own example of the defendant who removes, in public, the clothing of a woman in order to cause embarrassment or distress, there is clearly an indecent intent. Similarly, in *DPP v H* (above), there is a clear indecent intent, albeit the defendant's 'reason' for acting was to harm the baby rather than to satisfy a sexual urge.

Secondly, where the assault is objectively incapable of indecency then there will be no *mens rea*, and hence no indecent assault, irrespective of the state of mind of the defendant himself. Here, a secret, albeit undoubtedly

---

30   [1988] 2 All ER 221, p 228.

indecent, motive held by the defendant cannot be used by the prosecution to turn an objectively innocent act into an indecent assault. Examples of this second category would include cases such as *George* and *Thomas* (above).

The third category is the most interesting and may be likely to produce the greatest practical and theoretical difficulties. Where an assault, viewed objectively, is at most *capable* of being indecent, then the prosecution can adduce evidence to show, not merely that the assault was indecent, but also that the defendant committed it with an 'indecent intent'. The obvious example of such a situation is *Court* itself, although, as has been seen, the potential difficulties facing the trial judge in predetermining whether the circumstances of the case are 'ambiguous' or 'objectively innocent', may prove to be considerable.

In terms of the 'third category', it is essential also to note that it is not just the prosecution who may adduce evidence of the defendant's motive. If the prosecution are allowed to produce evidence of 'indecent motive' then it is only reasonable that the defence should be able to counter that with evidence of 'decent motive'. In *Court*, Lord Ackner cited with approval the decision in *Pratt* ([1984] Crim LR 41). There, the defendant had forced two young boys, who had been night-fishing, to strip and shine a torch on each other's genitals. Throughout the incident, the defendant was several feet away, and he touched neither boy. The trial judge ruled that the prosecution had to prove an 'indecent intent' and, consequently, he allowed the defence to adduce evidence of the defendant's 'non-indecent motive', namely that he was searching the boys for cannabis, which he believed they had taken from him on a previous occasion. The trial judge's direction was approved by Lord Ackner in the following terms:

> The defendant was entitled to put before the jury his explanation of his strange conduct in order to contend that the prosecution had not established that he intended to commit an assault which was indecent.[31]

However, given the House of Lords' own 'categorisation' of indecent assault, it is not easy to reconcile the principles established in *Court* with the actual decision in *Pratt*. For any defendant's non-indecent motive to be adduced in evidence, it must be accepted that his acts were in the ambiguous category. This clearly was the view of the trial judge in *Pratt* and it received the subsequent approval of Lord Ackner. But were Pratt's actions ambiguous at all? There appears to be a real tension between Pratt's motive and, say, the motive of Lord Ackner's hypothetical defendant who forces a woman to strip for the purpose of causing her embarrassment. The latter is viewed, rightly, as inherently indecent, and so the defendant would not be able to adduce his 'non-indecent motive'. But if this is correct, it is difficult to see how Pratt's actions were significantly different. It is quite feasible that his actions may

---

31   [1988] 2 All ER 221, p 231.

have been held to have been 'inherently indecent', in which case, his non-indecent motive would have been ruled inadmissible. In *Sargeant* (above), there can be little disagreement about the correctness of the defendant's conviction for indecent assault. But let it be supposed that another defendant had forced his victim to masturbate in a public place so that he (the defendant) could observe the victim's reaction for the purpose of his psychology thesis. This hypothetical non-indecent motive surely would be ruled inadmissible on the basis that the assault was inherently indecent. In these borderline ambiguous cases, trial judges are being required to draw increasingly fine distinctions, and uncertainty is likely to be the inevitable consequence.

3.2 Recklessness in indecent assault

As a result of the House of Lords holding that indecent assault requires an indecent intention, it would seem that recklessness has very little relevance to such a charge. However, there remains one situation where recklessness definitely is relevant to indecent assault, and one where it is likely to be held so if the appropriate circumstances arise.

3.2.1 Recklessness and consent

Notwithstanding the need for the prosecution to prove an indecent intent, recklessness remains relevant in relation to the defendant's state of mind about the issue of the victim's consent. In the overwhelming majority of indecent assaults, the defendant will know that the victim is not consenting to the acts in question. But what about the defendant who is reckless as to whether the victim is consenting or not? In such a situation, it seems that the courts will apply a subjective recklessness test, so that the defendant is guilty only if *he himself* had considered the possibility that the victim might not be consenting, but decided to continue with the act in any case. In *Kimber* ([1983] 1 WLR 1118), the Court of Appeal stated that a defendant would be reckless as to consent if he 'couldn't care less' whether or not the victim was consenting. But if the defendant himself believes, however unreasonable that belief may be, that the victim is consenting, then he lacks the requisite *mens rea*.

3.2.2 Recklessness and attempted indecent assault

Although there is no decided authority on the point, it would seem logical and fair to extend the decision in *Khan et al* (above) on recklessness in attempted rape to the offence of attempted indecent assault if the need should ever arise. Thus, suppose that a defendant admitted that he had intended to do an act which would, if completed, clearly have amounted to an indecent assault. He then does an act 'which is more than merely preparatory' to that indecent assault (for the purposes of s 1 of the Criminal Attempts Act 1981), but, for whatever reason, he fails to complete that substantive offence. The defendant then claims that he did not know whether the victim would have consented to the act or not, irrespective of the fact that he had failed to complete his act as intended. In these circumstances, it is submitted, there should be no difference in principle from the approach adopted in *Khan*: the prosecution must, of course, prove the *actus reus* of attempt, and they must prove that the defendant intended to commit the act, which, it is alleged, would have amounted to an indecent assault. However, it is then sufficient that, in respect of the victim's consent, the defendant had thought about the possibility that she might not have consented to the act, but was prepared to continue regardless. It should not be necessary to prove that the defendant knew that the victim would not have consented in order to uphold a conviction for attempted indecent assault. To hold otherwise would be to put a defendant charged with attempted indecent assault in a more advantageous position than a defendant charged with attempted rape. The potential anomaly would be even more acute if a single defendant were to be charged with doing acts that were more than merely preparatory to both rape and indecent assault. The defendant claims that he had thought about the possibility that the women might not consent, but that he did not know this for certain. Following *Khan*, the defendant undoubtedly would have sufficient *mens rea* for attempted rape. It would be inconsistent, not to say absurd, for that defendant not to have also the *mens rea* required for attempted indecent assault.

4   SENTENCING INDECENT ASSAULT

Indecent assault, whether charged under s 14(1) or s 15(1), is an offence which is triable either-way. Where a defendant is convicted on indictment, the maximum penalty available is 10 years' imprisonment. Where a defendant is convicted following summary trial, then the maximum sentence is six months' imprisonment or a fine not exceeding £5,000, or both.

In determining the appropriate mode of trial, courts should be aware of *Practice Note: National Mode of Trial Guidelines* ((1991) 92 Cr App R 142), where it was stated that, generally, either-way offences should be tried summarily, unless one or more of the 'specified features' exists and the court considers its sentencing powers to be insufficient. In the context of indecent assault, the specified features to be taken account of are: a substantial disparity in age between the victim and the defendant, and the assault is more than trivial; the use of violence or threats of violence; a relationship of trust or responsibility between the defendant and victim; several similar offences, and the assaults were more than trivial; where the victim is particularly vulnerable; and the serious nature of the assaults.

As with rape, one of the main controversies in sentencing indecent assault surrounds the precise level within the statutory maximum at which any particular sentence should be fixed. In common with many sexual offences, the Court of Appeal has attempted to provide guidance for sentencers faced with defendants convicted of indecent assault.

4.1   The guidelines

The major authority providing guidance for sentencing cases of indecent assault is *Willis* (above). This was the leading case (at least prior to 1994) on sentencing buggery, but insofar as an indecent assault is committed by a man on a boy under the age of 16, the Court of Appeal was of the opinion that 'much the same approach' is appropriate for indecent assault as for buggery. However, in a potentially far reaching statement, the court added:

> [I]t is not the label of indecent assault which is important but the nature of the act. In many cases it amounts to no more than putting a hand on or under the clothing in the region of the testicles or buttocks. Such cases are not serious. In some the assault may take the form of a revolting act of fellatio, which is as bad as buggery, maybe more so. Sentences should reflect the seriousness of the act constituting the indecent assault.[32]

It is arguable that finding the correct benchmark for sentencing indecent assault poses greater difficulties for the judiciary than it does in rape. Of course, in rape, there may exist a variety of external exacerbating features, but at least the physical act constituting the *actus reus* itself is limited to just two specific forms of penile penetration. In indecent assault, there exists not only the same potential range of external factors, but also a wide variety of acts and circumstances which can constitute the very *actus reus*. Thus, the judiciary must be aware of public attitudes whilst nevertheless trying to balance the seriousness of forced oral sex or the insertion of a bottle into the vagina of the victim, against the defendant who brushes his hand upon the victim's breast.

4.1.1   Contrast with rape

It is not, perhaps, surprising that, given the considerably different maximum penalties, plus the traditional view of rape as a uniquely serious sexual offence, that the judiciary have tended to draw a strong distinction between rape and indecent assault in sentencing terms. In *Pilgrim* ((1993) 14 Cr App R(S) 432), the defendant was convicted of indecent assault on a girl aged 15 after he had forced his penis into her mouth and ejaculated. The sentence of five years' imprisonment imposed by the trial judge was reduced by the Court of Appeal to three years. The court stated that a sentence of five years was more appropriate to rape than indecent assault. Furthermore, whilst the court

---

32   (1975) 60 Cr App R 146, p 149.

accepted that some indecent assaults were as serious, or even more serious than some rapes, this was not such a case. Specifically, there was seen to be no violence and the victim suffered no physical injury. The decision may be viewed as an example of the courts' general attitude towards indecent assault as being qualitatively different to rape, but also more specifically as an example of the absence of any aggravating features.

4.1.2   Aggravating features

As with aggravating features in rape, it would be unwise to try to provide an exhaustive list of all the factors which might be considered by a sentencer as relevant to the level of sentence, especially those which serve to increase that sentence. However, there are two issues which deserve mention in order to illustrate the courts' stance on such aggravating matters.

First, it is open to the sentencer to consider the effect of the indecent assault upon the victim, as a factor affecting sentence, but such information must be put to the court in an appropriate manner. In *Hobstaff* ([1993] Crim LR 318), the defendant had pleaded guilty to three counts of indecent assault committed over a two year period against his neighbour's young daughters. He had touched the girls' vaginas and had encouraged them to masturbate him and to perform oral sex. Counsel for the prosecution commented upon the horrific effects of the acts on the children, and the trial judge, in imposing a sentence of four years' imprisonment on each count concurrent, stated expressly that he had taken into account the effect on the children in determining the level of sentence. However, on appeal, Ognall J stated that it had been 'wholly improper' for prosecution counsel to comment upon the psychological trauma suffered by the victims where such comments had been unsubstantiated. Because these effects had been taken into account by the trial judge, the Court of Appeal reduced the sentences to three years' imprisonment. It is, of course, equally wrong for the sentencing judge himself to comment on psychological harm suffered by the victims if no evidence on that matter has been adduced.[33] This approach, we submit, is correct in principle: such a practice would not only introduce an unacceptable variable into sentencing practice, but it also is unjustifiable for sentencing judges to purport to take note of any issue not substantiated by evidence, and even more so if that may lead, *in extremis*, to the danger of trial judges speculating on the future possible effects upon a victim.

The importance of the approach adopted in *Hobstaff* was reiterated recently by the Court of Appeal in *Perks* ([2000] Crim LR 606). The appellant had been sentenced to four years' imprisonment following a plea of guilty on a single count of robbery. In reducing the sentence to three years, Garland J on behalf of the Court emphasised that where a sentencing court considers a

---

33   See, also, *R v O'S* (1993) 14 Cr App R(S) 632, pp 635–36, *per* Farquharson LJ.

victim impact statement, it must be in the proper form and conform to established guidelines. Victim impact statements are becoming increasingly common and the court stressed that several clear propositions concerning their use have now emerged. First, the sentencer must not make assumptions, unsupported by evidence, about the effects of an offence on the victim. Secondly, where a victim does suffer a particularly damaging or distressing effect, that should be made known to the sentencer. Thirdly, such evidence must be in the appropriate form (such as a witness statement under s 9 of the Criminal Justice Act 1967 or an expert's report) and made available in the proper manner to the defence. Fourthly, if the only evidence is that of the victim alone, it should be treated with care. Finally, opinions of the victim or the victim's close relatives as to appropriate levels of sentence should not be taken into account. However, the decision in *Perks* is also important for recognising that, rarely, the sentencer may take into account the impact upon the victim as mitigation, rather than aggravation. Thus, where the sentence passed on the offender aggravated the victim's distress, there might be some degree of moderation. Alternatively, the sentencer may take into account the victim's forgiveness or unwillingness to press charges, where that provided evidence that his or her psychological or mental suffering was very much less than would normally be the case. Neither of these 'mitigating' factors existed in *Perks* itself, but they can frequently be of importance in sexual offences, for example, where the parties were in a relationship and there has subsequently been a degree of reconciliation.

Secondly, abuses of positions of trust or responsibility are likely to be regarded as aggravating features. In particular, the courts have adopted a strict approach to taxi and minicab drivers. In *Bhatti* ((1992) unreported, 6 July),[34] the defendant, a taxi driver, was sentenced to three months' imprisonment after he had indecently assaulted his female passenger, aged 18, by touching her leg and kissing her forcibly on the neck. The Court of Appeal stressed the importance of the position of trust held by taxi drivers in relation to female passengers, especially in the light of the fact that drivers are often alone with women late at night with no other available source of help. On the facts, the court accepted that an immediate prison sentence had been necessary, but nevertheless felt it appropriate (as the appellant had spent eight days in custody without bail) to substitute a sentence of three months' imprisonment suspended for two years.

A similarly severe judicial attitude is adopted in relation to schoolteachers who abuse their positions of trust. In *Walters* ((1994) 15 Cr App R(S) 690), the Court of Appeal upheld a sentence of four years' imprisonment on a schoolteacher who had indecently assaulted several young girl pupils for whom he was responsible. In approving the sentence, Judge J stated:

---

34   See Rook, P and Ward, R, *Sexual Offences*, 1997, Sweet & Maxwell, p 8.

[T]his remains a case in which a man of very mature years in a position of trust systematically abused that trust in a most disgraceful, persistent and damaging way, targeting vulnerable girls who, for various reasons, he believed would be unlikely to report his conduct.[35]

An identical sentence was upheld in *Pike* ([1996] 1 Cr App R(S) 4), where the defendant, who had no medical qualifications, but held himself out as a hypnotherapist, carried out two (unnecessary) internal vaginal examinations of the complainant. On behalf of the Court of Appeal, Judge Gower QC approved the sentence imposed by the trial judge:

He [the trial judge] made the point that the applicant had obtained the victim's consent by ... 'sheer deceit' and that he had abused her trust in him. The learned judge ... expressed himself as satisfied that he had carried out the so-called medical examinations for no other reason than self-sexual gratification.[36]

4.1.3   Indecent assaults on consenting minors

It is clear that children under the age of 16 do give *de facto* consent to acts which constitute indecent assaults, even if such consent is regarded as legally invalid as a result of ss 14(2) and 15(2) of the Sexual Offences Act 1956. Whilst such consent will not provide a defence for the defendant's acts, it may operate as a factor for consideration in the level of sentence. An unusual, but illustrative, example of such a case can be seen in *Allen* ([1996] Crim LR 208). The defendant, a female aged 20 at trial, but 18 at the time of the offences, pleaded guilty to indecent assault and gross indecency on a child. The child, in fact, had been the defendant's 'girlfriend', and the incidents had occurred during the course of their relationship when the victim was aged 13. Letters from the victim adduced in evidence indicated that she had been a willing partner in the sexual acts. The defendant was sentenced to two years' imprisonment in a Young Offenders' Institution for the indecent assault, and one year concurrent for the offence of gross indecency with a child. On appeal, these sentences were reduced to 15 and eight months' imprisonment respectively. The Court of Appeal noted the defendant's age at the time of the offences, the lack of coercion (and, indeed, the willing participation of the victim) and the plea of guilty as all being relevant factors in reducing the sentences. The case is interesting for its relative rarity. Indecent assaults by females are rare in themselves, and even more so when committed on 'consenting' minors. Nevertheless, there remains, perhaps, a feeling that the sentences still err towards the harsh side. It is questionable whether comparable sentences would have been imposed upon young men who

---

35 (1994) 15 Cr App R(S) 690, p 692. See, also, *Cubitt* (1989) 11 Cr App R(S) 380, p 381, *per* Gatehouse J.

36 [1996] 1 Cr App R(S) 4, p 6. See, also, *Prokop* (1995) 16 Cr App R(S) 598, p 599, *per* Ognall J. For an abuse of a position of trust by an employer upon a potential employee, see *Singh-Marwa* (1995) 16 Cr App R(S) 537, pp 538–39, *per* Owen J.

committed similar offences against girls of the same age, or indeed by analogy with the offence of unlawful sexual intercourse with a girl under the age of 16, under s 6 of the Sexual Offences Act 1956.

4.1.4   'Minor' assaults

Once it is accepted that, in reality, the offence of indecent assault covers a wide spectrum of behaviour, it becomes inevitable that the judiciary must attempt to reflect the relative lack of severity in some assaults, by the level of sentence imposed.

The general view of the courts to 'minor' assaults may be taken as being expressed in *Williams (DW)* ((1992) 12 Cr App R(S) 671). The defendant had made a number of lewd suggestions to a stewardess on a train and he then touched her breast. In reducing the original sentence of six weeks' imprisonment to one of 10 days (the time that he had already spent in custody), Watkins LJ stated:

> In the ordinary way it cannot be doubted that loutish behaviour of this kind deserves to be punished ... in some instances ... by the infliction of a custodial sentence. But the facts of this matter have persuaded us, along with the fact that he was previously a man of good character and this was but one incident of offensive behaviour, that a custodial sentence was not called for ...[37]

Examples of such 'loutish behaviour', whilst rightly criminalised, are always likely to place sentencers in unenviable positions. On the one hand, they must be seen to be imposing a sentence which reflects society's disapprobation of behaviour which is offensive to women and which (if not sanctioned) can be regarded as being a further example of a patriarchal legal system reinforcing the stereotypical view of men being able to behave as they wish against women. On the other hand, sentences must reflect an objective awareness of the seriousness of the incident in question, so that the sentence does not become out of all proportion to the act. This is not to suggest that some indecent assaults should ever be trivialised, but it does indicate an appreciation of the breadth of such assaults, so that harsher sentences can more accurately reflect society's condemnation of more severe instances of the offence.

One particular manifestation of 'minor' assaults which is increasingly common and has caused difficulties for sentencers, is that of indecent assault committed by men pushing or rubbing against women in crowded places, most often on trains.

In *Neem* ((1993) 14 Cr App R(S) 18), the defendant was sentenced at Crown Court to 28 days' imprisonment and ordered to pay £250 compensation after indecently assaulting a young woman by rubbing against her in a crowded

---

37   (1992) 13 Cr App R(S) 671, p 672.

underground train. In the Court of Appeal, Macpherson J set out the following principle:

> Cases of this kind are usually dealt with in the magistrates' court. Simply for example again, in crowded places such as Wimbledon week and on the Tube trains, these things do occur and usually the case is dealt with by the magistrates and visited on conviction by a comparatively small fine. This case could have been dealt with by the magistrates. The man chose to go for trial and the learned judge took ... too serious a view of what had happened.
>
> On the other hand the indecent assault was persistent. He pushed himself against this girl's backside and, according to her, he started to get an erection, because she felt it. So that it was more than the first touch which may occur in cases of this kind.
>
> A sentence of imprisonment was ... *wrong in principle*. This man should have been fined and should have been ordered to pay a sum in compensation and costs.[38]

This decision highlights the difficulties facing sentencers in such circumstances. Whilst the incident in itself appears to have been regarded by the Court of Appeal as 'minor', there was also the aggravation of the act being persistent. Notwithstanding this aggravation, the court ruled that, on a first conviction for an offence of this type, a sentence of immediate imprisonment was wrong in principle.

Subsequent cases have challenged the extent to which the Court of Appeal in *Neem* was correct in seeking to establish such a principle. In *Townsend* ((1995) 16 Cr App R(S) 553), the defendant was convicted of, *inter alia*, indecent assault in circumstances very similar to those of *Neem*. He was sentenced to six months' imprisonment for the indecent assault and appealed on the basis that this was wrong in principle. In giving the judgment of the court, Glidewell LJ was of the opinion that the court in *Neem* had not been correct in seeking to lay down a principle for sentencing such defendants:

> Where ... previous decisions are specifically said to be guideline cases, then the court will ... follow the guideline cases. But that is not the situation here. What is clear is that as a matter of strict application to the doctrine of precedent, this court is not bound by a previous decision of this court in relation to sentencing, albeit the facts of a previous case may be very similar to those in the instant case.
>
> [W]e have concluded that the court in *Neem* was wrong in saying that as a matter of principle an indecent assault of this kind, for the first conviction, should not carry a sentence of custody. We think it is open to a sentencing court in its discretion to impose a custodial sentence for such an offence. We are not saying of course that it must do so; in many cases it is properly dealt with by a non-custodial sentence.[39]

---

38 (1993) 14 Cr App R(S) 18, p 20 (emphasis added).

39 (1995) 16 Cr App R(S) 553, p 558.

On the facts of the instant case, therefore, the court was of the opinion that the trial judge had been correct in imposing a custodial sentence. The victim had been caused distress, and was likely to be apprehensive when using the underground in the future. Furthermore, as Glidewell LJ stated:

> Conduct of this kind is not merely a nuisance, it is thoroughly degrading to the victim.[40]

Consequently, the custodial sentence was upheld, albeit the sentence for the indecent assault was reduced to three months' imprisonment. This can be seen again as reflecting the general attitude of the courts to 'minor' assaults committed by rubbing against a female victim on a train: the act should not be prevented, as a matter of principle, from attracting a custodial sentence, but the courts still attempt to impose a sentence which is commensurate to the seriousness of the incident itself.

4.2   Longer than normal sentences

Almost inevitably, there will arise in indecent assault (as in rape, above) circumstances whereby the sentencer wishes to impose a sentence which is longer than that which the facts of the case themselves merit. In these cases, there will often exist a tension between a desire to protect the public from the defendant, and what, objectively, may be viewed as a relatively minor incident in and of itself. The balancing act, which resolving such a conflict necessarily entails, was seen in *Webb* ([1995] Crim LR 965). The defendant pleaded guilty to indecent assault after he had sat next to his victim on a bus and, during the course of the journey, had squeezed her breasts and 'touched her up' under her skirt. The defendant had several previous convictions, including ones for indecent assault and indecent exposure. He was described, in a report made available to the sentencer, as 'inadequate' and 'immature', and it was noted that he lost his normal inhibitions and sought sexual gratification when he had consumed alcohol. A sentence was imposed of six years' imprisonment, passed as a 'longer than normal sentence' within s 2(2)(b) of the Criminal Justice Act 1991, and the defendant appealed on the basis that the sentence was out of all proportion to the offence. In upholding the sentence, Russell LJ stated the court's view that it was 'appropriate', for the reasons that had been given by the trial judge, namely the defendant's numerous previous convictions, the report as to his personality and the continuing threat that he posed to women.

A similar dilemma faced the trial judge in *White* ([1996] Crim LR 132). The defendant pleaded guilty to indecent assault, having been charged with attempted rape, after he had exposed himself to the victim, then chased and grabbed her from behind. The victim had managed to struggle free, but

---

40   (1995) 16 Cr App R(S) 553, p 558.

subsequently suffered nightmares, depression and loss of sleep, and remained nervous and depressed some seven months after the incident. The defendant had 27 previous convictions, including seven for indecent assault. The court received a psychiatrist's report which stated that the defendant was frustrated due to his inability to form relationships with women, that his offending was increasing and that he was unreceptive to treatment. The trial judge imposed a sentence of nine years' imprisonment as a longer than normal sentence. He stated that a term of five years would have been 'commensurate to the seriousness of the offence', but that the defendant was likely to commit further offences and the nature of his offending was becoming more serious. Conversely, the defendant had pleaded guilty, and 'credit' was given for this in terms of a reduction of one year from the possible maximum sentence for the offence. This reasoning was approved by the Court of Appeal, which upheld the sentence and rejected the arguments of the defendant that the original 'starting point' for the offence (five years) had been too high, and that the additional four years had been excessive.

Cases such as these[41] provide clear evidence of the difficulties facing trial judges when using the s 2(2)(b) power to pass a longer than normal sentence, in circumstances where the present offence is relatively minor and might have deserved a moderate or even low sentence *per se*, but the sentencer nevertheless wishes to 'protect the public'. At present, the authorities appear to suggest that whilst balancing the two competing interests – a sentence which is long enough to give adequate protection to the public, but still bears a reasonable relationship to the offence for which it was imposed – the judiciary is tending to favour the public protection criterion.

5 REFORM

The Criminal Law Revision Committee recommended[42] that there should no longer be separate offences of indecent assault upon males and females, but, rather, there should be a single offence irrespective of the sex of the victim. This proposal was approved by the Law Commission and incorporated into the draft Criminal Code Bill as cl 111:

> A person is guilty of an indecent assault if he assaults another in such a manner, of which he is aware, or in such circumstances, of which he is aware, as are–
>
> (a) indecent, whatever the purpose with which the act is done; or
>
> (b) indecent only if the act is done with an indecent purpose and he acts with such a purpose.

---

41 See, also, *Lyons* (1994) 15 Cr App R(S) 460 for a further example of the consideration of these issues.

42 *Fifteenth Report on Sexual Offences*, Cmnd 9213, 1984, para 4.8, Recommendation 19.

It has been stated (Law Com No 177, 1989, para 15.46) that cl 111 incorporates the effect of the decision of the House of Lords in *Court*. Indeed, given the wording of cl (b), it is open to argument that an even broader construction is possible, and that an assault which is 'indecent only if the act is done with an indecent purpose', could be interpreted as extending the offence to those cases where the act is objectively innocent, but the actor nevertheless had a secret indecent motive.

The clause also does not incorporate the present rule whereby the consent of a person under the age of 16 is not valid in law. In effect, there would no longer be an age limit below which a child could not consent as a matter of law, although, presumably, case law would develop to indicate an age below which there would be no consent *de facto*. In addition, if the indecency were to be 'gross', then separate specific code offences would be committed (see cll 114 and 115, discussed in Chapter 5).

Finally, the impact of the decision in *Brown*, insofar as it relates to a person's ability to consent to harm inflicted deliberately for the purpose of sexual gratification, was considered by the Law Commission in 1995.[43] In that paper, the Law Commission recommended provisionally that a person should be allowed to give a valid consent to injuries intentionally inflicted for sexual purposes within sado-masochistic acts, although consent would not be available where a 'seriously disabling' injury was caused, and neither would it be available to persons under the age of 18.

Subsequent to the above proposals, much more radical recommendations for the reform of indecent assault can be found in *Setting the Boundaries*. As was noted in Chapter 2, there was very strong support for the commonly held view that the current offence of indecent assault is deficient in several respects. In particular, the Report expressed concerns about its breadth, its potential severity and, in severe cases, its low maximum sentence:

> We recognised that other penetrative assaults could be as serious in their impact on the victim as rape and that they should not be regarded lightly. We thought the present law of indecent assault was inadequate to tackle these serious crimes. It is an offence which covers a wide spread of behaviour from touching to truly appalling violations, and the current penalty of 10 years is inadequate for the worst cases.[44]

In the light of this rationale, the Report proposes detailed changes to the offence of indecent assault. Recommendation 3 states:

> There should be a new offence of sexual assault by penetration to be used for all other penetration without consent.

43　Law Commission, *Consent in the Criminal Law*, Law Com No 139, 1995.
44　Home Office Consultation Paper, *Setting the Boundaries*, July 2000, para 2.9.1.

This should be defined as penetration of the anus or genitalia to the slightest extent, and, for the avoidance of doubt, surgically reconstructed genitalia should be included in the definition.

In circumstances where the means of penetration is not clear, the offence of sexual assault by penetration would apply.

This offence would be gender neutral in all respects. It could be committed by a man or a woman, on a man or a woman. Absence of consent/free agreement would be an essential element of the offence, and would have to be proven. That would be defined in the same way as for rape, discussed above. The offence would carry a maximum sentence of life imprisonment.

Finally, the Report proposes a less serious offence of sexual assault to cover those non-penetrative acts which nevertheless amount to unwanted sexual touching. Recommendation 10 states:

There should be a new offence of sexual assault to cover sexual touching (defined as behaviour that a reasonable bystander would consider to be sexual) that is done without the consent of the victim.

The Report was keen to move away from the requirement of 'indecency', which may be viewed as broad and uncertain. The proposed definition of 'sexual touching' follows that contained in the Sexual Offences (Amendment) Bill 2000, and essentially leaves the issue to be determined by the jury. The proposal should also clarify the *mens rea* requirement. There will no longer be a need to establish 'indecent intention'. Rather, *mens rea* is established by proving intent or recklessness as to the assault (or battery), as well as intent or recklessness in relation to lack of consent.

CHAPTER 7

PROSTITUTION: SOCIAL AND THEORETICAL PERSPECTIVES

1   INTRODUCTION

The law's censure and regulation of prostitution and prostitution-related activities is seen frequently as the perfect paradigm of a male-dominated, patriarchal society exercising control over women and autonomous female activity. Society is regarded as having a hypocritical fascination with the phenomenon of prostitution, highlighted by its general public and legal condemnation on the one hand and its private consumption of prostitution on the other.

According to Rudyard Kipling in a much (mis)quoted passage from *Soldiers Three*, prostitution is 'the most ancient profession in the world'. Contemporary writers rarely disagree. In fact, as Roberts has argued, the interest in the phenomenon may be taken a step further:

> [I]f prostitution today is the world's oldest profession, then men writing about it is certainly the second oldest ... [M]ale writers have been obsessed with the whore ... Whores were and are interesting women, the first to say 'No' to patriarchal ownership.[1]

The legal regulation of prostitution (and associated activities) in Britain today will be considered in the following chapter. But it is our contention that, given its seemingly inescapable presence within society, the purely legal controls cannot be understood fully unless the phenomenon of prostitution is first considered from a variety of contexts within which it has existed and continues to exist. It is essential, therefore, to appreciate at least in overview these historical, social, moral and theoretical perspectives, in order to grasp the role of the law in this area. The contextualisation of prostitution is perhaps more important than in any other 'sexual offence'.

1.1   The inevitability of prostitution

As a corollary to the apparent longevity of prostitution in many, if not all, societies, it has been argued that there is a certain 'inevitability' as to the existence of prostitutes, and that as a result, as Bresler has argued, legal intervention is futile:

---

1   Roberts, N, *Whores in History: Prostitution in Western Society*, 1993, HarperCollins – see 'Introduction', p xi.

One stands as much chance of ending prostitution by Act of Parliament as King Canute did of stopping the waves of the English Channel coming in ... merely because he ordered them not to.[2]

The 'reason' for such inevitability may not be difficult to find, as Bresler notes later:

[T]he simple truth is that from the beginning of time – and until the end of time – men have been going, and will continue to go, with prostitutes because they are seeking something which, for whatever reason, they cannot get elsewhere.[3]

It might be expected that such a realistic attitude to the issue would be confined to writers of academic opinion, but there are examples of authoritative recognition of the difficulty, or even futility, in using the law as a method of control in this area. Thus, Home Secretary CT Ritchie, as long ago as 1901, stated:

To get rid of prostitution by legal enactment or by official interposition is out of the question – so long as human nature is what it is, you will never get rid of it entirely ...[4]

Notwithstanding the important caveat that 'inevitability' is not necessarily synonymous with 'desirability' in terms of the existence of prostitution, the type of views expressed above do give rise to a number of fundamental questions. *Why* is prostitution inevitable? And, assuming that it is so, should the law nonetheless still try to exercise some control over it? (After all, there is a strong argument that theft always has been and always will be 'inevitable', but that is hardly a reason not to seek to control it.) If some legal control is to be exercised, is it sensible to distinguish between prostitution *per se* and offences related to prostitution? And again, *if* such a distinction is desirable, on what basis might it be made and is it sustainable in either theory or practice?

Finally, there is a strong consensus among some feminist and Social Interactionist theorists (see below) that the legal control of prostitution is biased against the prostitutes themselves. Although there has been a move towards criminalising certain activities of prostitutes' clients (see the discussion of the offences of kerb-crawling in Chapter 8), it remains true that the overwhelming legal intervention is against either the prostitute herself or those persons inexorably linked to her activities. The client himself remains relatively immune from criminal proceedings.

2   Bresler, F, *Sex and the Law*, 1988, Frederick Muller, p 49.

3   *Ibid*, p 51.

4   Home Secretary CT Ritchie, quoted in Weeks, J, *Sex, Politics and Society*, 1989, Longman, p 85.

2   PROSTITUTION IN HISTORICAL CONTEXT

Given that there is a certain inevitability in the incidence of prostitution, it is both useful and important to provide a brief account of the historical development of the phenomenon. This is important not merely as an historical exercise, but rather as a way to illustrate how and why both prostitution and prostitution-related activities have developed: how different societies at different times have dealt with the issues; political and legal responses to those issues; social attitudes, etc.

2.1   The move from matriarchy to patriarchy

In the period identified by Roberts[5] as 'pre-history' (that is, approximately 25,000 BC to 2,500 BC) many societies were matriarchal in form and based upon the religious and sexual authority of females. Certainly, whores existed, but, in fact, possessed religious authority and thus a large degree of social and political influence and power.

It was not until the decline of matriarchal societies and the consequent emergence of patriarchal systems that attitudes towards prostitution began to change. But, when they did, they changed dramatically and for the worse:

> Like the profession of prostitution, the division of women into wives and whores is as old as (patriarchal) history. It was ... around 2,000 BC that the first laws segregating the two put in an appearance.

> Already the gap was beginning to widen, between 'good' – docile and obedient – wives and 'bad' – sexually autonomous – whores.

> As the power of the male religious and political institutions grew, the patriarchal form of marriage in which the husband literally owned the wife and children drove the wedge between wives and whores even deeper ...

> While the domesticated female was sexually licensed – and therefore controlled – by her exclusive attachment to one man, the reverse did not apply. Men were not prepared to give up old freedoms and the double standard was born.[6]

2.2   Classical attitudes

'Freedom' of sexual behaviour reached its zenith in both ancient Greece (approximately 2,500 BC to 300 BC) and the Roman Empire (approximately 700 BC to 500 AD). All forms of sexual services, including female prostitution, were rife, and indeed often were encouraged and controlled by the authorities of the State.

---

5   *Op cit*, Roberts, fn 1, pp 1–11.
6   *Op cit*, Roberts, fn 1, pp 8–9.

The Greek city-States were the first to operate State-run brothels, although it is perhaps no surprise that these tended to be for the benefit of the State itself (in terms of revenue) and the clients (in terms of freely available and cheap sexual services), rather than the prostitutes who worked there.

Attitudes towards prostitution in this period predominantly were relaxed and favourable. Prostitution was viewed as both 'normal' and essential. In arguments that may be regarded as very early versions of the functionalist perspective, prostitution was seen as preventing adulterous relationships with married women, as maintaining the status of marriage, and as being essential to military morale.

Interestingly, the profession of prostitution was viewed frequently by the prostitutes themselves as desirous. Whilst, undoubtedly, many prostitutes were no better than slaves forced into cheap prostitution, for many more, it was an autonomous activity representing freedom of choice and economic self-sufficiency. Ironically, it was this element of autonomy and self-sufficiency, of a woman's right to break away from male domination, which arguably brought (female) prostitutes into conflict with patriarchal society. The classic 'double standard' of men desiring to utilise prostitution whilst, at the same time, not wishing to relinquish control of the female's activities, clearly existed then in the same way as it may be seen as existing still today. Indeed, the issues facing patriarchal society during the classical period may be regarded as representing the perennial problems of and conflicts within prostitution. These reasons would include, in particular, the desire to provide sexual services (for reasons of practicality or expediency), whilst desiring still to exercise some control over prostitutes' activities, and thus to create some balance between the State's interventionist role as opposed to a more *laissez-faire* approach. Insofar as the history of prostitution may be seen as a conflict between intervention and non-intervention by the State, little has changed in the last 3,000 years, and the task of the law is to continue grappling with those conflicts.

2.3   Prostitution and Christianity

With the decline of the Roman Empire (in approximately AD 450) and the subsequent emergence of the Christian Church, prostitution began to suffer its first real period of harsh and systematic repression. The Church's development as a power in its own right was to have a significant impact upon attitudes about and treatment of prostitutes and prostitution.

Some early Church pronouncements amounted to concerted attacks upon prostitution and on the sinful behaviour of prostitutes. Anti-prostitute campaigns were mounted, warning of the 'dangers of the flesh', and the sin of prostitution as one example of a sin against chastity whilst, at the same time, encouraging the availability of salvation through chastity. It was ironic, however, that, even at this time of severe condemnation and repression, the Church remained capable of taking a pragmatic view when necessary. The Church, from St Augustine to St Thomas Aquinas, believed it was an evil with which it had to live. Thus, prostitution was seen by some within the Church as a 'necessary evil', needed to siphon off man's sexual effluent. In reality, this was the Church's pragmatic face: condemning prostitution in theory, but recognising it *de facto* as an inevitable necessary evil.

2.4   Medieval Europe

Following emergence from the Dark Ages, and the commencement of feudalism in medieval Europe, prostitution once more began to thrive. This was seen especially in the rise of the so called 'camp followers' – large groups of prostitutes who travelled with pilgrims, went on Crusades and marched with a variety of armies across Europe. These camp followers, like a macrocosm of the single prostitute, were fulfilling the functional needs of a variety of temporarily misplaced males.

The general medieval period, of approximately the 11th–15th centuries inclusive, provides a classic illustration of the traditional contradictions which existed, and still exist, in societies' attempts to use the law as a method of regulating prostitution. For the most part, prostitution throughout Europe was very rarely illegal *per se*, but there were an increasing number of regulations being imposed which were designed to attack the perceived 'nuisance' aspects of prostitution. Across many of the main cities of Europe, therefore, there existed: regulations restricting the movements of prostitutes whereby they would be limited to certain areas of a city and restricted from other areas; regulations imposing 'dress codes' on prostitutes, so that they could be readily identified; and confiscation orders (of either monetary fines or property confiscation) for infringement of such regulations. However, in reality, such restrictions remained relatively insignificant. They were frequently ignored by the prostitutes themselves or by the authorities who were not opposed to 'turning a blind eye' in return for 'compensation'. Instead, it was still the Church and not the secular authorities which took a more severe stance on the issue of prostitution. As has frequently been the case, the Church at this time was seen as hypocritical in terms of the message it preached (the sinfulness of prostitution), when compared to the practices of many of its members.

2.5   The 16th–17th centuries

2.5.1   *The Reformation*

Throughout the course of the 16th century, Protestantism emerged as a counter-movement to the previous religious hegemony of the Roman Catholic

Church. In continental Europe, the main Protestant reformers of the time, most notably Martin Luther in Germany and John Calvin in Switzerland, were arguing for a new moral order to be established through the creation of theocratic States. The imposition of re-defined moral codes would be the central plank of this new morality. And, as Roberts has noted, prostitution was a key target:

> At the heart of the new Protestant image of man and society was a new sexual morality – one that was both more pragmatic and more repressive than that of the early Church ... Luther and Calvin proposed the upgrading of the patriarchal institution of marriage ... Procreative sex, within the confines of holy matrimony, was thus sanctified openly by the Protestant reformers ... Their goal was total chastity outside the married state; *they argued bitterly against the notion that young men's promiscuity was natural and inevitable, and that prostitution was therefore permissible.*[7]

2.5.2   Post-Reformation

The extreme moralism and repressive proposals of the Reformation were destined not to be permanent features of European society. By the late 16th and early 17th centuries, much of the formal legal control and suppression of prostitution existed more in theory than in practice.

However the lasting importance of the Reformation lay in its long term impact upon moral attitudes and, in particular, in its influence upon the emergence of a strong Puritan movement. In Britain, especially, much of the 17th century was marked by the classic conflict between 'moralists' and 'libertarians', with Puritanism developing into the most extreme version of the Protestant work ethic, together with its correlation of 'pleasure' and 'sin'.

The apogee of Puritanism/moralism was reached during the short lived period of the Puritan Commonwealth, from 1649 to 1660, following the English Civil War. It was a period highlighted by severe repression of all forms of 'entertainment', especially prostitution. Regulatory controls included severe restrictions on taverns (traditional meeting places for prostitutes and clients), prohibitions on prostitutes themselves, the closure of brothels and harsh penalties for infringements of such relevant measures.

Although the Puritan Commonwealth enjoyed only a relatively short lifespan, the impact of Puritanism *per se* was more significant. It succeeded in placing sexual morality more firmly onto the social (and thus political) agenda than previously it had ever been and, consequently, it set the scene for the future morality debate, which has survived in various guises to the present day.

---

7   *Op cit*, Roberts, fn 1, pp 111–12 (emphasis added).

2.5.3   The Restoration

The restoration to the throne of Charles II in 1660, after the Commonwealth, was marked by a return of sexual freedoms and openness in sexual mores almost to the point of over-indulgence. The aristocracy 'set the standard' for the acceptable level of sexual behaviour, and the rest of the population, buoyed up by the re-opening of the theatres and what today would be termed the restoration comedies, were more than happy to take these standards as their benchmark.

Although the period remained one of obvious and considerable class differences, there was at least a marked reduction in levels of hypocrisy. Prostitution existed in all strata of society, from royal mistresses, through exclusive brothels, and down to the traditional street-walker.

However, the relatively extreme sexual freedom and openness of the late 17th century was destined not to last. Sexual mores began to change as society itself (and attitudes therein) began to change, especially during the course of the 18th century.

2.6   The 18th century

The early decades of the 18th century were not too dissimilar to those of the 17th century in which the sexual freedoms had prevailed. There was a widespread variety of brothels, the 'high class' prostitution scene was thriving (especially in London), and prostitution at all other levels of society was tolerated, often openly.

But the real significance of the 18th century lay in the economic and social changes which were taking place and the corresponding moral changes which accompanied them.

For many centuries in Western Europe, societies had been based upon ruling aristocratic models, to whom the 'lower classes' looked for an example in terms of moral codes and values. Therefore, if the 'new' emerging middle class wished to challenge the traditional ruling class and establish itself as a viable alternative fit to rule, then it had to have some basis for so doing. To the emerging middle class, one obvious way of setting itself as that alternative, was to promote itself as the 'moral class' – the upholder of traditional family values, the respecter of sexual chastity/morality and the critic of immoral prostitution.

Hence, the philosophers of the Enlightenment developed further the Puritan ethic of hard work, especially the mother's role of educating children and inculcating moral and religious beliefs. This emergent 'middle class ethic' promoted a direct challenge to the perceived sexual promiscuity of the lower classes, in particular, with regard to the prevalence of prostitution. But, at the same time, the new ethic had not yet overtaken the sexual permissiveness of the old aristocracy, so that there developed a conflict between those who distinguished the 'virtuous wife' from the 'immoral whore', and those who (sometimes hypocritically) continued to pursue their 'need' for prostitution.

2.6.1   The economic factor

In addition to the emergence of the new middle class morality, the 18th century was important, indeed unique, for providing the genesis of two other phenomena, namely capitalism and the free market economy.

As feudal economies in Europe had experienced a gradual decline from about 1650 onwards, the capitalist economy, especially in Britain, had mushroomed. By the 18th century, the process of industrialisation was well under way, but was not yet sufficiently developed to cater for the masses of displaced peasants forced from the land and into the new towns. The result, inevitably, was extremes of poverty, hardship, disease and desperation. In such circumstances, it is not surprising that one of the weakest and most vulnerable groups in society, that is, women, should turn to prostitution as an activity which provided at least a vestige of economic hope, and thus survival: there was little realistic alternative.

Ironically, as Britain's relatively liberal monarchy of the time took increasingly less interest in State affairs, the 'capitalist philosophy' of trade and industry became the credo upon which society developed. Consequently, moral issues faded into the political background and prostitution was largely ignored, with very little concerted effort by the authorities to exercise control or impose a coherent set of legal rules on the activity.

2.6.2   The Societies for the Reform of Manners

As the State was seen as continuing to adopt an increasingly *laissez-faire* attitude towards morality, the moral stance was taken up by more informal non-State agencies. In the main, of course, these groups consisted of the new middle classes – eager to assert and impose their view of sexual morality. These resulting groups – the Societies for the Reform of Manners – were a logical consequence of the demise of the Puritan Commonwealth, and the subsequent lacuna which was seen to exist in relation to moral direction and ethical leadership.

In addition to seeking to seize the moral high ground, the Societies campaigned also against the blatant corruption of local constables (the body of men who patrolled the main towns and cities) and the magistrates, who all accepted bribes or demanded 'protection money' from prostitutes, brothel 'madams', and pimps, in return for not enforcing the regulations controlling prostitution.

Middle class moral reformers made up the membership of the Societies, and traditionally consisted of powerful citizens, lawyers, members of Parliament, magistrates and priests. Their 'clean-up' campaigns were widespread, and often very coercive in nature. On numerous occasions, the campaigns led to violence, sometimes against prostitutes themselves (or their pimps) and sometimes against a typical client-group, such as soldiers or sailors in garrison towns where prostitution was almost endemic.

Although most of the Societies had reached the height of their power and influence by about 1725, and, indeed, in the main were declining by the early 1730s, it was arguably their longer-term influence, rather than any obvious short term successes, which was of significance. In particular, the agitation engendered by the Societies, especially in relation to the more visible street prostitution, was an important influence in fostering a climate of opinion about prostitution. Admittedly, this opinion was largely one sided, that is, against prostitution and in favour of widespread reforms of sexual behaviour, but at least the Societies had succeeded (in modern parlance) in placing prostitution, and morality more generally, back onto the political agenda.

Similarly, the Societies were highly influential in shaping attitudes later in the 18th century in respect of concerns about public order. Unfortunately, as these concerns grew, the prostitute (as has frequently been the case) became an easy scapegoat to satisfy the apprehensions of the moral middle class. These attitudes were to lay the foundations for future moral vigilantism in the subsequent two centuries.

2.7 The 19th century

2.7.1 Early 19th century

By the early years of the 19th century, the full economic and social impact of the Industrial Revolution was beginning to be felt. Huge numbers of former peasants had poured, and continued to pour, into the new towns and cities in an attempt to find employment at a time when industrialisation and factory production were not yet sufficiently developed to provide adequate jobs. The results were inevitable: extreme poverty; no work (or, at best, work which paid subsistence wages or below); slum housing; homelessness; disease; and early death. Roberts highlights the desperate position:

> [E]ven in the factories, women were paid far less than the male workers, which put them at a disadvantage in the desperate struggle for survival: they were the poorest of the poor, underprivileged even among those who had nothing. *The social and economic conditions were ripe for the unprecedented boom in prostitution that ensued* ...[8]

Ironically, whilst poverty was an obvious 'side effect' of industrialisation, and therefore one obvious factor in influencing women into becoming prostitutes, there were other consequences resulting from industrialisation which were

---

8   *Op cit*, Roberts, fn 1, p 189 (emphasis added).

equally important in explaining the prevalence of prostitution. As a corollary to the creation of poverty, industrialisation produced also the infrastructure necessary for prostitution to thrive. There was wealth (albeit very concentrated) to be spent, an expanding client base and the physical opportunity in the sense of an increasing availability of venues where the parties could engage in prostitution. At the same time, an attitude was developing of enjoyment, amusement and revelry. This may seem somewhat paradoxical amid such poverty, but is perhaps typical of people's determination to 'forget their troubles' by recourse to whatever distractions are available. For some, prostitution was such a diversion.

As the conditions conducive to prostitution, especially among the 'lower classes', flourished, it was inevitable that there would be a corresponding moral reaction. Industrialisation and capitalism gave rise to the middle class bourgeoisie, but their strength was destined to lie not just in their economic and political power. Increasingly, economic and political influence gave rise to their moral and social values and ideologies. In this most polarised of class systems, the middle class divided female society in a now familiar way: the 'non-sexual', 'good' wife, as opposed to the sexual, dirty, 'bad' prostitute.

2.7.2   Mid to late 19th century

The 1850s and 1860s witnessed a further and stronger wave of industrialisation, with an increased number of factories, bigger cities and larger populations. One direct result of this process was the emergence of a set of new social conditions, especially the creation of a body of mass migrant workers, trade unionism and the decline of the traditional nuclear family and its values. Such fundamental changes rapidly impacted upon the existing Victorian moral orthodoxy: a moral panic was created, whereby the very essence of the bourgeois social order was perceived to be threatened with destruction.

The 'remedy' to this 'threat' was to take the form of a re-statement and re-emphasis of the traditional values of the middle class. This was to be based upon the centrality of the patriarchal nuclear family, with its belief in and respect for social discipline, the control of sexual behaviour and the Puritan work ethic. But the response of the middle class to the threat was not limited to merely a re-confirmation of traditional theoretical attitudes. Rather, their views had a much greater and more direct impact upon a number of legislative measures of the time. Even as early as 1839, for instance, public concerns about the nuisance of prostitution had resulted in measures such as the Metropolitan Police Act 1839 and the City of London Police Act 1839, which, *inter alia*, prohibited loitering for the purposes of prostitution and criminalised persons who knowingly permitted or suffered prostitutes to gather on certain defined premises, within the Metropolitan and City of London areas.

2.7.2.1 The Contagious Diseases Acts 1864, 1866 and 1869

By far the greatest impact of the middle class morality movements of the mid-19th century was the pressure exerted in influencing the passage of the Contagious Diseases Acts. Ostensibly, the Acts were 'public health measures', with the laudable aim of tackling the 'social evil' of VD (in particular, syphilis), which was a problem of almost endemic proportions amongst men of the navy and army in most naval and garrison towns.

The Acts provided for the compulsory examination, detention and treatment of prostitutes who lived in certain specified naval and garrison towns. It is interesting to note, however, that, whilst the treatment of syphilis *per se* was a praiseworthy activity, the legislation itself, as was often the case, was directed at the woman/prostitute, not the male participant in prostitution. And irrespective of the bias inherent in the Acts, it is arguable that the very philosophy underpinning the legislation was flawed. In particular, whilst syphilis was undoubtedly a grave concern, it was used by the moral instigators of the legislation as a symbol to encapsulate the corruption inherent in sexual behaviour. Syphilis embodied the middle class's dread of both sex and the working class. Sexual intercourse *per se* was dangerous enough, but this was exacerbated where sex occurred with a working class prostitute.

If the philosophy behind the legislation was questionable, it quickly became apparent that the Acts were subject also to misuse in practice, in the sense that they operated as a form of severe repression. Prostitutes (and even non-prostitute women who were merely suspected of engaging in prostitution) were deprived of their liberty. They were subjected to forced medical examinations. And the procedures imposed frequently caused illness, rather than prevent it as intended: infection was caused by the unclean medical equipment, and severe illness (and even death) was caused by mercury poisoning – one of the supposed 'treatments'!

2.7.2.2 Reactions to the Contagious Diseases Acts

Within a fairly short period of time from their enactment and implementation, the harsh workings of the Acts, together with the implicit assumptions about the existence of prostitution which they made, resulted in a strange alliance of early feminists, moralists and religious activists, all concerned to effect the repeal of the legislation. As Weeks has noted, the abolitionist movement was diverse and powerful:

> [T]he apparent acceptance of prostitution in the Acts evoked a strong response from feminists, led by Josephine Butler, and from social moralists, which was directed particularly against the State regulation of vice. Throughout the 1870s and 1880s the 'abolitionists' ... were a major social force, and the stimulus for the emergence of vigorous social purity organisations ...[9]

---

9   *Op cit*, Weeks, fn 4, pp 85–86.

The impact of Josephine Butler's campaigns, centred in Liverpool, should not be underestimated. Being both a feminist and a committed Christian, Butler was able to unite a range of perspectives and thus create a powerful, broad-based alliance seeking repeal of the Acts. But, as with many Victorian reformers in the realm of prostitution, Butler's combination of feminism and Christian belief did not always sit easily together. All abolitionists abhorred the economic deprivation which forced so many women into prostitution. Feminists were able also to recognise the severe repression of individual freedom which the Acts caused. But, at the same time, there existed the pervading element of Victorian Christian morality; an often overt condemnation of prostitution as sinful, and something to be eradicated in its own right.

2.7.2.3 Social Purity

By the mid-1880s, many of the original reform and repeal groups had either broadened into or been 'taken over' by the so called 'Social Purity movements'. These groups, not dissimilar to the Societies for the Reform of Manners in the previous century (above), consisted of a broad collection of religious, moral, feminist and middle class factions. Their shared common aim was to unite against prostitution, which was seen as the symbol of the general moral decline of the time. Butler herself had been a prime mover in the development of the single-issue repeal campaigns into the wider Social Purity movements. Indeed, the Contagious Diseases Acts themselves had been repealed in 1886, but the Social Purity groups, ignoring their original and specific abolitionist *raison d'être*, continued and, if anything, strengthened. The groups were no longer tied to abolition (that goal having been achieved), but turned instead to the wider objective of extinguishing all prostitution, on the basis of setting a higher standard of sexual morality for both males and females.

By the end of the century, Social Purity activists often patrolled the streets of many main cities, acting as early moral vigilantes and taking over the role of the police. It is ironic that such patrols frequently resulted in prostitutes becoming more secretive in their actions and more reliant on male pimps, which changes in behaviour often created a generally more dangerous working environment.

By the turn of the century, in the period approximately from 1890 to 1910, the Social Purity movement, and in particular the anti-prostitution lobby, had reached its height. At this time an amazing array of groups and ideologies were campaigning against prostitution. These ranged from conservative morality groups seeking the total repression of the sex industry (as being the 'work of the Devil'), through 'Butlerite' and feminist groups opposed to the 'female sexual slavery' inherent in prostitution, to early Marxist/socialist groups who saw prostitution as symbolising the rottenness of all capitalist, property-based societies.[10]

As ever in the history of prostitution, this period witnessed the orchestration of prostitution for solely ideological ends: prostitution was 'wicked' and thus to be eradicated; or it typified male domination in a patriarchal society; or it symbolised the deficiencies of capitalism. The prostitutes themselves and their accompanying circumstances were largely ignored.

3   THE 20TH CENTURY

Much of the first half of the 20th century, from about 1910 to 1950, was a period of relative calm in terms of discourse on prostitution. In historical context, the reasons for this inactivity are not difficult to find: within a period of only four decades the traumas of World War I, the Russian Revolution, the Great Depression, the rise of National Socialism and Fascism, and World War II, all meant that the public and the authorities had little time or inclination to debate the morality and immorality of prostitution.

3.1   The 1950s

Prostitutes and prostitution were placed firmly back onto the social and political agenda in the 1950s, most notably as a result of the Wolfenden Committee.[11] The Wolfenden Report was just one of a wide range of bodies and groups to identify a perceived general loosening of moral standards and decline of traditional (family) values in Britain at this time. Some 'evidence' for this moral decline was said to be found in the prosecution statistics for street offences over the relevant period. In the early 1940s, for instance, prosecutions for street offences stood at approximately 2,000 *per annum*. In 1952, this figure had soared to 10,000, and, in 1955, it stood at 12,000. Of course, these figures (like any statistics) do not necessarily 'prove' that there existed a greater incidence of prostitution or prostitution-related activity by the mid-1950s. The apparent rise could be due to a range of other factors, such

---

10   It is interesting to note that the Marxist view of prostitution remained the official ideology in the USSR until the collapse of Communism in the early 1990s. Officially prostitution (and, indeed, other sexual offences) did not exist in the USSR, because such crimes were manifestations of capitalist society. It was only with the advent of *glasnost* and *perestroika* under Mikhail Gorbachov that the converse reality of the situation became apparent. This gives some support to the view that prostitution does possess a degree of 'inevitability', regardless of culture, class and political ideology.

11   Much of the general background to the setting up of the Wolfenden Committee and its eventual report have already been discussed in Chapter 1, in the context of homosexuality. The fears about, and perceived threats of, homosexuality, were very much the fears and threats of prostitution.

as increased governmental pressure to tackle the issue of prostitution, and greater police activity 'on the ground'. Nevertheless, the figures did represent some evidence to explain why there was an increase in both official concern and public anxiety. The moral concerns over prostitution in the early 1950s could be 'explained' on very similar bases to the concerns about homosexuality: prostitution was increasing visibly on the streets of London (and other major cities); it created a bad impression, especially to foreign visitors; it was morally dangerous (presumably in the sense of possessing a potentially corrupting influence); and the participants were 'deviant'. One of the major anomalies in this reasoning has been noted by Weeks:

> It is striking that the estimated prostitute population of London in the 1850s of 50,000 was accepted with much less horror than the 2,000–3,000 or so in London in the 1950s. By the 1950s, there appears to have been a widespread worry that young men who went regularly with prostitutes might never learn the value of sex within marriage.[12]

Whilst the worry that young men who use prostitutes may never learn the value of marital sex is open to challenge on both grounds of logic and lack of empirical evidence, the statement is illustrative in another sense. The changes in attitude and perception about prostitution over the period of a century, indicate clearly that society's moral views can and do alter from generation to generation. It is clear that there were groups who held strong opinions against prostitution even in the mid-19th century, although the mass of the population appear to have been apathetic or, at most, ambivalent about the issue. But it is equally clear that, by the mid-20th century, a greater proportion of the population had vehemently held views on the matter, and were both willing and able to make those views known to the authorities.

3.1.1 The Wolfenden strategy

The central plank in the so called 'Wolfenden strategy' was the Committee's recognition of a 'public/private dichotomy', which could be used as the basis for distinguishing between private acts ('non-visible' and not to be criminalised) and public acts ('visible' and thus open to criminalisation). But even if this distinction is accepted (if only in principle), it inevitably would result in the proscription of many aspects of prostitution, as well as an explicit condemnation of prostitute women themselves, as Newburn has argued:

> Essentially the Wolfenden recommendations and their legislative enactment were a public denouncement of prostitution and an affirmation of the importance of 'normal' sexual relationships (monogamous and within the family) ... It was the 'ghettoisation' of one class of women, a reiteration of the division between 'normal' and 'deviant' and the embodiment of this division in an Act of Parliament.[13]

---

12 *Op cit*, Weeks, fn 4, p 240.

13 Newburn, T, *Permission and Regulation: Law and Morals in Post-War Britain*, 1992, Routledge, p 53.

Notwithstanding such forceful criticisms, the Wolfenden Committee remained convinced that if the purposes of the criminal law were, as they suggested, to protect from 'offensive and injurious' matters, to protect from 'exploitation and corruption' and to preserve 'public order and decency', then the public/private dichotomy was supportable in principle and the criminal law could justifiably be used to proscribe certain public displays of sexuality. Thus, the Committee's Report stated:

> The simple fact is that prostitutes do parade themselves more habitually and openly than their prospective customers, and do by their continual presence affront the sense of decency of the ordinary citizen. In doing so they create a nuisance which, in our view, the law, is entitled to recognise and deal with.[14]

3.1.2 The effect of Wolfenden

It can be argued that the legislation resulting directly from the Wolfenden Committee Report[15] suffered from much the same defect as have all regulations and controls in the history of prostitution, namely that, far from tackling the issue of prostitution *per se*, let alone the real underlying causes of it, the 1959 Act did no more than change the problem, by moving it to a different sphere:

> [The Act] drove prostitution off the streets by increasing fines and imprisonment. But simultaneously it led to a reorganisation of prostitution, contributing to a vast expansion of commercial prostitution agencies and call-girl rackets. By privatising prostitution, Wolfenden (who had recognised the danger but balanced it against the reduced public visibility) and the legislators had the effect of freeing prostitution for an increased rate of commercial exploitation.[16]

3.2 The 1960s to the present

Were the 'permissive sixties' and the 'swinging seventies' really as permissive and swinging as many historians, sociologists and politicians would have us believe? Can these two decades really be blamed as being the source of all our current 'moral ills'? There are no easy answers to such questions, although it cannot be doubted that the 'sexual revolution' of the 1960s had a huge impact upon subsequent social and moral values. Whether that impact was for good or bad remains a matter of interpretation.

From one perspective, the unparalleled consumerism which commenced in the 1960s can be seen to have challenged traditional ethical values: the old values of work and thrift were contested by the new 'young' values of pleasure and spending. Selling and advertising became the essence of the

---

14 Wolfenden Committee Report, p 87, para 257.
15 The Street Offences Act 1959, which is discussed in Chapter 8.
16 *Op cit*, Weeks, fn 4, at p 244.

modern consumer society, and to the businessmen and 'admen' of the 1960s and 1970s sex, became a commodity: a crucial means to the end of profit. Consequently, sexual activity became 'legitimised' for ordinary people in a way previously unprecedented. Sex was no longer regarded as something 'dirty', and the particular stigmatisation of prostitutes (as being synonymous with sex and thus dirtiness) began to be eroded. This relaxation of sexual mores, and the increase in sexual freedom and individual autonomy, led to an increased understanding and tolerance of the prostitute herself.

Paradoxically, a converse view exists which argues that, whilst increased sexual freedom had been *capable* of leading to greater toleration of and respect for prostitutes, this, in fact, did not happen in practice. Instead, the traditional 'double standard' in relation to prostitution, which has existed throughout history, continues to thrive. The authorities, and other groups who possess influence in society, feel threatened by increased sexual freedoms and, as has been seen in past eras, resort to repressive measures in order to re-assert *their* moral authority.

It is essential to recognise that the 'morality debate' throughout the 1980s and early 1990s has had a focus considerably wider than prostitution alone. The moral philosophy during the period of the Thatcher administrations (and, more recently, the Major administrations) was driven undoubtedly by a series of moral panics over a wide range of issues. These centred around concerns ranging across 'video nasties', child sexual abuse scandals, pornography, AIDS, and the more nebulous notion of the decline of the nuclear family. The 'solution' to these moral ills was the solution propounded by the 'New Right' ideology.[17] Here, the decade of the 1960s is presented as being the cause of all our present day moral ills; it was a decade without any moral probity or worth, the awful impact of which can be remedied only by a return to a 'golden age' identified by New Right ideologists as consisting of Victorian values, epitomised by the morality of the patriarchal family.

Much of the contemporary discussion of prostitution has centred around rights discourse, and seeks to incorporate analysis of a variety of (often competing) themes, such as human rights, individual autonomy, 'contract', and control, whilst still balancing traditional concepts of morality and patriarchy. A selection of the theories of prostitution will be considered in the following section.

---

17 See generally, eg, Levitas, R (ed), *The Ideology of the New Right*, 1985, Polity; and Scruton, R, *Sexual Desire: A Philosophical Investigation*, 1986, Weidenfeld and Nicolson. For an account of the related American ideology of 'New Puritanism', see, eg, Altman, D, *AIDS and the New Puritanism*, 1986, Pluto.

4 THE THEORISATION OF PROSTITUTION

If, now, it is clear that prostitution has existed in virtually all human societies at all times, there still remains the most fundamental question of how the existence of the phenomenon can be explained. In tackling this question, a number of related issues will arise. Central to these issues will be considerations such as: why do women become prostitutes?; why do men use prostitutes?; can prostitution be justified?; can controls on prostitution be justified?

It is unlikely that any one single theory can provide adequate answers to all of these questions (although each theory may purport to do so). Indeed, 'theory' may be an inappropriate term to explain each perspective, and it may be wiser to regard each theory as no more than a 'school of thought' upon the phenomenon of prostitution, where that school possesses a number of shared beliefs. Conversely, it should not be thought that these perspectives are necessarily mutually exclusive: there frequently exists a degree of overlap between the perspectives and consensus amongst the writers.

4.1   The functionalist perspective

4.1.1   Prostitution and sexuality

The functionalist model subscribes to the 'inevitability view' of prostitution, as described, for example, by Jarvinen:

> [P]rostitution is a normal and universal phenomenon, existing in all periods and all known societies. The functionalists consider prostitution as ... a natural and unavoidable social phenomenon ... which is relatively independent of the societal structure and level of development.[18]

Given the 'naturalness' and inevitability of prostitution, the prostitution/marriage dichotomy becomes of central importance to the functionalists. Married men want sex, in both quantity and variability, which they cannot always get within marriage. On this reasoning, it follows that, in all societies where the institution of marriage is relatively strong, prostitution will inevitably flourish. Indeed, if a society wishes to preserve the institution of marriage, then it can even be argued that the presence of prostitution is the price to be paid for that survival.

Functionalists may see this view of sexuality as supported by the fact that many men who use prostitutes are middle aged, middle class, married professionals: men who are perceived, and who perceive themselves, as

---

18   Jarvinen, M, *Of Vice and Women: Shades of Prostitution*, 1992, OUP, p 17.

getting from prostitutes something which they could not obtain within the confines of marriage.

4.1.2   Functionalist explanations

The preceding summary of sexuality leads naturally into the functionalists' 'explanations' of why men use prostitutes. Although several different notions exist, they are linked by the concept of 'sexual frustration'. Thus, a man's use of a prostitute may be occasioned by the inability or unwillingness of the man's wife or partner to satisfy his sexual desires (or, at least, certain aspects of them). Alternatively, there may exist an element of 'sexual isolation' on the part of the man. This may be 'short term', involving for example the man's absence from his usual partner due to reasons of work (sometimes exacerbated by the need to travel considerable distances from home through the requirement of employment); or 'long term', involving young single men, divorced men or widowers. In this last category, the man's inability to succeed in a 'non-commercial sexual relationship' is seen as a crucial factor in understanding prostitution:

> According to functionalism, prostitution is needed to satisfy the sexual needs of physically, emotionally or socially handicapped men. *Thus, prostitution seemingly fills important social functions in society.*[19]

The functionalist perspective is not limited to 'explaining' why men use prostitutes. It considers also the reasons why women become prostitutes. The several arguments which exist may be summarised as: the mental or emotional view (that prostitutes are 'feeble-minded or psychopathic or drug addicts'); the sexual view (they are hypersexual or lesbians with no emotional attachment to their male clients); the social view (they have suffered a traumatic childhood and/or sexual abuse, or they are alcoholic); and the economic view (prostitutes have high goals, but no other means of satisfying those goals). Whilst superficially diverse, all these views are linked by a common theme:

> A common denominator in all these assessments is that the prostitutes are characterised as deviant, as mentally, sexually or socially abnormal.[20]

4.1.3   Functionalism and control

Due to the fact that functionalists regard prostitution as 'inevitable', that is as normal and universal, it follows that it is an unrealistic social goal to try to eradicate it. If strict (or stricter) controls were to be introduced, the result would merely be different, more covert, forms of prostitution. This argument can, in fact, be taken a step further. Legislative control can be viewed actually as negative and harmful, in the sense that rigid regulation removes the 'safety valve' which prostitution provides. Without this safety valve there is a risk of

---

19   *Op cit*, Jarvinen, fn 18 (emphasis added).

20   *Op cit*, Jarvinen, fn 18.

sexual frustration (possibly even leading to an increase in the incidence of sexual offences), as well as a risk of an increase in extra-marital affairs, with consequential effects upon the status of marriage.

If control measures are to be adopted, therefore, they should not be aimed at prostitution *per se*, nor arguably even at activities such as soliciting, but should be reserved solely for the control of related social disturbances, such as accompanying criminality (for instance, the coercive activities of pimps) or associated problems, like drug use. By contrast, the law is seen as having no role in relation to purely private acts between consenting adult parties.

4.2 The feminist perspective

4.2.1 Prostitution and sexuality

One of the most prevalent themes in the feminist literature on prostitution is that prostitution is linked emphatically to the inequalities that exist between males and females in society. Thus, Jarvinen states:

> Prostitution consists of a supply and demand for remunerated sexual services; in all periods, men have answered for the demand and ... women ... for the supply ... [which is] reflective of the gender-skewed allocation of social, economic and political resources in the society ... The imbalance of power between men and women is reflected in the sexualisation of the socio-economically weaker gender.[21]

Similarly, Pateman has argued:

> Prostitution is an integral part of patriarchal capitalism ... Prostitutes are readily available at all levels of the market for any man who can afford one ...[22]

In feminist discourse, this economic imbalance, together with the inequality which results from patriarchal, capitalist systems, leads to the objectification of women. The prostitute woman is seen openly to be subject to male domination, with an overt financial relationship between the sexes which announces clearly to all that she has been, like any commodity, 'valued' and reified. Within this perspective there exists an inevitable correlation between the objectification and reification of females, and the commercialisation of the female body as a commodity. Nowhere is this process seen more overtly than in the transparent prostitute/client transaction, thus normalising the very phenomenon of prostitution.

A further strand of feminist thinking condemns the traditional patriarchal view of males having 'normal' sexual needs, but typical females as having little or no such sexual desire. By perpetuating this myth, it is argued,

---

21 *Op cit*, Jarvinen, fn 18, p 19.
22 Pateman, C, *The Sexual Contract*, 1988, Polity, p 189.

traditional male views categorise and criticise prostitutes as 'abnormal' women because they do possess erotic, sexual personalities. This may be seen as no more than a modern version of the archetypal 'good woman/bad whore' divide which has existed throughout history:

> Women's respectability is judged largely by their sexuality and, placed along a continuum, women are either 'good' or 'bad', virgins or whores. The ideological construction of the prostitute serves to divide and separate women into different categories.[23]

4.2.2 Feminist explanations

Feminist theory seeks to 'explain' prostitution from two quite different perspectives, namely the causes of women becoming prostitutes, as well as the reasons why men become the clients of prostitutes.

Several different explanations exist as to why women become prostitutes, but they are all related by the presence of a link between prostitution and patriarchal sexual ideology. Prime amongst these causes are 'economic reasons': prostitutes tend to be recruited from economically disadvantaged families, often with poor education and few employment prospects. Prostitution is thus a natural and rational alternative to low (or no) pay.

In addition, 'social rootlessness' is seen as an important factor. Many young women enter prostitution after drifting away from family, school, friends or their first jobs. They are lonely and socially marginalised, whereas prostitution sub-culture offers a recognisable and viable alternative.

Finally, there exists an element of sexual exploitation, whereby many feminists argue that prostitutes have suffered sexual abuse and/or incestuous relationships whilst they were young. No doubt, this is true in some cases, but it would be an error to over-generalise, as this account fails to explain why many girls who have been abused do not enter into prostitution in later life, and thus the causal link must remain at least questionable.

With regard to men who use prostitutes, feminist theory puts forward a number of 'explanations', which in many respects challenge the traditionally held beliefs about prostitutes' clients. To feminists, most clients are *not* sexually isolated or mentally or socially handicapped, as, for instance, functionalists have argued. Instead, many clients are seen as sexually experienced, often married and coming from all ages and social classes, especially higher classes.

Secondly, clients' motives are not always solely sexual in nature. Although clearly there often may be a sexual desire, there equally may well exist other 'motives': the excitement or 'danger' of a relationship with a prostitute; the non-demanding and impersonal nature of such liaisons; the desire not to be alone; the desire to be 'subservient'.

---

23 Chadwick, K and Little, C, 'The criminalisation of women', in Scraton, P, *Law, Order and the Authoritarian State*, 1987, OUP, pp 254–73, at p 254.

Interestingly, the patriarchal nature of contemporary society, with its traditional 'gender roles', provides two further, but contrasting, explanations, for men's use of prostitutes. The first of these is that some men have great difficulty in 'living up to' the demands of a patriarchal, gender-based society, in which they are expected to be dominant in a range of financial, social and sexual matters, without the opportunity of relaxing from these almost permanent obligations. Prostitution, however, does allow for such repose, even if only temporarily. Conversely, there are some men who will use prostitutes for precisely the opposite reason: to reinforce the stereotypical gender role, by convincing themselves of their own ability to meet the demands of our patriarchal society, which they would not be able to meet outside of a prostitute relationship.

4.2.3 Feminism and control

Feminist theory analyses the control of prostitution as the explicit control of certain types of women who are labelled as 'deviant'. In most societies where controls over prostitution exist, it is noteworthy that the bulk of control is exercised over the prostitute herself, rather than the male client. In patriarchal society, the traditional view of females is that asexuality and monogamy are the norms, whereas a prostitute is both sexual and polygamous. She is, thus, by definition 'deviant', and hence a natural and acceptable target for punishment or treatment. On this reasoning, it is only to be expected that the law will take an overt role in controlling the 'active' prostitute, by legislating for example against the act of loitering or soliciting in a public place, because such acts are outside the bounds of acceptable social behaviour. However, it is not necessarily easy to fit this analysis into the fairly strident measures which exist, and are taken against male clients, in relation to offences such as kerb-crawling.[24] In these offences, the initiative is being taken by the man, and the law's response can be seen as a reaction to the nuisance caused to local residents by *those* men.

4.3 The Social Interactionist (or constructionist) perspective

This perspective is less a single idea or concept, but more a collection of factors which serves to identify a number of themes running through prostitution. Within this fairly diverse range, three main themes may be identified: relativity, social control and classification.

4.3.1 Relativity

Social Interactionism views prostitution as a social construct, the definitions and constituent elements of which differ according to temporal and cultural

---

24 See the Sexual Offences Act 1985, ss 1(1) and 2(1), discussed in Chapter 8.

variances. Thus, in contrast to functionalism, for instance, which regards prostitution as normal, inevitable and universal, this approach sees the phenomenon as relative, that is as variable. Consequently, the precise meaning of 'prostitution' will depend upon the ways in which a number of factors are viewed.

First, prostitution is agreed, generally, to possess an element of 'commerciality', that is, that there exists a clear economic link in terms of a relationship between payment and the provision of sexual service(s).

Secondly, prostitution is 'non-selective', in the sense that the traditional view holds that an ability to pay is the only selection criterion applied by a prostitute. This factor may be doubted, as it is arguable that many prostitutes do in fact operate a 'vetting' process on several bases, such as the perceived dangerousness of some customers, the type of acts required by the client, the racial or social group of the client, etc.

Thirdly, there exists a criterion of 'promiscuity'. This criterion is used to distinguish the 'true' prostitute from, say, the 'kept woman' (who is paid by one man only), or the 'amateur' who may engage in a single, isolated act of prostitution.

Fourthly, and following from the previous criterion, there is an element of 'transitoriness' in prostitution, whereby prostitutes are distinguished from non-prostitutes because of the ephemeral nature of their associations and converse lack of long term relationships. Once again, this criterion may be questioned, as it is clear that many prostitutes do have regular customers, sometimes coinciding with those prostitutes who have a small clientele. Such women do not cease to be prostitutes merely because of the presence of such factors.

Finally, prostitutes are seen as possessing 'emotional indifference' in relation to their clients. Whilst the essentially impersonal and emotionally neutral nature of the prostitute/client relationship may represent the traditionally held view, there are instances of prostitutes holding emotional feelings of friendship and caring, especially for 'regular' clients.

What this diverse range of criteria emphasises is both the vagueness and relativity of prostitution as a phenomenon. Social Interactionist theory may deny the existence of a clear, universal conceptual definition, but the list of criteria is useful for highlighting the scale and spectrum of sexual relations which may fall within the ambit of the term 'prostitution'.

4.3.2   Social control

The second integral feature of a Social Interactionist perspective on prostitution is the focus on control ... The designations 'prostitutes' and 'customers' do not apply to naturally given categories of individuals with particular social or psychological traits; instead, they are the result of complicated social processes. The central question in a Social Interactionist analysis of commercialised sex is not why some people become prostitutes/customers, *but how certain people become defined as such.*[25]

The essence of this aspect of the Social Interactionist perspective, as Jarvinen makes clear, is to emphasise the 'how', rather than the 'why' of prostitution. If prostitution (including prostitutes and clients) can be identified and defined, then the authorities will be in a much stronger position to exercise control over the 'deviants'. The key objective in this perspective, therefore, becomes that of control. But control can only be exercised after the authorities have first identified the phenomenon and its constituent elements.

4.3.3 Classification

It follows from the previous two aspects, that Social Interactionists do not recognise a single, coherent phenomenon of prostitution, but rather different 'types' of prostitution. These types will depend upon how, precisely, the various activities of the parties are defined and classified. In particular, the varying classifications will highlight the different attitudes which exist in relation to alternative 'forms' of prostitution. This in turn will be seen to have a major impact upon the level of control or intervention exercised, both in theory and practice, by the authorities.

One particularly important aspect of classification is the element of 'publicness', which, although it is a term that can be used by theorists in a variety of ways, may be taken for present purposes as connoting a degree of openness or 'visibility'. Thus, different types of prostitution possess different levels of visibility, ranging from the prostitution of the comparatively visible street-walker, to that of the comparatively invisible call-girl working from a high class agency. But even this definition may be too simplistic, and a more complex social interaction may exist. The level of visibility, for example, may depend upon other factors such as to whom the prostitution is 'visible': the prostitution may be 'invisible' to 'outsiders' (that is, those persons not concerned with the transactions), but may be obviously visible to interested parties, such as the prostitutes themselves, the customers, pimps, hotel owners, etc. Conversely, some manifestations of prostitution are overtly visible (in the twin sense of being observable and known) to all in a particular community. Thus, 'red light' districts (such as King's Cross in London or Chapel Town in Leeds), or even a series of specific streets within a community, will be 'visible' sites of prostitution in these terms.

This element of visibility is linked inevitably to levels of control and tolerance, whether official or unofficial, of prostitution. In many respects the law takes a greater interest in visible forms of commercialised sexual activity (including specific manifestations such as soliciting), as compared with more invisible forms, where activities will be tolerated, or at least have a 'blind eye'

---

turned towards them. Consequently, as the Wolfenden Committee itself recognised, above, there should be little scope for legal intervention where private and discreet prostitution activities occur.

A second aspect of the classification of prostitution, is the level of 'exclusivity' which is seen to exist. In many respects, 'exclusivity', being linked inexorably to the criteria of promiscuity, non-selectivity and temporariness, lies at the core of the Social Interactionist view of control. On a supposed scale of 'exclusivity', street-walkers and cheap-bar prostitutes would operate at one end of the spectrum. They have numerous clients about whom they are non-selective, and the contacts are short lived and anonymous. Here, there exists 'low exclusivity'. At the other end of the scale operates the high class call-girl working from an organised, exclusive bureau. There will be a very selective (and limited) clientele, possibly even with a closer, longer term relationship forming. Here, there exists 'high exclusivity'. Based upon such a distinction, the use of the law as a mechanism of control is biased frequently against low-exclusivity prostitution, where it exercises a much more vigorous intervention. High-exclusivity prostitution escapes relatively untouched by the hand of the law. As has been seen throughout many periods in the history of prostitution, whilst the law may seek to exercise control over several forms of prostitution, it retains its most overt and heavy-handed intervention for the most vulnerable women.

4.4   The Liberal/Permissive perspective

This perspective can hold claim to being both the most straightforward and the most frequently held attitude towards prostitution. It represents a view popularised by the Wolfenden Committee, but maintaining its prevalence from the late 1950s through to the mid-1970s.

In a 1981 study of 25 Sheffield magistrates, Smart[26] found that, whilst all the magistrates agreed on the need for some legal, coercive intervention in prostitutes' lives, the type of intervention varied according to their perception of the problems and issues involved. Of the various views put forward, the Liberal/Permissive perspective was the most common:

> The magistrates who adopted this view ... argued that prostitution was only a matter for the criminal law when it became visible on the streets. The solution ... was a pragmatic recognition of the need for licensed brothels where people could get on with it *without causing a nuisance*.[27]

The kind of attitude typified in this statement is illustrative of several themes which have run through the entire prostitution discourse. In particular, the

---

26 Smart, C, 'Legal subjects and sexual objects: ideology, law and female sexuality', in Brophy, J and Smart, C, *Women in Law: Explorations in Law, Family and Sexuality*, 1985, Routledge, pp 50–70, at pp 61–62.

27 *Ibid*, p 63.

'visibility' of the prostitutes' activities was seen as a main justification for exercising control. The very essence of the liberal approach is that the law should not intervene unless and until there is an element of visibility or publicness, in which case, the law is then required to balance the competing interests of the prostitutes' individual autonomy against the wider public interest which inevitably occurs when acts are no longer in private. The views expressed above may also be taken as not condemning the activity or concept of prostitution itself, but rather that it is the unwarranted consequences of prostitution, namely the nuisance aspects, which cause the greatest concern and which the law should seek to control.

4.5   The Puritan/Authoritarian perspective

A number of magistrates in Smart's study adopted a point of view which was reminiscent of traditional authoritarian thinking and which has retained a strong presence in both general social attitudes and the literature on prostitution throughout many centuries:

> This category of magistrates were concerned to control not just prostitution but also prostitutes; they tended to be in favour of imprisoning women, felt the police 'did a good job', and saw no reason to reform the laws on soliciting ... The Puritan/Authoritarian discourse relied significantly upon three main axes: a Christian morality which sees prostitution as immoral and undermining of the value of family and social life; a Puritan ethic which condemns prostitution because it is assumed (mistakenly) to be a way of making easy money without really working for it; and an exaggerated concern over disease ...[28]

It was seen above that such puritan moral views are not new. Their origins can be traced back clearly to the early condemnation of prostitution by the Christian Church, through the Protestant reformers of the 16th century, through the purity movements and morality campaigns of the 18th and 19th centuries, to the moral entrepreneurial groups and New Right ideologies of the present century. It seems equally true to say that the ideological gulf which has existed between the liberal and moral/authoritarian perspectives looks set to continue.

4.6   The welfarist perspective

This perspective has as its origins the pseudo-scientific and biological 'theories' of criminality which were prevalent in the 19th and early 20th centuries in particular. These theories, whilst diverse in themselves, were linked by the belief that socio-economic factors were either irrelevant or, at best, played a very minor role, in explaining prostitution. Instead, criminal

---

28   *Op cit*, Smart, fn 26, p 57.

and deviant behaviour (including, for example, prostitution) could be proved by empirical scientific and biological explanations.

Although the 'theories' themselves are today almost entirely discredited, they remain of some interest for illustrating the impact of scientific knowledge on early criminological theory, as well as retaining a minimal influence on the welfarist model of prostitution. Two quite different theorists from the 19th century will serve to explain the concepts involved.

Parent-Duchatalet, a French 'sexpert', sought to 'prove' the inevitability of prostitution for some females, as Roberts has shown:

> [T]he woman who moved into prostitution started out with the sex trade in her blood: she was a 'certain kind of girl', whose natural inclinations towards 'idleness and licentiousness' led her into a life of disorder. This quickly developed ... into a 'period of debauchery' ... followed by the girl's entry into fully fledged prostitution. But Parent went further; he alleged that it was not simply the girl's natural disposition that led her off the straight and narrow, but also her family background. For here she had witnessed the 'disorderly relationships' that predisposed her to a life of prostitution.[29]

To Parent-Duchatelet, therefore, the female prostitute was destined to prostitution partly as a result of her natural inclinations and dispositions, but partly as a result of domestic background and familial upbringing. This 'inevitability' was a common theme in the so called scientific theories of the period, and failed to recognise fully the importance of wider social and economic factors.

A similar theory was proposed by Lombroso who, also in the late 19th century, popularised the notion of the 'born criminal'. His 'biological theory' encompassed the broad study of 'dangerous classes' in all types of criminal and deviant behaviour, including prostitution. In *L'uom Delinquente* (1876), Lombroso manipulated Darwin's evolutionary theory in order to argue that criminals and delinquents were degenerate throwbacks to our earlier, animal ancestry. Based upon this 'theory' Lombroso argued that prostitutes (like many deviant types) were 'scientifically recognisable' by their mental under-development, their physical deformities (especially in their genitals as far as prostitutes were concerned!) and their unusual bone structures. On the basis of this 'physical evidence', there existed again an inevitability towards prostitution which, irrespective of social conditions, it must be assumed these unfortunate women were powerless to prevent.

Such pseudo-scientific theories should be treated with ridicule, if not contempt. It is tempting to think that, in the late 20th century, these views would have few, if any, adherents. However, a worrying legacy from theorists such as Lombroso may remain in the form of the welfarist perspective. In Smart's study there was found to be some consensus on the opinion that

---

29 *Op cit*, Roberts, fn 1, pp 224–25.

prostitute women have psychological problems which are more important in explaining their prostitution than, say, social or economic factors:

> Prostitution was not usually seen as resulting directly from economic need or greed as with the two previous categories. Rather it was perceived of as *the result of some unresolved personality problem*.[30]

Although this may seem some distance removed from the early work of Lombroso, it highlights the fact that there continues to be a belief, if only in some quarters, that prostitution is capable of being explained on the basis of the personality problems of the woman. No doubt, there are some prostitutes who do possess personality disorders of one kind or another, but that fact cannot be used to create a generalisation about all prostitutes as it had been only 100 years ago.

4.7 The rights perspective

Much of the recent theoretical literature on prostitution has centred around the rights discourse.[31] In very general terms, there has developed a division between those who see prostitution as 'a right', a matter of sexual choice and freedom; and those who regard all prostitution as exploitative, corrupting and abusive.

Those on the pro-prostitution wing of the debate see prostitution essentially as a matter of sexual freedom and individual autonomy. This contractual conceptualisation of prostitution sees prostitution as an agreement freely entered into, whereby the consensual nature of the agreement removes all arguments pertaining to exploitation, corruption and coercion. The logical conclusion to this essentially libertarian and 'left-wing' perspective would be a de-criminalisation of most of the offences relating to prostitution, although it should be stressed that, given the consensual contractual analogy, any prostitution which was forced would, quite obviously, remain subject to legal control. Those who advocate the 'right to prostitution' seek to argue that there would be considerable advantages in removing legal restrictions (for instance, on brothels), in terms of health facilities for the workers, safety, and social status.

By contrast, those who see prostitution as embodying a violation of women's rights (often but not exclusively writing from a feminist perspective), deny that prostitution can ever truly be entered into 'freely'. Rather, it is a phenomenon which by definition involves corruption and

---

30 *Op cit*, Smart, fn 26, p 59.

31 For a discussion of the general issues, both for and against the 'right to prostitute', see Baldwin, M, 'Split at the root: prostitution and feminist discourses of law reform' (1992) 5 Yale Journal of Law and Feminism 47, pp 47–120; Barry, K, *The Prostitution of Sexuality*, 1995, New York UP; Edwards, S, *Sex and Gender in the Legal Process*, 1996, Blackstone, pp 165–77.

exploitation of females within a patriarchal society. The 'contractual right' analogy is rejected as false and inherently flawed: 'freedom of choice' is seen as a specious argument in societies where women continue to be subservient to men, and where frequently (for economic, social or cultural reasons) no real effective choice exists. The 'violation of rights' argument is best summarised by Edwards:

> For the protagonists of the view that prostitution is a human rights violation, such an interpretation is underpinned by the conceptualisation that prostitution is the institution upon which the sexual exploitation of women and children is built and which reduces women to a sexual commodity to be bought and sold and abused. There is a need to move away from the moral basis of prostitution legislation and to reframe future legislation along the basis of exploitation and harm. Any distinction between forced and free prostitution is artificial and specious.[32]

---

32 *Op cit*, Edwards, fn 31, pp 169–70.

CHAPTER 8

PROSTITUTION: STREET OFFENCES AND OFFENCES RELATED TO PROSTITUTION

1 INTRODUCTION

Prostitution *per se* is not, and never has been, a criminal offence in English law. Rather, as was noted in Chapter 7, the history of the control of prostitution in England has been a history of regulation and control in respect of the accompanying activities of both prostitutes and associated persons, where those activities may be regarded, in general terms, as constituting a 'nuisance'.

To adopt the terminology of the Wolfenden Committee, whilst prostitution itself may not, *inter alia*, offend against public decency or be exploitative, it is clear that a number of activities *related to* prostitution *may* infringe the perceived purposes of the criminal law, namely to protect the public from exploitation, corruption and 'offensive and injurious' matters, and to preserve 'public order and decency'.

In this chapter, we shall consider some of the more important and common offences involving secondary activities which are inevitably linked to the primary activity of prostitution. In the light of the perceived purposes of the criminal law, it is essential to consider whether offences such as soliciting, kerb-crawling, brothel-keeping and living on the earnings of prostitution are, in fact, relevant, effective and fair, or whether they represent an unnecessary, ineffective and discriminatory intrusion into individuals' autonomy and freedom of choice. Even where some intervention may be deemed appropriate, it will be important also to consider whether the current law is clear, efficient and equitable in terms of its operation and application.

1.1 Background to the modern law

Prior to the 1950s, the law pertaining to prostitution-related activities was diverse, with several different possible provisions being applicable.[1] In addition, there existed a wide range of local Acts and bylaws which, whilst not limited in their applicability to the activities of prostitutes, were often used to regulate the purported nuisance aspects of prostitutes' behaviour. This diversity of regulation led to fragmentation, inefficiency and inconsistency in terms of application and enforcement.

---

1   The Vagrancy Act 1824, s 3, eg, made it an offence for a common prostitute to engage in 'riotous or indecent behaviour' in a public street or place of public resort.

In light of these concerns, the Wolfenden Committee was keen to propose a re-shaping of the laws relating to prostitution so that: they were of general applicability; the requirement that somebody should be caused annoyance should (for the most part) be removed; and good order and decency should be maintained. In the latter respect the rationale of the Committee was clear:

> What the law can and should do is ensure that the streets of London and our big provincial cities should be *freed from what is offensive or injurious* and made tolerable for the ordinary citizen who lives in them or passes through them.[2]

It is equally noteworthy that many other jurisdictions appear to have adopted a rationale for prostitution-related offences which is similar to that adopted by Wolfenden. In Canada, for example, a 1985 governmental Special Committee identified nuisance to the public as a central consideration in the regulation of prostitution activities:

> Street prostitution increases traffic and impedes the flow of traffic as potential customers and simple onlookers cruise the streets. It increases noise in neighbourhoods, particularly in the early morning hours, as car doors are slammed or altercations occur between the various parties to the business.[3]

Such concerns led directly to measures, contained in Canada's Criminal Code, aimed at reducing the problem of street prostitution. In interpreting these provisions it is clear that the judiciary is also aware of the 'nuisance rationale', as Dickson CJC, for instance, has noted:

> The Criminal Code provision ... clearly responds to the concerns of homeowners, businesses and the residents of urban neighbourhoods. Public solicitation for the purposes of prostitution is closely associated with street congestion and noise, oral harassment of non-participants and general detrimental effects on passers-by or bystanders, especially children.[4]

It is worth noting also at this stage that, whilst the Wolfenden Committee was concentrating its deliberations upon the 'problem' of soliciting *by* prostitutes, there existed the converse problem of the soliciting *of* women *by men* for the purpose of prostitution. It had been widely assumed that s 32 of the Sexual Offences Act 1956 – soliciting or importuning for immoral purposes (see Chapter 2, section 4) – would cover such a situation. However, this was not supported by the earlier decisions on the interpretation of s 32, where, in particular in *Crook v Edmondson* (above), the Divisional Court held that the section did not apply to the situation where a man solicited a woman for the purpose of prostitution, because that was not an 'immoral purpose'. It was clear at the time, therefore, that not only was the law biased against women (in the sense that Wolfenden was considering only the issue of soliciting by, not of,

---

2   Wolfenden Committee, *Report of the Committee on Homosexual Offences and Prostitution*, Cmnd 247, 1957, HMSO, para 285 (emphasis added).

3   Special Committee on Pornography and Prostitution in Canada, 1985 (the Fraser Report), p 383.

4   Reference re: Criminal Code, ss 193 and 195 1(1)(c) (1990) 56 CCC (3d) 65, *per* Dickson CJC, p 73.

prostitutes), but also that the one possible enactment which might have been used against men soliciting prostitutes was being interpreted narrowly and thus creating a loophole.

2 LOITERING OR SOLICITING BY A COMMON PROSTITUTE

As a direct result of the Wolfenden Committee recommendations, Parliament enacted the Street Offences Act 1959. Section 1(1) of that Act provides:

> It shall be an offence for a common prostitute to loiter or solicit in a street or public place for the purpose of prostitution.

This somewhat innocuous-looking definition gives rise to a range of controversial issues, both in terms of problems of legal interpretation and wider concerns of public policy. Before examining the specific legal issues in detail, it is worth reiterating that to many writers the very existence and operation of s 1 is illustrative of the law's bias against female prostitutes. The section can be seen as an overt method of controlling women who are labelled by the State as 'deviant':

> Consequently, the ultimate purpose of prostitution control is to confine the sexual transactions within certain socially defined boundaries – by means of measures aimed at a group of 'deviant' women.[5]

2.1 Common prostitute

Section 1 of the 1959 Act can be committed only by a 'common prostitute', and it thus becomes imperative to know who can satisfy the criteria of 'common' and 'prostitute'.

2.1.1 Parties

It appears to have been accepted for some considerable time that the term 'common prostitute' refers to and is limited to females as principal offenders. This view received recent judicial support in *DPP v Bull* ([1995] 1 Cr App R 413). Here, the defendant, a male prostitute, was charged under s 1 of the Street Offences Act 1959. The magistrates dismissed the case against Bull on the basis that the section applied only to *female* prostitutes, and the prosecution's appeal was likewise dismissed. It was held on appeal that, when looking at the 'mischief' which s 1(1) was designed to remedy, it was clearly a mischief created by women prostitutes. Furthermore, the court considered it to be most unlikely that Parliament had intended s 1 to be applicable to males when there already existed (and continues to exist) the similar offence under

---

5 Jarvinen, M, *Of Vice and Women: Shades of Prostitution*, 1992, OUP, p 22.

s 32 of the Sexual Offences Act 1956, whereby males could be charged with persistently soliciting or importuning for immoral purposes.

However, in spite of this apparently unambiguous position, an anomaly remains. Thus there is clear evidence that, notwithstanding the apparent gender-specificity of s 1, many males (especially post-operative male-to-female transsexuals) are being prosecuted for and convicted of this offence.[6] As s 1 is an offence which can be committed by females only (as principals), and as English law at present clearly determines sexual identity by reference to one's gender biologically determined at birth, it follows that male-to-female transsexuals are being convicted of an offence which does not exist in law.

2.1.2   Prostitute

The terms prostitute and prostitution have never been defined by statute. Their definitions remain governed by the common law authorities.

The leading authority on the meaning of 'prostitution' is *de Munck* ([1918] 1 KB 635), where evidence was adduced showing that a girl aged 14 was paid to participate in a series of lewd acts with men. Although the nature of the acts themselves was not specified, there was medical evidence which proved that the girl was still a virgin and, on that basis, it was argued that there could not be prostitution, as that required the act of sexual intercourse *per se*. That argument was rejected by the Court of Criminal Appeal, where Darling J stated that 'prostitution is proved if it be shown that a woman offers her body commonly for lewdness for payment in return'.[7]

This generally accepted definition has been supported, and indeed extended, in subsequent cases. In *Webb* ([1964] 1 QB 357), the defendant, who ran a 'massage institute', was charged with several offences related to prostitution. Three women (ex-masseuses at the institute) gave evidence that part of their jobs involved masturbating clients, if the clients so wished. The trial judge defined prostitution for the jury according to the definition provided by Darling J in *de Munck*. The defendant appealed against conviction on the basis, *inter alia*, that the terms prostitute and prostitution did not extend to acts of indecency committed solely by the woman herself. This argument was rejected by the Court of Appeal, where Lord Parker CJ stated that there was no distinction to be drawn between activity and passivity on the part of the woman:

> [I]t cannot matter whether she whips the man or the man whips her: it cannot matter whether he masturbates himself or she masturbates him. In our judgment, the expression used by Darling J ... means no more ... than offers herself, and it includes ... such a case as this where a woman offers herself as a participant in physical acts of indecency for the sexual gratification of men.[8]

---

6   See Edwards, S, *Sex and Gender in the Legal Process*, 1996, Blackstone, pp 31–32.

7   [1918] 1 KB 635, p 637.

8   [1964] 1 QB 357, p 366.

The question of an alleged prostitute's passivity or activity has been considered in a number of Commonwealth authorities, as has the type of conduct which needs to be committed in order to amount to prostitution. For the most part these authorities are in accord with English law. Thus, in New Zealand, for example, Bain J confirmed in *R v Mickle* ((1978) 1 NZLR 720) that 'prostitution is proved if it be shown that a woman actively or passively offers her body commonly for physical acts of indecency for the sexual gratification of men'.[9]

The more interesting question concerns the type of act which has to be engaged in for prostitution to occur. It is now well settled that sexual intercourse *per se* is not necessary, whilst, conversely, most authorities do refer to the need for 'sexual gratification'. However, the phrase 'sexual gratification' itself is not without interest and it is clear that the courts will be prepared to impose some limitations upon this definition. Particularly useful guidance was given by Doyle CJ in the Supreme Court of South Australia in *Begley*:

> It does not follow ... that any conduct likely to cause sexual gratification of any type is prostitution. For example, it does not follow that a woman who performs an erotic striptease in front of men, or who allows an indecent film of herself to be exhibited, necessarily performs an act of prostitution, assuming of course that the element of payment is present. In the present case one has the combination of the masseuse being present in person (as distinct from represented in a film), engaging in physical contact with the client (in contrast to a striptease), that physical contact being a significant part of the whole process, and through that physical contact and the manner in which it is performed providing sexual gratification to the customer. It is the combination of these factors which satisfies me that the nude Thai massage as described ... was an act of prostitution.[10]

2.1.3   Common

The epithet 'common' is not merely an unnecessary and irrelevant addition to the offence, but instead imposes an important legal requirement. A *single* act of lewdness with a man on one occasion, for payment, may suffice to make a woman a prostitute, but she will not thereby become a common prostitute. In *Morris-Lowe* ([1985] 1 All ER 400), the leading decision on this criterion, Lord Lane CJ defined a prostitute as a woman 'who is prepared for reward to engage in acts of lewdness with all and sundry, or with anyone who may hire her for that purpose'.[11] On the facts of the case, the trial judge had ruled that the defendant had no defence by arguing that he had merely intended to entice a number of women into committing acts of indecency with him. But, on appeal, his convictions were quashed, as it was held that he was only

---

9   (1978) NZLR 720, p 722.

10 (1996) Supreme Court of South Australia (LEXIS transcript, para 28).

11 [1985] 1 All ER 400, p 402.

trying to procure a number of different women into *each* committing a *single* act of lewdness and that was insufficient to make the women 'common' prostitutes.

Of course, *Morris-Lowe* is not authority for precisely how many 'acts of lewdness' are necessary before a woman becomes a common prostitute. At most it says that a solitary act of lewdness will not suffice, but it does not say how many such acts will suffice. It should, in principle, be open to a woman to argue that she so infrequently practises as a prostitute, that she therefore fails to satisfy the 'common' criterion.

2.2 Loiter or solicit

By using two alternative verbs, s 1 in effect creates two different offences: one of 'loitering' and one of 'soliciting'.

2.2.1 Loiter

Loitering is, potentially, a very broad concept, and partly because of this breadth (thus making it easier to establish) it is more frequently charged than 'soliciting'.

There is no direct authority on the meaning of 'loiter' within s 1 of the 1959 Act, but there are some analogous statutory provisions which adopt the same word, and some useful persuasive authority may be gleaned from them.

In *Williamson v Wright* (1924 SLT 363), the Scottish High Court of Justiciary considered the word 'loitering' within the context of the offence of 'loitering in a street for the purpose of betting'. The court stated that loitering was indicative of a notion of 'lingering', and Lord Anderson held that loitering meant 'just travelling indolently and with frequent pauses'.[12] When applied to the activities of prostitutes, this rather generous definition becomes highly significant: it is clear that a prostitute will 'loiter', for example, merely by wandering along a particular stretch of pavement and pausing occasionally, perhaps in the hope or expectation that she will be picked up by a client. The prostitute need engage in no overt activity, and certainly no active approach towards potential clients is necessary. The criminalisation of such minimalist behaviour is difficult to justify.

2.2.2 Solicit

Essentially, the meaning of 'solicit' within s 1 of the 1959 Act is synonymous with its meaning in other criminal statutes, most noticeably s 32 of the Sexual Offences Act 1956. Consequently, a prostitute may solicit without use of the spoken word, but merely by the physical actions and bodily movements which she adopts (see discussion of *Horton v Mead* in Chapter 2).

---

12   1924 SLT 363, p 365.

2.2.2.1 Advertisements as soliciting

A specific issue which the courts occasionally have to consider is the extent to which an advertisement by a prostitute is capable of amounting to 'soliciting', and, indeed, what advertisement in this context actually means.

In *Weisz v Monahan* ([1962] 1 All ER 664), the defendant had displayed an advertisement in a glass case outside a shop. The advertisement indicated the defendant's services and availability as a prostitute. It was held by the Divisional Court that the defendant was not guilty as the word 'solicit' within s 1 required the prostitute's physical presence. Thus, Lord Parker CJ stated that in the context of this section 'soliciting ... involves the physical presence of the prostitute and conduct on her part amounting to an importuning of prospective customers'.[13] The effect of *Weisz v Monahan* is that a prostitute commits no s 1 offence by, in her absence, using any article to advertise herself, whether that be a card or, for example, the archetypal red light in a window.

However, the decision in *Weisz v Monahan* needs to be contrasted with that in *Behrendt v Burridge* ([1976] 3 All ER 285), where the defendant, a common prostitute, sat in the downstairs bay-window of a house for the purpose of advertising herself and her services. The window was lit by a red light and the defendant was dressed in 'skimpy' clothing. It was accepted that she had made no attempt actively to communicate with any passers-by, although it was proven that, whilst she was sat there, two men had entered the premises and one of them subsequently had sexual intercourse with her. The magistrates dismissed the charge, holding that there had been no soliciting, but merely an explicit form of advertising. However, on appeal by the prosecution, the Divisional Court restored the conviction, holding that, whilst the defendant had made no active approach to prospective clients (whether by any words or deeds), nevertheless, her presence in the circumstances was sufficient to amount to soliciting: she was tempting or alluring prospective customers by her physical presence. This decision must be regarded as stretching the meaning of 'solicit' to its utmost limit, and comes perilously close to soliciting by inactivity. If a prostitute were to place in her window a large photograph of herself, together with a written statement of the services that she was willing to provide, then, on the basis of *Weisz v Monahan*, she would appear to be 'merely' advertising, and thus would be not guilty of soliciting within s 1. But if another prostitute, dressed identically, sits in her window, she may be regarded as 'tempting' prospective customers and thus will be guilty. On any rational basis, this is a distinction without a difference, and we submit that 'soliciting' should require at least something more than mere physical presence.

---

13   [1962] 1 All ER 664, p 665.

It should be noted briefly that, where advertising is undertaken by a third party on behalf of a prostitute, rather than by the prostitute herself, then clearly that third party commits no offence under s 1. However, other offences may be committed depending upon the precise circumstances. Two such potential offences are conspiracy to corrupt public morals or, where the other party is a man and he receives money from the prostitute, living on the earnings of prostitution. The latter offence is considered in more detail below.

2.3   In a street or public place

A common prostitute only commits an offence under s 1 if she loiters or solicits in a particular venue, namely 'a street or public place'.

2.3.1   Street

Section 1(4) of the 1959 Act defines 'street' so that it *includes*:

> ... any bridge, road, lane, footway, subway, square, court, alley or passageway, whether a thoroughfare or not, which is for the time being open to the public; and the doorways and entrances of premises abutting on a street ... and any ground adjoining and open to a street, shall be treated as forming part of the street.

Due to the use of the word 'includes', it is clear that the list of places in s 1(4) is not exhaustive, and other places, structures or premises not on that list could be interpreted as being a 'street' or 'part of a street' as occasion demands. It is equally clear that even so-called 'private' roads, lanes, driveways, etc, are included in the definition if the public nevertheless has access to them.

2.3.1.1   Windows, balconies, etc, overlooking or overhanging a street

These types of structure are likely to be problematic when s 1 falls to be interpreted. When the section refers to '*in* a street ...', this, *prima facie*, seems surely to refer to the position of the prostitute herself, that is, it is the prostitute who must be in a street, etc, in order for a conviction to be upheld. However, because of the inclusive nature of s 1(4) and the adoption of the mischief rule, the courts have further extended the scope of the section. In *Smith v Hughes* ([1960] 2 All ER 859), the leading case on the extended interpretation of s 1(4), two prostitutes had attracted the attention of passers-by in a variety of ways. Their actions included tapping on a first floor balcony rail, tapping on both closed and half-open windows, leaning out of windows, hissing, indicating a price with their fingers and indicating the entrance to the building. It was held by the Divisional Court that, in all these instances, there was soliciting within s 1. The purpose of the Act, said the court, was to protect people who were walking in the street from being molested or solicited. Hence it did not matter where precisely each prostitute was or how she behaved, because, in each instance, the act of soliciting was 'projected to' and 'addressed to' someone in the street. Notwithstanding the purported application of the mischief rule in order to 'protect' the public, it is arguable that where, as here, there is potential ambiguity within the words of the statute, then such ambiguity should have been resolved in the favour of the defendant. The plain language of s 1(4) indicates strongly that it is the prostitute who must be in the street, not the person at whom the soliciting is directed, and, in that respect, *Smith v Hughes* represents a further example of clear statutory language being manipulated for the purpose of regulating the activities of prostitutes.

2.3.2 Public place

In the context of soliciting for the purpose of prostitution, there is no definition of the term 'public place' either in the statute or at common law. Instead, the meaning of 'public place' is determined as a question of fact and degree in each individual case.

Despite the lack of direct authority specifically within s 1, there are a number of cases dealing with the phrase 'public place' in other offences, and these are useful by way of analogy. One of the most detailed statements can be found in *Kane* ([1965] 1 All ER 705), in the context of both the old law of affray and the offence of being in possession of an offensive weapon in a public place:

> 'A public place' is a place to which the public can and do have access ... It matters not whether they come to that place at the invitation of the occupier or ... merely with his permission ... it matters not whether some payment, or ... small formality such as the signing of a visitor's book is required before they are allowed access. *The real question is whether ... access ... is restricted to a particular class of the public ... [I]t would be a private place and not a public place if access to it was restricted to members of the club or their guests.*[14]

It is clear also, from the opinion of Barry J, that the state of mind of the person who is authorised to control the premises in question may be of significance for the jury in determining this issue:

> It might well be that they [members of the jury] will arrive at a contrary conclusion if they take the view that this club was being run, and intended to be run, as a private club, but that, on occasion, the odd trespasser might have succeeded in effecting entry.[15]

The question of whether the determination of a place as 'public' is affected by the right of an occupier to restrict entry was considered expressly in *Waters* ((1963) 47 Cr App R 149). The issue for the court was whether the car park of a public house, over which the licensee exercised some control, was a public place for the purpose of the offence of being in charge of a motor vehicle in a public place when unfit to drive through drink. Lord Parker CJ stated:

---

14 [1965] 1 All ER 705, p 708, *per* Barry J (emphasis added).

15 *Ibid.*

If only a restricted class of person is permitted to have access or invited to have access, then clearly the case would fall on the side of the line of it being a private place. If, on the other hand, only a restricted class is excluded, then it would fall on the other side of the line and be a public place.[16]

It does not follow, of course, from any of the above general propositions that a place must remain exclusively public or private at all times. Thus, a particular place may be 'private' on some occasions, but 'public' on others, and this can be of considerable importance in respect of the types of venues often frequented by prostitutes. *Morris and Others* ((1963) 47 Cr App R 202) illustrates the general principle, albeit again within the context of affray. Here, it was held that a village hall, which usually was a private place, became a public place on the limited occasions it was let for functions:

The payment of 4 s gave a right to the purchaser to enter ... and, therefore, for the period of the dance – a restricted period – the public were entitled to pass in and remain for the duration of the dance, and the hall therefore had become for the period of the dance a place to which the public had access.[17]

Consequently, venues traditionally frequented by prostitutes – bars, night clubs, hotels, halls, theatres, etc – may legitimately alternate between their public and private uses. This can be of particular importance in relation to premises such as public houses and hotels, which undoubtedly become private at certain times, although when that precise time occurs can often be difficult to determine.[18]

2.4 For the purpose of prostitution

Section 1 requires that an ulterior intention be proved before a defendant can be convicted. The prosecution must establish that the defendant loitered or solicited *for the purpose of* prostitution.

It is frequently the case that no direct evidence of the requisite purposive element is available. In such situations, it is permissible for the court to infer the necessary intent from the surrounding circumstances. In *Knight v Fryer* ([1976] Crim LR 322), the defendant, a common prostitute, was observed to spend the afternoon in question in the doorway of a cafe in a red light district. Periodically, she would walk to the kerb, look in cars driven by lone men and then return to the cafe doorway. The magistrates acquitted her on a charge under s 1 on the basis that there was no evidence that she had been loitering for the requisite purpose. However, the Divisional Court allowed the prosecution's appeal, stating that, on the facts, it was open to the magistrates

---

16 (1963) 47 Cr App R 149, p 154.

17 (1963) 47 Cr App R 202, p 203, *per* Marshall J.

18 For a discussion of this issue in the context of a public house and the added difficulty of 'drinking up' time, see, eg, *Mapstone* [1963] 3 All ER 930, p 932, *per* Paull J.

to infer from the circumstances that she had been acting with the prohibited purpose.

Whilst the ability of the court to infer the necessary intent is of great practical significance, it should be emphasised that it is still incumbent upon the prosecution to prove that intent. This issue has received little direct attention in English courts, but a closely analogous offence was expressly discussed by the Alberta Court of Appeal in *R v Pake* ((1995) 103 CCC (3d) 524). There, the central issue for the court in determining the *mens rea* required for soliciting for the purpose of prostitution was to consider whether the relevant legislation was designed with the very wide objective of preventing the nuisance of men talking to prostitutes, or whether it was designed only to capture those persons who *intended* to engage in a transaction with a prostitute. The court held as follows:

> I think the meaning is clear. Without an intention to engage the sexual services, there is no offence ... Requiring intent to be proved will likely have little effect on the number of convictions. The finding of whether or not there was an intention is a finding of fact to be made by the trial judge based on all of the evidence. The intention of the accused may be inferred from the circumstances. In many cases, the content and context of the conversation will lead the judge to conclude that there was intention ... But even though the intention may be inferred, this does not diminish the requirements that intention be found.[19]

We submit that this position is indistinguishable from that pertaining to s 1. Intention (or purpose) to engage in an act of prostitution is a legal requirement, but if direct evidence of such intent were needed, then the section would be rendered redundant. The courts have avoided this difficulty by recognising the right to infer *mens rea*, whether that be from the words spoken or, more usually, the wider circumstances such as place, time and physical acts of the defendant.

3   SOLICITING BY MEN

The modern law relating to the control of prostitution-related activities has tended to centre upon the perceived nuisance aspects. However, the two major provisions, (s 32 of the 1956 Act and s 1 of the 1959 Act), were deficient in one important respect, namely how to deal with the nuisance of *men* who solicited women for the purpose of prostitution. Parliament first attempted to deal with this issue by passing s 32, but, as was noted in Chapter 2, the courts' interpretation of 'immoral purposes' (especially in *Crook v Edmondson*) did not necessarily extend to requests for consensual sexual intercourse with an adult female. Admittedly, this lacuna was partially filled by the decision in *Goddard*

---

19   (1995) 103 CCC (3d) 524, *per* Foisy JA.

(above), but that decision arguably rests upon the fact that the soliciting there was carried out in a manner which was 'unpleasant, offensive and disturbing'. Thus, if the man did not solicit in such a manner (or if the prostitutes themselves, as was often the case, did not find the behaviour unpleasant, etc), then no charge under s 32 could be substantiated.

It was equally clear that s 1 of the 1959 Act was inappropriate, as that section, by its very terms, was directed at the nuisance of soliciting by the female prostitute, not the male client.

The legislative response to these issues, bearing in mind especially that the most commonly perceived nuisance was that caused by men cruising red light districts in their cars for the purpose of picking up prostitutes, was the passage of the Sexual Offences Act 1985 and the introduction of two related offences of 'kerb-crawling' and 'persistent soliciting'.

3.1 Kerb-crawling

Section 1(1) of the 1985 Act states:

A man commits an offence if he solicits a woman (or different women) for the purpose of prostitution–

(a) from a motor vehicle while it is in a street or public place; or

(b) in a street or public place while in the immediate vicinity of a motor vehicle that he has just got out of or off,

persistently or in such a manner or in such circumstances as to be likely to cause annoyance to the woman (or any of the women) solicited, or nuisance to other persons in the neighbourhood.

3.1.1 Parties

Section 1(1) can only be committed, as a principal offence, by a male. Conversely, s 4(2) provides that the person solicited must be female. Of course, where a man solicits another man for the purpose of prostitution, a charge under this section is inappropriate. Instead, the relevant charge would be one under s 32.

Section 1 of the 1985 Act is equally inapplicable where a (female) prostitute solicits potential clients from her vehicle. But, in that case, there already exists a relevant charge, namely s 1 of the 1959 Act.

3.1.2 Solicits

The basic meaning of the word 'solicits' in s 1 of the 1985 Act is the same as when used in both s 32 of the 1956 Act (for example, *Horton v Mead*), and s 1 of the 1959 Act (for example, *Behrendt v Burridge*). The word was considered expressly within the context of the 1985 Act in *DPP v Ollerenshaw* ((1992) unreported). There, the defendant was charged under s 1 after a prostitute had called out to him, offering her services, and he had accepted, inviting her into his car. The Divisional Court quashed his conviction, holding that 'solicit' requires some element of importuning or asking on the part of the man. Given that there existed an agreement between the defendant and the prostitute for sexual intercourse, it could not be said that the defendant's invitation to the woman to enter his car was an act of soliciting. However, it was emphasised that a man will not automatically escape liability under the section merely because the prostitute happens to make the first approach: even where she does do so, the man may still subsequently solicit her:

> The finding here ... is that the mere acceptance of an offer [from the prostitute], no matter how well the man knew the district and no matter how anxious he was to have sexual intercourse with a prostitute, did not amount to soliciting.[20]

3.1.3   For the purpose of prostitution

To substantiate a charge under s 1 the prosecution must prove that the defendant had an ulterior intent, that is, that his *purpose* was to solicit a woman (or different women) in order to obtain her services as a prostitute. Proving such a purposive element by direct evidence may frequently be difficult, but, although there is no authority expressly on the point in relation to this offence, we submit that the courts will infer the necessary purpose from the surrounding circumstances, in the same way as occurs in s 1 of the 1959 Act. Indeed, there is strong persuasive authority to this effect from the decision in *Pake* (above), which expressly concerned the offence of a man soliciting for the purpose of prostitution.

The purposive criterion raises two other points of interest. First, under s 4(1), a man will only commit this offence if it can be proved that when he solicited a woman it was for the purpose of obtaining *her* services as a prostitute. It is no offence for a man to ask X if Y is available to provide her (Y's) services as a prostitute. Secondly, although the woman approached and solicited will usually be a prostitute, this is not a legal requirement. It is equally an offence under this section for a man to solicit a woman who is not a prostitute. The key question is whether the man was acting with the necessary purpose, not whether he knew the woman was or was not a prostitute.

3.1.4   Motor vehicle

The defendant must solicit 'from' or 'in the immediate vicinity of' a 'motor vehicle'. Whilst the overwhelming majority of vehicles pertaining to this offence will be cars, this is not necessarily so. Section 1(3) of the 1985 Act adopts the same definition as used in the Road Traffic Act 1988, so that 'motor vehicle' means 'a mechanically propelled vehicle intended or adapted for use on roads'.

---

20 CO/2197/90, quoted from Divisional Court hearing 5 December 1991, *per* Owen J (LEXIS transcript).

It is the norm in s 1 offences for the man to solicit 'from' the motor vehicle. It is irrelevant at what speed the vehicle is travelling; indeed, it may be stationary or even temporarily immobile.

3.1.4.1   In the immediate vicinity of

Although the man will frequently be 'in' the vehicle, and thus soliciting 'from' it, he will equally commit the offence if it is proven that he was 'in the immediate vicinity of' it when he solicited. Whether or not this is so is a question of fact and degree for the magistrates. Where the man clearly does not satisfy this criterion (because, for instance, he has parked his vehicle a considerable distance away), or where the evidence is not conclusive, an alternative charge under s 2(1) of the 1985 Act (see below) should be used.

3.1.5   Street or public place

The meanings of these terms are as discussed in relation to the offence of soliciting by a common prostitute. Section 4(4) of the 1985 Act adopts an identical definition to that used in s 1(4) of the 1959 Act (above). Similarly, 'public place' is not defined in the statute, but is a question of fact and degree and should be interpreted in accordance with the authorities on that phrase in analogous offences.

3.1.6   Persistently or likely to cause annoyance or nuisance

One of these two additional factors must be proved before a conviction under s 1 can be established. Thus a defendant must either have solicited 'persistently' *or* 'in such a manner or in such circumstances as to be likely to cause annoyance ... or nuisance'.

3.1.6.1   Persistently

This has the same meaning as when used in s 32, thus requiring 'a degree of repetition of either more than one invitation to one person or a series of invitations to different people'.[21]

3.1.6.2   Likely to cause annoyance or nuisance

An element of persistence does not have to be proved, providing this criterion is established as an alternative. Whether or not the defendant's act of soliciting is 'likely' to cause one of the prohibited outcomes is a question of fact and degree for the magistrates. In *Paul v DPP* ((1990) 90 Cr App R 173), it was held that it is permissible for magistrates to use their own local knowledge of a particular area in determining this matter. Indeed, there does not have to be any direct evidence of annoyance or nuisance actually being caused. Rather the magistrates may make this inference from their personal knowledge of the area (such as, in the present case, the facts that the area was known to be often

---

21   See, generally, *Dale v Smith*, and the wide interpretation adopted in *Tuck* (see Chapter 2).

frequented by prostitutes and the cars of potential clients, and it was known to be a highly populated residential area), and the Divisional Court will only overturn such a finding where no reasonable bench of magistrates could have come to that decision:

> Parliament has specifically used the word 'likely'. It has used that word ... with the intention that it should not be necessary to call evidence that a specific individual member of the public was in fact caused nuisance or ... annoyance. In my view ... the magistrates were perfectly entitled to infer that the conduct was likely to cause a nuisance without there being called before them any witness ...[22]

3.2 Persistent soliciting

Section 2(1) of the 1985 Act states:

> A man commits an offence if in a street or public place he persistently solicits a woman (or different women) for the purpose of prostitution.

The majority of the criteria necessary to establish this offence are identical to those which need to be proved in order to make a man guilty of the s 1 offence, as discussed above. Consequently, the parties to the offence, the meanings of 'street', 'public place' and 'persistently', and the need to establish a purposive *mens rea*, are all criteria identical to those in s 1.

3.2.1 Solicits

Although 'solicit' in s 2(1) is given the 'standard' interpretation, in common with most sexual offences, an explicit consideration of the word in the specific context of the present offence was made in *Darroch v DPP* ((1990) 91 Cr App R 378). The defendant was convicted under s 2(1) after he had been seen driving round and round the streets of a red light district and, on one occasion, had beckoned a prostitute over to his car. On appeal, the Divisional Court held that the act of persistently driving a car round and round a red light district was not soliciting *per se*, without some more positive indication, by act or word on the part of the man, that he wanted her to provide services as a prostitute. But the court went on to say that when the defendant beckoned the prostitute across to him, that act was capable of being viewed by the magistrates as 'soliciting', especially as they were entitled to use their previous knowledge of the defendant to rebut any possible 'innocent explanation' of his behaviour. However, in quashing the conviction, the Court held that whilst there was evidence of soliciting on the facts (namely beckoning the prostitute), the requirement of 'persistence' was lacking.

22　(1990) 90 Cr App R 173, p 177, *per* Woolf LJ.

3.3 Relationship between ss 1 and 2

It is clear that there is potential for considerable overlap between s 1, kerb-crawling, and s 2, persistent soliciting. However, s 1 was introduced to deal with the very specific problem of 'kerb-crawling', and thus it is the section which should be utilised where the defendant's soliciting occurs from or near a motor vehicle, out of or off which he has just got.

There are also important, if subtle, differences between the two sections. First, in one important respect, s 1 is wider in scope than s 2, as the former does not necessarily require an element of 'persistence', it being possible instead to satisfy the 'likely to cause annoyance or nuisance' clause. Secondly, however, under s 1, it is always incumbent upon the prosecution to prove that the defendant's soliciting satisfies the physical requirement of being from or near a motor vehicle. Whilst this may not cause too many difficulties in practice, it is nevertheless an additional factor to be established and, in future, an issue may arise as to what precisely 'immediate vicinity' means. Finally, where the motor vehicle criterion cannot be established, s 2 provides an obvious alternative charge. But, here, an element of persistence is always required, and *Darroch* indicates clearly that this may not be easy to establish in all cases.[23]

4 REFORM

In the context of prostitution and soliciting, the majority of the Criminal Law Revision Committee's recommendations were incorporated into the draft Criminal Code Bill. Many of the proposals amount to confirmation of the present law, although a few changes (some quite significant) would result from some of the clauses.

4.1 Prostitute

A 'prostitute' is defined within cl 122 of the draft Bill as follows:

> [A] person who, for gain, offers his body for sexual purposes to others or offers to do sexual acts to their bodies, whether or not he selects those to whom he makes his services available.

---

23 In those (probably very rare) cases where neither s 1 nor 2 can be substantiated, it remains possible to use the 'binding over' provisions of the Justices of the Peace Act 1361. This might cover the situation where there is no motor vehicle (automatically excluding s 1) and only one act of soliciting (no persistence and thus automatically excluding s 2). For a general discussion of the use of the 1361 Act in this context, see *Hughes v Holley* (1988) 86 Cr App R 130.

There are three points which are worthy of particular note in this proposed definition. First, the clause recognises expressly that a man can be a prostitute. Secondly, the requirement that the prostitute be 'common' is dropped and is replaced by a requirement that the prostitute must offer him or herself 'to others'. Because this is couched in the plural, it may be assumed that a person who offers his body to another on one occasion only will not come within the definition of 'prostitute'. Whilst this would appear, undoubtedly, to be the purpose of the clause, it is not entirely free from ambiguity. Thus, if a woman were to offer her body, for gain, to two men simultaneously, (the single sexual act to involve all three persons), but the offer is made on only one occasion, does this satisfy the definition? In this (admittedly unlikely) scenario, the woman has unquestionably made an offer 'to others', but, equally clearly, she has not done so on more than one occasion. This illustration, we submit, whilst satisfying the literal words of the clause, runs contrary to the purpose of the recommendation (namely to criminalise persons who offer themselves on more than one occasion) and thus should not fall within the ambit of the proposal.

Finally, the addition of a reference to 'selection' in cl 122, is an express recognition of the fact that many prostitutes are, in reality, quite selective of the clients they choose. The clause, therefore, would prevent the possibility of any argument to the effect that one is not a prostitute because she or he applies restrictive criteria to the clients chosen.

4.2   Soliciting offences

The primary soliciting offences, as proposed within the draft Bill, are contained in cll 135–38.

Clause 135 states:

(1) A woman is guilty of an offence if, being a prostitute, she loiters or solicits in a street or public place for the purpose of prostitution.

Clause 136 states:

(1) A man is guilty of an offence if he solicits a woman (or different women) for the purpose of obtaining her, or their, services as a prostitute, or prostitutes–

(a) from a motor vehicle while it is in a street or public place; or

(b) in a street or public place while in the immediate vicinity of a motor vehicle which he has just got out of or off,

persistently or in such manner or in such circumstances as to be likely to cause annoyance to the woman, or any of the women, solicited, or nuisance to other persons in the neighbourhood.

Clause 137 states:

A man is guilty of an offence if in a street or public place he persistently solicits a woman (or different women) for the purpose of obtaining her, or their, services as a prostitute, or prostitutes.

Finally, cl 138 states:

> A man is guilty of an offence if in a street or public place he persistently solicits another man or men for sexual purposes.

It should be noted that cll 137 and 138 would replace the present offence contained in s 32 of the 1956 Act, by distinguishing overtly between solicitation for the purpose of prostitution (which must be directed at a female), and solicitation for sexual purposes, which would be limited to acts directed towards males and thus effectively would operate as a control upon homosexuals. Potential difficulties with the operation of cl 138 have already been noted in Chapter 2.

5   LIVING ON THE EARNINGS OF PROSTITUTION

Whereas the rationale for the solicitation offences may be taken as a desire for the law to uphold certain perceived standards of decency and to prevent activities which amount to a 'nuisance', a different justification needs to be sought in relation to those offences which seek to punish people who live on the earnings of prostitution. Essentially, the rationale here may be taken as being a desire to proscribe an element of financial, sexual and emotional exploitation, as well as preventing corruption and controlling the wider coercive activities of many 'pimps'.

The law governing persons who live on the earnings of prostitution can be found in three distinct offences. As will be seen in the following sections the law in this area has never been rationalised. The offences frequently distinguish between the gender of the principal offenders, and considerably different criteria need to be proven in each crime.

5.1   Man living on the earnings of prostitution

Section 30(1) of the Sexual Offences Act 1956 provides:

> It is an offence for a man knowingly to live wholly or in part on the earnings of prostitution.

5.1.1   Burden of proof and trial judge's direction

Section 30(2) provides:

> For the purposes of this section a man who lives with or is habitually in the company of a prostitute, or who exercises control, direction or influence over a prostitute's movements in a way which shows he is aiding, abetting or compelling her prostitution with others, shall be presumed to be knowingly living on the earnings of prostitution, unless he proves the contrary.

This sub-section does not form part of the definition of the offence, but rather is an evidential provision upon which the prosecution may rely in appropriate circumstances. In *Clarke* ([1976] 2 All ER 696), it was confirmed by the Court of Appeal that the sub-section contains three quite distinct methods by which the prosecution can raise the presumption. The presumption will be raised if the prosecution prove that the defendant:

(a) was living with the prostitute; or

(b) was habitually in the company of a prostitute; or

(c) exercised control, direction or influence over her movements in such a way as to show that he was aiding, abetting or compelling her prostitution.

Where the prosecution relies upon s 30(2), it is incumbent upon the trial judge to explain and distinguish carefully between the three alternatives noted above (including drawing to the attention of the jury any evidence in support of any of those alternatives), but, once that is done, the burden of proof falls upon the defendant (on the balance of probabilities) to rebut the presumption that he was knowingly living on the earnings of prostitution.[24]

In *Grant* ([1985] Crim LR 387), the Court of Appeal held that, although the present case was not such an example (and thus the defendant's conviction on a single count under s 30(1) was upheld), a case could be envisaged where a prostitute's evidence-in-chief raised the presumption under s 30(2), thus imposing the burden on the defendant, and the presumption was then rebutted by the cross-examination of the prostitute. It therefore followed that, in principle, a conviction under s 30(1) was not inevitable merely because the defendant himself chose not to give evidence.

5.1.2 Parties

It is clear from the wording of s 30(1) that the offence can be committed as a principal offence only by males.

In this respect, the criminal law appears to have adopted the general proposition of English law that a person's gender is determined once, biologically, at birth. In *Tan and Greaves* ([1983] QB 1053), the Court of Appeal considered a range of prostitution-related offences, including the potential liability of one Gloria Greaves, a male-to-female post-operative transsexual. Gloria Greaves had been charged under s 30(1) with, being a man, living knowingly on the earnings of prostitution, namely the earnings of Tan, a female prostitute. In upholding Gloria Greaves' conviction, Parker J held:

---

24 See, generally, *Ptohopoulos* (1968) 52 Cr App R 47, where the court emphasised that it was essentially a question of fact as to whether conversation and association with a prostitute was sufficient to prove that the defendant was 'habitually in the company of' the prostitute.

> Gloria Greaves was born a man and remained biologically a man albeit he had undergone both hormone and surgical treatment, consisting in what are called 'sex-change operations'.[25]

It is interesting to note that this approach has not been followed universally in all jurisdictions. In *Cogley* ([1989] VR 799, Vict S Ct FC), the Supreme Court of Victoria declined to follow *Tan* and held instead that a person's gender was a question of fact to be determined in the circumstances of each case. This view would be welcomed by some commentators who regard sexual identity as a matter of individual choice, but it does introduce difficult questions of degree, for example, where a transsexual (born, say, male) is not yet post-operative, but genuinely regards himself as female. The present status of English law at least has the advantage of being certain, if not necessarily fair in individual cases.

5.1.3   Mens rea: *knowingly*

There are two distinct aspects to the requirement that the defendant must have 'knowledge'. He must know that the woman was a prostitute and he must know that he was living wholly or in part on the earnings of her prostitution. Thus, if a defendant and a prostitute live together, in circumstances where all domestic expenses are shared, he will not be committing an offence under s 30(1) if he does not know that she is a prostitute. Similarly, if the man wrongly believes that the prostitute with whom he lives, and shares expenses, contributes to those expenses from her 'legitimate income', whereas her income from prostitution is placed into her own private account, then, *prima facie*, he lacks knowledge as to the second aspect. Admittedly, it might be difficult to satisfy the court of the latter situation.

Because s 30(1) refers expressly to 'knowingly', it is submitted that no lower state of mind does or should suffice. The position in this offence is clearly different from, say, that of handling stolen goods, contrary to s 22 of the Theft Act 1968, where knowledge or belief is stated expressly as being sufficient *mens rea*. On this basis, nothing less than actual knowledge on the part of the defendant suffices. However, it is equally clear that direct evidence of such knowledge is not necessary, but that it can be inferred from the circumstances including what the defendant may say. In *Wilson* ((1984) 78 Cr App R 247), the defendant shared a flat with a prostitute. On being questioned by police, he was alleged to have said: 'I knew this would happen. I have been telling her to stop for ages.' It was held that this statement was capable of establishing the requisite knowledge.

5.1.4   Living on

There is a consensus of judicial opinion that the phrase 'living on' means 'living on parasitically'. This phrase, first used as a *dictum* by Lord Reid in

---

25   [1983] QB 1053, p 1063.

Shaw v DPP ([1962] AC 220), was cited with approval in *Stewart* ((1986) 83 Cr App R 327), where Mustill LJ said that 'the word "parasite" ... or some expanded equivalent, provides a useful starting point' for explaining to the jury the nature of the phrase 'living on'.[26]

5.1.5   Wholly or in part

If the defendant has no other means of financial support apart from the earnings of the prostitute, then it may fairly be said that he lives 'wholly' on those earnings. More commonly, the defendant (or possibly the prostitute) have other earnings, in which case, it can be said that he lives 'in part' on her earnings. The position would be complicated where the prostitute has two sources of income, one from prostitution and one from non-prostitution. Assuming that the man was even aware of the earnings from prostitution (and, of course, if he was not then he lacks the requisite knowledge), it would be difficult to prove that he lived on any money deriving from prostitution as opposed to the 'legitimate' source of earnings.

5.1.6   Earnings of prostitution

In many respects, this is the single most important criterion in the s 30(1) offence. Its precise meaning is both pivotal and a matter of some controversy. The central issue is well summarised by Rook and Ward:

> No problem should arise ... where the defendant lives with the prostitute and takes all or part of her earnings for himself. The position is also clear where the prostitute pays some or all of his rent, or buys food or drink for him. But the question which has troubled the courts for a generation is whether a person may be said to be living on the earnings of prostitution if he supplies goods or services to a prostitute.[27]

Two of the earlier cases to consider this issue are indicative of the differences of opinion which exist. In *Silver* ([1956] 1 WLR 281), the court was of the opinion that a person who supplies goods or services to a prostitute in the ordinary course of his business is living on the earnings of his own profession, not upon her earnings. However, this reasoning was rejected by a majority of the House of Lords in the leading case of *Shaw v DPP* ([1962] AC 220). There, the defendant was convicted of, *inter alia*, an offence under s 30(1) after he had produced a directory containing names, addresses, telephone numbers, some photographs and available services of prostitutes. He received payment from the prostitutes included, as well as some of the profits from sales of the directory. In upholding the defendant's conviction, Viscount Simonds rejected the reasoning in *Silver*, stating that such a view would exclude the very type of person (the pimp and protector) which it was designed to capture.

Viscount Simonds accepted that s 30(1) was not, nor should not be, all-embracing:

---

26   (1986) 83 Cr App R 327, p 332.
27   Rook, P and Ward, R, *Sexual Offences*, 1997, Sweet & Maxwell, p 298.

It does not cover every person whose livelihood depends in whole or in part upon payment to him by prostitutes for services rendered or goods supplied, clear though it may be that payment is made out of the earnings of prostitution. The grocer who supplies groceries, the doctor or lawyer who renders professional service, to a prostitute do not commit an offence under the Act.[28]

Instead, Viscount Simonds continued:

[A] person may fairly be considered to be living in whole or in part on the earnings of prostitution *if he is paid by prostitutes for goods or services supplied by him to them for the purpose of their prostitution which he would not supply but for the fact that they were prostitutes.*[29]

This proposition was considered and confirmed by the Court of Appeal in *Howard* ((1992) 94 Cr App R 89), where the defendant had produced and supplied cards and stickers used by prostitutes for the purpose of advertising their services, telephone numbers, etc. The defendant knew that his products were used by prostitutes in order to get clients and that payment to him came from the women's earnings as prostitutes. In upholding his conviction ,the Court approved Viscount Simonds' proposition:

I emphasise the negative part of this proposition, for I wish to distinguish beyond all misconception such a case from that in which the service supplied could be supplied to a woman whether a prostitute or not ... But a case which is beyond all doubt, is one where the service is of its nature referable to prostitution and nothing else. No better example of this could be found than payment by a prostitute for advertisement of her readiness to prostitute herself.[30]

Similarly, in *Stewart* ((1986) 83 Cr App R 327), Mustill LJ expressed himself as looking for a 'closer connection' than simply any person providing goods or services to a prostitute. Instead, he sought a close connection between the 'receipt of money' and 'the trade', although a more precise definition was not desirable. According to Mustill LJ, where goods or services are involved the test is:

... whether the fact of supply means that the supplier and the prostitute were engaged in the business of prostitution together: and the 'fact of supply' will include the scale of supply, the price charged and the nature of the goods or services.[31]

Whilst these types of test may well provide useful guidance, and indeed in most cases a reasonable jury could distinguish sensibly between a grocer and a producer of prostitutes' advertising stickers, there will inevitably be difficult

---

28 [1962] AC 220, pp 263–64.
29 *Ibid*, p 264 (emphasis added).
30 (1992) 94 Cr App R 89, p 93, *per* Lord Lane CJ.
31 (1986) 83 Cr App R 327, p 332.

cases. Suppose that a defendant sells, on a regular basis, expensive lingerie to two women. The first is a prostitute, whose particular clientele request such lingerie; the second is merely a woman with expensive tastes in underwear. Assuming that the defendant is aware of the prostitute's trade, none of the 'tests' identified above would lead to an obviously clear result, if he were to be charged under s 30(1). For example, he may still have supplied the items to the prostitute if she had not been a prostitute, in which case, basing his potential criminal liability upon her enhanced ability to pay seems arbitrary and unfair. Similarly, asking the question whether the goods supplied 'are referable to prostitution and nothing else', is also ambiguous: she may nevertheless have purchased the goods if she were not a prostitute, but if she could not otherwise have afforded them, should that influence a decision in respect of the defendant? Such complicated situations serve to show that, whilst the law pertaining to the provision of goods and services may be sound in principle, its application in fact can be highly problematic.

5.1.6.1 Prostitution

Whilst the precise relationship between the provision of goods or services and the 'earnings of prostitution' clearly can cause difficulties, it might be expected that there would be few problems with the requirement that the woman must actually have gained her earnings from the activity of 'prostitution'. Essentially, for the purpose of s 30(1), the courts adopt the standard definition of 'prostitution', as considered in *de Munck* and *Webb*, above. However, two interesting issues deserve specific mention.

In *McFarlane* ([1994] 2 WLR 494), the question for the Court of Appeal was whether a woman who operated as a 'clipper' – one who offers sexual services for reward and takes that reward in advance but never intends to provide those services – was acting as a prostitute, so that the defendant could be convicted of living on the earnings of prostitution. In upholding the conviction, the Court of Appeal approved the trial judge's ruling that being a 'clipper' could make a woman a prostitute. In reaching this decision, the Court noted that the essence of prostitution is 'the making of an offer of sexual services for reward', which 'Miss J' (the clipper) had done. Secondly, although it was arguable that the defendant had not exploited Miss J sexually, it was important to consider the wider context. In particular, when consideration was given to 'soliciting' in s 1(1) of the 1959 Act, if the law were to distinguish between a 'clipper' and a 'hooker', then convictions under that section would become very difficult to substantiate. Instead, as the mischief to be prevented is harassment and nuisance, any distinction between clippers and hookers is irrelevant.

The decision in *McFarlane* epitomises several of the interpretational difficulties inherent in prostitution generally. In particular, the question whether s 30(1) should be interpreted quite independently of s 1 of the 1959 Act becomes crucial. On one hand, it is arguable that the rationale of s 30(1) is to prevent *sexual* exploitation and, as that clearly does not exist in the present case, there is no basis for upholding the defendant's conviction. On the other hand, as the court preferred, it is sensible to treat 'prostitute' and 'prostitution' consistently, and to hold that a 'clipper' is not a prostitute would undoubtedly impede prosecutions under s 1.

There are similar differences of opinion with regard to the interpretation of the word 'offer'. If 'offer' means 'to make available', it is very difficult to see how a clipper does make herself available sexually. But if 'offer' means 'to promise something', then she does offer, as she promises sexual services (irrespective of her intention not to provide them).

In *Armhouse Lee Ltd v Chappell and Another* ((1996) unreported), the Civil Division of the Court of Appeal had to consider, *inter alia*, whether women who operated telephone 'sex chat lines' were acting as prostitutes. The proposal, by counsel for the appellants, that such women were prostitutes was rejected by the court:

> Mr Cordora's [counsel for the appellants] argument ... is that lewd discussions over the telephone offering sexual excitement in return for payment ... ought ... to be found to constitute prostitution ... For my part I would roundly reject the invitation. Consider the implications. Its acceptance would brand as prostitutes not merely those particular telephone women but also, for example, strippers. It would also result in many people involved commercially in such activities being instantly open to prosecution for living on immoral [*sic*] earnings. I see no warrant for any such extension of the criminal law. Rather ... a finding of prostitution requires at the very least both that the putative prostitute be at some stage in her client's presence and that her offer, whether intended to be fulfilled or not, is at any rate of some direct physical contact of a sexual nature between them.[32]

Whilst this *dictum* looks instinctively to be correct in principle, and Simon Brown LJ's concerns about over-extending the criminal law are understandable, a strict application of the proposition must cast doubt upon whether certain acts traditionally regarded as 'prostitution' are, in fact, so. Thus, suppose that X is a prostitute who solicits, *inter alia*, for a specialist clientele, namely men who wish only to watch the prostitute perform sexual acts upon herself, albeit the men gain sexual gratification from this. If X is in a public place soliciting for such a client, it would seem, *prima facie*, that she is *not* offering 'some direct physical contact of a sexual nature between them'. However it cannot be expected that, if such an argument were ever to be put before a court, the court would do anything but reject it. Indeed, on further reflection, the statement appears to be inconsistent with traditional views of prostitution, especially, for example, those in *Webb* (above), where it was held that 'it cannot matter whether he masturbates himself or she masturbates

---

32 Court of Appeal (Civil Division) hearing, 23 July 1996, *per* Simon Brown LJ (LEXIS transcript).

him'. But, equally, there is a general consensus of opinion that Webb is correct when it requires that a prostitute 'offers herself as a participant in physical acts of indecency'. We submit that Miss X, in the hypothesis above, satisfies neither the criterion of offering 'direct physical contact', nor that of being a 'participant in physical acts'. Admittedly, none of these general propositions, and certainly not the *dictum* of Simon Brown LJ, should be treated as if they were statutory provisions to be minutely analysed, but they do illustrate the difficulty of trying to agree a workable definition of 'prostitution' and then applying it to an almost endless range of human sexual activities.

5.1.6.2   Landlords and earnings

The law has long had difficulty in reconciling the position of landlords and the 'earnings of prostitution'. Does a man commit an offence under s 30(1) by letting premises or rooms to a woman known to him to be a prostitute and thereby receiving rent from her? The difficulty in answering this question is exacerbated by the fact that a prostitute may often use the same flat or room(s) as both living accommodation and for the purpose of her trade.

One potential way of considering the various possibilities which exist is to make a distinction between premises which are let solely for the purpose of prostitution, and premises which are let for the purpose of residential occupancy. As will be seen in the following sections, although the law does recognise such a distinction, the legal position is probably even more complicated than this twofold division suggests.

The first potential scenario is where the defendant-landlord lets premises to a prostitute solely for the purpose of her prostitution. According to the court in *Thomas* ([1957] 1 WLR 747), the defendant would be guilty where he let a single room, to a woman he knew was a prostitute, between the hours of 9 pm and 2 am. However, the court did suggest that this was so because the room had been let at a 'grossly inflated rent', the clear implication being that such a level of rent was a precondition for a successful prosecution in these circumstances.

However, later cases have cast considerable doubt upon whether an 'exorbitant rent' is a requirement where the letting is for prostitution alone. In this respect, the leading case now is *Stewart* ((1986) 83 Cr App R 327), where Mustill LJ, in the Court of Appeal, stated that 'if the letting was referable to prostitution and nothing else it was immaterial whether or not the letting was at a higher than normal rent'.[33] Furthermore, held the court, in those cases 'where the premises are let at a market rent with knowledge of the purpose to which they are to be put' (that is, for the purpose of prostitution only), then there may still be an offence by the defendant.[34] In this type of case, the jury should be directed to look at all the factors that are material to the individual

---

33   (1986) 83 Cr App R 327, p 334.
34   *Ibid*, p 333.

case. Such factors may include, but are not limited to: the nature and location of the premises; the duration of the letting and the hours of occupation; the lessor's role in, for example, furnishing the premises for the prostitute; the level and method of payment; and whether there is any personal relationship between the defendant and the prostitute.

The second scenario involves the situation where a landlord lets premises to a woman he knows to be a prostitute, for the purpose of her residential occupancy in those premises. In some earlier authorities, for instance *Silver* ([1956] 1 WLR 281), it was held that no offence was committed under s 30(1) where a defendant let premises to a prostitute for the purpose of her occupation, even though it was let at an inflated rent. In other words, the fact that a prostitute happened to use the premises where she lived also as the place where she practised her trade as a prostitute did not thereby render the landlord guilty of an offence under s 30(1). The position of the landlord's liability under s 30(1) in respect of lettings for residential occupancy was considered in detail by the House of Lords in *Shaw*, above. There it was held by the House of Lords that if a prostitute rents accommodation for residential occupancy at a 'normal rent', then the defendant (the lessor) commits no offence. This was justified on the basis that a prostitute is entitled to and must have somewhere to live, in the same way that she must eat, drink and be clothed. However, if the rent is 'exorbitant', then even though it may be a residential occupancy, the defendant may nonetheless be guilty, as Viscount Simonds explained:

> To the extent to which the rent is in excess of normal, he extorts it from the prostitute upon no other ground than that she is a prostitute.[35]

Similarly, Lord Reid stated:

> In reality he is not then merely acting as landlord; he is making her engage in a joint adventure with him which will bring to him a part of her immoral earnings over and above the rent.[36]

5.1.7   Advertising services of prostitutes

The more obvious types of advertising cases have already been considered. These would include the situation where prostitutes pay the producers of advertising magazines (for example, *Shaw*) or where they pay for a sticker to be placed in a shop window (for example, *Howard*). In respect of a defendant charged under s 30(1), however, such cases involve direct payment from the prostitute herself. The position is less clear where 'indirect' payments are involved. In *Ansell* ([1975] QB 215), the defendant placed advertisements for prostitutes in a magazine. He charged a fee to potential male clients for providing them with the names, addresses, services, etc, of prostitutes. The

---

35   [1962] AC 220, p 266.
36   *Ibid*, p 271.

prostitutes did not know of this arrangement and the fee was payable, even if the potential clients subsequently did not contact any prostitute with whose details they had been provided. It was held in the Court of Appeal that the fact that the money paid to the defendant came from the clients and not from the prostitutes themselves did not, in law, prevent that money from being the 'earnings of prostitution'. However, added the court, a jury should only convict if they were convinced that the receipt of money was 'so closely connected with the exercise by the defendant of direction, influence or control over the movements of prostitutes that it could fairly be said to be the earnings of prostitution'.[37]

5.2   Woman exercising control over a prostitute for purposes of gain

Section 31 of the Sexual Offences Act 1956 provides:

It is an offence for a woman for purposes of gain to exercise control, direction or influence over a prostitute's movements in a way which shows that she is aiding, abetting or compelling her prostitution.

5.2.1   Parties

The offence under s 31 can be committed as a principal offender only by a female. In line with the general view held by English law (see *Tan*, above), the fact of being female is determined at birth. There is no reason in principle why a man could not be charged as a secondary party to an offence under s 31.

5.2.2   For purposes of gain

Unlike s 30 (where the phrase 'living on' implies the actual receipt of financial payment or reward), there is no requirement in this section that the defendant must actually receive earnings. What is required is that the defendant must *act for the purposes of gain*; she need not actually receive gain. Consequently, the fact that a defendant may aid, abet or compel prostitution is not the offence *per se*; it must, in addition, be done for gain. The Criminal Law Revision Committee in 1982 gave as an example the case of a social worker who advised, or even assisted, a woman to continue being a prostitute for the purpose of benefiting her children. Here, the social worker seems unquestionably to be directing or influencing her movements, in a way which shows that she is aiding, etc, but, equally clearly, she has not done so for the purpose of her own gain, and thus there is no offence.

'Gain' is not defined in the statute. Obviously, it will extend to the 'normal' situation of direct financial gain, although it may extend also to indirect, non-financial gain. However, it may defined there seems no reason to suppose that it will be extended beyond gain to the defendant herself.

---

37 [1975] QB 215, p 223, *per* Roskill LJ.

5.2.3   Control, direction or influence

In order to be found guilty under this section, it must be proven that the defendant exercised 'control, direction or influence' over the movements of a prostitute. Until recently, there was very little English authority on the meaning of the words 'control, direction or influence'. In *R v O* ([1983] Crim LR 401), the defendant, O, lived with X, a prostitute, who was also her lesbian lover. O, who paid all the household expenses, was charged under s 31 with 'exercising *influence* over X'. The prosecution's evidence of 'influence' included the following facts: that O drove X to premises where prostitution occurred; that she paid the rent on those premises; that she escorted clients to those premises on one occasion; and that she placed advertisements for X. The trial judge (Neville J) accepted a submission of no case to answer and directed the jury to acquit the defendant. He ruled that influence meant more than simple encouragement, and that there was no evidence that O had compelled or persuaded X to act as a prostitute. In effect, this decision suggests that a woman cannot be guilty under s 31 unless she exercises some element of compulsion or persuasion upon the prostitute. Whilst this may be a reasonable interpretation of the words 'control' and 'direction', it is arguable that it is overly restrictive in terms of the word 'influence'. This issue was considered in detail in *Attorney General's Reference (No 2 of 1995)* ([1997] 1 Cr App R 72), where the Court of Appeal cast doubt on such a narrow interpretation. The defendant, who ran an agency offering sexual services for payment, had a wide range of responsibilities. These included paying rent on the premises, paying for telephone lines and advertisements, deciding which prostitutes went where and with whom, and taking commission from the prostitutes. The trial judge directed an acquittal, having ruled that, as there was no evidence of her possessing any sanction over the prostitutes, then it could not be said that she 'influenced' their movements. The Court of Appeal did not accept this restrictive interpretation of the word 'influence'. Rose LJ, on behalf of the court, stated that compulsion or persuasion 'may well be a necessary ingredient of control, and, possibly, direction', but 'influence' is indicative of neither compulsion nor persuasion, and nor does it impose a requirement of any form of sanction.[38]

5.2.3.1   In a way which shows she is aiding, abetting or compelling

There exists a clear relationship between this criterion and that discussed in the previous paragraph. There is no offence under s 31 if the prosecution merely establish one criterion, but not the other. It is not an offence for the prosecution to prove only that the defendant aided, abetted or compelled the prostitution of another woman, unless it is proved also that she exercised

---

38 *Attorney General's Reference (No 2 of 1995)* [1997] 1 Cr App R 72, p 76. For a critical commentary on the decision, see Birch, D [1996] Crim LR 663, pp 663–64.

control, direction or influence over that prostitute's movements (or vice versa). Thus, in *R v O*, above, there is little doubt about the fact that the defendant 'aided' X's prostitution, but without any evidence of 'influence' (albeit now that word may be interpreted in a considerably wider way), there is no offence.

5.3 Living on earnings of male prostitution

It is an offence under s 5(1) of the Sexual Offences Act 1967 where 'a man or a woman ... knowingly lives wholly or in part on the earnings of prostitution of another man ...'.

The majority of the criteria which need to be established for an offence to be committed under this section are identical to those in the other prostitution offences, discussed previously. In this section, therefore, we shall consider briefly only two specific issues which are worthy of note.

5.3.1 Parties

Unlike both ss 30 and 31 of the 1956 Act, this offence is not gender specific. It may be committed, as a principal offence, by either a male or a female. In common with previous offences, a person's gender for the purpose of s 5 is determined at birth. Thus in *Tan and Greaves*, above, it was held to be appropriate to charge one Brian Greaves (the 'husband' of Gloria Greaves) with the offence of living on the earnings of male prostitution, as, in legal terms, Gloria Greaves had been born male and thus remained male.

5.3.2 Sentencing

There is little direct authority on sentencing levels or policy in respect of s 5, although it may be expected, in the light especially of continuing concerns about young male prostitutes and the possibility of corrupting influences associated with such activities, that the courts may impose relatively high sentences. On conviction following summary trial, the maximum penalty is six months' imprisonment or a fine not exceeding £5,000, whilst the maximum penalty following conviction on indictment is seven years' imprisonment. In *Puckerin* ((1990) 12 Cr App R(S) 602), the defendant was sentenced to two years' imprisonment following conviction under s 5. He had been seen at railway stations in London, talking to young male prostitutes, introducing them to potential clients, driving both prostitutes and clients in his car, and placing money in to his pockets. The Court of Appeal, whilst expressing some sympathy with the trial judge's reason for imposing the initial sentence, nevertheless quashed that sentence and imposed a term of nine months' imprisonment:

> The learned judge can be excused for going to possibly rather excessive lengths in punishing this man for engaging in this very very sordid business. It is

disfiguring the streets of this country and other public places where it is conducted.[39]

However, added the court, it was important to look at the 'scale of the activity' of this defendant. There was no evidence that the activity had extended over a protracted period of time, nor that it had made him large sums of money (although both things may have occurred). Perhaps more importantly, there was no evidence that the defendant had coerced any of the young prostitutes into their activities, and there certainly was no suggestion on the evidence that any duress or compulsion had been exerted upon them. In light of these facts, the sentence would be reduced accordingly.

The decision is useful for providing some guidance in cases concerning men living on the earnings of young male prostitutes. Notwithstanding the undoubted element of nuisance (or even 'sordidness'), it seems that this may be balanced by the relative lack of profit and relatively small scale involved, as well as, more significantly, the lack of corruption or coercion. It should be expected that, where the defendant has led the prostitute(s) into the activities and/or exerts pressure for that activity to continue, then a considerably higher sentence, probably near to the maximum, will be imposed.

Finally, where any of the previous three offences (ss 30 and 31 of the 1956 Act, and s 5 of the 1967 Act) are committed by persons in the context of operating an 'escort agency' as a cover for prostitution, the courts have seen fit to impose a deterrent custodial sentence. In *Hassan El-Ghazzar* ((1986) 8 Cr App R(S) 182), the appellant was convicted on indictment under s 30(1), having operated a sham escort agency as a front for prostitution. The Court of Appeal upheld the sentence of 12 months' imprisonment and a fine of £2,000, adding that it was often not only appropriate, but also necessary in such cases, to pass custodial sentences. In *Ross and Viszkok* ((1986) 8 Cr App R(S) 249), the appellant Ross was convicted of offences under ss 31 and 5, and Viszkok was convicted of offences under ss 30 and 5. The appellants ran two 'escort agencies' over a period of three months. Clients, who were charged a fee of between £30 and £50, were put in touch with male or female prostitutes. A large number of prostitutes were available to the agencies and detailed records of their activities were found at the appellants' premises. The Court of Appeal stated that the sentencer should consider all relevant circumstances in reaching his decision. This would include, for example, the scale of the activity (such as the number of potential prostitutes and whether they were male and female), the level of profit, and the duration of the activity. Although the sentences for each appellant were reduced from 15 months' to nine months' imprisonment on the facts, the Court of Appeal confirmed the deterrence rationale in such cases:

---

39   (1990) 12 Cr App R(S) 602, p 603, *per* Watkins LJ.

[I]t has to be stressed that Parliament, by the scale of the punishment which it allows the courts to inflict, regards offences of this kind with the utmost seriousness and expects the courts to inflict punishments which are not only appropriate to the offence, but which will impress upon others who are tempted to commit this offence that they ought to desist from doing so. In other words, there should be an element of deterrence in sentences passed in cases of this kind.[40]

5.4 Reform

Setting the Boundaries proposes the replacement and enhancement of those offences currently contained in ss 30 and 31 of the Sexual Offences Act 1956, and s 5 of the Sexual Offences Act 1967. The recommendations emphasise the importance of exploitation, and distinguish between children and adults.

The Report was unanimous in believing that there should be a set of specific offences relating to the sexual exploitation of children, as this would 'set an unambiguous standard in society that it was wrong for an adult to expect to buy or deal in the sexual services of a child' (para 7.6.2). The proposals are found in two detailed recommendations. Recommendation 50 states:

> The review considers that the commercial sexual exploitation of children should be dealt with by specific offences in which 'child' should refer to any person up to the age of 18, and where sexual exploitation means the use of a child in prostitution or in the making of pornography.

Recommendation 51 states:

> It should be an offence to:
>
> buy the sexual services of a child;
>
> recruit, induce or compel a child into commercial sexual exploitation;
>
> participate in, facilitate or allow the commercial sexual exploitation of a child; or
>
> receive money or other reward, favour or compensation for the sexual exploitation of a child.

There was no unanimity in relation to the approach to be adopted in respect of sexual exploitation of adults. It is clear that the competing considerations of exploitation and the right of all citizens to a private life had to be balanced. Prostitutes may earn money for spouses, partners or other family members. This may or may not involve exploitation of the prostitute, but the current law does not distinguish between the level of exploitation involved. The review agreed that a financial relationship was the essence of such offences, but believed that application of the law through prosecution policies should be

---

40   (1986) 8 Cr App R(S) 249, p 250, *per* Watkins LJ.

determined by the level of exploitation. Thus, the level of 'abuse, pressure, force, deception and coercion' (para 7.7.3) should inform the decision to prosecute, not the definition of the offence. Consequently, Recommendation 52 proposes the introduction of modern gender neutral offences:

There should be offences of:

exploiting others by receiving money or reward from men and women who are prostitutes;

managing or controlling the activities of men and women who are prostitutes, for money or reward; and

recruiting men or women into prostitution whether or not for reward or gain.

6   BROTHEL-KEEPING

Although there exists a very wide range of offences in English law associated with and related to the general operation and management of brothels, we shall limit our discussion to one main offence, which is both of pivotal importance and which raises a number of interesting legal issues.

Section 33 of the Sexual Offences Act 1956 provides:

It is an offence for a person to keep a brothel, or to manage, or act or assist in the management of, a brothel.

6.1   Parties

It is clear from the wording of s 33 that the offence may be committed, as a principal offence, by either a male or a female. The question whether prostitutes *qua* prostitutes working in the brothel may be convicted as principals to this offence is a little more problematic and will be considered below.

6.2   To keep

There is no direct English authority on this point as it relates to s 33. However, in respect of the same offence in New Zealand, the Court in *Mickle*, above, held that to 'keep' a brothel requires the defendant to have 'conduct of the business accommodated therein'.[41]

6.3   Brothel

Whether or not premises are used as and amount to a 'brothel' is a question of fact and degree in the circumstances of each individual case. The word is

---

41   (1978) NZLR 720, p 723, *per* Bain J.

provided with no statutory definition, but rather its meaning remains governed by the common law. The leading common law authority is that of *Gorman v Standen* ([1964] 1 QB 294), where Lord Parker CJ defined a brothel as 'a house resorted to or used by more than one woman for the purposes of fornication'.[42] This definition contains three quite distinct and important elements, and it is incumbent upon the prosecution to establish each of them if there is to be a successful prosecution under the section.

6.3.1 A house

A brothel does not necessarily have to consist, in law, of an entire house or building. Of course, it may consist of an entire house, but, equally, it may be constituted by a room or set of rooms *within a house*, provided it is resorted to or used by more than one woman (see below).

In this respect, a particular difficulty which the courts have had to consider is where a building consists of a number of different, individual flats or suites, let to a number of prostitutes under separate lettings. The leading authority on whether such a building may be a brothel is *Donovan v Gavin* ([1965] 2 QB 648). The defendant owned a large house, in which he occupied a self-contained ground floor flat. Three further rooms on the ground floor were let separately to three different prostitutes. They each had keys to the main front door as well as to the doors of their own rooms. The tenancies had come into existence separately and at different times. The women used their rooms for the purpose of prostitution. On those facts, the Divisional Court held that there could be a brothel, even though individual rooms in the house were let to different prostitutes under separate tenancies. According to Sachs J, individual rooms within a house could constitute a brothel, provided they 'are sufficiently close to each other to constitute in effect what might be called a nest of prostitutes, be that nest large or small'.[43]

However, the decision in *Donovan v Gavin* should be contrasted with that in *Strath v Foxon* ([1956] 1 QB 67), where the defendant let the first and second floors of the building in question to one prostitute, and the third floor to a second prostitute. The only parts of the building which were shared by the prostitutes were a kitchen on the second floor, the street door and a staircase. The third floor of the building was separated by a strong door with a Yale lock, effectively making it self-contained. The Divisional Court held that, on the evidence, the magistrates had been correct to find that there were two separate lettings of two separate flats, with only very minimal joint usage. The court 'reluctantly' upheld the magistrates' finding that there was no brothel.

The decision in *Donovan v Gavin* should be regarded as representing the general rule on what constitutes a 'house' for the purpose of the definition of

---

42   [1964] 1 QB 294, p 303.
43   [1965] 2 QB 648, p 659.

brothel, with *Strath v Foxon* traditionally seen very much as the exception. Nevertheless, the contrasting cases illustrate the difficulties created by different types of lettings and how even quite minimal physical differences in the structural layout of buildings can affect decisions. It should also be noted that, even in 'exceptional' circumstances like those in *Strath v Foxon*, there may be alternative offences with which the defendant could be charged. In particular, such circumstances may often give rise to a charge under s 30(1).

6.3.2   Resorted to or used by more than one woman

In order to understand this criterion, a number of reasonably straightforward alternative scenarios need to be identified.

First, there clearly is no brothel if only a single prostitute uses the 'house' or premises, however numerous her clients may be. Secondly, the fact that two (or more) women happen to live in the same premises does not create a brothel if only one of the women uses the premises for her work as a prostitute. Thirdly, however, where premises are used by a 'team of prostitutes' on a 'rotating basis' (so that, in effect, there is only one prostitute present at the premises at any one time), a brothel may still be held to exist. This proposition was put by Watkins LJ in *Stevens v Christie* ((1987) 85 Cr App R 249):

> [W]here more than one woman resorts to premises for the purpose of prostitution then those premises are a brothel if there is a joint use of them as a team.[44]

Finally, the mere fact that one of only two women using the relevant premises is herself the tenant and occupier of those premises, does not prevent them from constituting a brothel.

6.3.3   For the purposes of fornication

It is essential to note that Lord Parker's generally accepted definition of brothel, above, refers to 'fornication', not, as might be expected, 'prostitution'. This distinction is important as the terminology is ambiguous and can lead to uncertainty. According to the *Oxford Combined Dictionary*, the accepted definition of the noun 'fornication' is 'voluntary *sexual intercourse* between unmarried persons'.[45] It cannot be supposed that Lord Parker intended the definition of 'brothel' to be given such a narrow scope. Such a limited definition would run contrary to the generally accepted legal view that a brothel can exist where women engage in any acts of sexual gratification. Indeed, in reality, many brothels cater for a 'specialist clientele', where acts of masturbation or oral sex, but not sexual intercourse *per se*, are provided. Therefore, 'fornication' (in its literal sense of 'sexual intercourse') is not an essential precondition of a brothel. Rather, it may be that Lord Parker was

---

44   (1987) 85 Cr App R 249, p 254.
45   *Oxford Combined Dictionary*, 6th edn, 1982, OUP, p 109.

using the word 'fornication' in its colloquial sense (namely to indicate any act of a sexual nature) or, more likely, that he wished to emphasise that payment was not a necessary condition for the existence of a brothel. To introduce a payment criterion into the definition of 'brothel' would raise almost insurmountable evidential problems for the prosecution; Lord Parker's definition at least has the advantage of removing that evidential burden.

In *Winter v Woolfe* ([1931] 1 KB 549), the defendant was the occupier of a dance hall where, allegedly, 'acts of lewdness and impropriety' took place between male undergraduates and women 'of the working class type'. Magistrates dismissed the charges on the basis that acts of gross indecency and fornication did not constitute prostitution, and that there was no evidence of any payment for the acts in question. This view was rejected by the Divisional Court, where a much broader interpretation to the word 'brothel' was applied:

> There was evidence ... that ... men were resorting to those premises for the purpose of ... fornication with women who resorted there for the same purpose ... That of itself is quite sufficient to justify the inference that these premises were being used for the purposes of prostitution.[46]

The decision may be criticised on two broad grounds. First, it is inconsistent with the generally accepted view (for instance, in *de Munck* or, more recently, in both *McFarlane* and *Armhouse Lee v Chappell*) that 'prostitution' requires some element of reward. Secondly, and irrespective of the first criticism, the definition is too broad as it brings within the ambit of the criminal law, via prostitution, non-commercialised sexual activities, which are very rarely the subject of legal control.

Such criticisms are forceful and it was arguable that, given an appropriate opportunity, the courts may review the decision in the light of more contemporary standards of behaviour. However, this proved not to be the case, and the decision was approved in *Kelly v Purvis* ([1983] 1 All ER 525), where Ackner LJ stated:

> [T]o constitute premises as a brothel it is not essential to show that they are in fact used for the purpose of prostitution, which involves payment for services ... A brothel is also constituted where the women ... do not charge for sexual intercourse.

Rather, concluded Ackner LJ, for the purpose of s 33, 'it is not essential that there be evidence that normal sexual intercourse is provided in the premises. It is sufficient to prove that more than one woman offers herself as a participant in physical acts of indecency for the sexual gratification of men'.[47]

With respect to the view of Ackner LJ, we submit that this view is both too wide and, more importantly, that it confuses two quite distinct issues. It is

---

46 [1931] 1 KB 549, pp 554–55, *per* Avory J.

47 [1983] 1 All ER 525, pp 528–29.

undoubtedly the law that prostitution does not necessarily require sexual intercourse *per se*, but rather that an act providing sexual gratification may suffice. However, whatever the nature of the requisite sexual act, it is entirely a different contention to suggest that prostitution can exist without some payment or reward. We submit that there is no direct authority which holds that there can be prostitution without such reward; indeed, the legal position is quite the reverse, and even the court in *Kelly v Purvis* accepted that 'prostitution ... involves payment for services rendered'. Once this proposition (that prostitution requires payment) is accepted, the absurdity of the above distinction becomes clear. Let it be supposed that Miss X and Miss Y were in the habit of soliciting men for the purpose of engaging in sexual acts with them. The women are not prostitutes, and there is no question of any payment being involved. Whatever view may be held about the promiscuity or otherwise of the women, it is clear beyond doubt that no offence under s 1 of the 1959 Act exists – the necessary element of reward is absent. If Miss X and Miss Y were, on a regular basis, then to return to the flat, which they share together, with men whom they had 'picked up', all the legal requirements for a brothel seem, *prima facie*, to exist: there is 'a house' which is 'resorted to or used by more than one woman' 'for the purpose of *fornication*'. This absurd conclusion should not represent the law; the fact that, literally, it appears to do so, is a direct result of the definition of brothel referring to fornication, and not prostitution.

6.3.4   To manage, or act or assist in the management

Section 33 utilises different verbs in order to proscribe a range of alternative activities by the potential defendant. The activities cited may be regarded as representing differing levels of involvement or even blameworthiness.

'Managing' is suggestive of some form of operational control. In *Abbott v Smith* ([1965] 2 QB 662), it was held that, if a defendant is to be guilty of managing a brothel, there must be 'some sort of evidence indicating the taking of an active part in the running of the business, something suggesting control ... [T]here must be ... something "a cut above" purely menial or routine duties, such as cleaning the stairs or answering the door'.[48]

'Acting or assisting in the management' of a brothel connotes a much wider range of actions than 'managing' *per se*. In *Gorman v Standen*, above, Lord Parker CJ explained the phrase as follows:

'Assisting in the management of a brothel' seems to me to contemplate ... the case of a man who runs a brothel not living there himself; he keeps and manages it but he has on the premises a woman who assists in the management.[49]

---

48   [1965] 2 QB 662, p 666, *per* Chapman J.
49   [1964] 1 QB 294, p 303.

In Lord Parker's scenario, therefore, the man would satisfy the requirements for both 'keeping' and 'managing' the brothel, whilst the woman would be guilty of 'assisting in the management'. However, whilst this is acceptable as a general statement of principle, it does not provide a detailed account of what one must do in order to satisfy the requirement of 'assisting ...', etc.

In *DPP v Jones and Wood* ((1993) 96 Cr App R 130), the defendants lived with 'K', a male homosexual prostitute who ran a brothel. The defendants gave assistance to K, which assistance included placing and paying for advertisements, providing lifts to the premises used as a brothel and generally providing a whole range of help short of sexual services themselves. The defendants appealed against their convictions for assisting in the management of a brothel, arguing that there was no evidence that they had taken any active role in running the business and, furthermore, that any duties they had performed were 'routine' or 'menial' and thus disclosed no control over the business. These arguments were rejected by the Court of Appeal, where Beldam LJ provided a thorough explanation of the meaning of 'assist' in the context of s 33:

> It is difficult to imagine an activity more helpful to a person managing a brothel than taking his advertisements to the local newsagents ... In my judgment it is not a necessary condition of the offence of assisting in the management that the person has to exercise some sort of control over the management. *That is the requirement of managing.* Equally ... it is not necessary to show that there was a specific act of management for that would be acting in the management. *Assisting is a wider concept.* No doubt not everyone who carries out some menial task at a brothel, like cleaning the stairs ... would be said to be assisting in the management, but that was not this case.[50]

6.3.4.1 Prostitutes and s 33

It follows from the previous authorities that a prostitute – merely by the fact, without more, of being a prostitute and providing sexual services in a brothel – does not satisfy any of the requirements under the section: there is no element of control or management, or even giving assistance to the management. However, it equally does not follow that prostitutes are automatically exempt from prosecution under the section merely on account of their status as prostitutes. Rather, if it can be proven that the prostitutes do acts which *go beyond the mere provision of sexual services,* then they may still commit the offence. In *DPP v Curley and Farrelly* ([1991] COD 186), the defendants were prostitutes who worked in a brothel. In the absence of the owner of the brothel, the prostitutes performed a range of tasks including the running of an appointments system, answering the telephone, locking up the premises, etc. The Divisional Court held that the magistrates had been wrong to conclude that there was no evidence of assisting in the management. There

---

50 (1993) 96 Cr App R 130, p 132 (emphasis added).

did not have to be some element of control by the defendants, and neither did there have to be an active role in the running of the business as a business.

6.4   Proof

By its very nature as a brothel, it is frequently the case that direct evidence of the use of premises as a brothel is unavailable or, at least, difficult to obtain. In common with several other sexual offences, this is legally irrelevant, as proof of such use can be inferred from the surrounding circumstances. Two examples will serve to illustrate the scope of the circumstances which may be utilised. In *Korie* ([1966] 1 All ER 50), it was held to be permissible, for the purpose of proving that the premises were a brothel, to adduce evidence that the premises were visited by known prostitutes. The principle was stated most succinctly by Chapman J:

> It is hardly to be expected that visual observation will be possible of what takes place ... in a particular room in a particular house. It must therefore be a matter of inference from the general surrounding circumstances what the purpose of a visit or a succession of visits is.[51]

Similarly, in *Woodhouse v Hall* ((1981) 72 Cr App R 39), police officers were allowed to give evidence of conversations in which an employee employed at the brothel offered to provide sexual services. This did not infringe the rule against hearsay, as the conversations were not admitted to prove the truth of their contents, but rather were admitted for the purpose of establishing the use to which the premises were being put.

6.5   Reform

The proposals for the reform of the law in relation to prostitution generally and the soliciting offences are contained in cll 122 and 135–38 of the draft Criminal Code Bill, and have already been considered above.

In relation to the three offences which, at present, fall within the general ambit of 'living on the earnings of prostitution', the draft Criminal Code Bill would effect a welcome rationalisation. The present offences under ss 30 and 31 of the 1956 Act and s 5 of the 1967 Act would be replaced by three new offences, which would make no distinction between men and women as principal offenders, and no distinction between male and female prostitution.

Clause 123 proposes that a person will commit an offence if 'for gain, he organises the services or controls the activities of more than one prostitute'.

Under cl 124, a person would commit an offence if 'for gain he controls the activities of a prostitute'.

---

51   [1966] 1 All ER 50, p 51.

Finally, cl 125 would make it an offence if:

... for gain, he does an act intending thereby to facilitate a meeting between a prostitute and another person for the purpose of prostitution, unless–

(a) he does so in the ordinary course of a trade, business or profession which does not include the facilitation of prostitution; and

(b) he does not charge a price exceeding that which he would charge if the meeting were not for the purpose of prostitution.

The main offence currently governing brothel keeping, namely s 33, would be replaced by cl 127, which states that a person commits an offence if 'he manages, or assists in the management of, premises in connection with their use, in whole or in part, for the purpose of prostitution by more than one prostitute'. The clause no longer makes reference to 'brothel'. One welcome consequence of this change is that the present definition of brothel as 'a house resorted to ... for the purpose of *fornication*' would be replaced by the phrase 'premises in connection with ... the purpose of *prostitution*'. This would narrow the scope of the offence as it stands at present and would remove the absurd anomaly that the word 'fornication' currently produces, as discussed above.

Finally, cl 126 provides that, for the purpose of, *inter alia*, cl 127:

... 'premises' includes, where parts of a building are separately occupied, any two or more of such parts as are occupied by prostitutes (whether one or more in each part) carrying on prostitution under common direction or control.

The effect of this clause would be to preserve the current law as represented in the decision in *Donovan v Gavin*, whereby a 'nest of prostitutes' can constitute a brothel. Indeed, it is arguable that the clause would go further and extend the present law by also bringing within the new offence circumstances, such as those which existed in *Strath v Foxon*. A future finding of separate lettings into separate flats with minimal joint use, would appear, on the wording of cl 126, to no longer operate as an excuse to a defendant under the new cl 127 offence.

INDEX